The Madness of the Saints

The Madness of the Saints

Ecstatic Religion in Bengal

June McDaniel

The University of Chicago Press
Chicago and London

June McDaniel is assistant professor in the Department of Philosophy and Religious Studies at the College of Charleston in South Carolina.

THE UNIVERSITY OF CHICAGO PRESS, CHICAGO 60637
THE UNIVERSITY OF CHICAGO PRESS, LTD., LONDON

Printed in the United States of America
98 97 96 95 94 93 92 91 90 89 54321

Library of Congress Cataloging-in-Publication Data

McDaniel, June.
The madness of the saints : ecstatic religion in Bengal / June McDaniel.
p. c.m.
Bibliography: p.
Includes index.
ISBN 0-226-55722-7. — ISBN 0-226-55723-5 (pbk.)
1. Hinduism—India—Bengal. 2. Ecstasy (Hinduism). 3. Bengal (India)—Religon. 4. Saints—India—Bengal. I. Title.
BL1153.7.B46M37 1989
294.5′42—dc19 88-35657
CIP

∞ The paper used in this publication meets the minimum requirements of the American National Standard for Information Sciences—Permanence of Paper for Printed Library Materials, ANSI Z39.48-1984.

Contents

Acknowledgments

I wish to thank several people for their help with this book. At the University of Chicago, I thank Wendy O'Flaherty, who read the manuscript in detail and gave much appreciated advice, criticism, and support; Clinton Seely, who read and criticized most of the Bengali translations; and Edward Dimock, for his useful suggestions. Funding for the field research came from the American Institute of Indian Studies, which provided the grant allowing me to live in West Bengal. This kindness was greatly appreciated. I also thank Prakash Desai, M.D., of the University of Illinois, for his helpful comments on those sections of the book dealing with psychology and medicine, and Larry DeVries of Regenstein Library at the University of Chicago for his suggestions on Sanskrit texts, folklore sources, and editing.

In West Bengal two figures stand out for their helpfulness. Narendranāth Bhaṭṭācārya, of the University of Calcutta, gave me much insight into Śākta texts and traditions. Sajal Majumdar, owner of a *pūjā* supply store, drove me on his motorcycle down jungle dirt roads and through labyrinthine Calcutta streets to interview holy men, women in possession trance, and psychiatrists. I owe both a debt of gratitude.

Also I thank the many holy men and women in Bengal whom I interviewed, who opened up to talk about their beliefs and experiences more than I ever expected. I was impressed by their openness and generosity to a stranger and by their willingness to share their religious experiences. I particularly thank Arcanāpurī Mā, Yogeśvarī Devī, Nikuñjagopāl Gosvāmi, Vṛndāvana Dāsa, Śivānanda Giri, Ambikā Bannerji, Tārānanda, and Swāmi Naciketasānanda for their detailed and useful descriptions.

Thanks go to Jim Denosky, husband and friend, for being consultant, critic, and all-around support system. His encouragement and interest kept the writing going during the slow times. Thanks are also due to my first source of inspiration for Indian philosophy and religion, Robert Garvin of S.U.N.Y. at Albany.

This research was inspired twelve years ago when some friends who had been in India for several years brought back their guru, a Bengali Kālī priest named Prahlāda Candra Brahmacārī. He was the first mad guru I ever met, and perhaps the most impressive one. He was short, with a large belly and a long white beard. He spoke no English, so we attempted to communicate by sign language and interpreters. He fell into ecstatic trances almost continually.

He would fall backward, chanting mantras rapidly, and go through a variety of mythological identities. At one moment he was baby Kṛṣṇa, claiming to be lost and asking for his mother; at another he was an all-knowing sage; in another he was a shy maiden, or a warrior. He would leap about, hiding behind the furniture and then jumping out. He would become frozen in the midst of his *homa* fire ceremony or pass out totally.

When I asked his devotees if he were ill, they said, "No, he is a madman [*pāgal*]. All of the real holy men are mad. This is what religious people are like in Bengal." After ten years and research in India, I have come to agree with them. Not all the holy men are mad, but the most respected ones are. I remained curious about the relationship of ecstasy and madness, but when I looked for books on religious madness in India, I found virtually nothing. This book seeks to remedy that situation.

Note on Translations

Most of the Bengali and Sanskrit terms in this book have been translated into English. However, there are not always exact translations available for these terms. The word *siddha* has been translated as "saint"—not an ideal translation (the Sanskrit word literally means a perfected one, or one with miraculous powers, or one who has achieved a goal). However, "saint" has the colloquial usage of *siddha,* which no other English term possesses.

Bhakti is translated as "devotion," while a *bhakta* is written "devotee," and a *bhakta siddha* is written as "devotional saint" (to distinguish him from a yogic *siddha* or a Buddhist *siddha*). *Ṛṣis* and *munis* are called "sages," while *sādhus, sādhakas, tāntrikas, avadhūts, aghoris,* and others are called "religious practitioners" or "holy men." *Sādhikās* and *bhairavīs* are called "holy women."

Sādhana is variously called "ritual practice," "spiritual practice," or "meditation"—depending on the context. *Kīrtana* is translated as "singing hymns," and *japa* is written as "chanting mantras." *Pūjā* is translated as "worship" or "ritual worship."

Both *pāglāmi* and *unmāda* are translated as "madness," although these states are usually distinguished in parentheses or footnotes. *Kṣepā* and *pāgal* are written as "madman." The states of *divyonmāda* and *mahābhāva* are called "divine madness," and the *sāttvika bhāvas* are translated as "ecstatic symptoms." Because the book explores the term *bhāva* in many different sections, I have allowed that word to remain. I hope that its many uses and meanings will not be too confusing to the reader.

ONE Introduction

Bhagavān [God] is mad, he has created all sorts of confusion
He has made the country mad
Such a madman as this, I have not found

O crazy mind
I haven't found the madman I desire
I haven't found any such madman
Thus I have not become mad.

—Untitled Bāul song,
sung by Boidyanāth Śarma,
Calcutta, 1984

O Crazy Mind

There is a nostalgia for madness in Bengal. The lovers, poets, and saints are mad, full of intense passion and desire for direct experience. A person may be mad for love or mad for God.

Madness (*pāglāmi*) has many connotations. There is insanity associated in indigenous Indian psychology with violent delirium and seizures caused by ghosts, ancestors, or other nonphysical beings, magic, or an imbalance of the elements. Madness connotes the unexpected, as in the Bengali proverb What will a madman not say? What will a goat not eat? (*Pāgal kī nā bole, chāgol kī nā khāe?*) It connotes affection, as a father may call his daughter "My little *pāglī.*" And it connotes the madness of the saint who is subject to intense emotional states and visions of God, whose life follows his experiences of religious ecstasy.

This book is a study of religious ecstasy in the Bengali devotional or *bhakti* traditions. These traditions are dedicated to religious experience, and the texts of Bengali *bhakti* give some of the most detailed accounts of ecstatic states in world religion. They describe states of trance and intense emotion—how they occur, their effects on the body and personality, the place of the ecstatic in the community and in the culture. Ecstatic states are described in theological texts, in handbooks of spiritual practice, in poetry and hagiography. They show the power of devotion in the lives of individuals, the ways in which direct contact with the sacred may disrupt and reorganize personality.

The Bengali devotional tradition is a history of people who are considered saints, incarnations of deities, and liberated souls. Their words change the course of the tradition, for their inspirations and revelations are believed to come directly from their deities. And their ecstasy is the sign of the truth of their words, for the divine presence is known to drive the person mad with love and passion.

Ecstasy in the devotional tradition differs from the more classical notion of ecstasy articulated by Mircea Eliade—the literal interpretation of the Greek root *ex-stē,* which is "to stand outside" or "to be outside." As Eliade states, ecstasy brings the shaman "beyond the realm of the sensorial": "it is an experience that brings into play and engages only his 'soul,' not the whole of his being, body and soul; his ecstasy manifests the separation of the soul; that is, it anticipates the experience of death."[1]

This definition necessitates a separation of self or soul and body, which *bhakti* does not require. In the classical definition of ecstasy, the soul leaves the body and returns, perhaps after visiting other worlds. Ecstatic devotees and gurus, on the other hand, may have visions while they are within the body or may participate in the identity or emotions of a deity through a spiritual body, or the physical body itself may become the dwelling place of the deity.[2] In this book, devotional ecstasy is defined as a radical alteration of perception, emotion, or personality which brings the person closer to what he regards as the sacred. It is manifested through word and bodily state, voluntarily or involuntarily. The ecstatic often passes through a stage of disintegration, but ultimately experiences an integration that brings parts of the self, or the self and the Divine, into a closer relationship or union.

The spiritual antecedents of the Bengali devotional tradition may be seen in some earlier Indian ideas. The perceptual or visionary form of *bhakti* ecstasy is comparable to the idea of *dṛṣṭi* or direct perception. The Vedic hymn is often called simply *mantra* or *dhīti,* "thought," implying that it is seen spontaneously in the mind and not learned.[3] The affective aspects of ecstasy are illustrated in one characterization of *bhakti* in the *Bhagavad Gītā* (9.29), spoken by Kṛṣṇa to Arjuna:

> Ye bhajanti tu māṃ bhaktyā
> mayi te teṣu cāpy aham.
> Those who worship me with devotion,
> They are in me, and I in them.

This reciprocity is seen in the idea of *darśana,* which includes both seeing the deity and being seen.[4] *Bhakti* as emotion is not only devotion, but sharing—a love relationship in which the devotee both gives and receives. Such reciprocity is also seen in the bodily transformations involved in *bhakti* ecstasy, when the person consciously creates or suddenly discovers a spiritual body (*siddha deha*). This body is an intermediate self, participating in the experiences of both the deity and the earthly person. The worshiper becomes a part of the deity's world of love and knowledge, while the deity is established within the heart of the worshiper. In ecstatic states, the spiritual identity becomes the dominant one, which may in turn affect the physical body (visions seen with spiritual eyes become materialized when the devotee leaves his trance). The inner states manifest in the physical body in the ecstatic symptoms—the *sāttvika bhāvas* and *bhāvera vikāras*—which show that the soul is not radically separated from the body. In shamanic ecstasy, the soul goes on a spirit journey through invisible regions to meet the dead or the gods and takes magical flight through the upper or lower worlds. In devotional ecstasy there is a permeability and openness uniting the person and the divinity, and a sharing of love between them.

Bengali *bhakti* ecstasy also differs from the definitions given by Gilbert Rouget in *Music and Trance,* in which he details the history of understandings of the term *ecstasy.* He contrasts trance, which involves movement, sound, company, sensory overstimulation, crisis, and amnesia with ecstasy, which requires immobility, silence, solitude, sensory deprivation, hallucination, no crisis, and recollection.[5] Yet devotional ecstasy occurs unpredictably, in group or alone, with noise or silence—the love of Rādhā and Kṛṣṇa can be recognized in *kīrtana* hymns and dancing, or while sitting in yogic meditation, or walking in the forest to bring water. The significant opposition studied here is not ecstasy and trance, but spontaneous and ritual devotional states.

In this study of ecstasy and ecstatics, three types of sources are used:

theological texts, biographies of ecstatic saints, and interviews with living ecstatics. These allow a comparison between the expectations of the religious tradition and the actual experiences of persons who belong to the tradition.

One interesting fact arising from such a comparison is the discrepancy between what "should" occur (the stages of religious development and gradual growth of insight and emotion) and what ecstatics actually experience (a chaos of states that must be forced into a religious mold, since they often do not naturally fit). As we look at the texts, we notice that the more personal detail is present in these stories, the greater the violation of ritual and theology. Human devotion does not always fit the ritual pattern, especially among the highly individualistic and idiosyncratic visionaries in this book. Indeed, this is why virtually all were mistaken for mad or possessed, and many had to undergo exorcism or Āyurvedic treatment to prove the religious origins of their passions and visions.

Both ritual and theology seek to order religious experiences. Ritual puts such experiences under human control, making the link with the deity subject to individual or group will. Theology rationalizes the experiences, justifies the rituals, and often centers on a story or past event that has forged the link with the sacred in which the group participates. Yet ecstatics are not necessarily dependent on the traditional rituals for their religious experiences.

William James, in *Varieties of Religious Experience,* contrasted two forms of recovery from disease: *lysis* and *crisis.*[6] One was gradual, the other abrupt, and he felt that these corresponded to the ways in which inner unification could occur in the spiritual realm. His emphasis was on spontaneous conversion, a sudden change in emotional excitement or "hot place in consciousness," which he found to be "firsthand and original," opposing the "imitative" types of experience associated with traditional religion. While he thought that religious ritual imitates such experiences, he also saw the ways in which spontaneous ecstatic experience must be limited and reworked to fit into a tradition. He quotes the *Treatise on Religious Affections* of Jonathan Edwards:

> Very often their experience appears like a confused chaos, but then those parts are selected which bear the nearest resemblance to such particular steps as are insisted on; and these are dwelt upon in their thoughts, and spoken of from time to time, till they grow more and more conspicuous in their view, and other parts which are neglected grow more and more ob-

> scure. Thus what they have experienced is insensibly strained, so as to bring it to an exact conformity to the scheme already established in their minds.[7]

Thus experience may come to imitate ritual. James also quoted John Wesley, who sought hopelessly for gradual sanctification in the 652 members of his society and was forced to recognize instantaneous sanctification ("practically if not dogmatically"):

> Had half of these, or one third, or one in twenty, declared it was *gradually* wrought in them, I should have believed this, with regard to *them,* and thought that *some* were gradually sanctified and some instantaneously. But as I have not found, in so long a space of time, a single person speaking thus, I cannot but believe that sanctification is commonly, if not always, an instantaneous work.[8]

Can ritual induce ecstatic states? Some of Karl Potter's findings in *Presuppositions of Indian Philosophy* may bear on this issue. He distinguishes between progress and leap philosophies as ways of attaining mystical freedom. According to the progress approach, there are causal relations between complete freedom and its necessary and sufficient conditions; thus a person may attain such freedom gradually. This is *jātivāda,* an approach emphasizing action, discipline, and ritual. According to the leap approach, there are no causal relations leading to the spiritual goal, and freedom is not ultimately gained by progress along the path of cause and effect. This is acausal *ajātivāda,* in which practice may be preparatory or additional but cannot coerce attainment. Like the Buddhist concept of *prajñā,* it is sudden knowledge or intuition, which does not depend on such contingent factors as circumstances and previous information.[9]

Potter finds both of these approaches in Indian philosophy, and both are present in Bengali *bhakti.* Those aspects of the devotional traditions that have incorporated yogic and tantric practices have also adopted the idea of a ladder to the deity—the assumption that bodily control and detachment can lead to spiritual control and attachment to the god or goddess. In *bhakti yoga,* the devotee may practice passion or passionlessness, visualize the paradise and a new spiritual body—in hope that these may bring the desired religious goal. For spontaneous ecstatics, ritual is the result rather than the cause; as Rāmakṛṣṇa Paramahaṃsa phrases it, the fruit comes before the flower.

These two approaches are important for Bengali devotionalism—the path of progression and the path of breakthrough. The path of progression is associated with James's *lysis* or gradual approach. It emphasizes order and harmony, and the divine is reached by self-control and obedience. The god is most present in the greatest purity—of self, of place, of statue. Such purity involves loyalty to lineage and tradition, acceptance of hierarchy and authority, and ritual worship and practice. Ecstasy is attained by faith and learning, by acceptance of *dharma* and avoidance of *siddhis* (powers) and self-glorification. Such a path is yogic and devotional, and called in Bengal *śāstrīya dharma,* the path of scriptural injunctions.

The path of breakthrough is associated with James's *crisis,* or abrupt change. It emphasizes chaos and passion, and the divine is reached by unpredictable visions and revelations. The presence of the deity is not determined by ritual purity—the god may be found in pure situations, but also at the burning ground, at the toilet, in blood and sexuality, in possession and ordeals. Initiation and lineage do not determine experience—often there is a "jumping" of gurus,—where different gurus are followed at different times. The criterion for status is neither yogic knowledge nor ritual skill, but rather *bhāva,* the ecstatic state that comes with direct experience of the divine. Such states are called *sahaja* (natural and spontaneous) or *svābhāvika* (unique to a particular individual). The path is more generally called *aśāstrīya,* or not according to the scriptures.

These two types of path run through the major traditions explored in this book; both are found among Vaiṣṇavas and Śāktas. Bāuls are voluntarily *aśāstrīya,* while holy women (*sādhikās*) have been largely limited to the *aśāstrīya* approach, as there is little opportunity for them to rise in the *bhakti* lineages (although in chapter 5 one woman is described who attained her status by being her guru's successor of choice).

While the ritual approach to Indian spirituality has been widely explored, the nontraditional or *aśāstrīya* approach has been mentioned only tangentially, largely in association with the "little tradition" of folk religiosity. However, it is not limited to worship of local deities and possession cults—the breakthrough aspect of Indian ecstasy runs throughout Bengali religion. In the mainstream devotional traditions, this approach is present in the lives of believers and saints, as James phrases it, "practically if not dogmatically." Spontaneous ecstasy has its own themes, its own order, which will be explored in the conclusion. For now, we shall look at one of the major manifestations of the breakthrough approach: divine madness.

Divine Madness

Divine madness is not unique to Bengal, or even to India. It has been explored in various traditions: in both Eastern Orthodox and Western Christianity, among the Hasids of eastern Europe, among the Sufis, in possession and trance dancers around the world.[10] Plato distinguished two types of mania in the *Phaedrus:* one arising from human disease, and the other from a divine state, "which releases us from our customary habits."[11] He noted four sorts of divine madness sent by the gods: the mantic, from Apollo, which brings divination; the telestic, from Dionysus, which brings possession trance (as a result of ritual); the poetic, from the Muses, which brings enthusiasm and poetic furor; and the erotic, from Eros and Aphrodite, which brings frenzied love. He states, "In reality, our greatest blessings come to us by way of madness, which indeed is a divine gift."[12] Greek playwrights showed divine madness to be a punishment from the gods, the "disease of heroes" or sign of the tragic hero, or a realm of illusion and error which may test or purify them.[13]

In India, divine madness is described among the Alvars and Tamil Śaiva saints of South India, the Marathi saints of western India, and in the genre of popular biographies of yogis and saints. There is a wide range of behavior that may come under the title of divine madness. For instance, such madness is not always ecstatic. In *The Deeds of God in Ṛddhipur,* Anne Feldhaus translates a biography of Guṇḍam Rāul, believed to be a divine incarnation by his Mahānubhāva followers. Rāul is abrupt, impolite, childish, irritable, and occasionally able to perform miracles (he could sit in the rain and not get wet, read minds, predict the future, and cure disease). However, he shows nothing that could be called an ecstatic state and shows no devotion himself—as he is God, he need not worship or identify with another. He is viewed as both divine and a madman, but not an ecstatic or *bhakti* saint.

David Kinsley, in "Through the Looking Glass: Divine Madness in India," finds the madman to be a spiritual hero, echoing the behavior of the gods.[14] Gods exhibit madness in their inconsistency, destructive acts, delight in enjoyment, and self-absorption; these actions show their freedom, transcendence of the world, and indifference to order. The devotional madman shows his total absorption in the divine, his renunciation, his imitation of or participation in a deity, his freedom and transcendence, and his not being at home in the physical world.[15] However, *bhakti* traditions tend to prohibit direct imitation of a deity. As one informant stated, "There is already a Kṛṣṇa—what need is there of another?" The more accepted goal is to be a close friend or beloved of the deity so overwhelmed with devotion that the physical world appears unreal and the transcendent world his true home.

Mad ecstatics tend to act in certain patterns. Sometimes the person is a trickster who does foolish or outrageous things, smiling mischievously, or he may be a hermit who stays alone in meditation, threatening visitors and potential disciples with magical vengeance or showers of rocks. He may be a lover in separation, crying, burning, and hallucinating, or a lover in union, dancing and singing in the beloved's presence. Indeed, across the various *bhakti* traditions, ecstatics tended to act more like each other than like members of differing belief systems.

Observers often confuse divine and ordinary madness. Spontaneous ecstasy can appear similar to ordinary madness—the person may demonstrate eccentric behavior, violation of social or moral codes, visual and auditory hallucinations, catatonic stillness, jumbled and chaotic or coded speech. However, while many Bengali saints are called madmen by their devotees and biographers, the realm of religious madness is generally considered a separate category from clinical madness. Psychiatrists interviewed in the Calcutta area stated that they never see patients with religious symptoms[16] and that such patients are kept within the family group or become holy people for their village.[17] In the most severe cases they might be taken to an exorcist (*ojhā*), who would try to exorcise a possessive ancestor, or to a tantric healer, who might give a metal amulet with spells or objects inside, or some Āyurvedic medicine, to discourage a mischievous ghost. There are also temples at which the disturbed person may be given mantras, special practices, and an iron bangle to wear on the wrist.

It is not difficult to differentiate ritual ecstasy from ordinary madness, for both are clear cultural models—the ecstasy is described and bounded by a preexisting theology, and the person may attain a defined state by mantra, visualization, or other spiritual practice. If the saint fits the tradition, his experience can be justified and validated by it.

It is, however, more difficult to differentiate religious madness from ordinary madness. Often the methods used are draconian; exorcisms can involve torture (in case the cause of the strange behavior is possession by a demon) such as tying the person down, burning him, hitting him with shoes or other objects. If the exorcism fails and the strange behavior remains, the person may be declared a saint by default. One cannot exorcise a god, for he would be more powerful than the exorcist. Indeed, only a deity is strong enough to resist the coercion of the exorcism. If no Āyurvedic cause can be found for the person's beliefs or behavior, sainthood is the only option remaining—by a process of elimination.

A less strenuous way to differentiate is judgment by a religious authority. Caitanya's divine status was announced by Śrīvāsa, a respected Vaiṣṇava. Rāmakṛṣṇa's female guru, Bhairavī Brāhmaṇī, convened a group of pandits at Dakṣiṇeśwar and demonstrated to them that Rāmakṛṣṇa had the eight ecstatic symptoms (*sāttvika bhāvas*) and had experienced *mahābhāva* (the highest ecstatic state for Vaiṣṇavas). As a result, Rāmakṛṣṇa was proclaimed not only a saint but an *avatāra* or incarnation of the deity. Often, passing holy men, brahmins, or even doctors may play this role of validator. However, for validation to occur, some of the ecstatic symptoms must be recognizably part of a specific tradition.

In popular folk belief, both the ecstatic and the madman have symptoms due to separation; however, the madman longs for his ancestral home, or money or a wife, or his lost job, while the ecstatic longs for his god. Separation (*viraha*) causes the same symptoms in both. It is the nature of the desired object that distinguishes the states. There are also differences in behavior, according to informants—the ecstatic appears to be harmful but instead ends up helping, while the madman genuinely hurts people by mental or physical violence. There is also a difference in control of states in folk belief: informants claim that the madman is forced into his abnormal behavior and cannot become normal if he tries, while the ecstatic chooses his states—he might be lost in trance, but he can emerge at will to argue with persons of different beliefs.

Holy men and women interviewed in Calcutta have distinguished the saint from the madman in both cause and behavior. The madman has a weak or defective brain, or his soul is in a bad body; he has no sense and will bite and hit; he is hostile and has many troubles. On the other hand, the saint is filled with the presence of Bhagavān (God); he is without any sense of the body—he has only the sense of divine presence and no others; his body is purified, and his appearance of madness is due to his visions of God; he talks to deities with words and gestures, and gets along well with animals; he can play with snakes and they will not bite him; he can swallow poison and it will not hurt him. Several holy men listed four qualities as the hallmarks of the saint: he is inert, *jaḍa* (he becomes lost in meditation, appearing like a corpse or a stone statue); mad, *unmāda* (he acts irrationally, for he is always in ecstasy); ghoulish, *piśāca* (he does not discriminate between pure and impure things, feeling love toward all); and childlike, *bālaka* (he acts like a child between four and eight years old). As a holy man interviewed in Bākreśwar stated, the one who has attained Kālī[18] is eternally in a state of apparent madness (*pāgal bhāva*) and has these qualities:

> In this state, the ordinary self does not manifest. The person is naked, acts like a madman, sometimes speaks as the goddess, and sometimes as a little child. One cannot tell a madman [*pāgal*] just because he goes to eat at the outhouse; many people here do that. There are many false holy men here, they are like imitation jewels, glass instead of diamond. . . . Only certain kinds of states are respected. When consciousness returns after a quiet trance, everybody comes to [the holy man's] feet and says, "O Bābā." But when he is in a true mad ecstasy [*mahābhāva*], people throw stones at him and say, "Go away."[19]

This informant mentions the false (*nakal*) holy man, who pretends to have ecstatic states, imitating those of others. Such a person is greatly scorned; the concept of imitation of ecstasy is widely known and universally despised. He also describes how intense ecstasy frightens people by its passion and resemblance to madness, while the milder trances are considered socially acceptable.

Ecstatic states and divine madness have been examined from a psychological perspective by opponents and proponents—by those who find ecstatic symptoms and mystical states to be forms of psychopathology and by those who are advocates of psychological breakdown as a path of spiritual growth. In "Mysticism and Schizophrenia," Kenneth Wapnick looked at the similarities and differences between ecstatic and mad states.[20] He found that both show a dichotomy between two levels of experience—one outer or social, the other inner or personal. Both show a breakdown of attachments to the social world, an experience of pain or terror as the person "entered the inner world," a feeling of peace following the end of the terror, and a "return" to the social world.

However, the mystical process is lifelong, while the schizophrenic episode tends to be shorter—and there is no evidence that recovered schizophrenics tend to explore such inner experiences voluntarily. Mysticism culminates in a state of unity, while schizophrenia has no such culmination. While the mystic generally maintains conscious control throughout, the schizophrenic has a breakdown in functioning and must be hospitalized.[21]

Wapnick suggests that the function of the religious discipline is to develop "muscles" to withstand the experiences of the inner world. These allow the inner and outer worlds to be joined, rather than separate and opposed as in schizophrenia, when conflict renders the person sterile and unproductive. Thus, mystical ecstasy and psychopathological states can be distinguished by goal, by adaptation to the social world, and by creativity.

These distinctions have been differently interpreted in India. Bengali understandings of divine madness are to a large extent based on pan-Indian understandings of the relationship of body, mind, and spirit. To better understand the organization of the person in India, we shall look at the medical system of Āyurveda.

Madness and the Indian Medical Model

In ancient India, both physical and mental disease were understood to come from outside the person, due to possession by a spirit or revenge by a ghost. Amulets were believed more powerful than medicine, unless the drug was considered an "internal amulet."[22] From the sixth century B.C. to the second century A.D. came a growth of medical schools, and medicine became more aligned with philosophy than with religion. Caraka, Suśruta, and Bhela brought out compendia based on theories of the elements and influenced by the Nyāya, Vaiśeṣika, and Sāṇkhya schools of philosophy. Caraka and Suśruta located the mind (with cognition and sensation) in the heart, while Bhela located *mānasa* (cognition) in the brain and *citta* (associated with feelings) in the heart.[23]

These writers were the major influences on the Āyurvedic system. Āyurveda (from *āyus,* life, and *veda,* knowledge), is the dominant system of Indian medicine, and it includes three possible sources of disease generally, and madness in particular. Endogenous (*nija*) diseases are biological imbalances, which are cured by herbs and drugs. Mental (*mānasika*) diseases result from negative emotion, mental strain, and an imbalance of *guṇas* or qualities and are cured by yoga and moral action. Exogenous disease (*āgantu*) is a result of outside invasion and includes god and ghost possession, which is cured by sacrifice or exorcism. Thus there are three major understandings of mad and ecstatic behavior possible: the biological, the psychological, and the spiritual.

These three areas are explored in a bit more detail. Endogenous disease arises through the humors, which are *vāyu* or *vāta* (associated with movement, nerves, muscles, and pain); *pitta* (associated with enzymes and hormones, digestion, and body temperature); and *kapha* or *śleṣma* (which regulates the other two, as well as liquids and plumpness). When these three humors have left their regular channels (*srotas*) they become faults (*doṣas*) and the person becomes ill. Madness is the intoxication of the mind by these *doṣas,* and it is relieved when the body is brought back to a homeostatic balance.[24] Endogenous disease includes astrological and karmic factors (interpreted by modern Āyurvedic physicians as hereditary and congenital factors), hormonal imbalances, brain tumors, old age, and degenerative diseases with mental symptoms.[25]

Diseases of *mānasa* are understood to be a disorganization of the mental elements, which are associated with passion and inertia. The causes of such an imbalance are called *vihara*—mental strain, improper activities, negative emotions, anxiety, strong instincts, loss of loved persons or objects, and association with hated ones. An imbalance may also be caused by improper yogic meditation, which causes the inner, spiritual bodies to go out of harmony with each other, or by too much study, which causes the folk disease called "study-*pāgal.*" Again, its cure is a return to a homeostatic balance. Passion and inertia must be subordinated to purity; the weak mind must be strengthened and desires disciplined. Proper meditation and prayer aid this balance, and yogic practices align mind and body.

Exogenous disease is the broadest category, for it includes the outside agents that affect the person. In this cateogory are drink, drugs, poison, accidents, unclean food, parasitic infections, and bites of rabid animals. However, the emphasis of Āyurveda has traditionally been on spirit invasion and the ways in which to deal with it.

If the problem is possession, the healer must find out what sort of spirit it is and whether it is acting on its own or as an agent for another. In some cases, it may even be difficult to determine that a spirit is the problem, for ghosts may influence people through their humors and imitate a physical disease. The spirit may be any of a variety of life forms. The victim may have been touched by a *gandharva,* seized by a *yakṣa,* smelled a *rākṣasa,* be ridden by a *piśāca,* seen by a god or ancestor, or cursed by a guru or ascetic. All of these cause exogenous insanity, especially by possession.[26] The infecting spirits can act on their own, because they want attention (usually in the form of a fruit or animal sacrifice), or because they want to play or to punish the person for a sinful, impure, or careless act. Or in their search for gratification they may act as agents of witchcraft and sorcery.

If a sacrifice will not get rid of the possessing entity, exorcism may be required. This can be a painful proceeding—it is assumed that the possessed person cannot feel pain, that only the ghost can—and torture chases it away as quickly as possible. The exorcist (*ojhā*) may also neutralize the effect of the evil eye and subdue, placate, or expel spirits by sacrificial rites. Blackford reports red pepper juice put into the eyes, sticks put into the ears puncturing the eardrum, and branding as techniques of exorcism.[27] Other folk cures include *jhār phuk* (blowing on the patient while reciting mantras) and the use of amulets and iron bracelets. An interesting description of the use of an amulet for a type of madness is given by J. C. Oman:

> His people had a servant who was afflicted in this way. Every six months or so the man used to become subject to a strange, morbid restlessness, and a mental inquietude which could only be allayed by his being visited and bitten by a serpent. Everyone looked upon him with repulsion as one allied with such a terrible reptile. He also inspired a sort of awe because of this connection. The man himself was generally unhappy, and when the paroxysms were at hand he was wretched and miserable.
>
> At last the sufferer consulted a wise sadhu, who gave him a *gânda tâwiz* (a peculiar malodorous amulet). When he had attached this to his person he experienced a sort of nightmare. Serpents seemed to crawl round him, to wind and coil about his limbs, and to hiss and dart at him. Even the ambient air seemed to be peopled with writhing serpent forms. For two hours or so this dreadful vision obsessed him, nearly driving him mad, and then the air cleared, as it were, and the ground at his feet resumed for him its natural appearance. He was cured forever; the mental shadows and the very real serpents passing entirely out of his life.[28]

Other cures for exogenous madness include pilgrimages (often to curing temples), fasting, religious rites and vows, jewels (especially astrological gems, to avert bad planetary influences), and sacrifices.

Caraka, probably the most influential writer on Indian medicine, says of insanity:

> Insanity is characterised by the perversion of mind, intellect, consciousness, knowledge, memory, desire, manners, behaviour and conduct. . . . Due to the perversion of mind, the pa-

> tient does not think of such things which are worth thinking; on the other hand, he thinks of such things as ought not to be thought of. Due to perversion of intellect, he understands eternal things as ephemeral and useful things as harmful. . . . Due to the perversion (loss) of conciousness, the patient is unable to have perception of burns caused by fire, etc. Due to the perversion of memory, the patient either does not remember anything or remembers things incorrectly. Due to perversion of desire, disinclination develops for things desired previously. Due to perversion of manners, the patient, who is otherwise normal, gets enraged. Due to perversion of behaviour, the patient indulges in undesirable activities. Due to the perversion of conduct, the patient resorts to such activities as are against the rules prescribed in religious works.[29]

He states of exogenous insanity, whose origin is external to the body:

> Some scholars hold the view that this type of insanity is caused by the effects of the sinful activities in the past life. Lord Punarvasu Ātreya considers intellectual blasphemy as the causative factor of this condition. Due to intellectual blasphemy the patient disregards the gods. . . . He also resorts to undesirable and such other inauspicious activities. The gods etc. cause insanity in him because of his own inauspicious activities.[30]

The patient is thus himself responsible for his madness—he cannot claim innocence and blame the gods:

> Neither the gods, nor *gandharvas,* nor *piśācas* nor *rākṣasas* afflict a person who himself is free from misdeeds. The primary causes of insanity in an individual are his own misdeeds, and other agents like the gods etc. act only as the consequence of these misdeeds. . . . The wise man should not blame the gods, ancestors or *rākṣasas* for diseases caused by his own misdeeds due to intellectual blasphemy. One should hold himself responsible for his happiness and miseries. Therefore, without apprehension one should follow the path of propitiousness. . . . Thus the power either to avert or invite the attack of insanity rests within the individual himself.[31]

Suśruta includes religious hallucinations (such as hearing *gandharvas* when they are not really present) as signs of impending death:

> The man who hears a variety of divine sounds, even in the absence of any of the celestial beings (such as the Siddhas, the

> Gandharvas etc.), or thinks that he is hearing the uproar of a city, or the moanings of the sea, or the rumbling of a rain cloud, without their actual presence or proximity . . . or assigns to them causes other than the actual ones, should be regarded as a doomed being.[32]

Āyurvedic psychiatry is a broad and sophisticated system, including in its modern form perceptual disorders (*indrīyārtha grahaṇa vikṛti*), thought disorders (*vicāraṇa vikṛti*), disorders of memory (*smṛti vikṛti*), emotional disorders (*bhāva vikṛti*), and behavioral problems (*ceṣṭā vikṛti*). It recognizes hallucination, obsession, amnesia, anxiety, elation, and depression. While there are cultural models and syndromes, there is a broad range of possible forms of insanity.

Many psychiatric patients in India do not fit clearly into the cultural models of the possessed or enchanted person; neither do they fit clearly into the Āyurvedic medical model. Rather, they show bits and pieces of various syndromes. G. F. W. Ewens, an English psychiatrist in India at the turn of the century, wrote of some of the insane patients he had seen. Few of them fit into a recognized cultural model, yet they were recognized as insane. One patient claimed that a *dhobi* (laundryman) in a tree was his enemy and tried to kill him; another was an uncrowned rājā; another was a king of yogis; another was blind and walked with a blanket on his head, for enemies would throw fire on his head. One patient was killed each night by attendants, but revived in the morning by a faqir; another felt that his insides were a river, and he required great amounts of food and drink; a third believed his shadow was God, and he would assault anyone who stepped on his shadow (as this would insult God).

Ewens found common hallucinations among the patients: that the food was poisoned, that beautiful women visited them at night, that they were attacked by insects and animals, that human faces would appear and talk to them, that small fires or bad odors would suddenly start. In one detailed case history, a Muslim hashish addict saw multicolored animals appear before his eyes, and he would get *behosh* (emotional). He was tormented by spirits who would sit on his chest at night, preventing him from sleeping. He would write phrases from the Koran in the dust and filth on the floor so that people could walk on it, for he claimed the Koran was at the root of his misery.[33]

Another case was a Hindu who threatened suicide and assault. He would sit naked, collecting rags and bits of paper. He destroyed clothing and other objects, and rubbed feces on himself and on the walls of the cell. He would curse the jail officials and accuse them of crimes. He claimed to be ordained by the gods to direct human affairs.[34]

Some of these cases may demonstrate cultural syndromes, but few Western psychiatrists would not recognize the symptoms. These patients were considered criminals when they committed illegal acts (such as murder), but not when they merely displayed symptoms that were deviant. Patients used religious imagery, but primarily to justify erratic behavior. In some cases, a yogi or faqir was believed to have magical powers; in one case, a man subject to fits of violence and incoherence would shout "Jai Devī"—he claimed that his outbursts were caused by worship of the goddess. Visionary experience was not that of a compassionate mother or mythic paradise, as saints have described. Rather, deities would appear in parts (disconnected heads and voices) and encourage violence, fear, and guilt.

Cultural syndromes are often seen in folk psychology. Deborah Bhaṭṭācārya found three Bengali categories of folk interpretations of madness: *tuktak, māthār golmal,* and *bhor. Tuktak* is sorcery, often due to the envy of neighbors. The person is struck by madness, disease, and misfortune, his personality changes, and he acts against his own best interests. In *māthār golmal* (the disfunctioning or confusion of the head), madness is seen in activity, anxiety, anger, sexuality, and sometimes burning sensations.[35] It is attributed to excess bile, which generates heat, or to shock. *Bhor* is possession by a ghost, which often occurs during religious festivals. It is expressed by rigidity and personality change.[36]

The madman is acultural, denying *dharma.* He has no home and lives on the street; he eats anything and does not bathe; he is naked and speaks gibberish. He does whatever he wishes, acting according to whim and his own inclination; he does not follow his social and religious obligations. Bhaṭṭācārya finds all of these forms of madness to be due to intrusions and the cure for madness to be a strengthening of the individual against such intrusions. While Āyurvedic psychology emphasizes individual responsibility, folk psychology speaks of madness due to illness and the actions of others.

Both Āyurvedic and folk understandings of madness are a useful background for studying the lives of the saints described in this book. When these saints first described their visions and trances, observers first viewed them through the medical, not the religious, model.

Like Western psychology, Āyurveda recognizes many types of insanity. And like Western psychology, it has great difficulty differentiating between mental imbalance and religious ecstasy, especially ecstasy that occurs unpredictably and outside the traditional religious situations.

Spontaneous and Ritual Ecstasy

The tension between spontaneous and ritual forms of ecstasy is not unique to the Indian tradition, but can be found in at least two other religious traditions—those of Buddhism and Christianity. In seventh-century Chinese Zen (or Ch'an) Buddhism, there was a conflict between the northern school of Shen-hsiu and the southern school of Hui-neng. The most well-known instance of this conflict is seen in poems intended to indicate the degree of enlightenment of their writers. Shen-hsiu wrote:

The body is the Bodhi tree (enlightenment)
The mind is like a clear mirror standing.
Take care to wipe it all the time
Allow no grain of dust to cling.

Hui-neng wrote:

The Bodhi is not like a tree
The clear mirror is nowhere standing.
Fundamentally not one thing exists
Where, then, is a grain of dust to cling?[37]

In the first poem, the importance of ritual practice is emphasized, while the second poem denies the efficacy of practice. Shen-hsiu's "Northern Zen of Gradualness" emphasizes meditation by purification of the mind, continual quieting of desires, and gradual ascent by disciplined repetition. Enlightenment is "acquired." According to Hui-neng's "Southern Zen of Suddenness," practice does not lead to enlightenment; rather, both are identical and meditation "contributes to the process of revealing one's enlightenment." Enlightenment comes suddenly, "in no way acquired, in no way caused." The goal is not a state of cultivated purity, but an experience of transcendence, a "breakthrough."[38]

In the *Sutra of the Sixth Patriarch,* these two approaches are symbolized by two Chinese logographs: *k'an ching* or "paying attention to purity," and *chien-hsing* or "seeing into one's true nature." The debate between these two schools was continued in the Japanese split between the Rinzai and Soto Zen schools.

The distinction between spontaneous and ritual religious experience also appears in the Roman Catholic tradition in the distinction between ascetical and mystical states. In ascetic or acquired experiences, the cause is human activity and repeated effort, and there is an increase in knowledge and virtue, as well as an inner purification. In mystical or infused experiences, the cause is divine operation, and the mystical graces come down like "rain falling from heaven." The operations of the gifts of the Holy Spirit lead to visions, mystical lights, and such extraordinary states as the mystical marriage and the unitive life.[39]

In *The Graces of Interior Prayer: A Treatise on Mystical Theology,* Poulain defines supernatural ecstasy as having two aspects: "the first, which is interior and invisible, is a very intense attachment to some religious subject; the second, which is corporeal and visible, is the alienation of the sensible faculties."[40] While basing his writings primarily on the experiences of Saint Theresa of Avila, Poulain also cites Saint Thomas Aquinas, who equates ecstasy with the Greek *extasis* and the Latin *excessus mentis,* the flight of the spirit. Ecstasy in the Catholic mystical tradition includes intense rapture, both brief and longer term, and intellectual visions (of the Trinity or of divine attributes). It may include the beatific vision, the direct view of God (although this is a debated point), and there are often spiritual sufferings during ecstasy—the pain of love (compared to a wound), a horror of sin, compassion for the damned, and the sorrow of the Crucified.

There are also ecstatic effects on the body: paralysis, weakness, trembling, rigidity, lowering of temperature, convulsions, and sometimes bloody sweat and inability to eat. Poulain describes how the ecstatic state is distinguished from the morbid state on the basis of knowledge gained in the ecstasy, such as moral sense, strong will, loving emotional state, acceptance of suffering, memory of the state, and the ability to act in the world.[41] While ecstasy cannot be produced "in a purely natural manner, by an intense concentration of the attention on a religious object," it may be simulated by conscious lying, overactive imagination, the devil's action, and inaccurate memory.[42] Such phenomena as fainting, hysteria, somnambulism, and hypnotic trance may also resemble ecstasy.

In Catholic theology, ritual practice can only lead to the ascetic virtues, and the person must depend on the action of the Holy Spirit for the infused graces. In Bengali devotion, both are believed capable of leading the person to the goal of mad, ecstatic love of the deity.

Bhakti, however, emphasizes ritual in a way different from Catholic mysticism. While Catholicism has unpredictable raptures and flights of the soul, *bhakti* attempts to control such events by visualization of paradises and spiritual bodies. Consciously induced love and vision take the place of infusion, drawing down the deity's grace. Both traditions emphasize ecstasies of divine love, but these are validated in different ways. While the Catholic ecstatic states are proved primarily by the moral actions they motivate, *bhakti* ecstasies are validated by their strength and persistence—causing the person to endure exorcism, medication, social rejection, and renunciation. Catholic mysticism has emphasized simple, intellectual visions of the divine attributes and Trinity, while Bengali devotional mysticism includes lush, sensual environments and physically attractive spiritual beings.

Ritual ecstasy is that state induced by following a discipline of spiritual practice, as taught by a guru of accepted lineage, and following statements in authoritative texts. Such ecstasy conforms completely to doctrine, with ecstatic vision arising from expectation and imitation of previous models. It is regulated behavior, according to rule, following tradition and religious practices, emphasizing purity and obedience to authority. Ecstasy is similar among different practitioners, who take identical paths to an identical goal. There is no room for madness here—it would be a failure of discipline, a break in concentration, a wrong word in the ritual. As the Vaiṣṇava devotee Jagadānanda Dāsa stated: "In the Western system, people try to invent things for themselves. In India, we try to follow previous people, to do what they did and get it down properly, the way that it was done before."[43]

However, spontaneous ecstasy is individual, different for different people. Trance may occur in meditation, but it may also occur while the person is eating dinner or working. In the biographies of Bengali saints, a vision or insight unique to that particular person is called *svabhāvika.* Such ecstasy is innate, native, not forced; the visions, revelations, and extreme emotional states come to the person without effort. Mad behavior may be a part of such spontaneous experience—the person may be overcome by passion for a god, or possessed, or in a trance. Such a state is not limited by textual rules. Its emphasis is on mystery and intuition, the limits of the conscious will.

Ritual and spontaneous states tend to oppose each other, but they may meet in the middle in two ways. One approach is the ritual seeking of spontaneous love—*bhakti yoga*—which creates conditions in which passion may best arise and be cultivated. In *bhakti yoga,* devotees attempt to induce love—both their own for the deity, and the deity's love for them—by ritual practice. The other approach is divine madness—*divyonmāda*—when the person loves the deity madly and passionately, and expresses this love in ritual action or in religious art forms (such as poetry, song, and dance). The expectation in *bhakti yoga* is that ritual is the trigger; in divine madness, ritual is the expression of emotion. In the former, ritual leads to spontaneity; in the latter, spontaneity leads to ritual.

In both cases, devotional ritual regulates the emotions. Ritual in *bhakti yoga* increases the practitioner's emotional intensity, giving traditional images and actions greater depth and meaning, while ritual in *bhakti* ecstatics lessens emotional intensity, expanding the focus from the vision of the deity to the worldly actions of worship and chanting. Rituals of worship are used to both increase and decrease ecstatic states.

Ecstatics are rare in modern India. The clear majority of religious practitioners interviewed during research for this book performed daily and periodic ritual, yet never had ecstatic experiences (or were unwilling to admit that they had them). These people were serious, dedicated, and respected by others of their traditions and were hopeful that they would one day experience such states of depth and intensity. These states were not understood to result from the practice itself, but rather from the grace of the deity, who might respect the devotee's religious commitment.

The ecstatic minority performed ritual as a means of ordering and stabilizing their lives. Visions and voices could appear at any time, but a life of ritual service and instruction of disciples provided an anchor, a social role, and a limited measure of control over events that had been chaotic, even violent, in the past.

For this approach, Rouget's analysis of the function of music gives an excellent idea of the function of ritual:

> The psychic upheaval that [trance] manifests thus obeys a purely internal logic of the state of consciousness. This means that the role of the music is much less to produce the trance that to create conditions favorable to its onset, to regularize its form, and to ensure that instead of being a merely individual, unpredictable, and uncontrollable behavioral phenomenon, it becomes, on the contrary, predictable, controlled and at the service of the group.[44]

To better understand both ritual and spontaneous ecstasy, we look at the Bengali terms for ecstatic states.

The Language of Ecstasy

Ecstasy holds an important place in Indian religious traditions. The most authoritative texts are revealed (*śruti*), seen, and heard by the sage, and later described or written by him. These arise from firsthand experience, unlike the indirect text based on memory (*smṛti*) and the systematic analyses and explications called *śāstra.* The language of revelation is vivid and powerful, its knowledge not acquired by the ordinary senses. The seer can say: "I have seen the Great Puruṣa, as golden as the sun, beyond all darkness."

When authors wish their texts to gain authority, they claim that the texts arise from that author's ecstatic experiences; they claim that they are revealed texts. The texts most generally accepted as revelatory are the Vedas, Brāhmaṇas, and Upaniṣads. Other forms of ecstasy are described in less universally accepted sources: Vaiṣṇava devotional texts, Śākta poems, magical tantras, the worship handbooks handed down from guru to disciple. Terms for ecstasy are used in this literature and in the oral tradition of practitioners and devotees.

The terms used by most Bengali informants to translate the English word *ecstasy* were *bhāva,*[45] *mahābhāva,* and *bhāvāveśa.* The *Samsad Bengali-English Dictionary* gives many definitions for *bhāva,* including: birth, existence, state, condition, mental state, mood, love, inner significance, imagination, meditation, ecstasy, and outburst of emotion. The Monier-Williams *Sanskrit Dictionary* has four columns of definitions for *bhāva.* The *Bāngālā Bhāṣār Abhidhān* has two columns, including as definitions the terms for essence, heart, imagination, divinity and yogic powers, passion, mental confusion, possession trace, and rapture.

To include definitions of *bhāva* in present usage, I asked Bengali informants encountered in a variety of locales what the word *bhāva* means. Many informants divided the meaning of the word into two categories: material and nonmaterial, or worldly and ordinary versus supernatural or spiritual. This section also divides their answers into two general categories, showing something of the wide range of understandings of the term. Some of the more technical definitions are further described in later chapters of the book.

Bhāva in the worldly sense is used to refer to mood, emotion, idea, state of mind, meaning. Although its use is secular, it still shows potential for a sacred dimension. Bengali informants have defined such *bhāva* as follows:

> *Bhāva* is that aspect of mind which deals with emotion and experience; it is a result of culture and personality. It is only emotion—it does not include images, which are only fantasy. Yogis may develop stages and faculties of *bhāva.* Any experi-

ence can be called a *bhāva,* but the highest *bhāva* is *brahma-bhāva,* a state of realistic expectations, a poise in which a stable equilibrium is established. (Psychiatrist)

Bhāva is a spontaneous response to natural beauty, often when alone, by seriously religious people. At that time, there are no worldly problems. It can occur in any time or place. There are local nuns who can deal very well with children; they do not have *bhāva,* but they are on their way to *bhāva.* (Psychiatrist)

Bhāva is sentiment or emotion. It depends on the context—it may be used for poetry and art, or for people—*dujon bhāva,* they are close. After fighting, children clasp fingers and say, "*Bhāva,* now we are friends." *Bhāva* is also inspired thought. (Grant administrator)

Bhāva is the person's first response to a stimulus, personal and idiosyncratic, which then becomes an appropriate response. It is spontaneous and normally subliminal, unless the person is well versed in introspection. *Bhāva* is a small gap which is different in different people. It is due to the *bhāva-saṃskāras,* the person's cardinal traits or inborn reactions. Normally these are submerged below the surface, but the person who practices a spiritual discipline may bring these behavioral traits to the surface. Sītārāmdāsa Oṃkārnāth is an example of a person who shows the fullest expression of these cardinal traits. (Psychiatrist)

Bhāva is thoughts and ideas. It is one's total thinking toward doing or obtaining something good; it means doing something good for others. (Bookseller)

Bhāva has a material and a spiritual meaning. Its material meaning is love between a man and a woman, but spiritual *bhāva* is love of God by a devotee with all his mind and heart. (Insurance salesman)

Bhāva is character or personality. After rebirth, if one looks back at one's old life, it is a *bhāva.* Different saris relate cloth and body in different ways; they cause different *bhāvas.* There is a soundless word inside which decides such preferences. *Bhāva* comes in waves and includes relations between people. It also includes bodily feelings, such as *bhālo bhāva* (to feel well) and *khārāp bhāva* (to feel ill). (Storekeeper)

Bhāva in the spiritual sense refers to intense inner experience. The deeper layers of the self are encountered and integrated, and the person maintains a vivid relationship to deity or Absolute. There are technical terms, such as the three tantric *bhāvas,* and the five Vaiṣṇava *bhāvas,* which are explained later. *Bhāva* in the spiritual (*ādhyātmika*) sense includes visions of the deity, mystical union, trances, and ecstatic symptoms. The following definitions are from Bengali informants, both laypersons and religious professionals:

> *Bhāva* is the religious experience of traditional holy men and women performing spiritual practices. It is taken seriously if they are part of a lineage. (Vaiṣṇava layperson)
>
> *Bhāva* is when different parts of the person come together, as when cooking Kashmiri chicken. Different spices are blended together to create a taste. In love affairs [*premer bhāva*], the parts of the soul are mixed together like spices. The soul and mind consult each other, along with the body, to decide about loving. Good worship [*pūjā*] creates good *bhāva* between the devotee and the goddess, if the person believes 100 percent. There is a relation of soul between the deity and the worshiper—they share the same actions, and adjust to each other, even if there was conflict between them at the beginning. (Śākta layperson)
>
> *Bhāva* is when a man surrenders completely before the deity with full faith. Worldly affairs become secondary. In the state of divine *bhāva,* there are no distinctions, no separate self. One can taste the pleasures of Kailāsa, and the nectar flows down onto the head. (Śākta practitioner)
>
> *Bhāva* is the combination of three aspects of the self. Together, these make up the subtle body [*bhāvamaya deha*], the body made up of *bhāva.* The subtle body becomes the perfected body [*siddha deha*] when it is purified by meditation and spiritual practice. *Bhāvas* are also purified in this way. Also, there is a relationship between *bhāva* and *rasa* [aesthetic enjoyment]. *Bhāva* and *rasa* added together equal bliss. Each *bhāva* requires a *rasa* to satisfy it. For instance, hunger is *bhāva* and pudding is *rasa. Bhāva* also can describe inner conceptions and intuitive thought. (Vaiṣṇava practitioner)
>
> *Bhāva* is very deep thought, deep in the heart, until one is lost within the self. The person becomes explosively pure in heart—he sees persons as other persons, such as all women as mother or sister. There are three stages of *bhāva* in the worship of Śakti—*bhāva,* possession by *bhāva* [*bhāvāveśa*], and deep trance [*bhāva samādhi*]. In *bhāva,* one becomes lost in

> memory and emotion. In possession by *bhāva,* one becomes lost from the material world and sees the heaven worlds. In the deepest trance of *bhāva,* one roams in the absolute [*ātman*]. (Śākta layperson)
>
> The precondition for *bhāva* is absorption in what the guru teaches about the form and qualities of the deity. You know what *rasagullās*[46] are. Here something is to be kept in melted sugar for a long time, and the qualities of the melted sugar are slowly absorbed into it. *Bhāva* is like this. . . . *Bhāva* is an evolutionary process, not to be acquired in a single day. The guru will set up the stage and supply the imagery. You are to be absorbed in it, to utter the names, Hare Kṛṣṇa, repeatedly until it takes your mind outside the realm of worldliness. Then *bhāva* will be aroused in you. (Vaiṣṇava practitioner)
>
> *Bhāvas* are of two kinds, pure and impure. That which leads the mind to Bhagavān, which leads one to the realization of Bhagavān, is pure *bhāva.* Its opposite is impure, that which leads men to worldly desires. . . . The person who has been possessed by divine *bhāva* will see the object of his worship all around, wherever he looks. There was a devotee in Vṛndāvana, and while he was preparing bread he became possessed by *bhāva.* His hand was on the burning oven; he was burnt, but he could not feel it. Someone saw it and he was rescued. Real *bhāva* makes one forget the material world. It is that condition in which one can forget and ignore his body of five elements. (Vaiṣṇava practitioner)

These informants' definitions of *bhāva* describe gradual degrees of inwardness. The worldly type deals with thought and emotion, spontaneous responses to beauty and other stimuli, outlook, personality, conscience, memory, and the beginnings of contemplation. As the person becomes more introspective and focused on a religious goal, the ecstatic aspect of *bhāva* emerges—the person becomes more integrated and surrenders before the deity; he tastes bliss, trance, aesthetic delight, passion for the god; he sees visions within his heart or all around him; he visits the heaven-worlds. Eventually, he reaches his highest goal: *ātmān,* the heavenly Vṛndāvana of Kṛṣṇa and the gopīs, or the paradise of Kailāsa, where Śiva and Śakti eternally dwell.

Bhāva includes not only inward states, but also their outward manifestation; a *bhāva* may be hidden or revealed. The ecstatic may leap and dance like a child or hide coyly behind a veil, acting a woman's role. Hidden states may be visible only to a few chosen disciples or to all observers.

Notes on Method

Ecstatic phenomena have been studied from a variety of perspectives. Those most prominent include the literature on mysticism, anthropology, classical and transpersonal psychologies, and ethnopsychology.

Mystical literature includes both older and favorable works dealing with mystical ecstasy[47] and more skeptical recent works.[48] Psychoanalytic studies tend to focus on the pathological dynamics associated with certain ecstatic states: schizophrenia,[49] denial and depression,[50] anxiety,[51] anorexia nervosa,[52] and regression.[53] Anthropological literature on ecstasy tends to emphasize trance and possession states, and often includes in-depth studies of individual cases.[54] Transpersonal psychology views ecstatic states as a special type of "altered state of consciousness" and seeks to find ranges of possible states that religious practitioners and others may enter.[55] On India specifically, work on ethnopsychology shows devotees and gurus in context, exploring indigenous understandings as well as Western conceptions of religious phenomena.[56]

In comparing the expectations of the religious tradition regarding ecstasy with the actual experiences of ecstatics and practitioners, I used three types of texts. The first type was theological texts, which would give historical instances of ecstasy in *avatāras,* sages, and devotees in mythical/historical situations and describe how these were understood in the tradition. Instances of faith and ritual practice were described in these texts, which would later become paradigmatic for followers. For this study, I chose texts that scholars considered significant and that the majority of followers claimed as the most important texts on religious experience. Vaiṣṇava devotees and practitioners felt that the *Bhāgavata Purāṇa* was the most important text on ecstatic states, followed by the *Caitanya Caritāmṛta* of Kṛṣṇadāsa Kavirāja, and the *Bhaktirasāmṛtasindhu* and *Ujjvala-Nīlamaṇi* of Rūpa Gosvāmin. Śākta devotees and practitioners generally felt that texts were less important than instruction from the guru, but the majority suggested the *Mahānirvāṇa* and *Kulārṇava Tantras,* and the songs of Rāmprasād, as well as the *Kathāmṛta* of Rāmakṛṣṇa Paramahaṃsa. Bāuls are much closer to an oral tradition and also do not emphasize the use of texts, but several suggested the songs of Lālan Fakir as best exemplifying *bāul bhāva.*

The second type of text used was sacred biography. The ones I used here are at an early stage in the biographical tradition—before the organization of a critical text or orthodox biography. They are not considered divinely inspired works, but rather journalistic accounts. Almost all are relatively recent—within the last 150 years—except for the biography of Kṛṣṇa Caitanya. This biography is used here as a theological text (based primarily on the *Caitanya Caritāmṛta* of Kṛṣṇadāsa Kavirāja) rather than as a saint biography—for its usage is different from the other biographies, and it plays a much more influential role in the Vaiṣṇava tradition. Indeed, Caitanya was viewed by many of his biographers as more of a deity than a human being, and there was more use of mythic elements and miracles in his biographies than in others.[57]

Lorenzen, basing his ideas on those of Weber, suggests that Indian hagiographies became important during 500–200 B.C., with the dissolution of Aryan social structures and the rise of new territorial kingdoms with urban centers and new social and religious movements. Such hagiographies appealed to the emotions of the general populace and served as a medium for new gods, heroes, and belief systems to enter into society.[58]

The Bengali style of hagiography appears to be less formal and less idealized than many other Indian lives of saints. These volumes are generally written by disciples who have lived with the ecstatic for some period of time and who carefully avoid coming to conclusions about events they do not understand. Quite frequently, the author states some curious action or phrase of the ecstatic and says outright that he does not understand its significance, but doubtless the guru understands better than he. The author tends to avoid elaboration, using a sort of realism comparable to the Bengali style of filmmaking and short story. However, there are patterns that appear in the lives of the ecstatic saints, which are described in the concluding chapter of this book.

The third type of text I used in this research was interview, generally taped and transcribed. I interviewed many religious practitioners who are not specifically mentioned in the book, who were asked about ecstasy (as *bhāva* or *mahābhāva*). They told stories, gave definitions, described their gurus or ecstatics known to them, and gave their own theories on what was really occurring with true saints (*siddhas*). Almost all practitioners I interviewed (over fifty persons) also mentioned false ecstatics—people who did rituals and pretended to go into ecstatic states, but really sought only status or money.

The longer interviews included in this book generally came from a single day of talking, although I may have visited the persons involved many times. I have written the stories in the same order as given by the person interviewed, although some repetition within the stories has been omitted. I found the interviewees through a network of informants, the most helpful of whom owned a *pūjā* supply store in Calcutta and knew the many religious practitioners, devotees, and renunciants who visited him. Interview questions were open-ended: "Could you tell me something about your life? Could you tell me the meaning of ecstasy [*bhāva, mahābhāva, bhāvāveśa*]?" While some religious practitioners were hesitant to speak or refused outright, most were glad that someone from so far away was interested in their beliefs and their lives; some bemoaned the fact that young Indian men and women were no longer interested in these issues. It was generally necessary to eat the *prasād,* the food or Ganges water that they offered, in order to speak with them.

The majority of ecstatics included in this book are people whose religious experiences began spontaneously. However, I did not originally choose them because they had spontaneous experience. Nor were they chosen for their madness. I used those biographies that gave the most detailed descriptions of ecstatic states for members of the devotional traditions of Bengal. Most of those chosen were major anchors of their traditions, who altered and validated traditional theology by their experiences. They were chosen for authenticity (the firsthand view of a devotee or an interview was preferred to second- and thirdhand sources) and for providing information about the childhood of the ecstatic, when ecstatic states often began. All of the ecstatics studied were respected: they had *āśramas* (temples or houses in which they were respected authorities) and disciples ranging from a few up into the millions. The ecstatics who were interviewed were chosen by my informants.

For the biographies, I deliberately chose non-Westernized saints in order to emphasize the native traditions. Therefore, such famous Bengali holy men as Vivekānanda, Yogānanda Paramahaṃsa, Śrī Aurobindo, and Rabindranāth Tāgore were excluded.

Some data were unavailable. I was unable to find any reliable Bāul or Sahajiyā biographies (although there were at least three competing oral histories of Lālan Fakir). Childhood data were scanty among Gauḍīya Vaiṣṇavas, and Rāmprasād's experiences must be deduced from his poetry, as he had no firsthand biographer.

I approached the various types of texts phenomenologically—looking for categories that arise from the material—without forcing the data into a preconceived mold. The respected elders in this approach are James, Eliade, and Van der Leeuw (whom Eliade called its "first authoritative representative").[59] While phenomenology has been understood in a wide variety of ways, from Hegel to Husserl, these three writers best show the orientation of this book: James on the value of spontaneous ecstasy, Van der Leeuw on the value of empathy,[60] and Eliade on respect for the sacred as a unique and irreducible category.

William James also emphasized the importance of religious pathology—the study of the extremes in order to understand the norm. He states:

> Insane conditions have this advantage, that they isolate special factors of the mental life, and enable us to inspect them unmasked by their more usual surroundings. They play the part in mental anatomy which the scalpel and the microscope play in the anatomy of the body. To understand a thing rightly we need to see it both out of its environment and in it, and to have acquaintance with the whole range of its variations.[61]

While James saw the study of the abnormal as a means to understanding the normal, this book studies the extremes of religious experience for their own sake. This is a study of the extremes in order to understand the extremes. It is the nature of such phenomena, being at the ends of the spectrum of human thought and action, that they are highly idiosyncratic and unpredictable. We approach the study of religious ecstasy with the following four points in mind: (1) There is a significant discrepancy between the theological concepts of ecstasy and the ways in which it actually occurs in the lives of Bengali ecstatics—that the theories and stages do not correspond to lived experience. (2) This gap is based on a distinction between ritual and spontaneous ecstasy, a distinction clearly seen in the biographies of ecstatic saints. (3) Divine madness is the highest goal of religious devotion—a state in which incorporation of opposites is more important than ritual purity and which includes elements of destruction and sacrifice as well as integration. (4) Despite the fact that divine madness is the highest state attainable on the devotional paths, it is extremely difficult to differentiate from ordinary madness, which is the least valued mental state, and from simulation. However, society has ways to distinguish these states.

TWO The Overflowing of Bhagavān

The Vaiṣṇava Tradition

> He was singing, dancing, and shouting at a tremendous rate; now falling to the ground, now jumping up, and now twisting his body in varied contortions as if in convulsions; in a word, he was conducting himself in such a manner that anyone not acquainted with the manners of the Vaisnavas would think that the man had gone "daft." But the madder a Vaisnava is, the holier he is deemed by the people.
>
> —Lal Behari Dey, *Bengal Peasant Life*

Your Disease Is a God: The Bhāgavata Purāṇa

Madness and ecstasy are intimately connected in Bengali Vaiṣṇavism. The highest ecstatic state is Rādhā's *mahābhāva,* which includes incoherent speech, irrational behavior, and all possible emotions experienced intensely and simultaneously. Rādhā's divine madness is a state so passionate and extreme that it is even a mystery to Kṛṣṇa, Rādhā's beloved and Lord. The great Vaiṣṇava saints are known for their visions, trances, and frenzies; most have been known as much for their ecstatic symptoms as for their devotion. Many have been seen by their non-Vaiṣṇava neighbors as madmen—suffering from the wind disease (epilepsy) or from possession by ghosts or demons. Ecstasy and madness are easily confused, for their symptoms are very similar—a chaos that disrupts the social or religious order.

The major figure in Bengali Vaiṣṇava ecstasy was Kṛṣṇa Caitanya, a fifteenth-century saint believed by his disciples to be a joint avatar of Rādhā and Kṛṣṇa. From the time of his conversion to Vaiṣṇavism at Gayā, his life was a long series of ecstatic states. Another major source for ecstasy among Bengali Vaiṣṇavas is the *Bhāgavata Purāṇa,* or *Śrīmad Bhāgavatam.* This text is their most authoritative scripture, describing the true character of Bhagavān, Lord Kṛṣṇa. Its author is believed by many to describe a direct vision of the deity (*bhāgavata-sākṣātkāra*). In his book *Viraha Bhakti,* Friedhelm Hardy argues that the *Bhāgavata Purāṇa* is the first ecstatic purana, changing the primary orientation of Vaiṣṇavism. He contrasts the earlier or "intellectual bhakti," with its stress on mental concentration, yoga, and meditation, with "emotional Kṛṣṇa bhakti" which emphasizes both agony and ecstasy.[1] Intellectual bhakti includes the "bhakti yoga" of the *Bhāgavad Gītā,* the loyalty and readiness to serve of the *Mahābhārata,* the Prahlāda of the *Viṣṇu Purāṇa* who meditates on the god, thinks of him, and remembers him. This is contrasted with the "emotional Kṛṣṇa bhakti" of the *Bhāgavata Purāṇa,* which describes the passion, confusion, and inner disturbance of love, and a Prahlāda who shows the bliss of love (*praṇayānanda*), as well as possession by Kṛṣṇa (*graha*), and the ecstatic symptoms of weeping, laughing, and singing.

Hardy finds the origin of the *Bhāgavata Purāṇa*'s emotionalism in the South Indian Āḻvārs, who wrote from the seventh-century A.D. onward. While their writing included both forms of bhakti, they placed a special emphasis on possession by the deity and on love-madness. In the *nāyaka-nāyikā-bhāva* songs, the girl is in love (explicitly or implicitly) with Kṛṣṇa. Nammāḻvār writes of love as "a disease of mind, too great even to think," which hurts the girl's heart, causing her to feel like ice and fire, and to "melt away" in suffering.[2]

Ecstatic symptoms may occur to the girl due to abandonment by or possession by Kṛṣṇa. These include tears, fainting, immunity to pain, mad dancing, anxiety, perspiration, sighing with a whirling heart, and incoherent speech. The girl is mentally disturbed, without clear understanding (*tēṟātum*), mad (*mayal*), and of ever-increasing insanity (*ēṟiya-pittu*).[3]

The Āḻvārs make use of the two meanings of *mā*—both Kṛṣṇa and mental disturbance. Love is a disease, and the disease is a deity, the only way to cure the disease (possession by Kṛṣṇa) is to worship him. As a friend states, "The disease [from which] she is suffering is a very exalted deity"; it is a "good disease."[4] The girl must recite Kṛṣṇa's names, take dust from his devotees' feet, and worship with fellow bhaktas in order to be cured. Here, spiritual practice does not induce the ecstatic state, but rather limits and channels it, bringing it into relation with tradition and society.

Āḻvār sources are not limited to love poetry; the bhakta devotee may be a demon, a madman, an idiot (*pēy, pittan*) in a state of frenzy (*veri*). Their status is shown in "God's Idiots":

Mumbling and prattling the many names . . .
while onlookers say, "They're crazy"
entering and not entering cities
standing still or swaying
before a laughing world
they dance, they leap
undone by feeling
And the gods bow down
before them.[5]

Bengali Vaiṣṇavas considered the *Bhāgavata Purāṇa* to be their most authoritative text, and its most important section was the Tenth Canto, which described Kṛṣṇa's childhood in Vṛndāvana. However, throughout the purana are descriptions of people in ecstatic states which are considered pleasing to Kṛṣṇa.

The most significant figure is Rādhā, whose states of longing and sorrow were more intense than those of any other gopī (cowherdess) or devotee. She would speak to trees, or to the skies, or even to insects:

> 11. A certain gopī who was musing over her union with Kṛṣṇa, saw a bee about her, and imagining that it was the messenger deputed to her by her Beloved Kṛṣṇa, addressed it as follows:
>
> 12. (The gopī said) Oh bee! O friend of a rogue (Kṛṣṇa, the treacherous paramour). Don't touch our feet (and try to win our favor by submissive bows) with your beard-like tentacles tinged with the saffron of the wreath of Kṛṣṇa that was pressed down upon the (saffron-painted) breasts of the rival women (of Mathurā). . . .
>
> 13. O friend of our Darling Lord . . . You are an honorable guest. Dear black bee! Please seek whatever you would like to have from me.[6]

The gopīs too, when left by Kṛṣṇa, spoke incoherently and also began to imitate him:

> 4. Singing aloud of Kṛṣṇa's glory in a chorus, they sought for him, like lunatics, from forest to forest, enquiring of the trees about that Lord (the Supreme Man), who, like ether, was pervading all the creatures from within and without.
>
> 5. "O Aśvattha! O Plakṣa! O Nyagrodha! (varieties of Indian fig trees). Have you seen the son of Nanda who has absconded, stealing away our hearts by his captivating smiles and bewitching glances?

> 14. Thus the cowherd women became bewildered in their vain search of Kṛṣṇa and raved in this way. With their hearts engrossed (and as if identical) with him, they began to emulate the divine sports of the Lord.
> 15. One of the gopīs who imitated Kṛṣṇa sucked the breast of another gopī who played the part of Pūtana. Another gopī emulating Kṛṣṇa, the baby, began to cry and kicked another gopī who acted the part of a cart (Sakata).[7]

Prahlāda would laugh, sing, cry, shout, dance about with hair standing on end and eyes half closed with tears, unconscious of his physical acts.[8] When Akrura saw Kṛṣṇa's footprints, his hair stood on end, he jumped from his chariot and rolled over and over on the prints.[9] Kṛṣṇa's queens in Dvāraka were so absorbed in him as to remain speechless, appearing as if dull-witted or like lunatics.[10] Nārada suggests that the devotee should appear as if unintelligent, childlike, or mad.[11]

This emphasis on ecstatic symptoms is not accidental—Kṛṣṇa himself states:

> 23. How can the heart be cleansed of impurities without the development of devotion? And can intense devotion be indicated if the hairs do not stand, the heart (is not) melted with intense emotion, and the tears of joy trickled down?
> 24. He is really overwhelmed with intense devotion whose voice is choked with emotion and oral expression is faltering, whose heart melts, who laments frequently, and laughs at times. Throwing away all bashfulness, he sings loudly and dances—such a person endowed with my devotion purifies the world.[12]

More specifically, he suggests:

> 29. (My devotee) though full of wisdom, should behave like a child. Though well-versed in a skill, he should assume dullness. Though deeply learned, he should show himself as insane. Though master of the Vedas, he should behave like an animal.[13]

The devotee is like a child, a dunce, a lunatic, like one haunted by a ghost.[14] He laughs, he screams, and he acts as if possessed.[15] The saint does not know if his transient body is sitting or standing, and his body acts according to karma or to the will of the Lord. He is as unaware as a man drunk on wine.[16] The passion and confusion of such states obstruct the sort of devotion oriented toward spiritual practice: "Hardly did they begin to describe (the deeds of Kṛṣṇa) when, remembering his dalliance with them, they could not proceed, as their minds were distracted by the vehement force of passion, O King."[17]

For Bengali Vaiṣṇavas, the *Bhāgavata Purāṇa* has the mythic authority of the revealed text. Two other types of major works describe Vaiṣṇava ecstasy. One type is the biography of Kṛṣṇa Caitanya, of which the most important is Kṛṣṇadāsa Kavirāj's *Caitanya Caritāmṛta.* The Caitanya Bhāgavata of Vṛndāvana Dāsa, another early account of Caitanya's life, also contains some detailed descriptions of Caitanya's trances. The other type of text consists of the treatises on religious affection, the *Bhaktirasāmṛtasindhu* and the *Ujjvala-Nīlamaṇi* of Rūpa Gosvāmin. These describe a ladder of religious emotion, going from the bottom (*sādhana bhakti*) to the top (the varieties of *mahābhāva*). Later in this chapter, theology and spiritual practice are described, and several biographies of Vaiṣṇava ecstatics are included. These are followed by a discussion of ecstasy and madness among Bengali Vaiṣṇavas.

Model for Madmen: Śrī Kṛṣṇa Caitanya

Mahāprābhu Śrī Kṛṣṇa Caitanya is the most important ecstatic figure in Gauḍīya Vaiṣṇavism. Believed by many Vaiṣṇavas to be either a joint incarnation of Rādhā and Kṛṣṇa (both deities together in one body) or Kṛṣṇa himself (and not a mere incarnation or *avatāra*), Caitanya's trances and fits of divine madness acted as the model for future god-maddened Vaiṣṇava devotees.

Ecstatic frenzy was most often seen in *kīrtana,* a form of worship using singing and dancing, which was popularized by Caitanya. Although later devotees sang of Rādhā and Kṛṣṇa, they began with *gaurcandrikas* (songs that relate Caitanya to Kṛṣṇa). It was his influence which revitalized Vaiṣṇavism in sixteenth-century Bengal. A short biography follows, using as major texts the *Caitanya Caritāmṛta* of Kṛṣṇadāsa Kavirāja and the *Caitanya Bhāgavata* of Vṛndāvana Dāsa.[18]

Kṛṣṇa Caitanya was born in Navadvīpa, just before a lunar eclipse in February, A.D. 1486. His mother was Śacī, wife of Jagannātha Miśra. He was named Viśvambhara (literally, "he who sustains the world") and nicknamed Nimāi and Gaurāṅga (because of his fair skin).

He was a restless, impulsive child, mischievous and aggressive. He joined a gang of boys, who would get into fights and bother people bathing and meditating in the Ganges. When Viśvambhara's older brother

Viśvarūpa became a renunciant, the house was plunged into sorrow. His parents had lost eight children, and now the oldest son was gone. Viśvambhara was also saddened, and he calmed down and became more studious.

At the age of eleven, his father died, and Śacī became entirely dependent on her son. But he was still impatient and would fall into tantrums, breaking everything in the house. He was a good student in spite of this, although vain of his learning, and at sixteen he began to teach Sanskrit grammar.

At about this time he married Lakṣmī, a local girl, and he became a popular teacher. At one point he fell into a trance during class, raving, shouting, rolling on the ground, finally becoming stiff. The cause of the seizure was debated by observers—too much ghee and rice, too much study, an evil spirit, the wind disease.

While he was on a trip to East Bengal, his wife died of snakebite, and he soon married Viṣṇupriyā. In 1508, he left for Gayā to perform a funeral (*śrāddha*) ceremony for his father's soul. He met Īśvara Purī at Gayā and took initiation[19] from him. Some time later he fell into an ecstatic state, and he returned home a changed person.

He came back dazed, falling into trances and calling out for Kṛṣṇa. He tried to teach his classes, but could not concentrate on the lessons. After several months of effort, he gave up teaching. The local Vaiṣṇavas were happy at his change of heart, for he now began helping them instead of insulting them as he used to do. Now he threatened non-Vaiṣṇavas, jumping at them out of trees and running after them.

He was commonly considered mad, subject to trances and wild behavior. His mother, Śacī, was told to tie him up and to apply Viṣṇu oil; however, any application of blessed oil or water made him worse rather than better. Luckily, the great Vaiṣṇava Śrīvāsa recognized his state as *mahābhakti-yoga*, a state of intense ecstasy.

A group of disciples began to form around Viśvambhara, including Śrīvāsa, Nityānanda, Advaitācārya, and Gadādhara. He is described as appearing to Śrīvāsa as a four-armed deity and to Nityānanda in six-armed form. Viśvambhara began to claim that he was Nārāyaṇa and Kṛṣṇa, that he was a master among Vaiṣṇavas. At this point he was twenty-four years old.

Viśvambhara now decided to preach the worship of Kṛṣṇa publicly. He held group worship with singing and dancing (*saṅkīrtanas*), converted the drunkards Madhāi and Jagāi, and put on dramas (in which he played the feminine leads, and at one point the actors nursed from his breast). The public worship became more boisterous, with the participants marching around town. When this was opposed by the Kazi, the local political leader, Viśvambhara led a mob to loot and burn the Kazi's house (at this point he identified with Narasiṁha, a warlike form of Viśnu).

He continued to fall into various *bhāvas* and decided to take vows of renunciation (*sannyāsa*). He bade farewell to his mother (few biographies mention his wife) and took his vows from Keśava Bhāratī at Katwa. He was named Śrī Kṛṣṇa Caitanya. He allowed his mother to determine his future home, and she decided on Purī because of its proximity to Navadvīpa.

Upon reaching the temple of Jagannātha at Purī, he fell into a trance and was seen by Vāsudeva Sārvabhauma, who took him to his house. Caitanya converted Sārvabhauma, stayed for a few months, and went to South India to preach and to search for his brother. In Rajahmundry he met the *śudra* (low-caste person) Rāmānanda Rāya, with whom he shared ecstatic states and conversations about Kṛṣṇa. Rāmānanda recognized Caitanya as the incarnation of both Kṛṣṇa and Rādhā.

On his return to Purī, he found new devotees as well as old ones. He would dance in ecstasy for Jagannātha, and at festivals, and he sent his disciples off to spread the word of devotion to Kṛṣṇa. He also traveled back to Bengal, and to Vārāṇāsī and Vṛndāvana, where his emotions were even more intense than in Purī, and where he discovered Rādhā-kuṇḍa (Rādhā's pool, where she would bathe).

The last twelve years of Caitanya's life were spent in a state of divine madness, according to Kṛṣṇadāsa Kavirāja:

> 87. As Rādhā spoke crazily in a state of madness [*unmāda*] when she saw Uddhava, so Caitanya spoke day and night.
> 88. He spent the last twelve years of his life in this way.[20]

He lived an ascetic life, eating little and often spending the night in meditation. He had strange physical symptoms of his intense love—his body would become distorted, stretched and compressed, sweat and blood oozing from his pores and saliva foaming at the mouth. Sometimes he was totally lost in ecstatic trance, sometimes he was half conscious, and sometimes he was in a normal state.

Caitanya became well known for his ecstasies. His love was not a peaceful state, but a continuous fluctuation between divine and human personalities, between love and loneliness. He was described as agitated and restless by Kṛṣṇadāsa, and his mind wandered due to the waves of ecstasy[21] within him. He would mistake his environment for Kṛṣṇa's Vṛndāvana, sing and dance, and then faint. He would later return to normal (*bāhya*) consciousness and ask, "Am I conscious? [i.e., *caitanya,* his name]. What have I seen in this near-dream state? What sort of madness have I spoken?"[22] Sometimes he would state his great love for Kṛṣṇa, and at other times he would deny that love, saying that his crying was deceitful and that he is a madman (*bāul*) whom nobody believes.[23]

His *bhāvas* were states of intense emotion and stress, which exhausted him:

> 35. Caitanya felt contradictory mental states, due to his different types of ecstasy, and there was a great fight [within him] between the ecstasies. Anxiety, restlessness, distress, anger and intolerance were all soldiers, and the cause of this was the madness of divine love [*prema-unmāda*].
> 36. Caitanya's symptoms of *bhāva* [made him appear like a] mad elephant. His body was a field of sugarcane in which elephants fought, trampling the cane. His state of divine madness affected his mind and body, causing fatigue, and he spoke possessed by *bhāva.*[24]

These moods were accompanied by bodily symptoms:

> 63. Caitanya's body was paralyzed, trembled, perspired, paled, wept and choked. He was thrilled. He would laugh, cry, dance and sing, running here and there, and sometimes he would fall unconscious on the ground.[25]

However, they led Caitanya to perceive Kṛṣṇa directly:

> 57. The symptoms of madness[26] caused the manifestation of Kṛṣṇa. In possession by *bhāva* [*bhāvāveśa*], the states of affection and sulking were awakened, [as well as] disrespect, pride, and sarcasm. Sometimes he blasphemed [Kṛṣṇa], and sometimes he honored him.[27]

Such states were poison and nectar in one, balancing and alternating the extremes of pleasure and pain:

> 45. While externally he appeared to be suffering from the burning of poison, internally he was in bliss.[28]

The *Caitanya Bhāgavata* of Vṛndāvana Dāsa was written in 1573 and was held in great esteem by the Gosvāmins of Vṛndāvana (followers of Caitanya who wrote about the nature of Kṛṣṇa's playfulness or *līlā*). It emphasized the similarities between the lives of Kṛṣṇa and Caitanya, and gave detailed accounts of Caitanya's ecstasies. Here is a long description:

> 148. When Prabhu cries, he cries for hours. He rolls on the ground, his hair completely dishevelled. 149. What person can remain hardened after witnessing such weeping, or not himself become agitated the same as Prabhu? When Prabhu laughs, he does so loudly, enjoying the bliss for hours. 151. When he is in the *bhāva* of a devoted servant, he does not know his own majesty; [then] he blurts out in a thick voice, "I conquer, I conquer!" 152. From time to time he sings, his voice loud; it sounds as if it will rupture the universe. . . . 157. From time to time all of his limbs shake violently and his teeth chatter like a child who is freezing. 158. On occasion his body breaks out in a great sweat and the perspiration pours off his frame, making him the very image of the Ganges. 159. Sometimes his body burns with fever, which is soothed only by applying sandal paste. 160. On other occasions he emits haunting, deep sighs, sending everyone away to remain alone. . . . 168. Sometimes he roars like ten million lions, but protects the ears of his followers. 169. When he moves about the earth unaccompanied, some see him while others cannot. 170. When overwhelmed with *bhāva,* he scares those upon whom he looks, and then laughing, chases away that fear. 171. Possessed by Kṛṣṇa, Viśvambhara becomes restless; there is no one who becomes more agitated in dance than he. 172. Overwhelmed with *bhāva* he grabs someone's feet, then again places his own on their head. 173. One moment he hangs on someone's neck, weeping then the next moment he mounts their shoulders. . . . 181. Hiccuping deeply, all his limbs dangle loosely; not able to stay calm, he falls to the ground. 182. His golden hued body at times appears different colors. From time to time his eyes appear to grow to twice their normal size. 183. Prabhu becomes superhuman as a Vaiṣṇava possessed. . . . 219. Śacī's son revealed all manner of delirium, which had been neither seen nor heard of in the *Bhāgavata.* 220. From time to time his entire body would become rigid so that he could not even bend over. 221. At other times

> his body seemed to be without bones, as if it were filled with butter. 222. At times his body appeared to grow two or three times its normal size. His natural condition sometimes seemed stout and sometimes feeble. 223. Sometimes he seemed drunk, swaying to and fro. Constantly in bliss, he laughed and rocked his body. . . . 227. With their eyes brimming, all the devotees beheld his amazing possession by Kṛṣṇa, his stunning dance.[29]

The *Caitanya Caritāmṛta* of Kṛṣṇadāsa Kavirāja is often considered the authoritative biography of Caitanya. It is a strongly theological work, describing the nature and function of Caitanya's incarnation, and it shows many events from Caitanya's life. Here it describes singing to the god Jagannātha:

> 67. Prabhu raised his arms and said: "Bol, bol," and the people, floating in *ānanda,* raised the sound of Hari. 68. Now he fell in a faint, and he had no more breath; and suddenly he stood up again and shouted. 69. He was like a śimula tree, thick with *puluka:* sometimes his body blossomed (with it) and sometimes it was thin. 70. Bloody sweat came out of every pore of his body, and he stuttered, "Jaja gaga mama pari." 71. It seemed that each of his teeth [was] separately trembling; his teeth chattered so, it seemed that they would fall out on the ground. 72. As time went on, the absorption in *ānanda* of Prabhū increased; the third watch came, and still the dancing was not ended. 73. A sea of *ānanda* rose up in all the people, and all the people forgot their bodies and their selves and their homes.[30]

When Caitanya raved with madness in Purī, he would fall into *bhāvas* and perceive himself in Vṛndāvana:

> 9. Suddenly Prabhu heard the song of Kṛṣṇa's flute, and absorbed in his *bhāva,* he left that place. 10. Though three doors were barred, absorbed in *bhāva,* Prabhū went outside. 11. To the south of the lion-gate, some cows of Telenga stayed, and going to that place, Prabhu fell unconscious. 12. And now Govinda, not hearing a sound from Mahāprabhu, summoned Svarūpa and opened the doors. 13. Then Svarūpagosvāmi, taking the bhaktas with him, lit a lamp and searched for Prabhu. 14. Searching here and there, they went to the lion-gate, and they found Prabhu among the cows. 15. His

> hands and feet were within his stomach; he had the shape of a tortoise. There was froth on his lips, his whole body trembled, and there were tears in his eyes. 16. Fallen unconscious, he was like a *kusmanda* fruit; externally he was stiff and rigid; inwardly he was overwhelmed with *ānanda.* 17. All around him the cows were sniffing his body, and when they were driven off, they did not leave the company of Mahāprabhū. . . . 20. When he regained consciousness, his hands and feet came out again, and his body was as it had been before. 21. Getting up, Prabhu sat down and looked this way and that, and said to Svarūpa: "Where have you brought me? 22. I heard the sound of the flute and I went to Vṛndāvana, and I saw in the pasture Vrajendra-nandana playing his flute."[31]

While his body would undergo the strange changes and distortions that are a result of *bhāva* (*bhāvera vikāras*), his mind would be focused on the love play of Rādhā and Kṛṣṇa. At Nīlācala Caitanya would dance and sing, wandering about in states of possession by *bhāva.* At one point he saw the sea at Purī and jumped in, mistaking it for the Yamunā. He fainted and was carried away by the waves. His disciples searched for him, and Svarūpa with some other devotees met a fisherman on the shore who displayed ecstatic symptoms. They asked about the cause of this condition:

> 44. And the fisherman said: "I have seen no man here; while I was casting my net, a corpse came into it. 45. I thought it was a big fish, and I brought it in carefully, and when I saw it was a corpse I was very much afraid. 46. I had to touch the body, to free the net, and at my mere touch the spirit entered my heart. 47. In fear I trembled, and water flowed from my eyes, my voice was choked, and I trembled all over. 48. I cannot tell whether it was a *brahman-daitya* or a *bhūta;* only on sight it entered a human body. 49. The body was tall—five or seven hands, and its arms and legs were three hands each. 50. The joints of the bones were loose and the skin was dangling, and when I saw it no life remained in the body. 51. As a dead body, he remained with his eyes rolled upwards, but sometimes he groaned, and sometimes remained unconscious. 52. I saw this in person; that *bhūta* has seized me, and if I die how will my wife and sons live? . . ." 61. Svarūpa said: "He whom you consider to be a *bhūta* is not a *bhūta*—he is Kṛṣṇa-caitanya-bhagavān. . . . 63. At his touch, prema for Kṛṣṇa

> arose in you, and considering him to be a *bhūta* or *preta*, you were much afraid. . . . 68. Prabhu was lying there upon the ground, and his body had lengthened; his body was white from the water, and covered with sand. 69. His body was long and inert, and his skin was loose."[32]

The disciples chanted Hare Kṛṣṇa in his ear, and he returned to a normal state. He was not happy to return to awareness of the outer world, preferring to watch Kṛṣṇa playing games in the water. However, the disciples were overjoyed and took him home. His emotions were continually shifting; as Kṛṣṇadāsa states:

> 59. Mahāprabhu was this way every day and night, with his ravings manifesting madness. 60. In a single day so many *bhāvas* were brought out, that if they were described with a thousand mouths, the other shore of them could not be reached.[33]

These shifting moods were considered to be Rādhā's emotions, in her states of intense passion. Caitanya's *Rādhā-bhāva* is his identification with her, and especially with her states of divine madness. The states are detailed in the texts on religious emotion.

Kṛṣṇa and the Passions of the Soul: The *Bhaktirasāmṛtasindhu* and the *Ujjvala-Nīlamaṇi*

The *Bhaktirasāmṛtasindhu* and the *Ujjvala-Nīlamaṇi,* two books by Rūpa Gosvamin, are studies of religious emotion that examine the ways in which the bhakta relates to Kṛṣṇa. The *Bhaktirasāmṛtasindhu,* or the Ocean of the Nectar of the Devotional Love, examines the earlier stages of religious emotion and the practices and systems of belief that develop it. The *Ujjvala-Nīlamaṇi* or Blazing Sapphire (its title also refers to the shining Kṛṣṇa) concentrates on more developed states of ecstatic devotion, the states of mystical love most clearly seen in Rādhā and the gopīs.

In the *Bhaktirasāmṛtasindhu,* divine love may arise from spiritual practice, or from the grace of Kṛṣṇa or his devotees: "This *bhāva* appears [in the hearts of bhaktas] in two ways: by intense absorption in ritual practice [shown in avoiding evil after attaining the state of firm devotion], and by the grace [*prasāda*] of Kṛṣṇa and his bhaktas."[34]

Attaining the state of *bhāva* by practice occurs more commonly, although both are infrequent. *Bhāva* is difficult to attain, as much practice is done only out of duty, without real love, and because Kṛṣṇa does not easily give his grace.[35] Spontaneous emotional states that occur without practice may also be due to penance in a previous life, but more generally they are seen as a gift of grace.

> 15. *Bhāva* which suddenly appears in the heart of an individual without any spiritual practice[36] is said to be due to the grace of Kṛṣṇa and his bhaktas. 16. This grace is given by Kṛṣṇa in three ways: verbally, by personal appearance, and by manifestation in the heart.[37]

Examples of these include Kṛṣṇa verbally blessing Nārada, the people of Kurujaṅgala overwhelmed by merely seeing Kṛṣṇa, and Śukadeva, whose devotion came spontaneously, while he was still in the womb.[38] The grace of devotees may also influence *bhāva*—an innate love[39] blossomed in Prahlāda by the grace of the sage Nārada, and enabled a low-born hunter to feel love. The sudden appearance of *bhāva* is highly valued, especially if it is believed to be a direct gift from Kṛṣṇa. When the more intense state of love, called *prema,* is given by Kṛṣṇa, this is called extraordinary grace (*atiprasāda*).[40]

The path of ritual practice described in the *Bhaktirasāmṛtasindhu* also leads to the goal of love of Kṛṣṇa. However, it is a longer and more complex process, involving two modes of worship—ritual action (*vaidhi*) and ritual emotion (*rāgānugā*). The worship that involves ritual action is a path of conventional obedience to Vaiṣṇava texts, without strong emotion toward the deity. It consists of following detailed rules of behavior, described in the *Haribhaktivilāsa* and other texts. The second type of practice is that of ritual emotion, and the person who follows it feels a desire to have the same emotions as those experienced by the people of Vraja, who knew Kṛṣṇa during his childhood. Their relation to Kṛṣṇa was a spontaneous love evoked by his beauty and grace (*rāgātmikā bhakti*). The practice of ritual emotion uses this spontaneous love as a model. The person visualizes the land of Vraja and enters into it imaginatively, seeing himself as a parent, friend, or handmaiden of Kṛṣṇa.

The person must serve Kṛṣṇa in both the physical body (*sādhaka-rūpa*) and the spiritual body (*siddha-rūpa*).[41] Ritual action deals with the outward behavior of the physical body—chanting, listening to scriptures, drawing Vaiṣṇava marks with whitish clay. Ritual emotion deals with inner behavior—building a spiritual body (or realizing its preexistence) in which to relate to Kṛṣṇa. Another distinction is that in ritual action, awe is aroused by Kṛṣṇa's grandeur and majesty, while in ritual emotion, love arises from his sweetness and beauty. Later Vaiṣṇava writings have detailed the techniques of making the spiritual body—focusing primarily on the ritual practice of the handmaiden (*mañjari sādhana*)—the creation of an inner body in the form of a thirteen-year-old girl, with a colored sari and a special service to Kṛṣṇa and Rādhā.

When these forms of practice grow real for the person, they become devotion with true emotion (*bhāva bhakti*)—a practice in which the person is deeply involved. The heart is said to be softened, and there are partial ecstatic symptoms: some pallor, tears, horripilation. *Bhāva* is a ray of the sun of religious love, and when it is evoked by spiritual practice, it follows the stages of firm faith, genuine liking, and attachment to Kṛṣṇa, and finally is called attraction (*rati*).[42] When this *bhāva* becomes deepened and coagulated or condensed, when the heart is softened by an attachment and a feeling of possession toward Kṛṣṇa, this state is called intense love (*prema*). In this state, the body and mind are directed only toward Kṛṣṇa, and there is a continual burning desire for him. Separation from Kṛṣṇa is misery, while his vision gives infinite pleasure. Reason is dissolved and melts into emotion, and the person forgets decorum—laughing, weeping, shouting, singing, dancing in ecstasy. He begins to show the subsidiary *bhāvas* (*anubhāvas*) and the symptoms of ecstasy (*sāttvika bhāvas*). These are discussed in greater detail in Appendix B.

This love intensifies until it reaches the highest states of ecstasy—*bhāva* or *mahābhāva*. This state is innately sweet, and it consists of two stages—enchantment or maturity (*rūḍha*) and complete enchantment or maturity (*adhi-rūḍha*).

In the state of enchantment, the passions are like a raging fire. Separation from Kṛṣṇa for even a moment is unbearable. It can affect the hearts of all present, like the rising of the waves of the sea. There is depression at the possibility of Kṛṣṇa's future unhappiness and a loss of consciousness (without fainting), with total concentration on Kṛṣṇa. The *Ujjvala-Nīlamaṇi* describes the state of enchantment in the maidens at the *rasa* dance with Kṛṣṇa:

> In the *rasa* dance, *rasa* was spread forth by the river of the gopīs' passion. That river bears the indescribable sounds of the stammering [of the gopīs like] gathering geese. It is covered with the movements of [their] shivering, darting here and there, and the ripples which are born of bliss are [their]

> huge goosebumps. It overflows with [their] tears, contains a sprinkling of [their] paralysis, and their passion repeatedly bestows ecstatic joy upon the world.[43]

It also describes how such agitation of the heart may be spread to others:

> O friends, the waves of the boundless ocean [of the gopīs' passion] sprinkled the Kurus, spun around the heads of the kings of the earth, made languid countless women in the heavenly abodes (who were faint from an excess of emotion); it flooded all people, overrunning the heart of Satyabhama by force, and it stunned Rukmiṇī, the greatest beauty of Vaikuṇṭha.[44]

The second stage of *mahābhāva* is complete enchantment (*adhi-rūḍha*), which has two types: loving bliss (*modana*) and passionate delirium (*mādana*). Loving bliss is found only in Rādhā's group of gopīs and gives both Rādhā and Kṛṣṇa a special kind of charm[45] when they are together. This state of bliss is also described in metaphors of nature:

> The desire tree of the joy of Rādhā and Mādhava shines eternally, sending forth incomparable soft, gutteral sounds, and it is expanded by the treasure of stillness [*stambha*]. This tree is full of blossoming buds [of gooseflesh] and for fruit it has the pearls of beads of perspiration. It holds the nectar of tears welling up, and although it is motionless, [yet] it is shaken by amorous play.[46]

In separation, love becomes fascination (*mohana*) and is shown in Rādhā in a variety of symptoms. She desires Kṛṣṇa's happiness, although she suffers from it; she is so unhappy that a wave of her sorrow upsets the universe, and the birds and animals weep; she desires death so that the elements of her body may serve Kṛṣṇa; and she becomes divinely mad (*divyonmāda*), with hallucinations of Kṛṣṇa and anger toward him. Fascination is seen in Kṛṣṇa when he faints at the loss of Rādhā, although he is in the arms of Rukmiṇī in his palace at Dvāraka. An example of Rādhā's state is given:

> Is it not amazing that Rādhā has become white due to her intense *rāga* [passion, also color] for you, while her teeth are clicking from her trembling, she is babbling, and her horripilated body defies the jackfruit?[47]

The more extreme effects of this state are also detailed:

> The human realm cried, the snake society became distraught, the assembly of the gods perspired and the inhabitants of Vaikuṇṭha shed tears. It is amazing, O Lord, how the snake of Rādhā's sighs of love wanders all around; and though it is full of joy, [yet] it has heated the universe, which has become troubled both inside and out.[48]

Divine madness is a state similar to fascination which results from a total concentration of the mind on Kṛṣṇa, like the mind of a yogin who contemplates Brahman. Rādhā's vision of Kṛṣṇa is so vivid that it appears as a perception. It is accompanied by incoherent behavior and raving. Such confused behavior is seen in Rādhā, after Kṛṣṇa has returned to Mathurā:

> She sometimes spreads a bed in the bower [when] she prepares the abode. She sometimes acts like a disappointed one, becoming angry and chastising the dark cloud. And sometimes she hurries to the trysting place and wanders about in the dense darkness. Distressed by the delusion of separation from you, what state has Rādhā not achieved?[49]

Types of raving include insulting Kṛṣṇa; accusing him of incompetence, cruelty, dishonesty, lust, and ingratitude; expressing jealousy and discussing leaving him; refusing to visit Kṛṣṇa because of his other women; and making anxious inquiry about him.

The climax of these states of divine madness, however, is seen in Rādhā's state of passionate delirium (*mādana*), which includes simultaneously all emotions of separation and union, all forms of passion and love:

> Delirium is the wine of love, with all *sāttvika bhāvas* and secondary states occurring simultaneously. Rādhā acts as if drunk with nectar and joy, feeling jealousy for unconscious objects that were near Kṛṣṇa and eulogizing objects that have touched him in the past, despite her being constantly in his arms. Passionate delirium (*mādana*) is called the origin of all types of bliss and *bhāva*.[50]

This experience of feeling all emotions at once is described by O. B. L. Kapoor:

> *Mādana* has the unique capacity of directly experiencing a thousand different kinds of enjoyment of union with Kṛṣṇa on only seeing him or recalling his memory. Yet these experiences are not imaginary (*sphurti*). The capacity to experience

> Kṛṣṇa in a thousand different ways involves the capacity to bring about his direct appearance (*avirbhāva*) in these experiences. What, however, makes *mādana* even more inconceivable is the fact that it presents these multifarious experiences of union simultaneously with multifarious experiences of separation (*viyoga*) involving craving (*utkaṇṭhā*) for union.[51]

The *Ujjvala-Nīlamaṇi* shows the range of divine love, from its nascent attraction (*rati*) to its greater intensity. This attraction may emerge spontaneously, not dependent on external causes, or it may be evoked by hearing about the lover, contemplating his good qualities and seeing things associated with him. Intense love is part of the person's essential nature (*svabhāva*).

Both the *Bhaktirasāmṛtasindhu* and the *Ujjvala-Nīlamaṇi* show the evolution of divine love, from its feeble and often forced beginnings to its later development. They catalog religious emotion, showing the importance of all emotional states, even negative ones, in relation to the deity. The more intense the state, the greater the ecstasy—and the madness.

Ritual Ecstasy: The *Siddha Deha* as Observer/Participant

The goal of most forms of Gauḍīya Vaiṣṇava ritual practice is ecstasy—to bring the person a direct vision of Kṛṣṇa, to have him become intensely emotionally involved in this vision, and often for him to assume a new identity as one of the dwellers in the paradise of Vṛndāvana. Even those practices that appear more indirect, such as watering *tulsī* plants and rolling in the dust of Vṛndāvana, have the goal of obtaining direct interaction with Kṛṣṇa and his divine associates.

According to Gauḍīya Vaiṣṇava informants, the most important forms of ritual practice are repetition of the names of Kṛṣṇa (*nāma japa*), repetition of mantra (*mantra japa*), singing hymns (*kīrtana*), worship of deities (*pūjā*), and visualizing Kṛṣṇa's activities (*līlā smaraṇa*). Chanting Kṛṣṇa's name is believed to evoke the direct presence of Kṛṣṇa, because the name is considered to be the magical jewel[52] that is identical with Kṛṣṇa himself.[53] Such chanting is the essence of all spiritual disciplines, which destroys bondage and gives realization. As Gaur Kiśora Dās Bābājī states:

> Bhagavān's forms are unlimited, and these cannot be known by imagination (*kalpanā*). As one chants the Harināma, the Lord's own form (*svarūpa*) will be manifested from within the letters of the name, and one's own true self (*ātmāsvarūpa*) will also be perceived. Along with that, one's service, etc, will awaken.[54]

Those who believe that Kṛṣṇa and his paradise will be revealed through the syllables of the name often place little emphasis on other forms of ritual practice, such as *līlā smaraṇa* (visualization and meditative practices). For them, the name reveals everything, and nothing more is necessary—visualization attempts to force the issue, to control the experience, unlike the natural flow of chanting.[55]

Repetition of mantra is similar to chanting Kṛṣṇa's name. The mantra, like the Name, is considered to be identical to Kṛṣṇa. However, the goal of the Name is to evoke Kṛṣṇa's presence, or a vision of his paradise of Vṛndāvana, while the goal of the mantra is to cause the devotee to enter the paradise and participate in the events there. According to Bengali Vaiṣṇava informants, the mantra acts as a key to the eternal Vṛndāvana. The Name or *mahāmantra* causes love of Kṛṣṇa in the devotee, but more is required for entrance into Vṛndāvana: one must receive initiation with an empowered mantra[56] from a guru who is himself initiated into that mantra.

Along with the mantras, various visualizations (*dhyānas*) should be done. For the guru mantra, the guru *dhyāna* describes the guru (one visualizes his body) often as an associate of Caitanya, with a golden complexion, wearing silk robes, with a shaven head. He has the Vaiṣṇava signs on his body, such as the sandalwood marks and a necklace made of *tulsī* wood around his neck. One may meditate on the guru's feet, placed on the thousand-petaled lotus upon the head. For the Kṛṣṇa mantra or the Caitanya mantra, Rādhā, Kṛṣṇa, Caitanya and Nityānanda are visualized on the red lotus of the heart.[57]

The Gopāla mantra is considered the main mantra in Gauḍīya Vaiṣṇavism.[58] That mantra is accompanied by the *kāma gāyatrī*.[59] The usual mantras given today by Vaiṣṇava gurus are the mantras of the *pañcatattva* (Caitanya, Nityānanda, Advaita, Gadādhara, and Śrīvāsa)—the guru mantra, the Gopāla mantra and *kāma gāyatrī*, and the Rādhā mantra and Rādhā *gāyatrī*.

The mantra should only be chanted mentally, as it loses its effect when pronounced out loud. The mantra helps develop the spiritual body and is believed to evoke the presence of the deity as tantric mantras do—they "call" the deity. While the Name purifies the person and evokes Kṛṣṇa's presence, the mantra establishes a relationship with him and allows him entrance into the eternal paradise of Vṛndāvana.[60]

Kīrtana is the loud singing of the names, qualities, and activities of the deity, generally as Rādhā and Kṛṣṇa or as Caitanya. Unusual powers are sometimes attributed to such songs—they may give superhuman strength and endurance, return youth to the aged, cure disease, and revive the dead. An example may be seen in Rām Dās Bābā of the Nitai Gaur Rādhe Śhyām subsect, whom one informant stated to have spontaneously created *kīrtanas* answering questions in the mind of his listening audience.

The *Bṛhat Bhāgavatāmṛtam* of Sanātana Gosvāmin gives several arguments for the superiority of singing *kīrtana* over visualization (it uses all senses and not just the mind; it may be done in a group; it benefits others). It states that singing Kṛṣṇa's name is the safest, easiest, strongest, and most direct means to attain to divine love; that it is dearest to Kṛṣṇa, and it infatuates him at once. Singing Kṛṣṇa's name directly evokes love into the devotee, and it submerges him into the ocean of bliss.[61]

Kīrtana is often seen as the song of separation of the soul and the god, the high point of love, and the natural flow of Kṛṣṇa's love in the ocean of bliss. It flows in the heart of the devotee by Kṛṣṇa's grace alone and cannot be gained by one's own effort. When Kṛṣṇa gives his grace, the heart overflows with love and becomes transparent, so that Kṛṣṇa's transcendental form may be seen.[62] This direct vision and encounter are described as the highest goal of devotional practice.[63]

Pūjā is the worship of pictures, statues, or objects that represent the deity. This worship consists of caring for these objects as one would care for the deity, were he personally present. Complete worship involves seeing to the needs of the deity throughout the day. The deity is awakened from sleep, offered greetings, fed, bathed, dressed, fanned, praised, given naps, and at the end of the day put to bed. This worship is ecstatic in the sense that, for the faithful believer, the deity is directly present and can reveal himself as alive within the image at any time. Ritual worship may be done with varying degrees of complexity, externally or mentally. Vaiṣṇavas feel that external worship is more effective because it engages more of the senses in the service of the deity. The more senses involved, the more absorbed in the deity the person may become.

Mental worship may be done in circumstances in which physical worship is impossible, such as lack of sufficient means, poor health, lack of a statue or other items, and so forth. It consists of the same activities as one performs in the external ritual, but it is done by visualization. Mental worship, if done carefully, is believed to be equally real. Stories abound of the mental food, eaten in a vision, which fills the person or is present when the person arises from meditation, and the colored dust thrown during a vision of Holi with Kṛṣṇa and Rādhā, which remains on the person when he returns to normal consciousness. An example is seen in the *Bhaktamālā* of Nābha Jī. During his meditation, when Raghunātha Dāsa ate a mental food offering of rice cooked in milk, he got a case of indigestion from it:

> He made his own body *bhāva rūpa.*
> In mental worship he partook of *dudha bhāta* [rice cooked in milk],
> and his inspired heart absorbed its *rasa.*
> Taking his pulse, the *vaidya* [doctor] said,
> He's been given *dudha bhāta.*[64]

The reality of mental worship is also seen in the *Bhakti-ratnākara,* in Narottama's mental service to Rādhā and Kṛṣṇa. The male devotee Narottama, in the body of a handmaiden (*mañjari*), was helping Rādhā's friends (the gopīs) by cooking milk:

> Narottama as a maidservant, with particular care
> Began to boil milk, as instructed by Rādhā's friend (Lalita),
> Seeing the milk boiling over, she became worried
> And took the pot of milk off the oven with her bare hands.
> The hands were burnt, but she didn't feel it.
> She gave the milk to the friends [*sakhīs*] with great happiness
> When she helped to feed Rādhā and Kṛṣṇa, her external consciousness returned.
> When she became aware of her burnt hands, she hid them
> But somebody close came to know of it.[65]

The Bengali Vaiṣṇava emphasis on *mādhurya,* the sweet aspect of divinity, shows itself in the worship as a preference for simplicity. The image is simply dressed as a cowherd boy, rather than in majestic jeweled ornaments and royal robes. The simpler dress communicates to the devotee the ready availability of the deity, his closeness rather than his distant grandeur.

The process of *smaraṇa,* literally "remembering," is a method combining visualization and meditation. It represents the transition stage between the mundane identity and the eternal, divine identity. It is through the process of visualization that the devotee becomes adapted to life in the paradise of Kṛṣṇa and his own eternal role in that life. In Rūpa Gosvāmin's characterization of *rāgānugā bhakti,* he prescribed *seva* or service with two bodies: the physical (*sādhaka-rūpa*), and the spiritual (*siddha-rūpa*).[66] The tradition following Rūpa feels that the physical aspect includes the body, speech, and mind of the devotee, while the spiritual body is a mentally conceived form serving Kṛṣṇa in the eternal Vṛndāvana.

Two forms of visualization (*līlā smaraṇa*) done by Bengali Vaiṣṇavas are meditations on Vṛndāvana and the actions of Rādhā and Kṛṣṇa, and on Navadvīpa and the actions of Caitanya. Both forms of meditation involve mental service in the visualized spiritual body, as instructed by the guru.[67]

In the *Vṛndāvana līlā,* the person visualizes himself as inwardly female, a handmaiden (*mañjari*) to Rādhā. This body is twelve or thirteen years old, wearing a certain color sari, in a certain residence, with a particular type of service, following the guidance of a handmaiden who is already a part of the paradise. This more experienced woman explains the details of service to Rādhā and Kṛṣṇa to the newcomer. In addition to this information, the disciple must memorize the layout of the heavenly Vṛndāvana: he must learn the location of Rādhā's house, her village, Kṛṣṇa's house and village, Rādhākuṇḍa (the pond in the forest where Rādhā and Kṛṣṇa meet), and the locale of the various bowers around Rādhākuṇḍa. Elaborate diagrams of all these localities are kept by various Vaiṣṇava gurus who specialize in teaching such visualization. Once this is learned, the disciple must learn the eternal activities of Rādhā and Kṛṣṇa. This set of activities is divided into the eight times that divide the twenty-four-hour day.[68] At each of these times, Rādhā and Kṛṣṇa have a specific action which the disciple must visualize in his spiritual body. He must fit himself, with his visualized body and service, into the appropriate scene.

As Narottama Dāsa Thākura writes:

> 1. Hari, Hari, when shall I in the future attain the state in which I shall become a *mañjari,* leaving my physical frame of a man, and apply sandalwood paste to the bodies of both [Rādhā and Kṛṣṇa]. . . .
>
> 4. Hari, Hari, shall I ever attain the state, in which after renouncing this world, I shall go to Vraja and be overwhelmed with extreme joy, when I shall see Vṛndāvana full of bliss and smear my person with the dust of the place; [when I] shall be overwhelmed with love. . . . When shall I, under the guid-

> ance of Sakhī, be entrusted with the performance of some service at the bower in response to my request, and shall be called by both [Rādhā and Kṛṣṇa] to come near them.[69]

Some practitioners include meditation on a minor war between Rādhā and her friends, and her rival Candrāvalī and her friends. One informant stated that his guru did not believe in Candrāvalī and that indeed even Kṛṣṇa was unimportant—for Rādhā was the true goddess, the infinitely beautiful one, whose mercy was the key to Vṛndāvana.[70] As several Vaiṣṇavas have said: "We are the true Śāktas, for we worship Rādhā, whom even Kṛṣṇa worships." By becoming her handmaiden, the devotee attains a bond with Rādhā and vicariously experiences her intense emotions.

In the visualizations of Navadvīpa, also called *Gaur līlā* (named after Gaurāṅga, a name of Caitanya meaning "fair-limbed"), the practitioner visualizes himself in Navadvīpa at the time of Caitanya. According to practitioners in Navadvīpa today, they see themselves as young male servants of Caitanya. They follow him through the day—wake him in the morning, help him dress and comb his hair, travel in a group with him, and share in his ecstatic states. This is a version of the ritual of the eight times (*aṣṭa kālīya līlā*), in which there are different visualizations for the eight parts of the day.

One form of Navadvīpa meditation is described in the *Bhakti Ratnākara,* in which Śrīnivāsa visualizes Caitanya:

> Navadvīpa is a beautiful place, adored by Brahma and the other gods. . . .
> Inside Navadvīpa is most wondrous Māyāpur
> By visiting that place, all sufferings vanish.
> There Gaur Sundara [Caitanya] is seated upon a wonderful throne
> He plays enthusiastically, surrounded by his dear ones.
> Śrīnivāsa sees [inwardly] that wondrous sight
> And stays near the Lord, at the Lord's command.
> He takes sweet-smelling sandalpaste
> And carefully smears it on the Lord's body, in wonderful designs.
> He puts flower garlands on the Lord's neck and joyously fans him.
> He drinks the nectar of the Lord's beauty, whose face is like a moon.

And he is beside him, forgetting his own identity,
Unable to control his trembling body.
His eyes flowing with tears of blissful love,
Many *bhāvas* are seen in him,
And he loses all memory and awareness of body.[71]

The meditation on Navadvīpa is described by practitioners as more emotionally intense than that on Vṛnadāvana, as Kṛṣṇa has taken on Rādhā's emotions in Navadvīpa, especially her mood of separation. All of the inhabitants of Vṛndāvana have become incarnate again in Navadvīpa. While the handmaiden body in Vṛndāvana is called the *siddha deha,* the devotee's body as visualized in Navadvīpa is called the *gaura deha* or *sādhaka siddha deha.* Singing hymns, listening to readings of the *Bhāgavata Purāṇa,* and chanting the name of Kṛṣṇa are also considered to be participating in Navadvīpa meditations, as Caitanya Mahāprabhu is believed to be present in these activities.

An earlier form of Navadvīpa visualization is the so-called urban mood (*nāgara bhāva*), in which the devotees saw themselves as married city women, in love with Caitanya as a man-about-town or *nāgara.* The women of Navadvīpa are described as having fallen in love with young Caitanya on sight, which is modeled on the gopī legends. A poem by Gokulānanda describes this *bhāva:*

> In company with his followers, Gaura the handsome and superb was going to the bank of the Ganges. Looking at that beauty all my bashfulness and decorum fled away, and I became restless. O friend! Manifold are the charms of Gaura's loveliness; I am a lady of a noble family, and yet I am so much perturbed, in a moment, have become mad, as it were. My heart is pierced through and through with the darts of the Bodyless One (i.e. the god of love): slander by men is at a distance (i.e. is of no concern to me). In the sea of Gaura's loveliness I shall throw down my life and my youthfulness: this is the desire of my heart.[72]

At times, the person may do two forms of visualization (*bhāvanā*) at once and take on two bodies. As Bhaktivinode Thākur writes in *Jaiva Dharma,* there are two divisions of the paradise of Goloka: Kṛṣṇa *pītha* and Gaura *pītha:*

> Those who are worshipers of Śrī Gaurāṅga-deva alone during the period of practice, serve him only in Gaura-pītha in their

accomplished state; and those who as practitioners, worship only Kṛṣṇa do so, when accomplished, in the Kṛṣṇa pītha. Those, however, who are worshipers of both Kṛṣṇa and Gaura during practice, are present, when accomplished, in both the pithas simultaneously, adopting the two bodies at the same time; this is the great mystery of the inscrutable simultaneous distinction and non-distinction between Śrī Kriṣṇa and Śrī Gaura.[73]

This is yet another application of the doctrine of *acintyabhedābheda*—a simultaneous identity and distinction, and a major doctrine of Vaiṣṇava theology. One may possess multiple bodies in several worlds, all in process—some becoming more real, some becoming less so. This doctrine is also seen in the functions of the spiritual body (*siddha deha*) as both observer and participant. As observer, it has a separate body from Rādhā and Kṛṣṇa or Caitanya, and it aids their actions. As participant, it feels the responses of the main characters more intensely than they do. The spiritual body both helps and experiences the lovemaking in the forest. Love at a distance is more powerful than direct love—as the *Caitanya Caritāmṛta* states: "[The companions of Rādhā] do not care for their own play with Kṛṣṇa, but they try to bring about the association of Rādhā and Kṛṣṇa, and derive from it a bliss which is ten million times deeper than what they could have enjoyed from their own association with him."[74]

Although visualization begins as mental exercise of imagination, if done in accordance with the teachings of the tradition it is believed to approximate the heavenly world. It is regarded as a fuzzy picture of the eternal paradise, which becomes clarified and distinct as the practitioner's mind becomes purified and his identity more firmly established. When the image becomes perceived rather than created, the eternal environment becomes the true one, and at death the soul remains there to live.[75]

The spiritual body is nonphysical, made of consciousness and bliss (*cidānanda*), and may take on a variety of forms—as a silent servant (flute, tree, or flower), a servitor (gardener, sweeper), a friend, parent, or consort. It is matured under the influence of the guru; as one informant stated:

The spiritual body [*siddha deha*] is a transformed body, achieved only by the grace of the guru. It is like a bird's egg—if you break it, only fluid will come out. You cannot do anything with it. But the bird can hatch it, and draw its child from it. In

> the same way, the guru aids in the attainment of the spiritual body. But it must be hatched like a bird, and discipline is necessary. Do mantra and meditation, and mind and body will be transformed, leading you to Kṛṣṇa.[76]

There are various types of perfection (*siddhi*). The perfection of true form (*svarūpa siddhi*) is the knowledge of the relationship between Kṛṣṇa and the soul, whose divine eyes are gradually opened to his handmaiden identity, while he dwells on earth. In the perfection of environment (*vastu siddhi*), the person is taken directly to Goloka by Kṛṣṇa's mercy and gains personal service to Rādhā and Kṛṣṇa.[77] In perfection by spiritual practice (*sādhana siddhi* or *āropa siddhi*) the identity is imposed by teaching and individual effort, while in the perfection of divine mercy (*kṛpā siddhi*) the identity is given by grace, and in eternal perfection (*nitya siddhi*) the identity is eternal or, in some usages, existing from birth in this lifetime.

All of the forms of ritual ecstasy described in this chapter are meant to lead the person to a direct encounter with Kṛṣṇa and to a great intensity of sorrow and joy. These states are seen in the lives of the Vaiṣṇava saints.

Biographies of Vaiṣṇava Saints

The Joy of Raw Eggplant: Siddha Gaur Kiśora Dās Bābājī Mahārāj and Gauḍīya Vaiṣṇavism

Gaur Kiśora Dās Bābājī was a member of the Gauḍīya Vaiṣṇava lineage and spent many years in Navadvīpa. Although he wore his begging bowl as a hat, did his worship in an outhouse, and would beat with an umbrella Vaiṣṇavas who wanted initiation from him, he was greatly respected by the Vaiṣṇava community for his detachment and devotion. It was believed that he spent thirty years in a state of intense love for Kṛṣṇa, roaming about the various groves of the heavenly Vṛndāvana as a confidante of Śrī Rādhā. He became well known as a perfected renunciant (*siddha bābājī*) and liberated soul (*paramahaṁsa*) in Vraja and Navadvīpa.[78]

He was born in a Vaiśya family in the village of Faridpur, in East Bengal. He was called Baṅgsidās and lived a householder life until his wife died when he was twenty-nine years old. At that time he took *bes* (a form of Vaiṣṇava initiation) from Siddha Jagannāth Dās Bābā, and later he took *kaupīn* (ascetic initiation, in which the person vows to wear only a single white cloth) from Bhāgavata Dās Bābā. He wandered for many years through villages in Vṛndāvana, continuously worshiping Kṛṣṇa. He learned the practices of ritual emotion (*rāgānugā bhajana*) and detachment (*vairagya*) from Siddha Nityānanda Dās Bābā of Madanmohan Thour.

In the year 1894, Jagannāth Dās Bābā ordered him to leave Vraja and go to Bengal. He lived in Navadvīpa from that year until his death. His behavior was considered unusual in Navadvīpa. He would beg dry foods from householders and offer it as ritual food to Bhagavān. He would cook in used and rejected clay pots and would cover himself with the clothing of corpses left on the banks of the Ganges. He ignored the opinions of others (who felt this behavior to be impure) and would use rejected and unwanted things. Sometimes he would wear a rosary of *tulsī* beads around his neck or have it in his hands for counting the names; at other times he would use a rosary (*mālā*) made of torn cloth with knots. He often roamed about naked or with his loincloth half untied.

In his *bhāvas,* distasteful foods became delicious to him. He would eat raw rice, or other grains, soaked in water or in Ganges mud. Lalitā-dīdī of Rādhāramanbagh witnessed him at worship:

> One day he picked up an unripe eggplant from the market and sat down at the base of a *jhao* tree at Baganbari. He cut the eggplant into pieces and dipped them into Ganges water and put a *tulsī* leaf on them. He offered them to his *iṣṭadevatā* [personal deity] and sang a song of offering: "*Bhaja pātita uddharaṇa, Śrī Gaur Hari.*" He then said, "I don't know the right method of cooking this, but please eat a little of this food." As soon as he said this, his voice became choked, and his body turned bright red and began to swell, while tears flowed from his eyes in streams, soaking his face and chest. Seeing these signs of love, Lalitā-dīdī was amazed. When the *bhāva* subsided nearly an hour later, he again sang a song. Putting [the image of] Śrī Gaura to sleep, he ate the unripe eggplant. His face showed expressions of great pleasure and happiness, more intense than one would make if tasting *pancamṛta* [a sweet drink, considered a delicacy].[79]

He would roam around Navadvīpa with an iron pot, begging for food. Often he wore the pot on his head. He went along the road saying, "*Jai Rādhe!*" and the local people thought he acted like a madman (*unmattavat*). Little boys would run along behind him, and he would play with them: "When he saw a boy who was dark, he would think of him as Kṛṣṇa, and the fair boy he thought of as Gaura. When the children would touch him, he would say, 'Look Mā Yaśodā, your Gopāl has punched me!' or 'Look Mā Śacī, your Gaura is making a face at me!'"[80]

Śrīpada Harimohan Śiromaṇi Gosvāmin, upon seeing him, recognized him to be a Vaiṣṇava saint. He told this to his disciple, Śrījukta Tārādāsī, and told her to see him. Since then, Tārādāsī developed an attraction for Gaur Kiśora, and Bābā also used to call her Mā. In Navadvīpa, he had three women friends: Bara Mā, Meja Mā, and Choto Mā, and even to his last days he would eat rice from only their hands.

He would often fall into trances, madly calling out names of Kṛṣṇa. Once when he was living at the Rānī's *dharamśālā* (shelter), he began to shout loudly, "Ha, Kṛṣṇa Caitanya." Other Vaiṣṇavas heard him yelling only these words for hour after hour. They thought that, unless they could change his mood (*rasa*), his throat would become torn and bloody. Several of them got together and began to shout, "Naraharir prāṇa Gaura." This changed the mood of Siddhabābā, who began to shout, "Raghunandana, Raghunandana" and then calmed down. Another time in that *bhāva*, he locked the door of his meditation hut from within, and he stayed for thirteen days yelling, "Ha, Kṛṣṇa Caitanya," crying continuously, slapping himself on the chest, and tearing at his hair.

He was concerned about a proper death:

> When he went for his bath, he would tie up [in a cloth] about eight or ten kilos of Ganges dust, and would do ritual worship while keeping it on his head. One day, Śrījukta Rādhādāsī Mātā of Baralghat asked him, "O Bābā, what is that on your head?" He smiled and replied, "Just see, Mā, your crazy child. It is not certain when or where he will die, and for that reason, he keeps this Navadvīpa Ganges dust on his head. If the body goes in any other place, then this dust of Gaura's Ganges will be there."[81]

Because he was disturbed by the people around him, he took to doing his meditation in unlikely places. For some time he stayed in the outhouse of Girishbābu and did his worship there. He also did his worship in the Rānī's outhouse, and purified it:

> A devotee went to do worship where Gaur Kiśora did his—in the outhouse of the Rānī's *dharamśālā* [a shelter for religious practitioners]. He perceived [*anubhāva kore*] that the bricks

and stones were all singing Kṛṣṇa's name [Harināma]. Seeing that by the power of Bābājī's chanting the name of Kṛṣṇa, consciousness [*caitanya*] had been infused even into unconscious objects, he left in amazement.[82]

Gaur Kiśora spent much time avoiding persons who wished to be disciples. He refused to have servants, and he cursed at his visitors; he would hit people who wanted to take initiation from him. Kedarnāth Bhaktivinode greatly desired initiation, and Gaur Kiśora would hide from him—often in the veranda of a prostitute's house near the bazaar. He considered it great fun to elude his pursuers.

Gaur Kiśora could not tolerate unsuccessful worship: "When there was no *nāma-sphurti* [manifestation of the name in meditation], he would often go to throw himself into the Ganges. He entered the water up to his neck and would only come out again when the name would appear."[83]

He would also threaten suicide when his readings of sacred text were disturbed by outside noises. He was intensely emotional, with moods of strong joy and sorrow.

In Navadvīpa, at times he would worship with Thākur Bhaktivinode at the birthplace of Caitanya, which had been recently found by Bhaktivinode and restored with images of Mahāprabhu Caitanya and his wife, Viṣṇupriyā. They would sing and dance, with their bodies undergoing the eight *sāttvika bhāvas:*

Sing, sing aloud O my mind
The blissful names of Nitai and Gaur
Be delighted, be delighted O my mind
[The] vision of Rādhā-Kṛṣṇa in sportive Vrindāban
Comes to me through the mercy of Gaur.
O say, say all, Gaur-Nitai![84]

Gaur Kiśora's divine madness was not recorded during childhood and adolescence—it is only described after he joined a renunciant Vaiṣṇava order. His purity was proved by his immunity to impurity, or even his conquest of it (such as causing an outhouse to resonate with mantras). He had inborn devotional love, like Kṛṣṇa's *gopīs,* and its spontaneous nature was shown in his *aśāstriya* (not according to *śāstras* or rules) behavior. He reversed many Vaiṣṇava rules about purity and proper worship techniques, but thought constantly of Rādhā and Kṛṣṇa, so he was a devotee and a liberated soul (*paramahaṁsa*), beyond the rules of even

Vaiṣṇava society, and his madness was a participation in Rādhā's state of divine passion (*divyonmāda*).

Dismemberment by Caitanya: Pāgal Haranāth and Shamanic Vaiṣṇavism

Pāgal Haranāth was a Vaiṣṇava of Sonāmukhī, considered by his devotees to be a joint incarnation of Caitanya, Advaita, and Nityānanda. His life included experiences of a shamanic flavor—dismemberment, death and resurrection, journeys in shadow form, trances and fevers, possession, miraculous powers. He shows a link between Vaiṣṇava religious experiences and those of an earlier Bengali stratum, of traveling souls and miracles.[85]

Thākur Śrī Haranāth Bāndopadhyāya was born in A.D. 1865, in Sonāmukhī, West Bengal. His father, Jayrām, was a pious man who worshiped a *śāligrāma śilā* (sacred stone in which Viṣṇu dwells) and built a large Śiva temple with his savings. As a child, Haranāth preferred animal friends to human ones and showed a variety of psychic abilities (he could always find hidden objects and knew in advance when a visitor would come). This disturbed his parents, who thought he was troubled by a spirit. They performed rites to appease spirits and ancestors, and made a talisman for him to wear.

As a child, Haranāth was frequently ill. One night, he awoke from a fever to find a small boy of great beauty kneeling on his chest. Haranāth wondered if this was his own soul, which had emerged from his body on its way to another world. The boy put his hand down Haranāth's mouth, into his chest, and extracted a small ball of clotted blood and placed it on the bed linens. In the morning, the fever had broken and the blood ball was gone, although a black stain from it remained.

Haranāth would fall into trances for hours at a time, and at school he would miss the roll call and questions addressed to him. At college, the janitors would find him still sitting in his seat hours after the class had gone. He was unable to pass his B.A. exams, although he tried several times.

At his first job, that of a schoolmaster in Ayodhya, he was often abstracted and detached. He only felt himself alive when he would sing hymns to Kṛṣṇa. He avoided people—he felt that his "waves of love" only extended to animals. He married, but was quite indifferent to his wife, Kusum Kumārī. He did not smile or speak unnecessarily. His condition was described by those around him as insanity.

In 1896, however, an event occurred which changed this behavior. On the road from Jammu to Kashmir, while in a tonga, he fell into a deep trance. The tonga wallahs laid him on a cot, wondering if he were dying. About ten hours later, he heard a bell ring and began to see visions. He was called by Gaurāṅga, whom he recognized as the child who had extracted the blood ball:

> When at the Lord's call I had come out of my body, I found Śrī Gaurāṅga standing before me and pointing out with his finger the world stretched before me. On turning my eyes toward it, I found that everything had become transparent. . . . I was able to see in and through mountains and trees, and in fact through everything and everybody. The hidden jewels at the bed of the ocean shed their luster before my eyes; I could see the life-sap flowing through the veins of animals, vegetables, and minerals also . . . she whose secret of nature lay revealed before my eyes, she was at this time an open book for me to read. . . . It was then I understood why the Lord wanted my body for His Līlā, for a Sannyāsī could never dance such a joyful dance with Prakṛti without shame being carried on him.[86]

Gaurāṅga told Haranāth that he had been watching him since his birth and that he wished to take over his body: "Your body is henceforth mine." Gaurāṅga divided Haranāth's body into sixty-four pieces and shook them out, cleansing the physical (*prakṛta*) dirt from them. He took the impurities from each and then reattached the parts by passing his hands over them. However, three parts were found to be missing. Haranāth said it was not necessary to find them—his mother would know him without them. But Gaurāṅga filled in these missing parts with earth from the nearby hills and told Haranāth to reenter his body. He did so, and his body urinated, thus announcing to the tonga wallahs that life had returned, after eleven hours. They also saw that his skin color had changed from dark brown to light gold and were frightened that he looked like a ghost. One asked, "How is it that you have become the color of the Europeans?"

Haranāth did not give a clear explanation of which parts were missing. However, when he was questioned as to how his present nonphysical (*aprakṛta*) body could create a physical son (he continued to live a householder life and had several children), he referred to the three earthly parts of his body.

He took a government job in Kashmir, in the Dharmartha Office, and spent much time traveling, preaching devotion to Kṛṣṇa, and singing hymns. He spent the last fourteen years of his life, the years 1913–27, in retirement in Sonāmukhī, surrounded by devotees and relatives.

Haranāth made a variety of claims about his identity, most frequently that he did not know who he was or what was happening to him. He felt that Hari played "various impossible games" through his body and that at times he was possessed by Gaurāṅga: "When I speak about Kṛṣṇa, I see him before me. I become Kṛṣṇa all over. What he says to me then, I myself do not know. Those who listen to my words concerning Kṛṣṇa at that time are not in this world of Māyā at all."[87]

Many of his disciples believed him to be a complex avatar—a combination of Advaitācārya, Nityānanda, and Gaurāṅga. Like Advaitācārya, he could explain sacred texts; like Nityānanda, he took the karmic burden of others' sins; and like Gaurāṅga, he filled his devotees with love. At various times, he claimed to be Gaurāṅga, Nityānanda, Hari, Hari's messenger, and Gopāl. He was called by others an avatar and a great saint (*mahāpuruṣa*).

In A.D. 1592, the Vaiṣṇava saint Manohardās told Śrīnivās Ācārya:

> A time is coming when an Avatar will be born at Sonāmukhī, who shall be the *bilās-mūrti* of the Lord, and whose mission in life shall be to make the whole world drunk with the extract of the sweet *rasa* contained in these *granthas* [leaves inscribed by the Gosvāmins]. The world will ring with His name and fame; he shall be Śrī Gouranga come again in *gṛhī's* [householder's] dress to push on the work which He had begun but left unfinished.[88]

Haranāth was widely believed to be this incarnation or avatar. While Gaurāṅga was on earth, he was limited by his renunciant role, which excluded women and worldly men. Thus it was necessary for him to return as a householder, to save women, Christians, Muslims, and princes.

"In the incarnation as Gaur, I had no pleasure; I associated with only one class and caste." Now there was more potential for joy: Haranāth could take on particular *bhāva* for each devotee. While in the dance of the *rasa līlā,* Kṛṣṇa divided himself into as many bodies as there were milkmaids; in *Haranāth līlā* Pāgal Bābā (Haranāth) divided himself into as many subtle bodies as there were devotees of his inner circle (*antaraṅga bhaktas*), to be with them in the dance of life.

Sometimes he called himself Nitāi, the mad *avadhūta,* rescuing souls and tasting love. He would impart intense religious love by touch, causing his devotees to act like madmen. He would also take on disease and sin by touch—getting fevers and pains by the first, and a temporary blackening of the skin from the second. His devotees had many stories of his clairvoyance—visiting people in his subtle body and telling them later of their wrong actions, writing replies to letters yet unmailed, knowing past and future.

Haranāth had his own interpretation of Vaiṣṇava theology. Chanting the name of Kṛṣṇa (*harināma*), which caused love of Kṛṣṇa, was the most important practice. Kṛṣṇa's name, he believed, was greater and more powerful than Kṛṣṇa himself, for it could approach sinners more closely and even be chanted by them. The goal was to reach Kṛṣṇa's home in the heavenly worlds, where souls with divine bodies[89] relate eternally to Kṛṣṇa through an intense love (*mahārasa*). This goal is reached through the grace of Nityānanda. As in Vṛndāvana, Rādhā is Kṛṣṇa's chief *śakti* (feminine energy of manifestation), so is Nityānanda Gaur's *śakti* in the physical realm—without the will of Nityānanda, Gaur does nothing. Nityānanda is Gaur's "second body," surrounding and helping him.

The sweetness of the name invokes Gaur and Nityānanda as well as Kṛṣṇa. The name is the ideal practice because of its *rasa:*

> When we talk of a "mango," the very name of the fruit reminds us simply of its exquisite sweetness, but when we actually hold a mango in our hands, first a doubt arises in the mind whether it is sweet or not, then we think of its bitter skin and hard stone. . . . Such is exactly the difference between Śrī Kṛṣṇa and His name. In the name there is only unalloyed sweetness. In Śrī Kṛṣṇa Himself there are qualities which inspire awe or even dread; that is why His name is so much sweeter than Śrī Kṛṣṇa Himself.[90]

Haranāth described his pen as generating love, much like Kṛṣṇa's flute. His love was also shown in his relationships with animals. He spent much time with snakes, birds, and other animals, to the point where he was called "zoo father" (*chiria bābā*). He suggested that his disciples also spend time in nature, avoiding people. He would also talk to the trees and rocks. When he returned to his garden in Sonāmukhī for his retirement,

> As He was entering and passing through His garden, the trees and plants had suddenly changed colour. They had as-

> sumed a pale yellowish tint, and were profusely dripping forth a sort of juice which looked like tears. Such a sight our Bro. N. C. Ghosh had never seen in his lifetime. Getting curious, He asked Thākur what the cause of this strange behavior of the trees might be. Haranāth's reply was characteristic. "You should know," said He, "these trees and plants are my fathers and mothers. They are shedding tears at seeing me return home after an absence of so many years."[91]

Haranāth had many *bhāvas* that he would take on, and for women disciples he would most often take on the role of an infant. He would cry for milk and butter, and sit on their laps, holding on to their saris. As one disciple states:

> At that time their breasts would overflow with milk, though they might be women actually barren, or long past childbearing age, and they would be given the opportunity to suckle him.[92]

He considered his title of madman (*pāgal*) to be an honor. He wrote to a disciple:

> I am a servant of the servants of Nityānanda, does it lie in my power to assume that title of *pāgal?* Out of blindness you yourselves have conferred that title upon me. *Pāgal* is Gouranga, another *pāgal* is His company, [they] dance, sing in sankīrtana and play the mridanga [drum]. Nitai and Adwaita are *pāgal*—*pāgal* are the disciples with them. If I get admission even in the last class of these *pāgals,* I shall be gratified in life after life.[93]

However, he referred to himself continually as mad (*pāgal*) and much admired a song by his disciple Pāgal Bhāi:

> The lunatic [*pāgal*] has laid a fine trap to catch lunatics
> Once he wept at Nadia, and made Nadia weep, and a stream of tears flow
> He flew to the country of the Oriyas, and remained in hiding
> Again issuing from the forest [at Sonāmukhī], the lunatic has begun a fine play. . . .
> The three lunatics [Gaurāṅga, Nityānanda, and Advaitācārya] have mixed together and become one. . . .

The catcher of lunatics runs to catch [them], beware,
beware, while there is yet time.[94]

Haranāth had many experiences that were not characteristic of mainstream Vaiṣṇavism. He was cured of a fever by a being (later identified as Gaurāṅga) who reached into his chest to extract a ball of clotted blood. He went through a period of death, dismemberment, purification of bodily parts, and rebirth. His material body became spiritualized. During this process, the world became transparent, and he spoke with the deity who was the agent of this change. He made otherworldly journeys in a subtle body and would also visit his devotees in the form of a shadow, which could become physical. He would be possessed by a deity and afterward have no memory of what he said; he would hear and respond to spirit voices. He would communicate with animals and plants, who were believed to understand and answer him. He had clairvoyant powers—he knew of past and future events, and events that occurred at a distance. He would cure the diseases of disciples by taking them into his own body, which would temporarily turn darker in color.

He is, however, clearly a Vaiṣṇava, advocating chanting and love of Kṛṣṇa, discussing Gaurāṅga and the paradise of Vṛndāvana, and believed by his devotees to be a joint avatar of Gaurāṅga, Nityānanda, and Advaitācārya.

The Storms of *Bhāva:* Vijayakṛṣṇa Gosvāmin and Yogic Vaiṣṇavism

Vijayakṛṣṇa Gosvāmin was a visionary who spoke to gods and ghosts, who was burnt in the flames of the name of Kṛṣṇa, who would fall into *bhāvas* continually and would share these states with his disciples. Between his preaching for the Brahmo Samāj and his own religious experiences, he influenced millions of people.

Vijayakṛṣṇa Gosvāmin was born in Śāntipur, West Bengal, in 1841. He came of a brahmin family, directly descended from Advaitācārya, the disciple of Caitanya. His father, Ānandakiśora, would often be lost in ecstasy while reading the *Bhāgavata Purāṇa*—shivering, in tears, with hair standing on end. Ānandakiśora's first two wives died, and in his old age he married Svarṇamayī Devī. Ānandakiśora died while Vijayakṛṣṇa was very young, and he was temporarily adopted by his aunt, Kṛṣṇa Moṇi. She died soon after, and he returned to his natural mother.[95]

Svarṇamayī had periods of madness. She would give away all her clothes and household items to beggars, and she would wear rags, while the household lacked food. She would never bargain with salespeople and was a devotee of Śiva. When she fell into a frenzied state later in life, she had to be tied up or she would run into the jungle.

By the age of six, Vijayakṛṣṇa fell into trances. He described a vision of his father's soul, who took him to the lunar sphere and asked him to be a great Vaiṣṇava saint and to uphold the glory of the house of Advaita. His relatives worried about him, as he would hear the voices of friends who had died of cholera, have dreams and visions of saints, and speak with the family deity Śyāmasundara. They took the child to a brahmin priest, who gave amulets and spoke mantras to drive away the spirit afflicting him. In 1850 he took initiation from his mother after his sacred thread ceremony.

He was not popular with the Hindus of Śāntipur, who were suspicious of his trances. They smeared his body with treacle and set wasps on him, burnt him with iron tongs when he went into ecstasy at a *kīrtana*, and threw old shoes at him while he was in trance. Ostracized by relatives and asked to leave town, he decided to go to Calcutta.

Vijayakṛṣṇa went there in 1859, to study medicine. He had completed a course of Sanskrit study in the village school and began to study Vedānta. He was married in that year to Yogamāyā Devī, when she was six years old.

He soon came into contact with Devendranāth Tāgore and the Brahmo Samāj. He joined them, discarding his sacred thread and rejecting the rituals of conventional Hinduism. In 1864 he was appointed high priest (*upācārya*) of the Brahmo Samāj and left his medical studies. He became a missionary and preacher, traveling throughout Bengal and speaking about the Brahmos.

However, within the Samāj itself there were many disagreements, and it was split into opposing camps. Vijayakṛṣṇa became disillusioned and grew interested in Vaiṣṇavism. He read the *Caitanya Caritāmṛta,* went to Navadvīpa, and began to sing Vaiṣṇava *kīrtanas* in the Samāj meetings.

In Calcutta, he had a vision of Mahāprabhu Caitanya, who gave him initiation. He then went to Benares and spent time with the yogi Trailaṅga Svāmī, who also initiated him. He joined many groups and tried their spiritual practices: Sahajiyās, Kartā-bhajās, Bāuls, Darveśis, Kiśori-bhajās. In 1883 he visited Gayā and underwent a radical change; he later called this his "day of regeneration." He took yoga initiation from a yogin of Mānsarovara Lake in the Himalayas and sat in meditation at the *āśrama* of Raghuvari Bābājī on Ākāśagaṅgā Hill at Gayā. There he fell into a trance lasting eleven days. He meditated on sound and *kuṇḍalinī* energy, and its perfection (*siddhi*) was when the Name resonated spontaneously in every organ of his body.

He continued the meditation for six months, often falling into darkness and despair. It created a great, unbearable heat so that he was continuously covering his body with mud or water. His *yogi-guru* told him to go to Jvālāmukhi and continue his practice there, where the heat continued. This flame was *nāmāgni,* the destruction of impurity, which emanates from the Divine Name. It is said not only to destroy impurities but also to restructure the body. Vijayakṛṣṇa stated that many painful dislocations occurred: limbs and features withdrew into the body, joints elongated, even parts of the body were rent asunder and then later put back together.[96]

He continued to perform a variety of spiritual practices and preach for the Brahmo Samāj until 1885, when he went into retreat at Geṇḍariā, a suburb of Dacca. It was a time of trials and temptations in which he did yoga, austerities (*tapasya*), and a meditation for gaining power over the gods (*devatā-siddhi*). At this time his guide was a nearby holy woman named Yoginī Mā.

He felt that religious practice was only the first stage in preparing the body for divine grace—practice must always fail unless grace is present from guru and god. He gained this grace in Geṇḍariā and was accepted after that time as a saint. From then he traveled, giving initiation and accompanied by a guru in invisible form.

He left the Brahmo Samāj in 1887, as he had come to accept image worship, mantras, the power of holy places, and the existence of deities. His disciples built him an *āśrama* at Geṇḍariā, where he lived in between pilgrimages. When his wife died in 1891, he moved to Calcutta and then to Purī. He had five children, three of whom were still alive when he died in 1899.

Vijayakṛṣṇa's mother was still alive while he was at the Geṇḍariā *āśrama,* and she lived there briefly. At one point she ran away, and he searched for her without success. He later heard some woodcutters discussing a naked woman resting her head on the body of a tiger in the midst of the jungle, and he immediately set off there. After speaking to the people in a nearby village, he went looking for her. He found her with a tiger, speaking incoherently to it, claiming to be Kālī, and offering to get it food. When she ran off into the jungle, he followed her; he wrapped her in his own upper cloth and began to cry. At first she did not recognize him, but he chanted to her the mantras that she had given him, and she gradually returned to a normal state. Vijayakṛṣṇa said of her, "She is in the state of liberation [*jivanmukta*]. People think she is mad when she is in a religious state, but really she is not mad. Because everything that happens in this state she remembers. Mad people do not remember."[97]

Vijayakṛṣṇa's visions and *bhāvas* were well known. They would occur at odd times, such as while eating:

> Thākur would sit together [with his disciples] and eat. While eating, he would often fall into trance [*bhāvāveśa*]. Suddenly he would sit completely motionless and weep continuously. When he would see visions of Vṛndāvana, he would repeat, "These gopīs have come," and overwhelmed with *bhāva,* he would speak with them. Each guru-brother stopped eating, sat quietly, and was deeply absorbed in listening to him. When he cried in trance he overflowed— and nobody ate.[98]

At one point, his disciple Mohini Bābu noticed that Vijayakṛṣṇa was late in returning from the outhouse. He asked Vijayakṛṣṇa about his lateness, and he replied:

> "I will tell you a mad story [about what happened]. Today, when I was about to enter the outhouse, I saw that Nārada, Vyāsa, and the rest of the sages, and Brahma, Viṣṇu, Śiva and the rest of the gods, appeared before me. Thus, I was not able to go into the outhouse. Finally, after repeated songs of praise, they disappeared. After that, I managed to finish in the outhouse, and when I came outside, before me appeared the sacred paradise of Vṛndāvana, and when I saw this the external world vanished [or, I lost consciousness]. This was the reason for the delay today. . . ." That day Thākur appeared as if intoxicated. From his body an unearthly light radiated out, and his face was filled with bliss.[99]

Sometimes his inner visions would become imprinted on his body:

> In the afternoon, at the time of the *Mahābhārata* reading, and at various other times, many amazing things happened. On Thākur's seat and on his own body, the forms of gods and goddesses were imprinted [*cāpā padita*]. There were various kinds of pictures, sometimes war chariots, and multitudes of

> soldiers, and temples. Sometimes the syllables of Rādhā and Kṛṣṇa, Rādhāśyama, Harerāma and others, and entire Sanskrit ślokas, were imprinted very clearly on his skin. Everyone could see this.[100]

Vijayakṛṣṇa Gosvāmin would often start group singing of hymns (*kīrtana*) by announcing that many gods, goddesses, and sages were present in a state of bliss, so that it was an appropriate moment for singing. However, he was violently against persons who imitated *bhāvas*—at one meeting taking a person by the neck and throwing him out into the street for "practicing religious pretensions" and displaying false *bhāvas*. Vijayakṛṣṇa knew the real state well:

> We used to feel that he would always dance in a new manner. In *bhāva,* sometimes he would remove the cloth from around his hips and use it as a veil, or sometimes he would shout, or sometimes he would become drenched with tears. Or sometimes sweat would fall from his body in streams. While dancing, this would be scattered all around. We too, though far away, were sprinkled with it many times. Though Bidhubābu and the guru-brothers would catch and protect Thākur while he was dancing, many times they were not able to deter him. Sometimes each limb would quiver fiercely, of its own accord. Sometimes, as soon as he raised a hand, it would begin to shake so quickly that we were astounded at seeing it. Sometimes he would only cry and sob. Or staring upward, holding a strand of matted hair, he would perform ritual worship (*ārati*) before someone, drenched in tears. Sometimes he would stand with folded hands while his body was covered with gooseflesh and did not breathe or blink, like a piece of wood, and he would only stare off into the distance. . . .
>
> Another day in Calcutta, at the Śyāmbazar residence, *kīrtana* singing was in progress. Thākur began to run about the room, ritually moving his hand toward an empty space. And bending down, he began to run as if lifting someone from the ground with his two hands, and he began to shout, "I am going." Later, he said that many gods and goddesses had done their full prostrations in the *kīrtana* room, and when he was running, he was raising them up. Then the maidens of Vṛndāvana came to take him.[101]

The devotees would dance in the waves of *bhāva,* which became a "sky-high typhoon." Their minds were overwhelmed with the apparently chaotic beauty of the various manifestations of *bhāva*.[102] Sometimes a *bhāva* would be shared with only one disciple, as in the village of Ichapura near Dacca. Vijayakṛṣṇa, with tears in his eyes, looked up at an image of Mahāprabhu, and began to tremble. The other Vaiṣṇavas started singing loudly, with drums and cymbals, and he began to dance. In a state of *mahābhāva*, he grabbed his disciple Lāl (who was in a similar state) and they leaped up and down. He took on a variety of roles—archer, wrestler, warrior—until he shouted "Jaya Nitai" and lost consciousness.[103]

He began a dust-throwing ceremony in Dacca in which a whole crowd was dancing wildly (*uddaṇḍa nṛtya*) and intoxicated by *bhāva* (*bhāvonmatta āvasthā*). He would leap roaring into the air, and the crowds were tossed by *bhāva* like a tempest. This would last six or seven hours. The shopkeepers on the street were spellbound.[104] Seven children fainted, one remained unconscious for twelve hours, and a teenager roamed the streets for a week asking "Where is my Kṛṣṇa?" and crying continuously.[105]

Vijayakṛṣṇa was quite verbal about his visions. He would give a strange, deep laugh which caused others to shiver, and point into the empty air: "Look, there comes the mad one, there he stands! But he wants to go away—catch him! . . . There is an eye in his forehead which is so dazzling, it is like the sun."[106]

He would stand trembling, describing visions of the Mother, yogis, sages, and ghosts he had known. He alternately laughed and cried, then fell into a trance that would last for hours. Dinners would remain uneaten—visitors would find themselves absorbed in *bhāva*, senseless with food in their hands, sobbing in the waves of *mahābhāva*. Some persons would find themselves possessed by spirits, others would lose consciousness or have visions of gods and goddesses, lights, geometrical shapes, and persons.

Possession by *bhāva* was continuous at these meetings, and the villagers thought it was due to the presence of ghosts. Visitors at the Brahmo Samāj compound were caught up in the hymns, and they fell on the stairs, in the streets, corridors, grass, under the trees. They would dance and sing, take on strange forms,[107] and fall to the floor. Vijayakṛṣṇa would go into trance and counsel his disciples on their visions:

> The different forms that you all see in meditation should not be considered as imaginary, or as illusions. Persons doing meditation must see many visions. In the first stages, these visions are shifting and temporary. As the mind becomes more pure, still, and transparent, these visions become clearer and more enduring.

> In the beginning, the vision appears as a sort of picture, a painted canvas, appearing from time to time in flashes. Later it is seen vividly, as a clear-cut image that appears alive. Then you can hear the image speak to you, and it can answer your questions. It is then concrete, with hands and feet, and you can watch it moving these limbs in gestures as you communicate.
>
> Spiritual practice may bring visions not only of our gods and goddesses, but also of the forms worshiped by other religions. All of these forms may be revealed to you, whether you seek them or not. These are the forms in which the deity is conceived all over the world. Do not think that I am indulging in imagination—this is a very direct experience, a direct truth. If you disregard these [visions] as imaginary or illusory, you miss the path of spontaneity [*sahaja*]. . . .
>
> Once yoga starts properly, you will see things which are strange, wonderful, supersensual—things you cannot imagine in your so-called normal state. A person's life becomes blessed by having these visions.[108]

Vijayakṛṣṇa describes a natural (*sahaja*) practice in which there is no inner ritual or meditation on a fixed mental form; rather, divine forms reveal themselves spontaneously. The person is pulled by an inner urge, so strongly that he barely maintains social customs.[109] He praises the women of Vṛndāvana for their spontaneity (*svabhāvika bhāva*) in relation to Kṛṣṇa, admiring their natural love which could not be gained by many, even after much worship and meditation. Devotional love (*prema-bhakti*) is an irresistable force that draws the devotee to Kṛṣṇa whether or not he does ritual practice. And the practice (*sādhana*) itself should be spontaneous—*mantras* should be heard rather than chanted.

In the state of perfection (*siddhi*), every organ of the body sings the divine name. Chanting the name of God is a practice that may lead to perfection; the mind should be empty, without voluntary acts of imagination or visualization.[110] Chanting can lead to a manifestation of divine form (*rūpa*), but Kṛṣṇa should determine which of his infinite numbers of forms he will show.

When breath and chanting are perfectly harmonized, strange changes may occur to the body:

> The sound of it resonated within him, and he felt exhausted from the flow of power. He then felt as if his hands, feet, and head were shrinking and collapsing into him, as if some centripetal force were trying to draw them inside . . . he felt as if

> his nerves, muscles and limbs were being wrung, and that he would be compressed into a tortoise shape. He heard the sound of the Name coming continuously from within, and also from outside. Though it was painful, he did not want it to end. Then he completely lost the sense of body. Gradually the tremendous force of the flow of the Name [*nāma*] subsided, and his body was returned to its normal shape.[111]

Vijayakṛṣṇa felt it was imperative to keep chanting during this process—or the body may be reduced to a lump of flesh. Sometimes when the Name penetrates the body, the joints separate and the body elongates, the limbs may separate from the body and then return to their exact places. He insists he has seen such cases.

According to Vijayakṛṣṇa, devotion is not obtained by effort, but descends without apparent cause. The more it has been repressed in the person's life, the greater will be its intensity. It is this descent of grace which leads to the full realization of Bhagavān. There are two ways to gain admission to paradise: the initial vision of Bhagavān, and the disinterested love of persons. In this state, all of creation becomes filled with joy and music, and in the rays of light one learns the secrets of creation.

The guru, too, may give this grace. Vijayakṛṣṇa refused to give initiation to disembodied spirits, although they wished for it. However, when he took a bath in the Yamunā in Vṛndāvana, they licked the drops of water from his body and cast off their own dark and suffering bodies, rising in light.[112]

Vijayakṛṣṇa was a yogi who tried many paths and who was a visionary and ecstatic from childhood. His father would fall into Vaiṣṇava bliss, while his mother was subject to periodic fits of madness and had to be tied down. He performed *kuṇḍalinī* yoga rather than the ritual practice of the handmaiden (*mañjari sādhana*), yet had thousands of Vaiṣṇava followers, many of whom thought him to be an avatar. He had spontaneous trances and raptures, even in impure situations, and saw visions of gods, ghosts, and sages. While his divine madness was initially socially unacceptable, it later came to represent a return to Hindu orthodoxy and a strike against the Brahmo Samāj. Instead of a madman, he was later seen as a neoconservative saint.

Against Universal Destruction: Prabhu Jagadbandhu and *Harināma*

Prabhu Jagadbandhu, called the world savior, gathered a large number of followers to proclaim the power of chanting Kṛṣṇa's name (*harināma*).

Chanting the Name would avert the great destruction at the end of the Kālī Yuga and lead to salvation of the earth and to universal liberation (*mahā-uddharaṇa*). His followers believed him to have experienced all of Rādhā's states of *mahābhāva* and to have gone beyond them to a state of absolute sweetness—a child *bhāva* beyond Caitanya's *Rādhā bhāva.*[113]

Prabhu Jagadbandhu was born in 1871, in the village of Dāhākārā, in Murśhidābād, Bengal. His father, Dinanāth Cakravarti, was a scholar of Nyāya philosophy, and his mother, Vāmā Sundarī, died before he was a year old. He was cared for by a maidservant, Urmilā Mā, who died a year later; he was then given to his Aunt Rasmaṇi Devī. She then died, and at the age of four he was given to a cousin, Digambarī Devī, in Govindapur, while his father remained in Dāhāpārā. When Jagadbandhu was seven, his father died, and he performed a funeral (*śrāddha*) ceremony. He was given to an uncle, who soon died, and then to his cousins, Tāriṇī Bābu and Gopāl Bābu, who arranged for his education.

He stayed in Govindapur until the age of eleven, when the Padmā River washed away his house; a new house was built in Brāhmankāṇḍā, near Faridpur. He took the sacred thread at age twelve, observing strict ascetic behavior (*brahmacarya*), speaking little, and living alone in a room. He was a shy, absent-minded child who would never touch anybody or allow others to touch him. He always kept his entire body wrapped up in cloth.

He briefly went to high school in Ranchi, where his cousin worked. As a high school student, he arose at three o'clock in the morning to worship the family deity, Rādhā-Govindajī, and he slept no more than four hours a night. He never spoke or read textbooks, and his relatives were worried about his sanity. Although he was harmless, their cook felt threatened and poisoned him. He became extremely ill, but survived. His cousin felt that perhaps Ranchi was not a good environment for Jagadbandhu and sent him to Pābnā to live with another relative, Golokmaṇi Devī.

In Pābnā, Jagadbandhu totally rejected study (the textbooks were full of ignorance, *avidyā*), and he poured his full energy into religious devotion. As a biographer states:

> Exactly like Śrī Gouranga, he entirely gave himself up to Hari Kīrtana and all the signs of *bhāva* and *mahabhāva* began to appear and disappear like waves upon that ocean of bliss. So great became the effect of kīrtana upon him, that wherever he heard the sound of kīrtana, be it a house, river, or pathway . . . he invariably used to fall into trance.[114]

By the age of sixteen, Jagadbandhu stood out in a crowd—he was six feet tall, with white skin, blue eyes, and red lips. He decided that his task was universal liberation, to rid the world of its anxieties. He had apocalyptic visions of world destruction and decided to struggle against the forces of the Kālī Yuga, using the name of Lord Hari (Kṛṣṇa) as a weapon. In an effort to save the world, he would frequent and organize parties for religious singing.

His guardians tried to keep him from singing, but to no avail. While singing, ecstatic symptoms (*sāttvika bhāvas*) would emerge (tears, sweating, horripilation, shivering), and he fell into trances lasting days and nights. Townspeople mistrusted him, feeling him to be a bad influence on their children, and he was beaten several times.

While at Pābnā, Jagadbandhu became involved with a *darvesh* named Hārān Kṣepa, a holy man who was considered a madman by the townspeople. He lived poorly, dressed in rags, and claimed to read the past and future and to heal diseases. He ignored caste and saw himself as both Hindu and Muslim. Jagadbandhu would publicly hug and kiss him, and sleep in his bed. He called the Kṣepa "Buḍā Śiva," saying that he was perfect from birth (*nitya siddha*) and in his true form the Advaitācārya of *Caitanya līlā*.

Jagadbandhu began preaching his own interpretation of Vaiṣṇavism, speaking out against initiation, which had become a hereditary profession. In place of secrecy and whispering in the ear, he called for public *harināma* among all castes and sects. At nineteen, he began to go on pilgrimages and gave his first photo to devotees. He traveled through northern India and later returned to Brāhmankāṇḍā. There he built a cottage, complete with *pañcavati* (a group of five sacred trees) and vines from Vṛndāvana. He cut off all communications with his remaining family and lived an ascetic life. He soon had a large number of boys as followers. He spoke against illiteracy, useless talking, and lust, telling the students to keep their distance from each other and not to take food tasted by another. He would prophesy their future and also tell them their secret sins, which he could perceive due to his third eye. He included among his followers boys from the Dom and Caṇḍāla subcastes (*jātis*). He described his reasons for singing: "The whole nature awaits spiritual emancipation. It was only through the Lord's name that this could be effected. Besides, there are many bodiless souls in our atmosphere. They also wish to hear the songs in the name of the Lord."[115]

At nineteen, he also converted a poor, depressed low-caste group, the Bāgdīs of Faridpur, to Vaiṣṇavism. Their leader or *sardār,* Rajani

Dās, felt that only Christian missionaries would help them obtain food and education, and then only if all were baptized. Jagadbandhu called on Rajani before the mass baptism and spoke to him as an equal. He invited the entire caste for blessed food (*prasāda*). All the Bāgdīs came the next day, attempted to sing *kīrtana,* and took the food. As they were leaving, Jagadbandhu took out a bundle of new clothes and gave a piece to each Bāgdī, and tied beads of *tulsī* wood around their necks. He told the leader: "Rajani, you are no longer a Bāgdī *sardār,* but henceforth you will be a *Mohānta,* and your name is Haridās, as Lord Hari has been merciful to you. All of your castemen should form a hierarchy of their own, and will be known as the *Mohānta sampradāya.*"[116]

To Jagadbandhu's followers, this act showed him to be the true world savior (*mahā-uddharaṇa*), for he prevented the Christian baptism and created a new Vaiṣṇava lineage.

Jagadbandhu led great singing groups, accompanied by long drums and cymbals, through the streets of Faridpur. These created a vibration in the air with the name of Hari, in order to dispel the spirits of destruction. He often visited Navadvīpa and Vṛndāvana, and spent his time in Navadvīpa in continuous week-long *kīrtanas,* saying "Sleep is death" to his dozing followers. In many villages, the singing would attract two or three thousand followers. At Barisal he led a group of six thousand people, mostly Bengali brahmins. While in Calcutta, he turned the Doms of Rāmbāgān into enthusiastic Vaiṣṇavas with his singing parties, and he fought an epidemic of plague there by chanting the Name.

When he was restrained by relatives from going to *kīrtana,* he would leap until he hit himself against the walls and fell unconscious. He would roam about alone, singing, and from time to time people would beat him or attempt to drown him. Once when beaten, he was found by a devotee, who sang the Name over him. The devotee noticed that he made dancing gestures even while lying on the ground, and soon ecstatic symptoms (*sāttvika bhāvas*) emerged and he regained consciousness.

At this time he began to make claims about his identity—that he was Rādhā-Kṛṣṇa, a spiritual king, and Hari Mahāvatarana (a great incarnation of Hari). He stated that he had the bodily signs (*lakṣaṇa*) of Rāma, Kṛṣṇa, and Rādhikā.

In 1899 he went into retreat at Śrī Aṅgina, a thick jungle with wild animals and thorn plants near Faridpur (then called Goalchamat). There he wrote the *Harikathā,* about the meaning of Kṛṣṇa and Caitanya. His followers could not make sense of it and did not wish to read it, but he insisted that they do so. In 1901 he stopped writing letters to disciples and became more gloomy, ceasing to smile. He was in a frenzied condition ("brought about by his deep sorrow for the fate of men") and would disappear without warning. He spoke unintelligibly, including such sayings as

> Am I nobody to you? Shall I be wafted away? . . . I am your body, hands, feet, life, mind and everything. Obey my words, chant Harināma and hearing that, let me mix myself up with the dust, with everything on earth, with the sky. . . . I belong to Harināma, and to nobody else; if you do not sing Harināma and be true men, I will never come out of my room. I shall transform myself into stone by being closeted in my cottage. All of you sing Harināma and preach it.[117]

He briefly returned to normal, and then in 1902 he took a vow of silence which lasted seventeen years. He confined himself in a dark thatched hut in Goalchamat, and a single disciple served him as attendant. When he refused food for more than a week, the disciples would hear of it and enter the hut, begging him to eat. He would not leave the hut, although disciples claimed to receive instructions from him in dreams. People who visited him would occasionally be allowed in, and they would perceive him as Kṛṣṇa, Rādhā, Gaurāṅga, and Śiva. He saw his disciples in 1916, going out into his yard for a few minutes. He had no sacred thread or white cloth; he came out naked, wearing only rubber shoes. He had gained weight and no longer had long hair. When three devotees came to touch his feet, he struck them with the bolt of a door.

In 1918 he emerged from seclusion, acting like a young child and walking with difficulty (his biographer, Navadvīp Ghosh, calls this "simulated paralysis"). He appeared shorter and had to be carried on a chair. At first he was mute, but began to lisp a few words. He would cry like a child, play with dolls and toys, and alternately abuse people nearby and then serenely smile at them. He passed stool and urine while lying in bed, and his eyes never appeared to focus on anybody. Even at this stage he gained disciples, who considered him the embodiment of all deities and their most cherished god. Many disciples continued to see him in dreams.

He ate little and roamed naked, sometimes without his rubber shoes. When he was carried, *kīrtana* processions would follow him. His followers would discuss their various understandings of his life, which they often called *paṅgu līlā,* "a life of vicarious suffering."

In 1921 he fell while being carried to his rickshaw and fractured his thigh bone. A doctor bandaged it and told him to keep still, but he would beg passersby to move him and help him walk. Another doctor changed the bandage, leaving one end of the fractured bone piercing the skin. Jagadbandhu's temperature rose, he foamed at the mouth, and died. The body did not begin to decompose until the sixth day, at which point it was decided that he would be buried (as he had led the life of a renunciant and did not require burning).

Jagadbandu claimed that he was not born of flesh and blood, that his mother had not been pregnant, and that he had never been in her womb. He predicted his condition in later life: "Someday you will find me in a state of senselessness and stillness resembling that of a dying person. See that at that time no wicked person comes near and annoys me. It is you who will then be the guardians of my body."[118]

This state was interpreted by his disciples as child *bhāva,* the thirteenth great state or *nirvikalpa jñāna.* They interpreted his books to mean that Rādhā's state was the tenth state, and that the union of Rādhā and Kṛṣṇa in Caitanya was a still higher state (the eleventh as shown in his dislocation of joints, and the twelfth in his tortoise-*bhāva,* when his limbs were drawn into his body). Higher than the *mahābhāva* of Rādhā and Caitanya was Jagadbandhu's state of *mahācaitanya*—a sweetness beyond ego and jealousy such as those of Rādhā.

Kṛṣṇa's *rasa līlā* dance saves too few—most gopīs were dismissed, and not allowed to be near him. Even Candrāvalī was excluded, and she was an eternal aspect of Kṛṣṇa. Jagadbandhu wished to save all beings, and in his theology combined Vaiṣṇavism with an original creation by sound and light. He stated:

> The beginning of the eternal and endless is Govinda—the Ultimate Being. He incarnated as Śrī Kṛṣṇa and Śrī Gourāṅga. By combining in myself all the sweetness and beauty of those two *līlās* and taking the collective power of the two, I have come as Hari Puruṣa Jagadbandhu. That I am that very Being—I represent in myself both of them with something new—is yet unrevealed to the world.[119]

He predicted that he would change the world, continent by continent, abolishing drinking and cow slaughter. His followers await his resurrection, believing that their deity will rise from his apparent death. At that time, he will reveal his great revelation, which will prove his status as savior of the world.

Jagadbandhu's disciples, who call themselves the Mahānāma lineage (*sampradāya*), claim that he is an incarnation of Caitanya, as Jagadbandhu spread the chanting of the Name, converted low castes, prostitutes, and evil men to Vaiṣṇavism, and became agonized if people did not chant with him. Also it was believed that he made true predictions and averted the disasters of the Kali Yuga. Some followers view him as a joint avatar of Gaurāṅga and Nityānanda, as Jagadbandhu wrote that he combined all *līlās* within himself.[120] His followers chant "Jaya Jagadbandu Hari" to hasten the Mahāuddharaṇa Yuga, a time of universal liberation.[121]

Prabhu Jagadbandhu's eccentric behavior began in childhood and continued throughout his adolescence, when he developed the grandiose goals of saving the world and fighting off universal evil and destruction through the power of his chanting. By his teens, all six of his caretakers had died (including both of his parents, relatives, and servants); one can understand why he did not want people to touch him or go near him. He was subject to spontaneous trances and extremes of emotion, and charismatic enough to attract large numbers of devotees. The belief in his devotion, and even in his divinity, could incorporate his irrational behavior, breakdown, and regression; it was simply assumed that his divine emotions were too strong for his physical body. He was never initiated and practiced no ritual or meditation besides singing the Name, yet he was considered by devotees as saint and savior.

The Freeing of the Waters: Madness and Ecstasy in Bengali Vaiṣṇavism

> Vidyāpati says, "Listen, O precious lady! In a prolonged thirst, one drinks water profusely."
>
> —Sukumar Sen, *The History of Brajabuli Literature*

The love of Kṛṣṇa is a liquid love. Devotees float in the seas of *rasa* and the tides of *bhāva;* the mind melts, flowing like ghee or oil; the spiritual thirst is quenched by "drinking the nectar" of the *Bhāgavata Purāṇa* through the ears. Vaikuṇṭha was inundated by Kṛṣṇa's mercy, while Navadvīpa was flooded in the currents of love and singing started by Caitanya, which covered the town and poured out into dancing. As the folk saying goes, "Bengal was swept by a flood of *bhāva,* Śāntipur was almost sunk, and all of Nadia was swept away by the tide."

Nature, too, was influenced by the liquid love. The *Bṛhat Bhāgavatāmṛtam* of Sanātana Gosvāmin describes the effect of such divine love: the Yamunā runs in high tides, the trees flow sap, the people cry, the nursing mothers find that their flow of breast milk increases.[122] Nature itself is ecstatic—the rivers have their hair standing on end (as rising lotuses which blossom in rapture), the trees shed tears of joy (in dropping flowers full of honey), and the mountains are melted.[123]

The devotees are intoxicated by drinking Kṛṣṇa's love, which makes their feelings as soft as butter. The influence of Kṛṣṇa's love can melt hard hearts, fill dry souls with an ocean of love, and cause people to float in seas of joy. At the *rasa* dance, when the milkmaids' love reached its most intense state, it melted and flowed into the current of the Yamunā River.[124]

Liquid is often used as a metaphor to describe ecstasy. It shows the person to have a special kind of permeability. Normally, orthodox Hindus are very careful about maintaining boundaries of the self, for there is great potential for the entrance of impurity through dirt, blood, excrement, and corpses. The person must avoid the dangerous entrance of defilement. Madness, according to Āyurvedic theory, is caused when the person is most open and vulnerable—during childbirth or improper sexuality, while passing impure places, during punishment or war.[125]

If heart and mind are not strong enough, protection against defilement (a greater impermeability) may be given by an amulet or by prayers. Spiritual power is gained by self-control and strict concentration. The violation of boundaries brings many possibilities of disorder: witchcraft, poisons, charms, evil planetary influences, sexuality, family stresses, spirit invasions, the loss of spiritual energy and substance.

Yet Vaiṣṇavism, in its metaphors of fluidity and openness, encourages permeability. The controlled, contained person is hard-hearted, like stone; his mind must be melted, and he must be open to the movement of liquids: nectar, waves of *bhāva,* the ocean of aesthetic enjoyment (*rasa*), the continuous thought of Kṛṣṇa, like oil poured forth. Self-control and ritual order cannot be maintained.

In Āyurvedic medicine, fluids are associated with elasticity and change. *Vāta,* the wind element (associated with diseases of the nerves), is cured with oil that has been blessed or empowered.[126] Oil massage (*sneha*) and sweating (*sveda*) are preliminary Āyurvedic treatments, making the body pliable and permeable so that it will accept the medicine. As one physician stated, "The patient's body will break when we want to curve it—it will break like dry wood when there is no *sneha* and *sveda* [therapy]."[127]

Liquids link the systems together, keep the bodily channels running smoothly, and connect the physical and spiritual aspects of the person.

Madness is an imbalance of fluids or a "bad wind," a spirit that is swallowed or inhaled, a weakness of nerves. According to Caraka, ordinary madness (*unmāda*) occurs when the humors (*doṣas*) are made impure or weakened and their flow is obstructed, especially in the cardiac region. Such impurity can result from food, situation, persons, or the actions of ancestors and ghosts in exogenous insanity. Madness is basically an obstruction or blockage of proper flowing in the body.[128]

The "divine madness" of the Vaiṣṇava is an overflowing of *bhāva*—not an obstruction or blockage, but a flooding. *Bhāva* is a liquid that enters the heart and condenses into spiritual love (*prema*). It is induced by too much purity rather than not enough, from ritual practice or from the grace of Kṛṣṇa and his devotees. It has no treatment; like Rādhā's love, it should be ever-increasing. Its entrance depends on the hardness of the heart, which has several grades. It may be like a lightning bolt (strong and never soft), like gold (melted at high temperatures), like shellac (melted at low temperatures), like honey and butter (melted in sunshine), or like nectar (always liquid). The hard, brittle heart is resistant to such love, while the softened one becomes full, causing the person to faint or show other ecstatic symptoms. Aesthetic experience too is associated with fluids. *Rasa* is sap and essence, the sweet liquid that enters the person in appreciation of the beauty of dance, music, and drama.

The change of permeability in Vaiṣṇava ecstasy allows for exposure to impurity with no ill effect. As the person becomes more open to love of Kṛṣṇa, he becomes less open to situations that might negatively affect others.

Siddha Gaur Kiśora Dās Bābājī would wear cloth taken from corpses and worship in an outhouse; he used rejected pots and drank from old clay cups, and hid from disciples at a prostitute's house. A devotee found that, rather than making Kiśora impure, the bricks of the outhouse had had consciousness infused into them and were chanting the name of Kṛṣṇa. Vijayakṛṣṇa Gosvāmin had visions of deities while at the outhouse or during a meal. In the sacred town of Navadvīpa, even the dogs are pure. Rādhāramaṇ Caran Dās had a death festival for his dog, Bhakta Mā:

> On the fourth day [after her death] was Bhakta Mā's death festival [*ciṛā mahā-utsava*]. On the fourteenth day was the customary preparation for feeding Vaiṣṇavas [*Vaiṣṇava seva*], and the Vaiṣṇavas of the large monasteries were invited the next day for lunch at noon. At Rādhāraman Caran Dās's request,

> Navadvīpa Dās went around everywhere looking for Bhakta Mā's [dog] relatives. As soon as he saw them, he threw himself down on the ground before them, and wrapped some cloth around their throats, and invited them to the festival.
>
> The next day, cooking for the festival began in the early morning. By noon, the Vaiṣṇavas knew that it was for a dog, and nobody would come; his pleading was to no avail, and many people criticized him. As the time approached, the dogs began to arrive in groups—they did not quarrel [among themselves], and they also sat down in a row. Bābājī Mahāsaya had a piece of cloth around his neck, and with their consent, he humbly gave out leaf plates to the dogs. A basin of lentils, various vegetable dishes, curds, and other dishes were mixed together and distributed.
>
> The place was full of the sound of *harināma* and ululation; the dogs remained still, and not one of them bent his face to the leaf. When the distribution [of food] was over, Bābājī Mahāsaya said with folded hands, "Tell them to be seated."
>
> Then a black dog came, and sniffed the sacred food [*mahāprasāda*] on all the leaves, and then they all ate. Another leaf was spread for the new dog, and none of the dogs made a sound. The distributors walked before each dog and offered food, and when each dog was finished eating, he turned his face away. They drank water from clay cups, and Bābājī Mahāsaya [Rādhāramaṇ Caran Dās] signaled [for them] to bring their leftovers. Navadvīpa Dās took their *caraṇāmṛta* [the water in which their feet had been washed]. Bābājī Mahāsaya signaled again, and they each left and returned home. Nobody could remain unmoved at such an event.[129]

Devotional love can make even the most impure into good devotees: the dogs displayed perfect manners, probably better than those of some human Vaiṣṇavas, who might speak or move during the meal. The influence of love can reverse impurity: the fear of contaigon can be turned around into "building the kingdom" and purifying the world.

Another form of purification, fire, is seen where love in separation is so intense that the heart burns, as in the case of Rūpa Gosvāmin in the *Bhaktamālā:*

> That great one (Rūpa), firm in his bhakti, remained standing
> though without awareness of his body, so it appeared.
> Śrī Gusāiṃ Karṇapūra came behind and observed him, then
> he went close by.

> Feeling his breath, he realized
> It was like a flame of fire that scorched his skin.[130]

Certainly one of the strangest stories of the fires of the heart was the story of Siddha Kṛṣṇadāsa of Ranabaṛī, who was branded at Dvāraka during the pilgrimage there—a violation of Gauḍīya Vaiṣṇava *sādācara* (proper behavior).[131] In a dream, he was rejected by Rādhā for joining the ranks of Satyabhama (Dvāraka was her city), and she renounced him as a devotee. He was heartbroken:

> Losing all hope, he returned to Ranabaṛī and gave up eating. In the fire of his past action, and in the flames of separation from Rādhā, his heart began to burn. It is said that Bābājī spent three months in this state and that after that the internal fire was ignited externally. For three days, he gradually burned from the feet up to the head, and he was transformed into ashes. I heard from the carrier [*vāhana*] of Siddha Jagannāth Dās Bābā, named Bihārīdās Bābā, that Siddha Bābā was at Ranabaṛī. In a house not far away, at the end of the night, he called Bihārīdāsjī and said, "O Bihārī, see what is happening inside that house." Bihārīdās, after some searching, came to know that the Ranabaṛī Bābā's body was burning. . . .
>
> [Jagannāth Dās Bābā] broke down the door and entered the house, and he saw that the fire had moved up to his throat and that moreover it was not rising higher. He told Bihārījī to bring some cotton. From the dark field, Bihārījī brought some cotton, and when he gave it to Siddhabābā, he twisted it and made three wicks. As soon as he put these on the head of Ranabaṛī Bābā, the head burst into flame and the whole body was burnt into ashes.[132]

One Vaiṣṇava informant at Navadvīpa used fire as a metaphor, comparing visualization (*bhāvanā*) and realization (*upalabdhi*):

> Realization will not come in the first stage. Have you seen wet wood? If it is put in the oven for a fire, it will cause smoke because it is wet; so long as it is not completely dry, no fire will be produced. The guru gives a mantra to persons who are like wet wood, whose bodies have stored wetness because they have enjoyed [sensuality]. [As they dry], the smoke is visualization; when they are the best fuel, and have fire, this is realization.[133]

Rādhā in her separation from Kṛṣṇa was said to be entranced (*bhāvāveśa*), and her sighs caused a grove to burn. Vijayakṛṣṇa Gosvāmin burned in the fires of the Name (*nāmāgni*). He stated:

> When the Name takes place with every rhythm of your breathing, a burning sensation may start. Gradually, with the increase of *nāma,* the feeling of burning increases, and it seems as if every particle of the body is on fire. The burning sensation makes the person run about madly. This experience happened to me when I was initiated into renunciation [*sannyāsa*] by my guru, Paramahaṁsajī.[134]

The Name (*nāma*) may cause madness as well as fire:

> I repeated Kṛṣṇa's name incessantly, and my mind became unhinged. I could not be calm—I became mad, and so I laugh and weep and dance and sing. . . . Once, my mind was calm, but in the name of Kṛṣṇa my rationality has disappeared.[135]

Such madness signifies entrance into the celestial world. As a Vaiṣṇava of the Gauḍīya lineage stated,

> "What is madness? It means total absorption in something other than that which is generally accepted as reality. When someone is totally absorbed in something that is limited to his own perception, and [is not available to] the perception of others, he is called mad."[136]

He suggested that the way to tell, the "test" of the internal world, was in the quality of *rasasvāda,* that is, the intensity of the experience of "tasting *rasa.*" Ecstasy always contains devotional love (*bhakti rasa*), while ordinary madness does not. In the handmaiden identity (*mañjari bhāva*), the person becomes nondifferent from Rādhārāṇī by being her female servant and thus experiences her emotions. He explained that this was seen as madness to those who cannot feel the mood (*rasa*).

Certainly *rasa* is a major concept in the ecstasy of Bengali Vaiṣṇavas. In its abstract use, it was originally a critical principle that emerged in debate about the nature and function of drama. Its meanings expanded to cover a wide range of experiences. Dramatic *rasa* is the mood that fuses the separate elements of a play into an integrated whole and includes the *vibhāvas* (the causes of emotion, the persons and events presented), the *anubhāvas* (the effects or external signs of emotions), and the *vyabhicāribhāvas* (the transitory, accompanying emotions). Edwin Gerow lists four qualities of *rasa:* a sense of unity; an immediate awareness (the subject is grasped without interpretation); an impersonal affective side; and a generalized situation that avoids such aspects of "partial awareness" as "mine," "his," or "now."[137]

Rasa is depersonalized, opposed to history and to individual acts—the actor's own feelings are irrelevant. What is most significant is impersonality (*sādhāraṇikārana*), the distancing of the aesthete/devotee from his object of admiration.

In *bhāva,* the person experiences his own emotions; in *rasa,* he experiences those of another person. *Bhāva* is firsthand—the person may be overcome, entranced, confused, but he is feeling personally. There is no inner separation between the person and his own emotional reactions. *Rasa* is different. It is closer to empathy, or perhaps a sympathetic identification—the person feels somebody else's emotion indirectly, through projection, and a sort of rapport. It is disinterested, impersonal, generic—and common to others who perceive the same situation, whether on stage or in meditation on a heavenly paradise.

If individuality is present, the emotion is *bhāva.* If individuality is negated in favor of experiencing a type, or a stereotype, it is *rasa.* The actor is often compared to a puppet, who acts without individual will. Idiosyncrasy and character are considered to be obstacles, for *rasa* destroys time, space, and individual identity. Ultimately, even the portrayed characters are negated, for they revert back to their origins as archetypal emotions. As Gerow states, "In it, Rāma and Sītā are no longer Rāma and Sītā, who manifest love and terror, but love and terror themselves, not understood, but directly and intuitively perceived."[138]

We may define *bhāva* as the religious extreme of the personal, while *rasa* is the religious extreme of the impersonal. Kṛṣṇa is Rasarāja, the impersonal Lord of *rasa,* which is beyond time, space, and person, while Rādhā is Mahābhāva, the Lady of Great Emotion, who is the essence of personal feeling. In the *Caitanya Caritāmṛta,* Kṛṣṇa wished to become incarnate as Caitanya so that he might feel the intensity of Rādhā's emotion.

Rasa needs *bhāva.* Without *bhāva,* it runs the risk of depersonalization.[139] Helene Deutsch, a Western psychoanalyst, has written of a borderline personality type called the "as-if" personality. A person with this personality type is detached, unable to feel his own emotions, so he imitates the emotions of others. This is done both in hopes of feeling as they do and as a means of adapting to the environment. Such emotion is quite impersonal; life situations are seen as a stage, and these people observe the emotions of others and act as if they feel an appropriate emotion. To varying degrees, they understand and experience the emotions of others. But they maintain an inner wall and feel what is appropriate rather than what is individual and spontaneous. Like the *rasika* (the appreciator of *rasa*) or the actor, they feel impersonally. Life becomes a drama, but not a world of individual meaning.[140] Too much distance from personal emotion can create a wall behind which the individual and his own emotions can be lost.

The issue of impersonality and distancing is extremely important in certain forms of Bengali Vaiṣṇava meditation. In the *līlā* visualizations, the devotee is the observer, as one of Rādhā's handmaidens, or he may be one of Caitanya's friends, who feels "as-if" he experiences the feelings of Rādhā or Caitanya (who feels "as-if" he experiences Rādhā's emotions). Such feelings are not merely vicarious, but consciously distanced. When there is a lessening of distance—such as acting out Kṛṣṇa and Rādhā's activities on earth, having men dress as women, or experiencing the Sahajiyā transmutation of *rasa* from abstract essence to personal liquid—the orthodoxy disapproves. Many Vaiṣṇava writers emphasize the evolution of the personal into the impersonal, of *bhāva* into *rasa.*

Vaiṣṇava concepts of ecstasy and madness may be seen in four categories, in descending degrees of religiosity: (1) divine ecstasy (*mahābhāva*); (2) ecstatic symptoms (*anubhāva, sāttvika bhāva, vyabhicāribhāva*); (3) *rasa* induced by the wrong objects (*rasābhāsa*); and (4) secular madness, without any component of *rasa* (*unmāda, pāglāmi*).

Mahābhāva is a state of intense emotion in which ecstasy is at its highest point. It appears as madness because the person (Rādhā, or the person who shares in her emotions) is overwhelmed by love and cannot function in normal society. One stage of *mahābhāva* is called divine madness and includes raving and irrational behavior. However, Rādhā's passion focuses totally on Kṛṣṇa, and her mood is pure erotic love.

The ecstatic symptoms that do not share in Rādhā's emotions are considered to be developmental, symptoms of maturing into a *sthāyībhāva* (a permanent role in relation to Kṛṣṇa). The *sāttvika bhāvas* and *anubhāvas* have been detailed earlier in this chapter and in Appendix B. The *vyabhicāribhāvas* are transitory emotions that express intensity and include sickness, insanity, and epilepsy.

Insanity is a transitory emotion associated with both emotional and physiological causes. Śāradātanaya in the *Bhāvaprakāśana* finds the causes to be loss of the beloved in superior persons, frustration of desire in middling persons, and loss of wealth in inferior persons. Vidyānātha lists its main symptom, nondiscrimination between animate and inanimate creatures, as due to planetary influences, excessive emotion, humors, and supernatural agents. Sarveśvarācārya lists its symptoms as doing actions that cannot be forecast by others, knowing things as different from what they really are, loss of mental unity, intense emotions, hallucinations, and delusions. Bhāratamuni and Hemacandra list the same symptoms: unmotivated laughter, weeping, reading, singing, dancing, sitting, standing, lying down, running, raving, smearing the body with dust and ashes, wearing rags or soiled clothes, using earthen pots, and so forth as ornaments, imitation of others, and other senseless acts.[141] It is also associated with epilepsy.[142]

Both madness (*unmāda*) and epilepsy (*apasmāra*) are seen as species of disease, but they have different associated moods (*rasas*). Epilepsy is associated with horror and terror, while insanity is associated with charm and loss of the beloved. This distinction is made by Sārṅgadeva in the *Saṅgīta Ratnākara,* while the *Nāṭyadarpaṇa* of Rāmacandra and Guṇacandra associates madness with the erotic mood of separation.[143]

For the Vaiṣṇava, the mood (*rasa*) would be the most important distinction between these two states. Thus, while Caitanya's symptoms might resemble epilepsy, this state would not be possible—his *rasa* is erotic, not associated with fear and terror, and this attribution would create a conflict of *rasas.* He could not be an avatar and at the same time subject to possession by a ghost or a bad planetary configuration. Again, opposing *rasas* can inhibit each other, and Caitanya's emotions must be too strong to be suppressed.

The problem of conflicting *rasas* is seen in the next category, *rasābhāsa.* This is a "semblance" of *rasa* or *bhāva,* which is excited by inappropriate objects. It is a damaged or mutilated type of emotion, which does not produce satisfactory enjoyment. It includes emotions that conflict with each other (for instance, parental love and wifely love), suppressing each other rather than blending together. It may be *rasa* toward a different deity, such as Śiva or Kālī. In this case it may be ecstatic, but it is still *anurasa*—emotion with no reference to Kṛṣṇa and thus a false emotion. Or the emotion may be tainted by pride or power, or the presence of the majestic or the comic. Such emotions may be conflicting or merely incomplete. The *rasa* may be present, but the cause must be determined.[144]

If there is no religious emotion present, then the lowest category of interpretation arises—secular madness. Such insanity has no divine component and as such is considered an ordinary disease. It may be due to desire and greed, or to humor, planets, or spirits. Rather than an error of *rasa,* it is a total lack.

Do such categories fit the experiences of the Vaiṣṇava saints? In the biographies of many saints, the first two categories are blurred (the term *mahābhāva* is used loosely, as equivalent to the *sāttvikas*) and opposed to the last category of ordinary madness as "wind disease." The idea of conflict of *rasas* is rarely seen in the popular literature.

The major texts on religious affection are based on Caitanya's life and actions, and could be seen to fit his experiences. But the stages of intense love require an identification with Rādhā and a sharing in her emotions. Many Vaiṣṇavas do not have such a focus on her—they do yoga toward Kṛṣṇa or chant his Name, and have visions of Vṛndāvana as a celestial paradise of lights, or become possessed by Kṛṣṇa and Caitanya, or have visions of them. Other Vaiṣṇavas have a different focus on Rādhā—she is their Śākta goddess, or their mediator to the high god Kṛṣṇa, who is too powerful to approach.

The Gauḍīya Vaiṣṇava Gaur Kiśora dās Bābājī did not discuss his inner experiences—the success of his handmaiden—identification was deduced from his irrational and peculiar actions, which were seen as divine madness because of their focus on Kṛṣṇa and Caitanya. He also had traditional Vaiṣṇava initiations and was part of an accepted lineage; thus, behavior not specifically Vaiṣṇava (such as wearing his begging bowl on his head) was interpreted as eccentric rather than mad. Even his impure behavior shows only the detachment of the liberated *paramahaṃsa.*

Pāgal Haranāth was not part of an accepted lineage and as such had much more trouble being accepted. His authority came not from tradition, but from his claims of psychic ability and his disciples' support of these claims, as well as their belief in his love for them. His spiritual development was not a ladder of love, but rather a long period of madness ending with a death and rebirth experience, interpreted in a Vaiṣṇava framework. Once he was clearly a Vaiṣṇava, the title Pāgal became a compliment.

Vijayakṛṣṇa Goswāmin was a yogi who had investigated many paths: Bāul, Sahajiyā, Kartā-bhajā, and Brahmo Samāj. Radical experiences in *kuṇḍalinī* yoga led him to Vaiṣṇavism. He never identified with a female body, but saw perfection as a state in which the body resonated with Kṛṣṇa's name, and the person could see creation as full of light and music. He felt meditation to be passive—a situation in which one waited for the divine revelation of Kṛṣṇa's grace. His ecstatic paralysis, mad dancing, visions, and trances were initially seen as mad, but were later interpreted as the spontaneous descent of *bhāva,* when he began to be seen as a saint.

Prabhu Jagadbandhu was believed by his followers to have experienced Rādhā's states of love and to have surpassed them, entering the state of a child. He was recognized as a world savior while still in his teens, and his later breakdown, with its incoherence and isolation, was believed by his disciples to be consciously chosen. Even his death was only an illusory veil that hid his status as savior and delays his final revelations.

All of these saints showed ecstatic behavior, which could be interpreted as madness. Yet in each case, the religious components were strong enough to outweigh the secular, and the apparently mad behavior was seen as ecstasy.

Divine madness is not an aberration, as is ordinary madness—it expresses the highest religious goal of Vaiṣṇava theology. There is no horizon beyond ecstatic madness for a human being in these texts—there is no sobriety beyond the intoxication.

The Vaiṣṇava desires to live eternally in the heavenly Vṛndāvana. That world may be perceived spontaneously, or given by the grace of god or guru, or created by visualization. It is reached by love for Kṛṣṇa, a "liquid love" with waves of passion and tides of *bhāva.*

The flood of *bhāva* washes away the old personality and brings forth the new spiritual body of the bhakta. As in Āyurveda, where sweating and oiling are necessary to make the body permeable to medicines, so the flooding of emotion makes the person capable of entering a nonphysical world.

When Bhagavān overflows, the universe is created—it is his love and play, streaming like a fountain, which creates an infinity of worlds. When the person overflows, ecstasy is created—an infinity of emotional states which shift, conflicting and harmonizing. The personal reflection of Kṛṣṇa's play is the emotional *bhāva* of the devotee in ecstasy.

The ecstatic flows with love, and he overflows. The emotions of the cycles of separation and union are so intense that varying emotions are expressed chaotically or, like Rādhā, simultaneously. It is the pressure of these emotions that requires the creation of a spiritual body; as one Vaiṣṇava informant stated: "The physical body can hold only so much love [*prema*], after that, one needs a spiritual body."

Until the excess love can be organized into a spiritual body, it will overflow into ecstatic symptoms. However, even when the spiritual body is formed, it still participates in Rādhā's state of love-madness, as the visualized handmaiden body in heavenly Vṛndāvana or the visualized *Gaur* body of the eternal Navadvīpa. For both earthly and heavenly bodies, the highest state is one of passionate and divine madness.

THREE

Nursing the Baby-Husband: The Śākta Tradition

Dark mother always gliding near with soft feet
Have none chanted for thee a chant of fullest welcome? . . .
Approach, strong deliveress
When it is so, when thou has taken them
    I joyously sing the dead
Lost in the loving floating ocean of thee,
Laved in the flood of thy bliss, O death.
—Walt Whitman, "When Lilacs Last in the Dooryard Bloomed"

The Strands of Śāktism

The Śākta tradition is a syncretistic one; it contains elements from tantric Buddhism, Vaiṣṇava devotion, yogic practice, shamanism, and worship of village deities. Śāktas may be ecstatic in many ways: they may be in a state of divine madness for the Mother; they may feel Śakti inwardly in the form of *kuṇḍalinī,* or as a possessing entity; they may see her on her great throne in the paradise of Kailāsa or on the Isle of Gems; they may struggle with her for her blessings and conquer her in magical ritual; they may merge with her as an aspect of the Self.

Popular Śāktism has a strong devotional orientation. It has no authoritative written tradition, as Vaiṣṇavism does, no series of commentators, no texts which are known and followed by all priests and devotees. Rather, it is primarily an oral tradition, organized by saints, temples and *āśramas,* and sacred places (*śākta pīṭhas*) which are believed to have great power. Śākta informants claimed that books taught nothing, and were dead and unnecessary; only individual experience was important, and only in the guru-disciple relationship could there be a transmission of power and brahman awareness (*brahmajñāna*).

Both tantric texts and Śākta practitioners have claimed that the god

Śiva and the goddess Śakti (or Kālī) are identical, different aspects of the same unity, like milk and whiteness or fire and heat, and that worship of one is the same as worship of the other. However, in the iconography, Śakti dances on Śiva's prone body. And Śākta worship appeared clearly dominant in the streets of Calcutta. As one informant stated:

> Look at how the *devīs* [goddesses] are worshiped—out in the streets, with noise and color and big statues and shrines [*pāṇḍāls*]. Then look at worship to the male gods—in the house, only a few people, nothing elaborate. What are the biggest worship ceremonies [*pūjās*]? Kālī, Durgā, Saraswatī *pūjās*. The goddesses are more important to us. They have great power.[1]

Several informants brought up the image, attributed to the medieval Śākta saint Kṛṣṇānanda Āgambāgīśa, of Śiva lying on the ground, with Kālī's foot on his chest and her tongue sticking out. Less traditional Śāktas said that this showed the place of Śaivism in Bengal (trampled beneath the worship of the goddess); they associated it with the local sports teams (in which the women were consistently winning, while the men's teams were consistently losing). More traditional Śāktas said that sticking out the tongue was an expression of Kālī's embarrassment at stepping on her husband while destroying the world. One informant had a variation on this theme:

> Śiva was born from the goddess Kālī. She is the only uncreated being. Śiva was needed for creation, so she created him by her own action. She created sperm in her womb and made love to herself. She made a mistake in creating the world and started to destroy it. Brahma told Śiva to stop the destruction—so he stretched himself down before her. To avoid killing him, she stopped destroying the world. Śiva insisted that she re-create the destroyed part, so she vomited it out. She had swallowed the whole world. That is why her tongue is sticking out when she stands on Śiva.[2]

This mixture of Śiva as offspring and husband of the goddess is a common theme in Bengal. If the Great Mother is the creatress, everyone is her child—including her husband. This theme is harmonized in the story of Mālancamālā, from the *Ṭhākurdādār Jhuli* stories of Dakṣinaranjan Majumdar. It may be briefly summarized:

> A king heard this prediction for his infant son—that he was fated to die, but would live if married to a girl born on a cer-

> tain day. The only girl in the kingdom with that birth date was Mālancamālā, who was poor and of low caste. Having no choice, he married the infant prince to her, but the infant died soon afterward. In a rage, he built a funeral pyre for the child and cut off Mālancamālā's nose and ears. She and the baby were thrown into the fire. In the midst of the fire she sat, with the baby prince on her lap. She asked several times, "Is my husband dead or asleep?" Voices in the wind first answered "dead," but later they said, "asleep." She smiled and took the child in her arms, and pressed it to her breast. The blood that gushed from her nose and ears (which had been cut) was licked by ghosts and demons. The demons tried to take away the body, and tempted her in various ways; they took over the wood of the funeral pyre, so that it grew hands and feet and walked. The apparitions continued their threats. She stated: "Be witness, O gods, here is my baby-husband in my lap. If I am chaste and devoted, O you tempters, do but touch me and you will be reduced to ashes; I am Mālancamālā and no other, you are an evil spirit, leave! O night, if thou dost not pass away, with my baby-husband in my lap, here do I solemnly say, I will transform the stars to fire and the flowers to stars!" The night was frightened, and left trembling. By morning, the apparitions were gone. The baby in her lap was gently moving its hands and feet. Mālancamālā went off to find it food.[3]

There are many tantric elements included here: the identification of the human woman with the goddess (here as the *satī,* the chaste wife); the ritual of *śava-sādhana* (sitting at night with a corpse until it comes to life); the powers (*siddhis*) gained from self-sacrifice; the magical transformation of substances (she turns ashes and sand to milk and food); the power of the mother/consort in relation to the son/husband.[4] It is the attitude of a heroine (*vīrācāra*)—the stance that brings spiritual success.

Tārāpīṭh is a *śākta pīṭha*[5] and also a *siddha pīṭha,* a place where a holy man is believed to have attained the state of perfection (*siddhi*). Legend has it that both Gautama Buddha and Vasiṣṭha-muni attained perfection at Tārāpīṭh—Vasiṣṭha upon a seat made of five skulls (*pañcamuṇḍa āsana*). However, it was the recent saint Vāmākṣepā who made the place famous. Though few tantras actually mention Tārāpiṭh as a *śākta pīṭha,* it is popularly believed to house the Devī's third eye, and it has gained a patina of both age and notoriety (as a center for tantric ritual).

The conflict in the images of mother and consort may be seen in the myth and secret ritual at Tārāpīṭh. There are two rituals of worship at Tārāpīṭh, for day and night. The daytime worship of the goddess is an offering of food. This is offered to the Tārā image, which has a silver face and long black hair, and wears a Benarasi sari. However, there is an inner statue which is unveiled only at midnight, in secrecy; the sari is removed, and beneath it is the image of a nursing mother—Tārā nursing Śiva Mahādeva. This was described as the "real" image of Tārā by an informant, who told the myth of Tārāpīṭh:

> Kālī was created from the third eye of Durgā and had as her husband Mahādev. When the great ocean was churned, it created poison, and if this poison had spread, all creation would have been destroyed. Śiva decided to swallow the poison to save the universe. The poison did not go to his stomach, but caught in his throat. Kālī knew that only her breast milk could save him. But she said, "I cannot nurse my own husband. I must change into another form." So she turned into Tārā and fed her breast milk to Mahādev. She took him on her lap and gave him the breast so that he would survive. The milk countered the poison, and Mahādev survived. But a little bit of the poison got into the breast, and this is the reason for the dark ring around the nipples in women's breasts.[6]

While for Vaiṣṇavas, the mingling of parental and erotic love is forbidden, a conflict of religious moods (*rasābhāsa*), for Śāktas these moods can unite. It is the heroic Śākta (*vīra*) who has ritual intercourse with the Mother (as incarnate in a human woman) and who then becomes her beloved child, later to join her after his death.[7] Yet there is also a tension in the love of wife and mother, seen in the tantric alternation of celibacy and ritual sexuality, in symbolic aggression toward the mother image (as we shall see in the famous case of Vāmākṣepa's throwing his urine onto the Mother and cursing at her), and in the tantrika challenging the Mother to a fight for power.

Tension also occurs between the three major strands that run through the worship of Śakti and that have different theologies and practices. These three strands are the yogic, the devotional, and the magical. The yogic strand emphasizes knowledge, and in its highest state the person enters the ocean of wisdom of *brahman*. The goal is monistic: Śiva and Śakti are ultimately one, and in meditation the yogi realizes his unity with them. Ecstasy is also seen in deep trance (*samādhi*), in the visions and bodily symptoms of *kuṇḍalinī* yoga, and in the powers (*siddhis*) that often accompany meditation. The devotional (*bhakti*) strand emphasizes love of the goddess, usually as mother, although sometimes as wife or daughter. It is dualistic: the goddess creates and destroys, and other deities are either her emanations or inferior to her. The worshiper seeks to become divinely mad (*divyonmāda*), so full of love that the physical world becomes irrelevant. The magical or shamanic strand emphasizes power, and its highest state is *siddhi lābh kore,* the attainment of *siddhi* or perfection. Kālī *siddhi* means that she comes when the practitioner calls, to do his bidding. This strand is polytheistic: other deities may be called for magical purposes or possession, and *yoginīs, ḍākinīs,* and other entities may be worshiped.

For the yogic strand, *haṭha yoga* (control of the body) is a beginning, but *mantra yoga* and *kuṇḍalinī yoga* are more highly valued. These involve the dissolution of the physical body in favor of a subtle one and the raising of the goddess Kuṇḍalinī in the form of a snake. There is great emphasis on the power of mantra, which is considered to be a conscious entity when empowered.[8] It is believed to exist in the body in unmanifest form, and needs to be awakened and perceived. The seed mantras (*bījas*) may invoke deities and resonate the cakras, as seen in *kuṇḍalinī* yoga (described in greater detail in the section on Śākta ecstatic ritual). Yogic meditation involves visualization of diagrams (*yantras*), although in Bengal there is greater use made of statues (*mūrtis*). There is also visualization of the deities Śiva and Kālī, often in their paradise of Kailāsa. Its goal is merger with these deities, after the eight steps of Pātañjala yoga. This goal is often called *brahmajñāna* or *brahmabhāva* and refers to knowledge of the formless state in which all distinctions are destroyed. In some cases, *brahmajñāna* is interpreted as a substance, a liquid that descends from the lotus of the mind and causes bliss with its drops of light. This may result in a state of religious madness (*pāgal bhāva*) in which all distinctions disappear. The precursors of the yogic strand are Śaivite yoga and the early Buddhist *sahajiyā* yoga.

The devotional strand involves personal love of the goddess, who has created the universe and is infinitely beautiful inwardly, although her outer forms may reflect death and destruction. The devotee wishes to remain the child and worshiper of the goddess forever, at death entering her paradise, which is called Kailāsa, or Maṇidvīpa, or Pañcākāśa. The worship of the goddess is described in the *Devī Bhāgavata,* as well as in Śakta poetry and the manuals associated with goddess worship. The major goddesses of Bengal are Kālī, Durgā, and Tārā, with village worship of Manasā the snake goddess, and Śītalā the cool one, the goddess of smallpox. The desire to become mad with love (*divyonmāda*) for the goddess is comparatively recent. Goddess worship was more yogic and shamanic, an esoteric cult, until its popularization by such poets as Rāmprasād Sen and Kamalākānta in the eighteenth and nineteenth centuries. This Neo-Śākta revival brought the new custom of public worship of Kālī and a synthesis of yoga and bhakti. Madness then became a sign of devotion, the worshiper being a mad child of mad parents. Other *bhāvas* were also popular; sometimes Devī was the wife, who represents the mystery and creative potential of woman, or she was the daughter, the sweet child who is taken away to marry and live in her husband's distant village. This is the mood of separation (*viraha*), which is also seen when the worshiper is separated from his beloved mother. The child *bhāva* was emphasized in the songs of Rāmprasād, which are sung on Durgā Pūjā.[9] The village goddesses tend to inspire the fearful *bhāva* rather than bhakti love—like the other goddesses, they must be propitiated or they will have their revenge. Devotion toward Kālī and Tārā is often associated with the magical strand, although its ecstasy is like that of the Vaiṣṇava—tremors, thrills of joy, hair standing on end, tears.

The strand of music and shamanism emphasizes power and the conquest of the goddess—she may be manipulated by prayers and tears, but the approach of the hero (*vīra*) is to struggle with her, to coerce her favors, to prove his strength. Perfection is sought primarily through the ten manifestations of Devī (*daśa mahāvidyās*), who grant different types of powers. Ecstatic visions of the goddess alternate with visions of spirits and hell worlds, and the burning ground may appear full of frightening entities. Madness in such a situation is a danger—it is believed to be the result of fear or of committing an error in the ritual; the magician becomes persecuted by his own servants, who may control him. The background of this strand is in the magical texts, such as the *Atharva Veda*, the worship of local deities by exorcists (*ojhās*), and tantric Buddhist magic. Also associated with the shamanic strand is possession (*bhor*) by a deity, in which the person goes into a trance (either spontaneously or as a result of ritual), and the deity speaks through the person's mouth. In Bengal, women are most often mediums, while men are often possessed during ascetic rituals, such as hook swinging, in which the person's endurance shows that Śiva is present in his body.

Each of these strands has its own authority (*pramāṇa*) to distinguish true saints from those who imitate religious states and from the insane. The yogic tests examine whether the person is performing serious ritual practice and whether he has gained strong concentration or miraculous powers, especially if his practices have been arduous. Age is a proof used primarily by disciples—if their guru is now three hundred years old, this proves his sincerity as well as his superiority over other gurus of lesser years. Often years are added by disciples, who claim that their guru will not admit it but that he lived in the 1700s, or that he was born consciously in this life (which thus becomes an extension of the previous life). The combination of age and miraculous powers is particularly attractive and often associated with the unpredictable behavior of the perfected (*siddha*) yogi. The madman and the imitator generally do not devote time to meditation and austerities, and are unable to manage miracles.

In the devotional strand, the proof is the saint's love for the goddess, and secondarily his or her love for disciples. It is the quality of his *bhāva* which is studied—its intensity, its passion, its ecstatic qualities. Neither miracles nor age is part of pure Śākta bhakti; rather, absorption in love for the goddess is the decisive criterion. It is difficult for the false *sādhu* to imitate horripilation and changing skin color, although he may make great claims of love and devotion. There is an intermediate area with states of insanity, however; the states known as god madness (*prema pāgal* and *ṭhākur pāgal*) may be seen by Śāktas as both devotion and insanity.

For the shamanic strand, success in possession is gauged by a worthy god (often local deities are slightly snubbed, and ghosts and demons positively avoided) and the ability to exorcise unwanted entities from others. Madmen tend to be possessed by entities whom people wish to avoid, while persons who imitate possession (*bhor*) are often low-caste village women, and urban Hindus do not believe that high gods would go near them. Many women are possessed by Kālī, who is more believable as a possessing entity, since she would not be so particular about her vessels as would a deity concerned with purity. The other major proof is magical ability, especially in healing and knowledge at a distance.

Madness and ecstasy for Śāktas may best be examined by looking at the goals and techniques of these three strands. All three are seen fused in the life of the saint Rāmakṛṣṇa.

Model for Madmen: Rāmakṛṣṇa Paramahaṃsa

There were those who danced, and were convulsed with laughter, crying Bravo to the illusion of the world. There were naked men living with the dogs on beggars' scraps, who no longer distinguished between one form and another, and were attached to nothing. There were the mystic and drunken bands of Tantrikas. Young Rāmakrisna observed them all.

—Romain Rolland, *The Life of Rāmakrisna*

Rāmakṛṣṇa includes both the singular dedication of devotion to a deity and the universalism of Vedānta, combined with yoga and tantra. Although he performed many forms of spiritual practice, he remained a priest of Kālī, and asked her for advice and regarded her as Mother long after his experiences of Vedānta, Christianity, and Islam. Major sources for this short biography include the *Śrī Śrī Rāmakṛṣṇa Līlā-Prasaṅga* of Svāmī Śāradānanda[10] and the *Rāmakṛṣṇa Kathāmṛta* of Mahendranāth Gupta.[11]

Rāmakṛṣṇa was born in 1836, in Kāmārpukur, West Bengal, under an auspicious constellation. His father, Kṣudirām Chatterji, headed the only Brahmin family in a village composed mostly of blacksmiths and other low-caste people. Kṣudirām worshiped the god Raghuvīr with tears, changing skin color, and other ecstatic symptoms; he also had visions of Śītalā and Viṣṇu Gadādhara ("holding the mace"), who predicted Rāmakṛṣṇa's birth. Rāmakṛṣṇa's mother, Candrādevī, could not count money or understand worldly matters, and her husband often feared that she would be considered mad. She, too, had visions of deities and light, and felt that she had been impregnated by the light of the god Śiva when she was forty-five years old (almost a year before Rāmakṛṣṇa's birth, when his father was sixty-one years old). Continuous visions caused her to wonder if she were possessed, but Kṣudirām verified her visions with his own. About this time Kātyāyanī, their eldest daughter, was possessed by a ghost and acting strangely.

Rāmakṛṣṇa was named Gadādhara, after his father's vision of Viṣṇu Gadādhara, and grew up to be a willful child, indulged by his aging parents. He was curious and disobedient, and enjoyed acting and staying with women, wearing female dress and ornaments so well that he was mistaken for a female. At the age of seven, he fell into a trance at the sight of cranes. In that year his father died, and he grew closer to his mother. He had two brothers and two sisters at that time.

Rāmakṛṣṇa enjoyed playing dramatic roles, both onstage and off, and being the center of attention. When he heard that his Aunt Rāmsila was often possessed by the goddess Śītalā, he said, "It would be very nice if the spirit who possessed aunt would possess me."[12] He would memorize songs and poems about deities and fall into further trances. When he was eight years old, he fell into a trance, suddenly possessed by the goddess Viśālakṣī, and during a performance in which he played the part of Śiva, he was possessed by the god.

He moved to Calcutta at the age of seventeen, at the urging of his older brother, to study and to serve the deities of wealthy families. Soon after, the Kālī temple of Rānī Rasmaṇi was consecrated at Dakṣiṇeśwar, and he began to spend time meditating there. When he was nineteen years old, he was appointed priest of the Kālī temple by Mathur, the son-in-law of Rānī Rasmaṇi. It was difficult for them to find a priest, as the Rānī was a *sudra,* a low-caste woman, and few brahmins wished to work in a temple sponsored by a low-caste widow. However, Rāmakṛṣṇa found it a good place to begin in his Śākta tantric practice.

He worshiped in the five trees behind the temple (*pañcavati*) and was initiated in the Kālī mantra by a Śākta guru. He would see the snake of Kuṇḍalinī amid a wall of fire around his seat, with the letters of mantras in bright colors. He had little food and sleep, and would cry for long periods of time. He sang the songs of Rāmprasād and Kamalākānta, without his cloth and sacred thread, and saw fire and light, and the world turning to liquid silver and mercury. He states:

> I practised the discipline of the Tantra under the bel-tree. At that time I could see no distinction between the sacred tulsi and any other plant. In that state I sometimes ate the leavings from a jackal's meal, food that had been exposed the whole night, part of which might have been eaten by snakes or other creatures. Yes, I ate that stuff. Sometimes I rode on a dog and fed him with luchi, also eating part of the bread myself. I realized that the whole world was filled with God alone. One cannot have spiritual realization without destroying ignorance, so I would assume the attitude of a tiger and devour ignorance . . . . I had all the experiences that one should have, according to the scriptures, after one's direct perception of God. I behaved like a child, like a madman, like a ghoul, and like an inert thing.[13]

Experiences and visions followed each other rapidly. He describes them:

> Oh, what a state of mind I passed through! I would open my mouth, touching, as it were, heaven and the nether world with my jaws, and utter the word "Ma." I felt that I had seized the Mother, like a fisherman dragging fish in his net.[14]

The goal of his meditation was to gain a vision of the Mother. However, this did not occur until he attempted suicide, and then he saw Kālī as an ocean of consciousness, which swallowed him up. He described the scene:

> I determined to put an end to my life. When I jumped up like a madman and seized [a sword], suddenly the blessed Mother revealed herself. The buildings with their different parts, the temple, and everything else vanished from my sight, leaving no trace whatsoever, and in their stead I saw a limitless, infinite, effulgent Ocean of Consciousness. As far as the eye could see, the shining billows were madly rushing at me from all sides with a terrific noise, to swallow me up! I was panting for breath. I was caught in the rush and collapsed, unconscious . . . within me there was a steady flow of undiluted bliss, altogether new, and I felt the presence of the Divine Mother.[15]

The attainment of his goal did not cause him to abandon his practice; rather, it made him desire the Mother continuously. He alternated separation and union with Kālī, and had strange symptoms in each. In separation, he would collapse or remain paralyzed, suffer burning sensations, and throw himself on the ground, rubbing his face against the floor and wailing. He had hallucinations of persons emerging from his body, including two young boys who would dance about and then return. As Rolland states:

> He saw demoniac creatures emerging from him, first a black figure representing sin; then a sannyasin, who slew sin like an archangel. . . . He remained motionless, watching these manifestations issue from him. Horror paralysed his limbs. Once again for long periods at a time his eyes refused to close. He felt madness approaching, and terrified, he appealed to the Mother. The vision of Kali was his only hope of survival.[16]

However, in union he would identify with the Mother, decorating himself with flowers and sandal paste. As priest, he saw the statue as alive—he would stagger up to Kālī's image, embrace it, laugh and joke with it, hold its hands, and dance with it. He would put the statue to bed at night and lie down next to it, or he would stay up all night talking and singing.

Mathur thought he was insane and arranged to have him treated by an Āyurvedic doctor in Calcutta; however, the treatment did not work.

He continued to throw earth and money into the Ganges (because he regarded both as worthless), and he took the leavings of the poor, cleaned outhouses with his hands, and ate the excrement of others.[17] He could not keep his clothing on. At this time, he would also make grandiose claims: "One who became Rāma and Kṛṣṇa is now within this case [showing his body]. But His advent this time is secret."[18]

Rānī Rasmaṇi and Mathur tried to cure Rāmakṛṣṇa's insanity by sending a prostitute to him at Dakṣiṇeśwar (assuming his derangement to be due to continence). However, Rāmakṛṣṇa later said that he saw the Divine Mother in the woman, and that his genitals became contracted and entered completely into his body, like the limbs of a tortoise.[19]

His mother, Candrādevī, heard of his visions, and she was horrified by his sharing food with jackals and dogs: "When he was told that the Divine Mother sometimes assumed the form of a jackal, and that the dogs were the carriers of Bhairava, he regarded the remnants of food taken by those animals as pure and sacred, and partook of them as prasada without the slightest hesitation."[20]

She believed his problem was celibacy and arranged a marriage for Rāmakṛṣṇa. He chose Śāradā Devī, of the village of Jayrambati; she was then a child of five, while he was twenty-three years old. He stayed a while with her in Kāmārpukur and then returned to Dakṣiṇeśwar, where he was again sleepless and delirious, full of burning and various *bhāvas*.

He was aided by Bhairavī Brāhmaṇī, an elderly holy woman who came to see him at Dakṣiṇeśwar. She was adept at both tantra and Vaiṣṇava spiritual practices, and declared that his state was not ordinary madness, but *mahābhāva,* or religious madness. She stated: "My son, everyone in this world is mad. Some are mad for money, some for creature comforts, some for name and fame; and you are mad for God."[21]

She asked Mathur to arrange a conference of scholars to prove Rāmakṛṣṇa's status as a saint. She argued for him before Vaiṣṇavacaraṇa, a Vaiṣṇava scholar, quoting the *Caitanya Caritāmṛta* and other scriptures, and he agreed that this was indeed a case of divine madness and that Rāmakṛṣṇa was an avatar. The pandit Gauri was convinced that Rāmakṛṣṇa was greater than an incarnation—that he was Bhagavān. Rāmakṛṣṇa himself was relieved that he was not suffering from a disease.[22] These views did not change his symptoms, but they did change the way others treated him.

The Brāhmaṇī taught him tantric practices (*tantra sādhana*) from texts. He had visions of Māyā first nursing a child and then crushing it, of *kuṇḍalinī* rising, and of the origin of the universe in a triangle of light.

He then practiced two forms of Vaiṣṇava practice, called the *vātsalya* and *mādhurya bhāvas*. He was first a woman friend of the Devī, dressed in sari and ornaments, who served and fanned her. At this time, he forgot that he had a male body. He was then the mother of Rāmlālā, a metal statue of Rāma that belonged to a wandering holy man named Jaṭādhāri. Rāmakṛṣṇa later described to his devotees how the little statue would dance, jump on his back, insist on being taken in his arms, run in the fields, and play pranks. He saw himself as a woman and mother. Jatādhāri finally left the statue, which he had served devotedly for many years, with Rāmakṛṣṇa.[23]

In *mādhurya bhāva,* the mood of erotic love, he identified with Rādhā in her states of divine madness. He had a vision of Rādhā and wore a sari, gold ornaments, and artificial hair for six months:

> He regarded himself as one of the gopis of Vrindavan, mad with longing for her divine Sweetheart. At his request, Mathur provided him with a woman's dress and jewelry. In this love-pursuit food and drink were forgotten. Day and night he wept bitterly. . . . Śrī Ramakrishna's anguish brought on a return of the old physical symptoms: the burning sensation, an oozing of blood through the pores, a loosening of the joints, and the stoppage of physiological functions.[24]

He further described his experiences:

> *Mahābhāva* is a divine ecstasy, it shakes the body and mind to their very foundations. It is like a huge elephant entering a small hut. The house shakes to its foundations. Perhaps it falls to pieces . . . . I was unconscious for three days in that state. I couldn't move. I lay in one place. When I regained consciousness, the Brāhmaṇī took me out for a bath. But my skin couldn't bear the touch of her hand; so my body had to be covered by a heavy sheet. Only then could she hold me with her hand and lead me to the bathing-place. The earth that had stuck to my body while I was lying on the ground had become baked. In that state I felt as if a ploughshare were passing through my backbone. I cried out, "Oh, I am dying! I am dying!" But afterwards I was filled with great joy.[25]

When Totāpurī, a naked mendicant with matted hair, came to Dakṣiṇeśwar, Rāmakṛṣṇa was initiated as a renunciant (*sannyāsī*) and adopted a Vedāntic view. He experienced the formless aspect of the Mother, *nirvikalpa samādhi.* Totāpurī himself had a vision of the Divine Mother, which lasted through the night and morning, when he had an attack of dysentery so severe that he attempted suicide. He realized that *brahman* was actually Śakti and that the Mother was the source of the light he saw. Rāmakṛṣṇa saw the Mother as both form and formless, but her command to him was that he remain in *bhāvamukha*—the states of ecstasy and vision that gave him access to both worlds. Rāmakṛṣṇa later described the state of *bhāvamukha* as living in the "ripe I," in continuous awareness of all states, rather than the Vaiṣṇava alternation of separation and union. He felt the *bhāvas* to be important: "God is realizable by *bhāvas* alone. Can he be realized when one is lacking in them? Do you know what a *bhāva* is? Establishing a relationship with God and keeping it bright before our eyes at all times."[26]

The Mother's command came after a long trance, which followed Totāpurī's vision of the Mother and his subsequent departure:

> After the departure of Totapuri, Śrī Ramakrishna remained for six months in a state of absolute identity with Brahman. "For six months at a stretch," he said, "I remained in that state from which ordinary men can never return; generally the body falls off, after three weeks, like a sere leaf. I was not conscious of day or night. Flies would enter my mouth and nostrils just as they do a dead body's, but I did not feel them. My hair became matted with dust.[27]

For certain periods, Rāmakṛṣṇa performed the spiritual practices of Islam, Christianity, and several other faiths, and traveled on pilgrimages. He largely ignored his wife, although he gave her spiritual instruction when she visited and at one point worshiped her as an incarnation of the Goddess, in the Ṣoṛaśī Pūjā. He implied to his disciples that he had married her because of his delicate stomach—he needed someone to cook for him.

As disciples came to him, Rāmakṛṣṇa put a greal deal of energy into teaching. He would still fall into trances and dance in bliss, and observers would laugh, weep, and fall on the ground. He would lose consciousness at the touch of metal or coins and appear drunk at the mention of wine. He developed throat cancer and died in Calcutta in 1886, at the age of fifty, surrounded by disciples.

Rāmakṛṣṇa stated of tantric practice:

> The devotee assumes various attitudes towards Śakti in order to propitiate Her: the attitude of a handmaid, a "hero," or a child. A hero's attitude is to please Her, even as a man pleases

> a woman through intercourse. The worship of Śakti is extremely difficult. It is no joke. I passed two years as the handmaid and companion of the Divine Mother. But my natural attitude has always been that of a child toward its mother.[28]

Indeed, woman must be propitiated; she is linked with gold as a major threat and compared with death itself:

> The Tantriks sometimes use a corpse in their religious rites. Now and then the dead body frightens them by opening its mouth. That is why they keep fried rice and grams near them, and from time to time, they throw some of the grains into the corpse's mouth. Thus pacifying the corpse, they repeat the name of the Deity without any worry. Likewise, the householder should pacify his wife, and the other members of the family.[29]

Viewing women as the Mother is a way to reduce their fearfulness:

> I am very much afraid of women. When I look at one, I feel as if a tigress were coming to devour me. Besides, I find that their bodies, their limbs, and even their pores are very large. This makes me look upon them as she-monsters. I used to be much more afraid of women than I am at present. I wouldn't allow one to come near me. Now I persuade my mind in various ways to look upon women as forms of the Blissful Mother.[30]

Another way to avoid the danger was by "identification with the enemy," by losing the male identity:

> How can a man conquer passion? He should assume the attitude of a woman. I spent many days as the handmaid of God. I dressed myself in women's clothes, put on ornaments, and covered the upper part of my body with a scarf, just like a woman. With the scarf on I used to perform the evening worship before the image. Otherwise, how could I have kept my wife with me for eight months? Both of us behaved as if we were the handmaids of the Divine Mother.[31]

Such identification came easily to Rāmakṛṣṇa, who would enter into both dramatic and ritual roles. His identifications came in stages, as Rolland describes:

> He became the person of Rama by stages, through the people who served Rama, beginning with the humblest, Hanuman.

> Then in reward, as he himself believed, Sita appeared to him. This was his first complete vision with his eyes open. All his succeeding visions came by the same successive stages. First he saw the figures outside himself, then they vanished within himself, finally he became them himself.[32]

In his visions and identifications with the Divine Mother, his roles fit those of both Vaiṣṇava and tantric madmen:

> A man who has seen God sometimes behaves like a madman: he laughs, weeps, dances and sings. Sometimes he behaves like a child, a child five years old—guileless, generous, without vanity, unattached to anything, not under the control of any of the gunas, always blissful. Sometimes he behaves like a ghoul: he doesn't differentiate between pure and impure things, he sees no difference between things clean and things unclean. And sometimes he is like an inert thing, staring vacantly: he cannot do any work, he cannot strive for anything.[33]

The madman has no discrimination: he cannot distinguish between home and elsewhere, between deity and self. He stated: "Sometimes the paramahaṁsa behaves like a madman. When I experienced that divine madness, I used to worship my own sex organ as the Śiva-phallus."[34]

But his hidden power may be seen in his worship, as in this story quoted by F. Max Mueller about a wandering holy man (*sādhu*):

> An itinerant sadhu came once to the Kali temple of Rani Rasmani, and seeing a dog eating the remains of a feast, he went up to him and said, embracing him, "Brother, how is it that thou eatest alone, without giving me a share?" So saying, he began to eat along with the dog. The people of the place naturally thought him mad, but when standing before the temple of the Goddess, he began to chant forth some hymns in praise of Kali, and the temple appeared to shake through the fervor of his devotion. Then the people knew him to be a great sadhu. The true sadhus roam about like children or madmen, in dirty clothes, and various other disguises.[35]

The childlike aspect of madness is associated with the matured ego, as both are beyond social conventions, ideas, or purity and impurity. At times the madness shows an alienation from the body:

> A man who has realized God shows certain characteristics. He becomes like a child or a madman or an inert thing or a

ghoul. Further, he is firmly convinced that he is a machine and God is its Operator, that God alone is the Doer and all others are his instruments.[36]

There is even the Western analogy of the "screw loose":

> When he is in samādhi, he becomes unconscious of the outer world and appears inert. . . . He is not aware of filth as such. Even rice and other cooked food after a few days become like filth. Again, he is like a madman. People notice his ways and actions, and think of him as insane. . . . One reaches this state of mind after having the vision of God. When a boat passes a magnetic hill, its screws and nails become loose and drop out. Lust, anger, and the other passions cannot exist after the vision of God.[37]

Alienation from the body is seen in Rāmakṛṣṇa's tendency to refer to himself as "this case" or "this body," and his tendency to split his personality into fragments, which he could then watch. Such visions were often tied to his physiological state:

> At that time a naked person, emerging from my body, used to go about with me. I used to joke with him. He looked like a boy, and was a paramahansa. I can't describe to you all the divine forms I saw at that time. I was suffering then from indigestion, which would become worse when I saw visions; so I would try to shun these divine forms and would spit on the ground when I saw them. But they would follow me and obsess me like ghosts. I was always overwhelmed with divine ecstasy and couldn't tell the passing of day and night. On the day after such a vision I would have a severe attack of diarrhoea, and all these ecstasies would pass out through my bowels.[38]

Sometimes such visions came about as a result of spiritual practices and had strong sexual overtones:

> This is a very secret experience. I saw a boy 22 or 23 years old, exactly resembling me, enter the Sushumna nerve and commune with the lotuses, touching them with his tongue. He began with the center at the anus and passed through the [other] centers . . . at his touch they stood erect . . . and last of all, the 1000-petalled lotus in the head blossomed. Since then I have been in this state.[39]

At times his body was hypersensitive, identifying with the bodies of others:

> A blow given to a man in the street by a furious enemy left its physical mark on the flesh of Rāmakrisna. His nephew saw his back red and inflamed at the sight of a man whose back was scored with the whip. And Girish Chandra Ghose, whose witness is unimpeachable, has certified to the fact of his stigmata.[40]

He identified himself as an *īśvarakoṭi,* one for whom spiritual practice was unnecessary. He describes them:

> The Incarnations of God belong to the class of the Isvarakotis. . . . Their ego is not the "thick ego" of worldly people. The ego, the "I-consciousness," of worldly people is like four walls and a roof: the man inside them cannot see anything outside. The ego of the Incarnations and other Isvarakotis is a "thin ego"—through it they have an uninterrupted vision of God. Take the case of a man who stands by a wall on both sides of which there are meadows stretching to infinity. If there is a hole in the wall, through it he can see everything on the other side. If the hole is a big one, he can even pass through it. The ego of the Incarnations and other Isvarakotis is like the wall with a hole. Though they remain on this side of the wall, still they can see the endless meadow on the other side. . . . Again, if they will, they can pass through the big hole to the other side and remain in samadhi. And if the hole is big enough, they can go through it and come back again [to the worldly place].[41]

The *īśvarakoṭi* is this way from childhood, thus the lack of necessity for practice:

> Fruits first, flowers next, as is the case with the creepers called gourds . . . whatever practice they are seen to undertake for achieving perfection in matters spiritual, is for the purpose of showing people that they will have to undertake similar practices in order to achieve similar results.[42]

Rāmakṛṣṇa distinguishes five types of *siddha:* the *svapna* (who gains perfection in a dream); the *mantra* (whose mantra leads him to perfection); the *haṭhāt* (whose perfection is gained suddenly, as when a poor man finds a treasure or marries into a wealthy family); the *kṛpā* (perfection is gained by the grace of god or guru); and the *īśvarakoṭi* or *nitya siddha,* who is like a gourd or pumpkin creeper—the fruit comes before the flower, and the fruit of meditation is present before its practice, a reversal of the typical situation. The practice of the *nitya siddha* is to set an example for humanity, as Rāmakṛṣṇa has done for all later Śāktas.

The Path of the Kulācāra: The *Mahānirvāṇa Tantra* and *Kulārṇava Tantra*

The major texts of Śāktism are tantras and devotional poetry. Tantras include all three strands, although there is often an emphasis on the yogic aspect, for many tantras are handbooks and instruction manuals for the practitioner. They are usually in the form of discussions between Śiva and Śakti: in the *āgama* texts he speaks to her, and in the *nigama* texts she speaks to him. The major topics include creation and dissolution of the universe, ritual worship of deities, attainment of supernatural power, and the nature of union with the supreme being. There are tantric rites for the five systems of Hindu worship (*pañcopāsana*)—toward Viṣṇu, Śiva, Śakti, Gaṇapati, and Sūrya. There are both Vedic and tantric rituals for the worship of some of these deities. Most tantras belong to the medieval and late medieval periods (eighth through fifteenth centuries). This section focuses on Śākta tantra as a source for understanding Śākta ecstasy.

The two tantras most frequently cited as authoritative, by both Śākta ritual practitioners and laypersons, are the *Mahānirvāṇa Tantra* and the *Kulārṇava Tantra,* both texts of the Kulācāra school of Śāktism. They make an interesting contrast of texts: the *Mahānirvāṇa Tantra* is a "doctored" text, questionable in its author and origin, while the *Kulārṇava Tantra* is an older and more reliable source, with many details not included by the *Mahānirvāṇa Tantra.* One of the major areas of difference is the topic of ecstasy and madness; this is mostly avoided in the *Mahānirvāṇa,* but in the *Kulārṇava* is emphasized as the central aspect of tantra.

The *Mahānirvāṇa Tantra* was first published by the Ādi-Brāhmo-Samāj in 1876, in Bengali script, with a commentary by Kulavadhuta Hariharānanda Bhārati, the tantric guru of Rāmmohan Rāya. The text is incomplete, ending with a statement that this is the first half of the tantra. Arthur Avalon, also known as Sir John Woodroffe, published an English translation, and claimed to have seen the second part (in the hands of a Nepali pandit). There is much debate about whether the tantra is spurious, perhaps written by either Rāmmohan Rāya or his guru. Rāya had two criteria for judging an authentic text: either it must contain elaborate commentaries, or quotations from it should be given in later compilations and essays. Yet in this case he ignored these rules.[43]

The text endorses rituals that would not be threatening to a Western outlook, such as *kuṇḍalinī* yoga (interpreted as monism), and the rituals of *puraścarana,* which lead to the dissolution of the sinful body and the creation of a celestial (*deva*) body. Ecstasy is the yogic visualization of a deity:

> 51. Seeing (in his mind's eye) and meditating upon the water as Fire, the worshipper should draw it through the nose by *Iḍā* and expel it through *Piṅgalā* (into his palm), and so wash away all inward impurity. . . .
> 52. Then let him meditate morning, midday and evening upon the Great Devī Gayatrī, the Supreme Devī, as manifested in her three different forms and according to the three qualities.
> 56. In the morning, meditate upon Her in Her Brahmi form, as a Maiden of ruddy hue, with a pure smile, with two hands, holding a gourd full of holy water, garlanded with crystal beads, clad in the skin of a black antelope, seated on a swan.[44]

Initiation is an ecstatic event:

> 140. Immediately upon initiation into this mantra, his soul is suffused with Divine Being. What need then, O Deveshī! for such a one to practise various forms of *sādhana?*[45]

The images of heavenly worlds are described, as are the promises of the tantric practitioner's future greatness:

> 39. He becomes in learning like Bṛihaspati himself, in wealth like Kuvera. His profundity is that of the ocean, and his strength like that of the wind.
> 40. He shines with the blinding brilliance of the sun, yet pleases with the soft glamor of the moon. In beauty, he becomes like the God of Love, and reaches the hearts of women.
> 41. He comes forth as a conqueror everywhere by the grace of this hymn of praise. Singing this hymn, he attains all of his desires.[46]

However, conflicts arise in the areas of the forbidden—wine, women, ecstatic intensity. Wine is the symbol for divine intoxication and ecstatic bliss, and in this text it is alternately desired and feared. At first wine is associated with bliss:

> 38. O Kula-rūpini! Infuse into the essence of this excellent wine which produces full and unbroken bliss, its thrill (*sphuraṇa*) of joy.
> 39. Thou who art like the nectar which is in Ananga (*Kāma*), and art the embodiment of Pure Knowledge, place into this liquid the ambrosia of *brahmānanda*.[47]

It is glorified as a form of the goddess:

> 105. Wine is Tārā Herself in liquid form, is the Saviour of beings, the Mother of enjoyment and liberation, who destroys danger and diseases, burns up the heaps of sins, and purifies the world.
> 106. O Beloved! She grants all success, and increases knowledge, intellect and learning, and O Ādyā! She is ever worshipped by those who have attained final liberation, and those who are desirous of attaining final liberation.[48]

This is undercut almost immediately:

> 114. The understanding of men is clouded by the drinking of wine, whether in small or large quantities, according to the difference in the quality of the wine, to the temperament of the individuals, to the place where and the time when it is taken.
> 115. Therefore, excessive drinking is to be judged, not from the quantity drunk, but from the result as shown in difficulty of speech, and from the unsteadiness of hands, feet and sight. . . .
> 118. The King should severely chastise and fine the man who is unsteady in hands, feet, or in speech, who is bewildered, maddened, and beyond himself with drink.[49]

This pattern of affirmation and negation continues through the text. Perhaps the most peculiar description is that of the Bhairava-cakra, which totally omits mention of any ecstatic elements. Indeed, persons who are a part of the circle do not transcend caste, but instead become the best of brahmins.[50] After giving the ritual for sanctifying the wine, the text tells its readers not to use it, because it is the Kālī Yuga. For this reason, too, they should not perform sexual rituals, but instead meditate on the Devī's feet. The *cakra* is a fearsome thing—ghosts and demons run away in fear, and the gods visit the place, which is more holy than all other shrines. But the major event described is eating sweets and not worrying about the food's impurity. Oblique reference is made to the practitioner's *śakti,* who must be his wife according to the Śaiva rites; however, the interaction with the woman (*śakti seva*) is not described.[51] The Tattva Circle is also totally devoid of ecstasis—the participants sit on attractive carpets, chant mantras, and eat sweets, and do not require a wine jar or long ritual.[52]

The Victorian hesitation of the *Mahānirvāṇa Tantra* may be contrasted with the more earthy *Kulārṇava Tantra.* Arthur Avalon partially translated this text and omitted almost all ecstatic details. However, the Bengali edition is more descriptive of Kula attitudes toward both ecstasy and madness.

The *Kulārṇava Tantra* is an important text of the Śakta Kulas—Avalon calls it the most frequently cited text in the tantric literature. It emphasizes the secrecy of the Kula path, stressing that it is only for those who have studied in previous lives. For external instruction is of little avail; knowledge should dawn without being taught. The *Kulārṇava Tantra* organizes its discussion of ecstasy around two rituals: the states of piercing (*vedha*) which arise in initiation, and the states of ecstatic joy (*ullāsa*) which reveal themselves in the ritual *cakra* (circle of people).

The tantra mentions several types of initiation and gives etymologies for the term *dīkṣā.*[53] The initiation by ritual, or *samayā-dīkṣā,* includes *abhiṣeka* (sprinkling with water) and fire pit. The *sādhikā* or *varṇa-dīkṣā* has the disciple place letters on his body, then dissolve these in the *ātman;* this induces a state of bliss. The *kalā-dīkṣā,* which also withdraws letters from the body, leads to the state of *divyabhāva* and meetings with *yoginīs.* Initiation by touch, or *sparśa-dīkṣā,* is done without ritual—the guru's touch is compared to a bird nourishing its young by the warmth of its wings. *Vāg-dīkṣā* is initiation by word or mantra, and in *dṛk* or *carya-dīkṣā,* the guru gazes into the disciple's eyes (as a fish is thought to nourish its young by sight).[54]

Śāmbhavī-dīkṣā is instantaneous knowledge that arises from the guru's look, speech, or touch. Mental initiation (*māno-dīkṣā*) has two aspects: the *tīvra,* which gives liberation by ritual, and the *tīvratara,* in which the guru's thought frees the disciple of his sins. Of this, the *Kulārṇava Tantra* states:

> 61. O Śāmbhavī! Released from external awareness, the disciple instantly falls and rolls on the ground, a state of divine *bhāva* arises in him and he comes to know everything.

> 62. O Īśvarī, that joy which he experiences at this initiation by piercing [*vedha-dīkṣā*], he is unable to describe afterward.[55]

It is the *vedha,* the piercing or impact from the guru's power, which causes ecstasy in the disciple during initiation. A variety of different symptoms arise:

> 64. Bliss, trembling, new birth, the spinning of the head, sleep, and fainting, O Kuleśvarī, these are the six states of *vedha.*
> 65. O Kuleśvarī! These six conditions arise due to the *vedha* initiation. Wherever the person who experiences this may be, he is liberated, there is no doubt about it.[56]

There is also a special initiation called the *siddhābhiṣeka,* which may be performed by external ritual or internally, in which the disciple encounters the guru's power directly. It causes liberation and rebirth as Śiva after death. It is described alchemically: "O My Beloved! As the iron struck by mercury becomes gold, so does the person struck by [this] initiation attain to the state of Śiva."[57]

One may gauge the validity of the initiation if the mantra given by the guru appears to have consciousness (*mantra-caitanya*). This proves the lineage of the guru and is seen in the mantra's effects on the initiate:

> 64. O Kuleśvarī! When a mantra which is conscious is chanted even once, the knots of the heart and the heart area are untied, the practitioner is no longer tempted by the wealth and majesty of Māyā, his limbs become elongated, and he cries tears of joy.
> 65. His hair stands on end, his body becomes as if possessed [*āveśa*], and he stutters. When these signs are present, one can be sure that the mantra has been handed down by tradition.[58]

Because the mantra is believed to be conscious, as a person might be, it is subject to similar personality problems. A mantra may be angry, lazy, apathetic, ashamed, or young, adolescent, or old. It may be intoxicated, without affection, hungry, proud, and cunning. It will only induce ecstasy when these traits have been altered.[59]

The guru causes ecstatic states in the disciple directly, through the techniques of *vedha,* and his knowledge of the *cakras,* states of consciousness, and the inner geography of the spirit. He should be able to give spontaneous joy and remove the pleasures of the senses. From his touch should flow bliss, from his sight, liberation, for his glance burns up sin. He is also present at the other major ecstatic ritual, the *cakra.*

The secrecy of this rite is always emphasized:

> 84. O Devī! *Kula*—ritual should always be kept secret, as a woman does not reveal her pregnancy by her lover.
> 85. The Vedas, purāṇas, and śāstras display themselves like prostitutes, but this wisdom is secretive, like a daughter-in-law.[60]

In the *cakra,* the male and female participants exchange food and drink. However, they must be sure that all others present are *kula* initiates, otherwise, the mantras would turn away their faces and the gods would curse them. Food and wine become sacred *prasāda* and are accompanied by mantras and worship of Bhairava. The wine causes exhilaration, and all spontaneous actions are considered as the actions of Bhairava; indeed, after taking his blessed food, the yogis are considered to be Bhairava himself.[61]

Behavior at the *cakra* is reinterpreted:

> 59. In this state, discussion shows the fruit of mantra practice, sleepiness is deep trance [*samādhi*], bad actions are worship, union with (one's) consort is liberation, one takes food as if it were a sacrifice to Bhairava, and conversation, O Iśāṇī, is seen as the chanting of hymns.
> 60. The contact of bodily parts is *nyāsa* [ritually placing a god in the body], taking food is the pouring of oblations on the ritual fire, observation is visualization [*dhyāna*], and sleeping is like embrace [*bandhana*].
> 61. In this way, whatever actions are performed by devotees in a state of ecstatic joy (*ullāsa*) are considered virtuous.
> 63. Enthusiasm, bliss, increase in knowledge, poetry, speech, playing on the flute and the vina, weeping, falling down and getting up again, yawning, walking, even various bad acts;
> 64. All of these actions, O Devī, are called yoga.[62]

In the *cakra,* states of bliss are induced by both ritual and wine, and the states of intoxication caused by both become extreme:

> 67. Intoxicated by passion, the women take shelter with other men, treating them as their own. Each man also takes a new woman [*śakti*] and treats her as his own, when in the state of advanced ecstatic joy.

68. Seized by delusion, the men embrace other men.
69. The women are confused and ask their husbands such questions as;
70. "Who are you, who am I, who are these other people, why are we here, is this a garden, or our home, or an inner courtyard?"
71. O Śāmbhavī! The yogis take the food from each other's plates and dance about with their drinking pots on their heads.
72. The devotees fill their mouths with liquor and have the women drink it from their mouths. They also put spicy food in their mouths and put it into the mouths of their partners.
73. The women who are not in their normal senses [*behuśa*] clap and sing songs whose words are unclear, and they stagger while dancing.
74. Yogis who are intoxicated with alcohol fall upon the women, and the intoxicated *yoginīs* fall upon the men. O Kulanāyikā! They are induced to perform such actions, to fulfill their mutual desires.
75. When this state of ecstasy [*ullāsa*] is not accompanied by perverse thoughts, the bull among yogis reaches the state of godhood (*devatā-bhāva*).[63]

There is also a fairly long section describing the states of ecstasy induced by the *cakra*. The first five may be translated as birth, childhood, youth, maturity, and later adulthood. The sixth state (*unmanā*) is agitation or excitation, and the seventh state is called *manollāsa* (extreme exhilaration) or *anavasthā* (the state beyond states, or state without qualities or locale). These states grow with practice and initiation:

81. In the sixth ecstatic state, which is called the *unmanā ullāsa,* the devotee often swoons.
82. When this occurs with a strong desire to experience the ultimate [*parabrahman*], the devotee may enter the seventh state of ecstasy, called the *anavasthā* [the state beyond all states].
83. In this condition, he is beyond control by body and senses.
84. In the state of this highest swoon[64] he takes on the form of the greatest mantra,[65] and this state of swooning brings [him] to the root of liberation.
85. He gazes outward but looks inward, and his eyes are unblinking. This is the *śāmbhavī mudra.*
86. This is the greatest of *mudras,* the true form of the bliss

> of union (*samarasa*), expressing the nature of the self. By means of this, the devotee truly becomes Śiva. There is no doubt about this.
>
> 87. Persons engaged in self-study can know some of this bliss. But this state is beyond description and must be experienced, as the pleasure of drinking sugared milk must be experienced.
>
> 88. By means of concentration, this great joy causes god possession [*devāveśa*]. This stage is called the vision of *brahman* [*brahmadhyāna*], and it is visible through horripilation [and other such symptoms].
>
> 89. Those persons who are absorbed in concentration cannot describe this state. Men of virtuous actions and intelligence become absorbed in this bliss.
>
> 90. Such men cannot tolerate even a moment's interruption of this state, and if this happens, they become saddened and confused. This state [of *brahmadhyāna*] is the great fruit gained by your devotees in the seventh state of ecstasy.[66]

These states arise from the *cakra* rituals, which include identification with Śiva and Śakti, as well as from the use of the five *makaras,* the forbidden things. Among these, special attention has been given to drinking alcohol.

The *Kulārṇava Tantra* mentions three types of drinking: the *divya* way is in front of Devī, the *vīra* way is with ritual hand positions and postures, and the *paśu* way is drinking arbitrarily, according to one's own desires.[67] It becomes more specific for those who are fully initiated:

> 100. He should drink and drink, and then drink again, until he falls to the earth. If he gets up and drinks again, he will have no rebirth.
>
> 101. The Devī is satisfied by [his] exhilaration; Bhairava himself is satisfied [or he becomes Bhairava] by swooning; and all the Devatās are satisfied by [his] vomiting.
>
> 102. One should satisfy all three of these. Even world rulers cannot feel the bliss that Kula yogis gain from *divya* drinking.[68]

Drinking bestows bliss, miraculous powers, liberation, and other abilities. By the mere sight of such wine, all sins are destroyed, and by its smell one gains the fruits of one hundred sacrifices. Its touch gives the reward of visiting millions of shrines. The true wine-drinking refers to the nectar in the crown of the head, and wine is associated with the intoxication of religious ecstasy.

Sexuality is also important:

> 107. Without the nectar of *bhaga* and *lingam* [vagina and penis] I am not satisfied, even if [offered] thousands of jars of wine and hundreds of piles of meat.
>
> 108. This world does not bear the mark of the *cakra,* lotus, or thunderbolt. It bears the mark of *lingam* and *bhaga.* Thus, the world [reflects] the form of Śiva and Śakti.
>
> 109. When there is a union of Śiva and Śakti, the devotee experiences deep trance [*samādhi*].[69]

The *kula* path unites yoga and *bhoga* (enjoyment), its adherents claiming the best of both worlds. The ritual links wine, women, and forbidden foods with the divine, and all things become allowable. The mere mention of the Kulācāra caused thrills in those who have experienced its joys: "When the *kula* is praised, [those] whose hair stands on end, whose voices shake with emotion, and who shed tears of joy, they are the best of devotees."[70]

The *kula yogi* also finds socially permissible a wide range of behaviors, many of which are frowned on by his community. Like the Vaiṣṇava devotee of the *Bhāgavata Puraṇa,* the *kula yogi* behaves as a madman or is disguised in a variety of ways. He may act impolitely or aggressively, and such acts are seen as a result of impulse:

> 67. O Kuleśvarī! They do not [express] their self-knowledge at once. Among men they live as if they were intoxicated, dumb, and inert beings. . . .
>
> 72. O Maheśvarī! Although they are liberated, the *kula yogis* play like children, behave like idiots, and speak like drunkards. . . .
>
> 74. He goes about in different guises; at times like a righteous person, at times like a fallen one, at times like a ghost or demon. . . .
>
> 82. Who can straighten the course of a winding river, or stop its flooding? And who can stop the man who wanders peacefully and sports as he chooses?[71]

His behavior is partly a result of his ecstatic states and partly a desire to avoid interaction with worldly people: "Such a yogi lives in a way that causes worldly men to laugh, feel disgust, revile, and avoid him."[72]

The *Kulārṇava Tantra* spends little time on social ethics, preferring to emphasize the ecstatic and mad behavior of the *kula yogi* and the details of initiation, yogic meditation, and worship. The intoxication of the *cakra* is believed to lead to liberation, while the mad public behavior hides states of ecstatic trance, possession, regression, and confusion under the guise of proper tantric actions (*ācāra*).

However, there is little that practice can do for those who are not ready for states of bliss. Such action is of little avail: "Divine knowledge [*kulajñāna*] emerges of its own accord[73] as a result of practice done in previous lives, without instruction, as one needs no instruction to know what he has dreamed.[74]

These two tantras describe different types of ecstasy. The *Mahanirvāṇa Tantra* emphasizes yogic practices—the visualization of symbolic images and merger with their deities. It includes worship of the goddess in her many forms and both supports and denies the rituals of meat and alcohol. The *Kulārṇava Tantra* also includes yogic details, describing the ecstatic states in initiation (such as instantaneous knowledge, fainting, and rebirth) and the states of joy (*ullāsa*) in the circle, the feelings of intoxication and bliss. However, it also emphasizes loving worship of Śiva and Śakti, and the use of wine and flesh, as well as the use of mantras for spells of love and death. Thus, both tantras show the presence of the three strands—of yoga, devotion, and magic.

Ritual Ecstasy: The Descent of Brahman Wisdom

> In every Indian cremation ground the refulgent and divine halo of Bhairavas and Bhairavis is yet to be seen mingling with the light of the flames of funeral pyres, rending apart the waves of nocturnal darkness and illuminating the wide expanse of heaven. Dead and putrefying corpses submerged near cremation grounds are still brought to life by the force of the sādhaka's mantras, and made to render aid to sādhana and siddhi . . . the throne of the Daughter of the Mountain is still moved by the wondrous, attractive force of mantras.
>
> —Śrīyukta Śiva Candra Vidyārṇava Bhaṭṭacārya Mahodaya

The three strands may be seen in the study of Śakta tantric ritual. Such ritual is complex, and it includes many elements. Bhakti is seen in the loving worship of Devī and her ten forms; yoga is seen in the exercise of *kuṇḍalinī* yoga; magical rites of death and sexuality are seen in the reverse (*vāmā*) path, in the burning ground at midnight.

The devotional strand emphasizes love of the goddess as a personal deity. Popular Śākta devotion is a relatively recent phenomenon, but dedication to the goddess has been mentioned in many older Śākta texts.[75] Devotional practices are specifically described by the Devī in the *Śrīmad Devī Bhāgavata Purāṇa,* a late medieval work considered a major Śākta text:

> He always meditates on Me with a constant vigilance and actuated by a feeling of Supreme Devotion; he does not think himself separate from Me but rather thinks (to) himself "that I am the Bhagavatī." He considers all the Jīvas as Myself, and loves Me as he loves himself. . . . He becomes filled with devotion to Me whenever he sees My place, My devotees and hears the Śāstras, describing My deeds, and whenever he meditates on My Mantras, he becomes filled with the highest love; and his hairs stand on their ends out of love to Me, and tears of love flow incessantly from both his eyes; he recites My name and My deeds in a voice, choked with feelings of love for Me.[76]

The highest state is one of total surrender:

> He sings my name loudly and dances, being intoxicated with My love, and has no idea of egoism and is devoid of his body-idea, thinking that the body is not his. He thinks that whatever is Prārabdha (done in his previous lives) must come to pass and therefore does not become agitated as to the preservation of his body and soul. This sort of Bhakti is called the Para Bhakti or the Highest Devotion.[77]

He may get final liberation, although this is not sought, and wisdom is equated with devotion:

> He gets immediately dissolved in My Nature of Consciousness whose heart is really filled with such Parā Bhakti or All Love. The sages call the limiting stage of this devotion and dispassion as Jñāna (knowledge). When this Jñāna arises, Bhakti and dispassion get their ends satisfied. . . . That man enjoys there all the objects of enjoyment, though unwilling and, at the end of the period, gets the knowledge of My Consciousness. By that he attains the Final Liberation for ever. Without this Jñāna, the Final Liberation is impossible.[78]

While they are on earth, devotees of the goddess should display ecstatic symptoms:

> With hearts filled with love and with hairs standing on their ends, all should satisfy Me frequently with tears of love flowing from their eyes and with voice choked with feelings and with dancing, music and singing and with his whole body filled with joy.[79]

In ecstatic states and in the states after death, the devotee goes to the paradise of Maṇidvīpa, the Isle of Gems, and he takes on female form:

> O Himavan! Nothing remains at any time unavailable to him who worships thus the Bhuvaneśvarī Devī. After quitting his body, he goes to the Maṇi Dvīpa, My Place. He gets the form of the Devī, and the Devas constantly bow down to him.[80]

For service to the Devī, this feminine form is believed to be preferable to the male form. Brahma describes his visit to the paradise, accompanied by Viṣṇu and Śiva:

> Seeing us standing at the gateway, the Devī Bhagavatī smiled and within an instant transformed us three into females. We looked (like) beautiful and youthful women, adorned with nice ornaments; thus we greatly wondered and went to Her. Seeing us standing at Her feet in feminine forms, the beautiful Devī Bhagavatī looked on us with eyes of affection. We then bowed to the great Devī, looked at one another and stood before Her in that feminine dress. We three, then, began to see the pedestal of the great Devī, shining with the lustre of ten million suns and decorated with various gems and jewels. . . . Thus full one hundred years passed away in seeing the various glories of the Devī in the auspicious nectar-like Maṇi Dvīpa; as long as we were there, Her attendants, the Deva girls adorned with various ornaments, gladly considered us as Sakhīs. We too were greatly fascinated by their enchanting gestures and postures.[81]

Indeed, manhood alienates the worshiper from Bhuvaneśwarī, as Śiva states:

> O auspicious one! How can we understand Thy sport? O Mother! We are transformed into young women before Thee; let us serve Thy lotus feet. If we get our manhood, we will be deprived from serving Thy feet and thus of the greatest happiness. O Mother! O Sire! I do not like to leave Thy lotus feet and get my man-body again and reign in the three worlds. O

> Beautiful faced one! Now that I have got this youthful feminine form before Thee, there is not a trace of desire within me to get again my masculine form. What use is there in getting manhood, what happiness is there if I do not get sight of Thy lotus-feet![82]

Like the Vaiṣṇava practitioners of the handmaiden ritual (*mañjari sādhana*), the Śākta devotees may become inwardly female and worship the goddess by personal service. Many tantras stress the details of this service—washing the goddess's hair, oiling her, putting on her dress, ornaments, and the red cosmetics *lac* and *kumkum*. There is a direct communion between devotee and goddess, and this relationship is considered to be superior to liberation.

In Bengal, devotion to the goddess is strongly associated with her ten forms (*daśa mahāvidyās*). The goal of devotion to these forms for many devotees is *siddhi lābh kore*—the attainment of perfection—and the different forms of the goddess give different perfections. The two most important of the forms are those of Kālī and Tārā.

According to Śākta informants, Kālī is the goddess of liberation; she is called Kaivalodayinī—she who gives escape (*mukti* or *kaivalya*) from the illusory world. She controls the gray area between life and death, and her devotees will not be reborn. The liberated person (*mukta-puruṣa* or *mukta-nārī*) will gain the Mother's blessing and stay on her lap forever, in her home in the five heavens (*pañcākāśa*).

Tārā Mā is the goddess of supreme knowledge; she is called Jñānodayinī—she who grants the ability to know and realize the Absolute. She is a philosopher and guide, and her devotees gain knowledge of the arts and occult sciences (generally listed as astrology, palmistry, the solar system, and poetic inspiration). In worship of Tārā, biological urges are destroyed by fire. She has eight forms—the *aṣṭa-Tāriṇī.*

The other manifestations are less important, sometimes called *vidyās* rather than *mahāvidyās.* Ṣoḍaśī, Bhuvaneśvarī and Cinnamastikā grant the gifts of *rajas*—wealth and heaven—while Dhūmavātī, Bagalā, and Kamalā grant the tamasic gift of power in magical and destructive acts.

The aspects of the goddess show many elements of ecstasy and madness. Some found in the *Kālī Sahasranāma* (the thousand names of Kālī), with the translations of a devotee, include Kāmārtā (the ecstasy of passion), Madanāturā (she who is intoxicated by Kāma), Mattā (the mad one), Pramattā (she of cosmic insanity), Atimattā (she who is intoxicated by her devotee's love), and Mahāmattā (she who is overflowing with intoxication). She is also Mātaṅgī (mad with a furious love) and Madirāmedaronmādā (intoxicated by drinking the cosmic wine of divine love).[83] The *Lalitā Sahasranāma,* more often used in the southern Śrī Kula school of Śaktism, also gives the names of the goddess. These include Nirvāṇasukha-dāyinī (she who gives the bliss of *nirvāṇa*), Mada-śālinī (she who is full of the bliss), and Mada-ghūrṇita-raktākṣī (she whose eyes are turned inward in ecstasy). She is also Mattā (mad or intoxicated), Mādhvī-pānalasā (in a state of divine inebriation), Bhāvajñā (one who experiences *bhāva*), and Muktinilayā (the abode of liberation).[84]

There is also devotion to minor goddesses, but of a style different from the devotion to deities who can grant liberation. In the *Devī Bhāgavata,* the goddesses Manasā, Śītalā, Caṇḍī, and Ṣaṣṭhī are called *siddha yoginīs.*[85] They grant boons rather than ecstasy to their disciples and are not generally associated with being ecstatic themselves (although the *Devī Bhāgavata* gives a derivation of the name Manasā as "she who meditates on God with her mind and gets rapture in her meditation on God.")[86] They reward worshipers and punish nonbelievers. Manasā is the goddess of snakes, Śītalā is the smallpox goddess, Maṅgala Caṇḍī is a warrior goddess, and Ṣaṣṭhī rules over childbirth. The sixteen mothers, the tantric *mātṛkās,* are also worshiped at Vedic sacraments. The Vaiṣṇavite Rādhā is often worshiped as a Śākta deity, either as the powerful mediator to a distant Kṛṣṇa or as the universal goddess, as in the *Rādhā-tantra.* The Vaiṣṇavite poet Pratāpa-rudra writes:

> For your sake, O Rādhā, I have worshipped you. I have accomplished all that I had desired. Among your limbs may I become the full limbs (i.e. the two breasts). Among your ornaments, may I become the pair of anklets. . . . Another desire do I entertain in my heart: I may remain on your feet as a tiny speck of dust. But if I am not allowed to remain as a speck of dust, then I guess, you do be gracious to Pratāpa-rudra out of your own accord.[87]

In Bengal, Durgā is Durgātinaśinī—one who destroys suffering. As Vāmādurgā, she is worshiped with her children, the demons; to worship her as Jayadurgā, the devotee dances naked, abusing the deity, threatening her if she does not accept his offering of burnt fish. The image of Jagaddhātrī is more often seen—wearing a snake as a sacred thread, four-handed, riding a lion.[88] There are also many forms of Kālī, including Siddhakālī, whose body overflows with nectar; Dakṣiṇakālī, wearing a garland of human heads and having sex with Mahādeva, who appears to be a corpse; Guhyakālī, with large belly and matted hair, and Śiva in the form of a child; and Bhadrakālī, who is emaciated with hunger, who weeps and says, "I am not satisfied."[89]

Popular devotion focuses on the great festivals of worship.[90] There are long rituals of worship, with flowers and ghee and Brahmin priests, and lights and fireworks at night. Large Śākta temples, such as those at Kālīghat and Dakṣiṇeśwar, also attract great crowds. In some temples there is singing of hymns to Kālī (*Kālī kīrtana*), when both priest and worshipers sway in semitrance. However, most ecstasy and madness is found among the devotees and tantric practitioners, in their rituals at the burning ground, temple, and jungle.

Among devotees, ecstatic madness is believed to intoxicate the person so that he can perceive only the goddess. The body is suffused with sweetness, while the mind is confused and the heart melts. The Śākta states of divine madness are characterized by confusion, passion, and loss of self-control: trembling, laughing, weeping and crying out before the goddess, rolling on the ground. *Prema pāgal* and *ṭhākur pagal* are intermediate states, in which the deity's name is invoked, but the behavior is too extreme even for devotion and may involve fear and other negative emotions toward people. Among the Śāktas of the shamanic strand, ecstasy is the controlled spiritual state and madness the uncontrolled one—where the Śākta magician is himself controlled by his captive spirits, who may enter or possess him. In the ecstatic state the person may be possessed by a spirit he chooses, while in madness a stranger may visit and take over. Should the Śākta not conquer sexuality and death, but rather become subject to lust and dread, he is widely believed to be vulnerable to insanity and breakdown.[91]

Devotional poets such as Rāmprasād Sen used the imagery of *kuṇḍalinī* yoga in many of their poems, both as background to a devotional relationship and as the major action of the poems, in which *kuṇḍalinī* is called the Divine Mother. Modern practitioners of *kuṇḍalinī* yoga see it as one of the major forms of ritual practice by which to approach the Mother. A Śākta informant in Calcutta, priest of a Bagalā image, described the process:

> The goal of practice is for positive and negative to meet—at the union of Śiva and Śakti, fire comes out. The Kuṇḍalinī goes up the spine until it reaches the *ājñā cakra* [the energy center in the forehead]—then it becomes Kula-kuṇḍalinī. There are four lotuses inside the center in the forehead. The

> Śakti goes through the *ājñā cakra,* through a small hole, and then she spirals out into [the paradise of] Kailāsa. If the hole is too small, the *vajroli mudra* [a yogic exercise] can force the Śakti through.[92]

There is often a combination of yogic and devotional practice in which the deity is both visualized and loved, seen as an aspect of the devotee, yet capable of helping him and giving grace. It may be seen in the meditative aspect of worship and in the elaborate *puraścarana* or worship of the deity with mantras. Practices that combine Śākta tantrism and yoga include *bhutaśuddhi,* in which bodily purification is based on identification with the deity and the elements of the body are transformed and involuted, and *nyāsa,* in which syllables, deities, sages, and so forth are placed in different parts of the body so that it may be sanctified by their presence. The worshiper may become identified with the deity or transfer the deity's identity into a statue or image, to awaken it.

The yogic strand is seen in the practices of *kuṇḍalinī* yoga. The upward path of *kuṇḍalinī* incorporates elements of tantric Buddhism, haṭhayoga, and devotion. *Kuṇḍalinī* Śakti is the wife of Śiva, who lives in the *sahasrāra* lotus in the head, and when they meet, the yogi is filled with bliss. The ordinary body is dissolved into a visualized subtle body of channels and lotuses, and the individual self is dissolved into the deity. The person visualizes these lotuses or *cakras,* each inhabited by a deity, as connected by nodes (*granthis*) and channels (*nāḍīs*), through which passes the vital air (*prāṇa*). This becomes his celestial body, which he perceives by intuition (*sākṣajñāna*).[93]

Like other yogas, *kuṇḍalinī* yoga begins with Patañjali's eight steps and makes use of hand and body positions and breathing exercises (*prāṇayama*). However, their goal is not the one-pointed concentration of *samādhi,* but the awakening of the goddess Kuṇḍalinī, who lies asleep near the bottom of the spine in the *mūlādhāra cakra.*[94] As she arises, the channels (*nāḍīs*) associated with the external sense organs stop functioning, and the person's attention is focused inward. Elements and qualities are fused and incorporated, and liberation is reached when Śakti unites with Parama-Śiva in the thousand-petaled lotus above the head.

There are a variety of ecstatic symptoms associated with *kuṇḍalinī* yoga. The goddess may be seen as a lightning flash or a chain of lights. Swāmī Viṣṇu Tīrtha gives a long list of symptoms: shaking and trembling of the body, hair standing on end, involuntary *kumbhaka* (deep breathing), laughing, weeping, stammering, fearful visions, loss of semen, involuntary yogic postures, fixation of sight, cessation of breath, revolving eyeballs, vibrations in the spinal cord, convulsions, and the feeling that one does not possess a body. Other symptoms include waves of bliss, hearing mantras, the body falling on the floor and rotating like a grinding stone, or squatting on the floor crosslegged and jumping from place to place like a frog, feeling as if dead or paralyzed, making animal sounds (jackals, dogs, tigers, birds), jerking and tossing of the body, a feeling of spirit possession, glossolalia, intoxication, energy and endurance, visions of deities, and magical powers (*siddhis*).[95]

Usually the yogi is an observer of the scene, in which he watches the snake of Kuṇḍalinī uncurl and rise along his spine. Or he is led upward, "as a rider guides a trained mare by the reins."[96] However, at times he identifies with the goddess and travels upward himself:

> The *sādhaka* in *laya-siddhi-yoga,* thinking of himself as Śakti or the female principle of creation, feels himself in union [*saṅgama*] with Śiva and enjoys infinite pleasure. . . . On their union nectar flows, which runs from *brahmarandhra* to *mūlādhāra,* flooding the *kṣudra-brahmāṇḍa* or microcosm, i.e. the body of the *sādhaka,* who becomes forgetful of all in this world and immersed in ineffable bliss.[97]

This bliss is felt as sweetness, and the yogi participates by observation of the divine couple, as in the Vaiṣṇava handmaiden ritual (*mañjari sādhana*), or by identification with one or both of the participants.

Different *cakras* are associated with different qualities—fulfillment of desires, magical powers and sexual attractiveness, liberation. Kuṇḍalinī may rise with a variety of movements: antlike (slow and straight), froglike (by leaps and bounds), snakelike (zigzag), birdlike (flying up and down), and monkeylike (reaching the top by a few jumps). The yogi may hear different sounds—drumbeats, ringing bells, the sound of the *vīṇā* (a stringed instrument). This ascent is called *ṣaṭ-cakra-bheda,* the piercing of the *cakras.* It is guided by the chanting of mantras, and when the yogi's mind and life energy (*prāṇa*) are merged in the mantra, he experiences total union, as in the merger of Śiva and Śakti. In many cases, the yogi depends on the grace of the mantra and its deity. The mantra continues automatically, as *ajapa japa*—it chants itself.[98]

There is great danger of madness in the practice of Kuṇḍalinī yoga.

When the goddess does not manage to rise and meet Śiva, but becomes trapped along the way, the yogi may be subject to visions, voices, headaches and bodily aches, insomnia, even mental breakdown. In this case, madness is an incomplete religious experience.[99]

The shamanic or magical strand turns away from the social concerns of bhakti and the traditional imagery of yoga. For this path, instinctual desire may be as correct a state as the purity of the yogi. The reverse (*vāmā*) path of Śāktism is found in the path of the hero, the *vīrācāra*. It includes rituals that reverse the normal values of the culture and emphasize impurity and struggle, yet evoke states of vision and extreme emotion. Two major rituals involved deal with death and sexuality.

The corpse ritual (*śava-sādhana*) occurs on the new-moon night. The tantric practitioner should go to a lonely spot—a burning ground, empty house, hill, or riverside. There he must take an attractive young corpse, which has died of snakebite or by violence. It is placed facedown on a blanket of deer or tiger skin, and the tantric sits on the corpse and contemplates the goddess. He sees many terrible sights and temptations, and if his determination is shaken, he will go insane. He may draw a diagram (*yantra*) on the corpse's back, and he calls down the Mother to grant his wishes. If ghosts and demons appear, he calls to her with greater fervor—and she comes down to save her child. If he is successful, the head of the corpse will turn around, and Devī will speak through the corpse's mouth.

In some variations, the corpse ritual is performed with an assistant. The dead body is bathed and consecrated, and fed alcohol and cooked meat. The worshiper identifies with the goddess, and the corpse becomes her cosmic seat. Mantras awaken the corpse, and the *tāntrika* binds him with spells to grant boons. Corpse and ritual objects are then thrown in a running stream.[100]

The *Kālī Tantra* describes yet another variant of the ritual:

> 8. At the root of a bilva tree, having carefully placed a corpse on his own lap, he does the *narasiṁha-mudra*. Observing the corpse, he will chant the *mātṛkā mantra* and the *puṭita mantra*.
>
> 9. Having chanted these one thousand times, he will become master of all miraculous powers.
>
> 10. Carrying the corpse to the root of a banyan tree and worshiping the goddess there, he will chant mantras while lay-

ing down and become the master of all miraculous powers [*siddhis*].

11. Holding the belt of hands [*karakāñjī*], decorated with a necklace made of skulls, with markings of ash from the burning ground and decorated with this ash, chanting mantras even once at the burning ground, he will become the master of all powers. . . .

35. Bowing before Śiva and Śakti, he places markings [on his forehead] and he becomes the greatest of heroes.

36. In the graveyard at night, he will become the true form of Unmattānandabhairava [in the form of] Digbasana, if he chants the *mātṛkā-varṇas*. He will be pure, wearing ashes, with loose hair, and skull and sickle in his hands.

37. He will hold all miraculous powers in his hands.

38. If he performs worship, than *ḍākinīs, yoginīs,* and worldly women will appear, and he will become the master of all powers. . . .

40. He who worships Pārvatī without the corpse ritual will live a terrible life in Naraka [a hell-world] until the great destruction at the end of the world.[101]

Such practices may be associated with the tantric Buddhist contemplation of the horrible (*aśubhabhāvanā*), such as decaying corpses. Some variants include elements of the Tibetan Buddhist *chod* rites, in which the *tāntrika* at the burning ground offers his own body as a sacrifice to the spirits present, and the corpse raising (*ro-langs*), in which a corpse is brought back to life and made to answer questions; often pieces of the body are taken for future use. In some cases, the tantric practitioner lies on the corpse mouth to mouth, breathing life into it, repeating mantras. When the corpse's tongue protrudes he must bite it, or the ghost will devour him and the land will be devastated.[102]

What is the ecstasy of death? There seem to be two forms which such proximity to corpses and burning grounds provide. One is the "samādhi of horror."[103] Here the person discovers radical detachment and total distaste for the world—he is catapulted into a realization of its true, ghastly nature (this would be close to a Buddhist response). The other form is the realization of total dependence on the Mother, when the *tāntrika* is overcome with fear at the phantoms that he sees. When he calls out in desperate panic for the Mother, she comes and rescues him. Thus the ecstasy of the burning ground may be total detachment, or total dependence, evoking the extremes of emotion and emotionlessness in the practitioner.

The precursor to this ecstasy may be madness. Max Mueller quotes a story told by Rāmakṛṣṇa:

> Two persons, it is said, began together the rite of invoking the Goddess Kālī by the terrible process called "śavasādhana." . . . One invoker was frightened to insanity by the horrors of the earlier portion of the night; the other was favoured with the vision of the Divine Mother at the end of the night. Then he asked her, "Mother! why did the other man become mad?" The Deity answered, "Thou too, O child! didst become mad many times in thy various previous births, and now at last thou seest me."[104]

Another area of secret, "reverse" ritual is sexuality. Tantras call such practices *latā-sādhana, nāyikā-sādhana,* or *maithuna;* these may be separate rituals or incorporated into the group worship in the *cakra,* which includes other forbidden acts such as drinking wine and eating fish and meat. Tantras tend to be curt, emphasizing the ritual aspects of *latā-sādhana,* and making no mention of emotion toward the woman. Devotional love is toward the Mother, while the consort is strictly a ritual object, used to gain power. As the *Kāmākhyā Tantra* states:

> 35. [The practitioner] will bring a *siddha yoginī* [or a prostitute], and a ritual circle [*kula-cakra*] will be established.
>
> 36. Then the practitioner will joyfully worship the Devī, [especially] her *yoni-pīṭha* [genitals].[105] Then he will sing hymns sweetly and chant mantras continuously, while looking at his partner [*śakti*].
>
> 37. That person who chants mantras continuously while in this state, he will be lord of all miraculous powers in the Kālī Yuga.[106]

Three varieties of sexual ritual are given in the *Māyā Tantra:*

> 1. O wife of Śiva, I will speak of the principles of *latā-* or *nāyikā-sādhana,* so listen to this.
>
> 2. If the practitioner chants mantras on the woman's hair one hundred times, on her forehead one hundred times, on her *sindur*-dot one hundred times, on each breast one hundred times (as there are two of them, this adds up to two hundred in that area), on the navel one hundred times, on the

genitals one hundred times, and while having sex with the woman three hundred times, this totals one thousand mantras, then he will become lord of all powers. . . .

4. I will discuss another type of practice, which is difficult to perform. Bring a woman while she is menstruating, and at midnight worship your personal deity [*iṣṭadevatā*] within her genitals.

5. After that, the practitioner must chant mantras 336 times daily, for three days. By means of this, he can gain the fruit of one thousand corpse rituals. There is no doubt about it.

6. Here is another type, please listen with a receptive mind. First, to gain perfection in the four paths, he will chant mantras 108 times. Then he will worship his personal deity in the genitals [*yoni*] of a woman who is not his own.[107] Then he will worship Mahāmāyā 108 times, using a new flower (or menstrual blood).

7. After that, he will offer a burnt offering, and chant mantras 108 times. He becomes devoted to the practice [*samayācāra*], and he is always absorbed in Mahāmāyā.[108]

8. If he does this daily for sixteen days, he will become rich, strong, an orator and a poet, and dear to all. There is no doubt about it.[109]

The sexual ritual is seen as extremely important in many texts; the *Kulāvalīnirṇaya,* for example, states that it is the only means by which the aspirant may become perfected (*siddha*).[110] Like the offering of blood (*puṣpa*),[111] it gives a vital energy that combines pure and impure, and allows the practitioner to transcend his normal limitations.

While informants had many stories of corpse rituals,[112] few had anything to say about sexual ritual. Less traditional Śaktas suggested Promode Chatterji's book, *Tantrābhilāsir Sādhu-sangha,* as a reliable source. This book claims to be an autobiography, the memoirs of the author while he was a wandering holy man. Chatterji discusses a visit to a tantric ritual meeting (*cakra*), to which he was invited after he met an *aghorī bhairava tāntrika* (a follower of the Śakta *vāmācāra* path) in Bākreśwar. The following describes the ritual, at the burning ground on a stormy night:

I went near Aghorībābā's cottage and saw people sitting in meditation, unaware of my presence. There was no light, except for occasional flashes of lightning, and I sat down in the back. Incense was burning, and a low-caste [*caṇḍāla*] attendant

> brought a jar of wine and placed it on the ground. . . . Each person had a skull [to be used as a drinking bowl] and a copper pot. What was perhaps most amazing was their ability to ignore the swarms of mosquitoes that attacked them. Aghorībābā strode into the circle, completely naked, and all present bowed their heads. The Bāul got up and led Aghorībābā to the seat reserved for him—a tiger skin. . . . When Aghorībābā sat down, Maheśwarī Mā took off her clothing and bowed at his feet, offering him various items. The place was totally silent. She stood before him like a statue, and he then worshiped her, touching her body ritually and smearing it with sandal paste. They both remained in meditation. As I got more involved in the ritual, the mosquitoes bothered me less.
>
> After a long period of trance, the *aghorī* extended his arms and embraced the woman [*bhairavī*], and she sat down on his lap. It was not erotic, but rather it evoked a sense of holiness and sweetness[113] and I felt a continuous ecstatic mood.[114] The other participants began to chant mantras. . . . Then Khaṇḍa Bhairavī whispered mantras in Aghorībābā's ear, and he finally showed signs of outward consciousness. He took some wine in the skull cup, offered it first to his partner, and then drank it himself. Then came the turn of another couple—Siddha Karolī Bhairava and his partner [*bhairavī*]. They repeated the same ritual as Aghorībābā, and after about half an hour the woman sat on his lap and both drank some wine. Then the other couples followed.
>
> The wine jug went around the group three times and was finished by the *aghorī*. Then a plate of meat and fish was passed around, and the men and women fed each other. The couples appeared to be in a state of great bliss.
>
> Maheśwarī Mā returned to the Aghorī's lap, and they looked like a statue of Śiva and Pārvatī. While the other couples began to act intoxicated and lustful, they remained absorbed in trance. . . . At the end, I found myself rooted to the spot, and in a flash of lightning saw the scene as divine: light-figures of naked gods and goddesses in the midst of their divine play, surrounding a large statue of Hara and Gouri, as still and profound as the Himalayas. I was not sure how long I remained in this state, but when I returned to normal consciousness, the sun was rising in the eastern sky.[115]

The magical strand combines a variety of techniques: the yogic *bhūtajaya* (manipulation of the elements), Vedic sacrificial rites and spells, shamanic travel to other worlds, visions of heaven- and hell-worlds, and encounters with deities and entities.

The *Śiva Sutra* states: "By contemplation on the nature of the *pañca-bhūtas* or five cosmic elements, the Yogi gains the capacity to analyze and separate them, and thus to find out how the universe and the objects within have been built or put together through their instrumentality."[116]

This ability is based on the withdrawal of consciousness from the channels of prāṇic flow (*nāḍīs*). Various types of powers are gained, including complete control over perception (*dhīvaśat*). Such knowledge is inherent, a part of one's nature, and it rises to the surface when the person's mind is emptied: "The supreme knowledge [*vidyā*] which arises [in one's consciousness] by adopting proper means, is *svabhāvika* and can exist only in a void state, beyond manifestation, *śivāvasthā*."[117]

Some magical practices show Buddhist influence and emphasize the illusory nature of magical phenomena. Buddhist magic made use of *ḍākinīs*, witches, *vajra-yoginīs*, mantras, magical looks, and sight of the faces of deities. Many tantras incorporate Buddhist images with images of Hindu deities: *gandharvas, apsarases, vidyādharas* (themselves magicians), *yakṣas*, and *nāgas*. The magician could worship them and gain celestial beauty and power, invisibility, long life, and knowledge of the language of animals.

Magic also includes exorcism and possession. The exorcist (*ojhā*) must determine if the possessing spirit is vegetarian or carnivorous, if it is a local victim of murder or suicide, if it has been sent out by other sorcerors. The Santal witch detector (*jān guru*) becomes possessed and speaks in tongues, and later in the tribal language, to find the invading spirit. The exorcists will admit failure when they encounter a god in the apparently possessed person. The Śākta may also seek to become possessed by a deity in order to heal, prophesy, or approach the deity.

Śākta tantric healers may also incorporate astrology, palmistry, and the use of herbs and jewels into their cures. This mixture may be seen in the temple/pharmacy of a *piśāca tāntrika*, an exorcist of sorts, who makes his living by making amulets (small metal cylinders tied on to the arm with strings, containing mantras and various magical ingredients) and chasing ghosts and demons away from their victims.

This syncretism may be seen in the following description, taken from field notes, of his temple or Kālī *bāṛi*:[118]

> On Kālī Pūjā, in front of his temple, were two oil paintings about five or six feet tall. On one side was a painting of Rāma-

kṛṣṇa, on the other side was a picture of Vāmākṣepā. They were the guiding figures, the patron saints of the goddess. In front of the temple was a *bali,* where black goats are sacrificed. It is painted red with two white dots on the horns, which project upward. It was full of rock and ash, with ropes, candles, and incense lying around it.

At the temple door were two skulls painted red, with white dots on their foreheads. Near them were large iron bells, a trident hung with iron bracelets (as cures for madness), and heavy grates with locks. The statue of Kālī Mā within was black, and she wore a nose ring, a silver crown, bracelets, and a necklace of silver skulls wound with wreaths of red flowers. Her eyebrows and eyeliner were red, and she wore a red sari. She stood upon a Siva who had white skin and light brown hair. In front of her was the *devī ghat,* a red water pot decorated with flowers, and behind her was a pair of black antelope horns projecting from the wall. With her on the black altar were a jackal (who accompanies ghosts and demons), a statue of Nandi, several *Śiva lingas,* and conches. Small bowls and dead flowers were strewn upon the red mosaic floor.

Its older Śākta substratum was evident in the back room—full of dusty, gray-brown human skulls and bones, painted masks, old coconuts and iron pots, and dead animal parts. Above them was a large picture of Kālī's feet, dark blue but red on the bottom. Nearby was a picture of a skeleton in meditation, sitting upon a corpse; in his navel was a red mandala of Kuṇḍalinī.

In the next room, the mood shifted. There was one picture of Kālī done in a primitive style, amid numerous pictures and photographs of Hindu saints. There was a print of Caitanya (carrying the body of Haridās, from an incident in the *Caitanya Caritāmṛta*), and several prints of the Sacred Heart, with thorns and rising fire in the chests of both Margaret Mary Alacoque and Christ. Between two of these pictures was one of a yogi with a trident. There was also a picture of Sūrya as a charioteer with horses, surrounded by the planetary deities.[119]

The reverse path involves several types of struggle with the Mother and her followers. In its ecstatic aspect, the goal is direct encounter with the goddess, via vision, possession, or willpower. The Śākta seeks to be dominant, rather than submissive, before the deity.

Ritual ecstasy includes the practices of the three Śākta strands: the yogic exercises and meditations on Kuṇḍalinī, the bhakti worship and devotional practices, and the magical rituals with corpses in the burning ground. All evoke ecstatic states and risk madness. The proximity of the states of bliss and insanity may be seen in the lives of the saints.

Biographies of Śākta Saints

Divyonmāda for Tārā: Vāmākṣepā

Vāmākṣepā (Bāmdeb) was the great holy man of Tārāpīṭh. An informant stated:

> The first saint of Tārāpīṭh was Vasistha-muni. He became perfected [*siddha*] at Tārāpīṭh. He sat on a seat[120] made of five skulls: human, monkey, snake, mongoose, and vulture. These are put on the earth near a *bael* tree. One needs power and stamina for such a meditation—an ordinary man may become mad or crippled if he sits on it. After a lapse of several hundred years, Bāmdeb of Āṭlā became divinely mad [*divyonmāda*] for the goddess Tārā. Bāmdeb was a saint from birth. He made Tārāpīṭh more famous than Vasiṣṭha-muni.[121]

Vāmākṣepā was born in 1837, in the village of Āṭlā near Tārāpura (or Tārāpīṭh) in Birbhum. He was named Bāmācaraṇa by his father, Sarvānanda Chatterji, and his mother, Rājkumārī Devī. He was the second son and had a sister who was later widowed. Because of the sister's religious zeal, she was called *kṣepī,* madwoman. As a child, he was subject to tantrums: when a Kālī image would not answer his prayers, he would roll on the ground, screaming and crying. Thus, even as a child he had the name "mad Bāmā," or Bāmā-kṣepā.[122]

He had little interest in studies, and the family was too poor to afford schooling for him. His father was a professional singer, and Bāmā would often sing songs with him. Bāmā's father was an ecstatic, falling into *bhāvas* while he sang, so that he would forget who and where he was. Even in his daily life he spent so much time in *bhāva* that his wife would beg him to pay some attention to *saṃsāra* so that they would not starve. He called his father a yogi, and when Bāmā rolled on the ground screaming "Jaya Tārā!" his mother became upset, but his father smiled. Sarvānanda also took Bāmā for his first visit to the great cremation ground at Tārāpīṭh.

Bāmā took initiation from the family guru and had his sacred thread ceremony at sixteen years. His father died soon after, and his mother asked him to get work, to keep them from poverty. However, he was absentminded and indifferent toward work and found it difficult to keep a job. He spent much time at Tārāpīṭh, the great burning-ground and shrine of the goddess Tārā Mā. He spent days and nights there, singing and dancing before her image, in the midst of its skulls and bones, half-burned corpses, dogs, jackals, and vultures.

In 1864, Brajabāsī Kailāspati came to Tārāpīṭh as a *sannyāsi* wearing red cloth and *tulsī* beads, who would eat with dogs and jackals. People thought him a *piśāca siddha* (a *siddha* capable of black magic). When Bāmā began to follow him and do as he did, the villagers began to call him Bāmā Mleccha (without caste). Kailāspati was rumored to have brought a dead *tulsī* tree to life, walked on the floodwaters of the Dvāraka River, lived underwater and flown in the sky, and instructed ghosts and demons. When he would give Kailāspati his hookah, Bāmā often saw spirits assembled, who would later jump into trees or disappear into the darkness. Kailāspati explained that they had done meditation in this burning ground in past lives, but died being afraid and came to him for advice.

Bāmā's actions became upsetting to the villagers. He saw a boy in the road who claimed to be the Nārāyaṇa deity of one of the houses, who asked Bāmā to take him with him and give him a drink. Bāmā dipped the stone idol given to him by the boy into the river; then he went back to the village and took all the roadside statues of deities with him, installing them on a sand altar at the river's edge. The villagers were furious that their deities had vanished, even a deity that had been inside a house. Bāmā hid in the hut of "Śrī Guru Bābā" and blamed it on Nārāyaṇa. Kailāspati returned the statues to the villagers, who watched their statues more carefully after that.

In a dream, Bāmā saw Tārā, who told him to set fire to the paddy in the village. He set the fire with the coal from Kailāspati's hookah and saw himself as Hānuman setting fire to Lanka. The fire spread through the village, and the villagers spent much time trying to put it out. In the midst of the flames he saw the goddess Tārā, and he danced in ecstasy before her. He told the villagers that he would atone for the fire by jumping into it, which he did shouting, "Jaya Tārā." They could not find his burnt body, but he was later seen running to Kailāspati's hut. They wondered if he were a ghost, or somehow alive, or had himself learned magic. Bāmā himself later said that he felt Tārā Mā's hands lift him out of the fire and throw him into the forest.

Bāmā's mother tried to have him locked up, as she thought him mad, but he escaped to Kailāspati. She feared Kailāspati, and only watched from a distance. Bāmā called her "small mother" (*choto mā*), and he called Tārā "big mother" (*baro mā*).

Bāmā took initiation from Kailāspati and saw a great light condensed into the form of the Tārā mantra, which was his personal mantra. He saw a demoness with long teeth and fiery eyes, and later the environment was transformed—the bushes became *ḍākinīs* and *yoginiīs,* and he heard the voice of Tārā, who told him that she lived forever in the *salmoli* tree and that she would be its fiery light. The tree shot forth flames, and he saw a blue light, which took on Tārā Mā's form. Wearing a tiger skin, she stood on a corpse with four arms, matted hair, three eyes, and a protruding tongue. She wore snake ornaments and an erect snake on her head. She embraced him and vanished at dawn.[123] Some accounts say that this was preceded by a vision of Kailāspati walking on water in the form of Bhairava, who was wearing wooden sandals. Bāmā also learned about religion from Vedagya Mokṣyānanda, who taught him religious texts—the Vedas, purāṇas, and tantras.

Bāmā was subject to mood swings, alternating devotional love and exhilaration with anger and hatred. He would curse Tārā and her ancestors, throw bones and skulls, and frighten away visitors. He would call Tārā *strī,* meaning earthly woman or prostitute, and say that she was a demoness who had harmed him and that he would have his revenge by calling down a thunderbolt on her head. He would rage and then sink into a trance.

Bāmā became the priest at Tārā's temple in Tārāpīṭh, and his stay there was marked by confrontation. He roamed about the cremation grounds happily, making friends with the dogs, naming them and spending time with them, and sharing his food with them. He would eat the food to be offered to the deity before the worship ceremony (*pūjā*) was finished, thus making it impure. The caretakers of the temple were angry at this and beat him severely. He insisted that Tārā Mā asked him to take the food in this way. After this, the temple owner, the Rānī of Nātore, had a dream:

> She dreamt that the stone image of Mother Tārā was leaving the temple of Tārāpīṭh and going to Kailāsa. Tārā Mā looked very sad, with tears flowing down her face, and she wore no mark on her forehead. She was bewildered and emaciated. Her back was bleeding and full of cuts, and vultures and jackals followed behind her, lapping up the blood from her wounds.
>
> In fear, the Rānī asked, "O Mā, why do you show me these terrible things, and why are you leaving us?"
>
> The goddess answered, "My child, I have been in this sa-

> cred place [*mahāpīṭha*] for ages. Now your priests have beaten my dear mad son, and as a mother I have taken these blows upon myself. See how my back is bleeding—I am in great pain. . . . For four days I have been starving, because they have not allowed my mad son to eat my ritual food for four days. So I have refused to take their offerings of food. . . . My child, how can a mother take food before feeding her child? You must arrange for food to be offered to my son, before it is offered to me, at the temple. If not, I will leave there permanently."[124]

Bāmā got his job as priest back, and people began to visit him, to come as devotees, or simply to see him.

He performed worship after this, and a crowd gathered to see it. Bāmā did not follow the traditional rituals; he sat straight before the image and said laughingly, "So girl, you are having great fun, you will enjoy a great feast today. But you are just a piece of stone, without life, how can you eat the food?" He then ate all the food offered to the goddess and asked an assistant to sacrifice a goat—again, without the traditional rites. He did not say any Sanskrit mantras, only a few in Bengali. He threw some leftover food to the Mother, saying, "Well, Mā, take that."

He took a handful of flowers marked with sandal paste and stood before the goddess. He cursed her and threw the flowers at the body of the statue. He wet the flowers with his tears. Although these flowers were thrown in a haphazard way, with abuses rather than mantras, they arranged themselves into a neat and beautiful garland around the neck of the goddess, and the observers were amazed at the *mantra-hīna* (mantraless) worship of the madman, Kṣepā-bābā. He then went into a trance, which continued all day, and he emerged from it on the next day. He was not a priest who followed schedules—often the time for worship would pass and nobody could find Kṣepā-bābā anywhere. He would later be seen in trance under the hibiscus tree, or in the jungle, having arguments with the goddess.

Nīlamādhava, a villager, wished to know if Bāmā was a saint, so he hired the prostitute Sundarī to seduce Bāmā. On seeing her, Bāmā said, "Mā, you have come." He then began to suck her breast so vigorously that blood came out. In pain, Sundarī began to shout, "Save me!" His devotees were shocked to see a prostitute there and told her to leave.[125]

A variety of stories about Vāmākṣepā are told by Bengali Śakta *bhakta*s. They say that he drank liquor and ate human flesh from corpses, that he had supernatural powers, that he was in a continuous state of *bhāvāveśa* for his entire life. Perhaps the story most often repeated was his unique worship of the image in the Tārā temple, when he took his own urine in his hand and threw it at the image, saying, "This is the holy water of the Ganges." Alternative stories say that he answered a crowd's protests by saying, "When a child urinates or defecates while sitting on the Mother's lap, is she defiled? Can a mother think that she has been defiled by her loving child?"

Another story told by many informants describes his mother's death ceremony:

> Bāmdeb was in the Tārāpīṭh burning ground, amid rain and thunder, meditating. Eight miles away, over the river Daroga, his mother died. Bāmdeb knew instantly, for he heard her voice as she died. He swam the river during the storm to get her body and swam back with her body to get her cremated at Tārāpīṭh, a holy place. The family and relatives objected, but he would not listen and shoved them aside, taking the body. Ten days after her death, there were last rites and food for hundreds of people. Rain clouds gathered, and a storm broke. But Bāmdeb made a circle with a bone, and no rain fell inside that circle. All around was pouring rain, but in the circle all was dry.[126]

Because of his continuous *bhāva,* normal etiquette could be rejected. He would share the food offered to him with dogs, jackals, crows, and low-caste people, all from the same leaf, and would eat temple offerings on the burning grounds, sharing it with whoever or whatever wished to eat. He would smoke hashish and drink liquor from the broken neck of the bottle, or from a skull. Yet he became respected and was called Śrī Śrī Bābā Vāmākṣepā. It was believed that he had gained perfection and had regained all past memories. He was harsh to disciples who did not appear sufficiently dedicated:

> One person came and asked for initiation, saying that he wanted to renounce the world. Bāmā told him to bathe in the river. When he returned, Bāmā gave him a kick and told him angrily to leave and never come back. Bāmā's disciples protested, and he told them that this man was still thinking of his business in Calcutta while taking his ritual bath.[127]

He also had unique curing techniques; these stories, too, were told by several Śākta informants:

> A person came to Bāmdeb with a swollen scrotum. He had no money and said, "I am in great pain because of this." Bāmdeb stared at him and then kicked him in the scrotum. At first the man doubled up in pain, but then he was cured. . . . When a devotee was bitten by a snake, Bāmdeb took the poison into himself, and he turned blue in trance.[128] He cured another patient by squeezing his throat, although it looked to his devotees as if he were trying to murder him.[129]

His rituals were famous for their sacrilegious (*aśāstrīya*) character, but as they were done in a state of *bhāva,* they nevertheless had great powers—to cure illness, to stop epidemics and natural disasters, to affect crowds. At the Kālīghat temple, while in a state of *bhāva,* he tried to lift the statue of the Mother and take her on his lap. When stopped by the priests, he shouted, "I do not want your jet-black Kālī. She looks like a demoness coming to devour [someone]. My Tārā Mā is beautiful, with small feet. I do not want your black Kālī—my Ākāśa Tārā is good enough for me."[130]

People would call on him, asking him to pray to their household images, to enliven them with his *bhāva.* He would fall into trance when he visited their statues, and often he performed neither worship nor chanting of mantras. He would loudly call into the air for the Mother, and many observers saw the statue appear to take the form of a human being. He could create such a powerful mood that even sarcastic people who came to laugh at him found the scene impressive.

Bāmā, who practiced a form of *kuṇḍalinī* yoga, was interviewed by Promode Chatterji. The author tells some of Bāmā's ideas in his book of interviews with saints, *Tantrābhilāsir Sādhu-saṅgha:*

> Mā is asleep in the *mūlādhāra cakra*[131] and should be awakened—if she is not awake, who is there to give one liberation? Only she can do this. . . . The first sign of the awakening of Kuṇḍalinī is that the person does not feel satisfied with the ordinary state of life—one gets a great urge within to get over this confinement. . . . The awakening of Kuṇḍalinī gives men great pleasure, a kind of pleasure that ordinary men never attain . . . as you pass through and move from one *cakra* to another, you feel[132] the manifestations of the varied *bhāvas* of Kuṇḍalinī Śakti. But what is important, as a result of Kuṇḍalinī Śakti's functions in every *cakra,* is the kind of *bhāva* it creates, a different *bhāva* in each place, and the feeling of these *bhāvas* brings such a state of bliss that it cannot be described.[133]

He felt that the soul departs the body through the spinal channel at death, through an aperture[134] in the skull, and it enters a state of emptiness and peace, *nirvikalpa samādhi.* This is the home of Tārā Mā, which is beyond the material world, the heaven worlds, and the home of Kālī. Tārā's grace is necessary to reach this state.

Even in later life, he retained the madness of his youth. He would walk through monsoon rain and thunder, calling on the Mother or cursing her. At one point, he gathered all the warm clothes and shawls that he could find, which had been donated by his devotees, and set fire to them. As the flames rose high up in the air, he began shouting happily, "See how bright is Tārā Mā's image in the flames." His followers tried to stop him, but he told them that he was performing the ritual fire (*homa*) with clothes.

Shortly before his death, he became withdrawn and spent most of his time in trance and meditation. He ceased to talk with his disciples, speaking only rarely about death and Tārā Mā. His love-hate relationship with her continued until his death in 1911.

Vāmākṣepā was a Śākta with strong shamanic tendencies, who became the symbol of devotion for millions of Bengali Śāktas. Divine madness was present in him from childhood, when he would have tantrums because the stone image of the goddess would not speak to him. He was associated with impurity (sharing food with jackals, eating the flesh of corpses, refusing to bathe, using urine in ritual, performing corpse rituals, and daily consuming wine and hashish) and shamanic powers (reading minds, acquiring knowledge at a distance, perceiving ghosts, spirits, *ḍākinīs,* and *yoginīs,* having skill in nature-magic and healing). His healings often incorporated aggressive acts: one patient was cured by being kicked in the scrotum, another by being strangled. His techniques of worship also included aggressive elements: he would curse both goddess and devotees, and set fires in which to have visions. Yet he is the saint seen by many Śāktas as the ideal child of the Mother, more faithful to his goddess than any other devotee.

Skin Like Vermilion Mangoes: Nityagopāl

Nityagopāl, known more formally as Yogācārya Avadhūta Jñānānanda Deva, was born in Panihati, Bengal, in 1856. His parents were Janamejaya Basu and Gourīmaṇi, Janamejaya's third wife. Both were described as religious people. Nityagopāl was conceived after his mother went to Benares to pray to Vīreśvara Śiva for a son (as Gourī already had two daughters). Nityagopāl was born prematurely, before the lying-in room had been built. He was a tiny infant, at first lost amid the rags and blood at birth. When he was found, Janamejaya's mother thought Gourī had given birth to a girl, and she left the child on the floor and bewailed her misfortune. But a nurse noticed that the child was male, and then all rejoiced.[135]

As he grew older, he would fall into trances, and his mother thought him diseased or insane. After three days in trance at the age of two years, he was thought to be dead, but a passing holy man told his parents that he would return to normal. He lived separately from his father, as astrologers had predicted the father's death soon after he met his child. Indeed, the father did finally see the child when he was about three years old, and the father died shortly afterward.

Nityagopāl did well in school, although he often arrived late due to his trances, and he was given much attention by his widowed mother. When Gourī shut him up in a room one day for his mischief, he had a vision of Rāma and Lakṣmaṇa, Śiva and Durgā, Rādhā and Kṛṣṇa. Then the goddess Ādyā Kālī took him in her lap and nursed him at her breast. When his grandmother heard him laughing, she opened the door, and the deities disappeared.

Gourī died when Nityagopāl was eight years old, after she had a vision of Kālī. After this, he moved to Calcutta to live with his grandmother. He studied religious texts, until in his teens financial problems caused him to drop out of school and become a government worker. His grandmother tried to pressure him into marriage; she dressed him up in costly dress and kept him in the house, inviting the prospective bride and her relatives. When they arrived, he took the clothing off, put it on his head as a turban, and sat naked before the visitors. They asked if he were mad, and he answered, "Yes." He never married.

One day at the temple of Trikoneśwar at Kālīghat, he saw a yogi in trance, who initiated him into renunciation (*sannyāsa*). The yogi was Paramahaṁsācārya Śrīmad Brahmānanda Svāmī Mahārāj. After the initiation, Nityagopāl locked himself in his room, watching it glow different colors. His neighbors accused him of madness. He had a vision of Kālī in which she was ornamented, with her head reaching to the sky; she was laughing and shaking the heavens. After this, he began to travel and lead an austere life. He went on pilgrimage, seeing gods and hermits and sages. He practiced a variety of austerities—eating only clay and water, wearing little clothing, meditating while standing in deep water. In later life he stated that these practices were not necessary to reach *samādhi*, but were *bhāvas* assumed for the sake of others. He lived primarily in Calcutta, Navadvīpa, and Vārāṇasī.

He claimed to be neither Śākta nor Vaiṣṇava, and stated: "Bābājī Mahāsaya, I regard Kālī as Mother, Śiva as Father, Ganesh as brother, and Kriṣṇa as Husband. I cannot behave like a wife of this iron age." [136]

His spiritual states were recognized by Rāmakṛṣṇa, whom he would often visit. Although there was rivalry between the devotees of the two, they could share spiritual states and understand each other:

> With Rāmakriṣṇa in Dakshiṇeśwar, he would fall into *bhāva*. When Hriday, Rāmakriṣṇa's nephew, tried to touch him to bring him out of trance, Hriday's tongue came out of his mouth elongated. Rāmakriṣṇa realized that Thākur was contemplating Śrī Śrī Nrishingha Deva, so had the people sing a hymn in praise of the avatar, and Hriday returned to normal. [137]

They would fall into trances together and speak in a language not intelligible to others. Rāmakṛṣṇa would call him Śankara, Nitya Paramahaṃsa, or Nitya-haṃsa. In some cases, Nityagopāl was less traditional than Rāmakṛṣṇa; when a low-caste boy brought sweets (*jilāpis*) to Rāmakṛṣṇa, the latter rejected the gift and ordered the spot where they lay washed and cleaned with cow dung and Ganges water. The low-caste boy was so upset that he thought of suicide, but Nityagopāl offered him shelter. When Rāmakṛṣṇa heard this, he said, "I shall grant My grace to a chosen few, but Nitya will prepare cakes with rotten cow-dung." [138] However, Rāmakṛṣṇa did direct people to Nityagopāl for *mantra* initiation.

During singing of hymns (*kīrtanas*) Nityagopāl would have ecstatic symptoms: bristling hair, trembling and shivering, babbling like a child, teeth chattering violently. His skin would swell, taking on the color of vermilion mangoes. His disciples describe his limbs lengthening and shortening, and his skin turning white and dark, red and blue. He would dance in two styles—in a feminine manner, softly and sweetly, and vigorously, like Śiva. [139] He was subject to possession trance as well. At the temple of Bhāvatāriṇī, the *Caṇḍī* of the *Mārkaṇḍeya Purāṇa* was being read. Nityagopāl became possessed by the goddess Caṇḍī and began to dance. Blood gushed out of his mouth as he went about in trance-dance. Disciples said that at a later Kālī *kīrtana*, he assumed a female form and said: "I, your mother, am here to deliver you. . . . You shall have to observe no practices whatsoever for the achievement of your supreme end. I shoulder the whole responsibility."[140]

Nityagopāl would lisp "Mā, Mā," and act like a child sucking at his mother's breast; his disciples would see the forms of deities in him—Ardhanārīśvara, Śiva and Durgā, Rādhā and Kṛṣṇa, Kālī and Nitai-Gauranga. At a Kālī *kīrtana,* one disciple saw him as Mother and, in *bhāva,* jumped onto his lap and began to suck at his chest. Another disciple saw him as the four-handed Tārā from the waist up, with bright blue skin, matted hair, and three eyes. Nityagopāl stated that he assumed all *bhāvas* for the guidance and enlightenment of others.

He felt that he could perceive all phenomena: "As fire permeates a flintstone, so do I pervade the Universe as consciousness . . . even a tiny ant, that moves in an impenetrable cave of the Himalayas, is within the ken of My vision. Mine is an unobstructed vision everywhere."[141]

At one point he ate a whole potful of raw goat meat sacrificed to Ānandamayī Kālī of Nimtala at Calcutta. When he drooled in *bhāva,* devotees would take it as ritual food (*prasāda*), saying that it was intoxicating and tasted like wine.

In his book *Divya Darśana* (divine vision), Nityagopāl gives a visualization of himself:

> Nityagopāl is supremely beautiful. His brilliant splendor is like champaka flower and molten gold. Bliss is emanating from his lotus face. His circular face is manifesting heaps of light, surpassing millions of suns. His beauty is supernatural. His matchless *mahābhāva* is incomparable. He is the Lord of Wisdom and the Bliss of Knowledge. All divine ecstatic states flow from him. . . . He is all-powerful, nothing is impossible for him. In order to attain him, I meditate on his Image of Knowledge.[142]

He interpreted his name in a non-Vaiṣṇava way: *nitya* indeed meant "eternal," but *go* meant "heaven," "paradise," "religion," or "virtue" rather than "cow," and *pāl* merely meant "preserver." His approach to religion was a universalist one. He felt that there were three forms of *samādhi:* merger, in which the soul enters the absolute by concentration; devotional union associated with ecstatic states; and spontaneous meditative union due to revelation by the deity. Merging comes as a result of meditation on Kuṇḍalinī, while in devotion, the devotee gains the *bhāva* of the Supreme Śakti or Prakṛti (a feminine identity), to have divine union with Kṛṣṇa in the heart or with Śiva in the other *cakras.* The devotee may identify with Rādhā or her other forms—Durgā, Kālī, Gourī, Bhuvaneśvarī, Sītā, Ṣoṛaśī. Such love creates a religious madness in which the devotee weeps and laughs at the same time, and speaks like a child.

Spontaneous remembrance of the deity does not evolve out of prayers, repeated practice, or meditation, but is an inborn attachment. As one dos not gain love and devotion toward his parents by practice, so love toward the deity is natural and spontaneous. It is primarily a blissful union: "But the unification of the individual soul with the Supreme Self is the true, perfect or highest union. And the enjoyment of the bliss [pleasure] from this unification may be called spiritual copulation [*ādhyātmika-maithūna*] out of which comes the daughter, the supreme peace."[143]

He emphasizes the state of absorption, in which the person is like a corpse or an inert object. With the mind concentrated, the breath is suspended and the body paralyzed without sensation. This is "divine deafness and blindness." However, the intense love associated with absorption also creates intoxication, boyishness, and madness.

Nityagopāl died in 1911, regarded by his disciples as a hidden avatar. He is buried at Mahānirvāṇ Math in Calcutta, where his full-size statue is worshiped and given offerings each day.

Nityagopāl was a yogi, a Śākta *avadhūta,* who equated Śākta and Vaiṣṇava paths. He had a few visions in childhood, although most are described after his initiation. His disciples claim him to be *nitya siddha*—a person enlightened from birth, for whom spiritual practice was unnecessary. Most of his visionary and possession states took place during hymns, although many spontaneous experiences were described. Madness was a necessary claim to keep him from marriage, and in later life it was a part of his devotion.

The Burning Ground of the Heart: Rāmprasād Sen

Rāmprasād is the great poet of the burning ground (*śmaśāna*), who turned Kālī from an esoteric symbol into a devotional goddess. His songs are sung by lovers of Tārā and Kālī, who believe him to have experienced all of the states about which he wrote. He is said to have died of an overdose of *bhāva.*

There is little data on Rāmprasād's life—he had no devotees who wrote biographies. Also, some debate has occurred over whether there were really two different writers named Rāmprasād. However, most Śāktas believe there was only one writer, a great devotee and saint, and the major events of his life were consistently repeated by informants. Later Śāktas have written biographies of Rāmprasād, and these are used here.[144]

Rāmprasād Sen was born in Halisahar, West Bengal (then called Kumarhatta), in the year 1720, in a Vaidya Śākta family. His father, Rāma Rāma Sen, was an Āyurvedic physician, and his mother, Siddheśvarī, was the second wife. She also bore a son Viśvanāth, while the first wife had borne three children.

Rāmprasād went first to Vidyānidhi's Sanskrit school, where he learned grammar, literature, and Bengali poetry. He was a bright child who rarely needed to study. His father then sent him to a Maulavi, to learn Urdu and Persian—the languages of the Muslim rulers. Although his father wanted him to be a physician, Rāmprasād was more interested in language and literature.

He was married to Sarvanī, and both were initiated into the Kālī mantra by the family guru, Madhvācārya. Rāmprasād learned Śākta ritual practice from several gurus; many stories include Kṛṣṇānanda Āgambāgiśa as one of his gurus (although he died in the fifteenth century). Rāmprasād spent much time in Śākta worship and meditation.

When his father died, the burden of maintaining the family fell on Rāmprasād's shoulders. Initially he rebelled against this and sang to the Mother:

> I will not take your name again, for you hurt me;
> I call upon you repeatedly, but you cannot hear;
> Why should the son suffer while his Mother is alive?[145]

However, he soon found a job as a clerk in Calcutta, for Durgā Caraṇa Mitra of Garanhati. However, he would feel love for Kālī during office hours and would sit staring ahead, sometimes writing poems to Kālī in his account books. He would spend hours in a trance state. Fellow workers accused him of absentmindedness and inefficiency (according to some versions, dishonesty), and when the landlord looked at the account books to verify this, he was impressed by the poetry written there. He gave Rāmprasād a monthly pension of thirty rupees to go home and write poetry full time.

When Rāmprasād retired to write, he spent long hours meditating in his room or neck-deep in the Ganges. The boatmen on the river would pause to listen to his hymns. During one of his evening hymns on the Ganges banks, he was overheard by Mahārāja Kṛṣṇacandra of Nadia.

The mahārāja called him to Kṛṣṇanāgar and made him his court poet, giving him the title "Kavirañjana." Many of Rāmprasād's later songs are refutations of the charges of another court poet named Ayodhya Gosvāmin (Anju Gosāin), who condemned Śāktism and wrote satirical songs about it. Rāmprasād was a universalist, equating Śiva, Kṛṣṇa, and Kālī. Although he could also sing Hindi classical music, the Muslims at court preferred to hear his Śākta songs.

The mahārāja granted him thirty-three acres of rent-free land for his family, which initially allowed them to prosper. His mother organized the household, and his wife worked by her orders. But after his mother's death, the situation grew chaotic. The land was not well supervised, there were poor crops, and the rents were not collected. Some land was flooded by the Ganges. Rāmprasād and his family often went without food, and they prayed to Kālī to save them from starvation. Despite the chaos, he spent his time in trances and visions.

He planted five trees, and in their midst he built a ritual seat[146] using the skulls of a monkey, jackal, mongoose, snake, and human. On this he worshiped the Mother at midnight. He practiced various forms of Śakta ritual practice, including the corpse ritual. When some nearby bamboo fence fell down, he was helped in repairing it by his daughter, Jagadīśvarī, whose work on the fence continued although she was called away. He took this as one of the manifestations of Kālī.

At one point, his wife, Sarvanī, perceived Rāmprasād's Kālī statue as alive, with heartbeat and breathing. She screamed and fainted. Rāmprasād came in, took away the Kālī statue, and put his wife in its place. He began to worship her, singing devotional songs. Both sat in trance for the night.

After the death of Kṛṣṇacandra, Rāmprasād became detached from his family and from the world, and spent all his time in meditation. He stopped visiting and entertaining visitors. He spent all of his time in the house or amid the five trees. After his wife's death, he was tended by his daughter-in-law, Bhagavatı Devı, and his son Rāmdulāl. He also had the poor blacksmith Bhajahari, who waited on him. His death in 1766, during the yearly immersion of the Kālī statue, was described in the *Tantra-tattva:*

> It was only when, after having worshipped the Devī . . . he went to throw that image of the Mother of the world into water, and after having placed the Mother's image on the bank of the Ganges, descended into the water until it reached

> his waist . . . then, keeping his eyes fixed on the Mother's image without, he went into Samādhi, having made the Saṁsāra Mudra, and called the Mother within from without. Then immediately the Mother . . . knowing the approaching end of the son's play, appeared all full of smiles in his heart. The fear-dispelling look of the Blissful Devī dispelled the fear of existence. The dance of love of the Dancing Kālī opened the door of his heart. His body, tired with the overflowing bliss of love, began to lose all self-control. His eyes, closed with bliss, filled with tears; then it was that, bringing to an end his beloved Sādhana, the Sādhaka sang to his heart's content for the last time in his life to the ringing chords of his heart.[147]

Rāmprasād's state of mind and religious experiences may best be gauged by his poetry. He wrote such epics as *Kālīkīrtana, Śivakīrtana,* and *Kṛṣṇakīrtana,* but his shorter poems are most well known. Sometimes he is a petulant child, complaining about his mother's lack of affection, and sometimes he is the tantrika practicing the complexities of Kuṇḍalinī yoga. He describes his ecstasies in the first person:

> Black clouds have risen in the skies of my heart,
> The peacock of my mind dances playfully and promenades.
> The sound of the Mother echoes like thunder in the
> mountains,
> And her soft smile of blissful love flashes like lightning.
> Tears flow endlessly,
> Which quickly remove the fearful thirst of the *caṭaka.*[148]
> There are many more births,
> Rāmprasād says, he will not be born of a womb again.[149]

At times he is a universalist, associating divine madness with the saints of all traditions:

> Make me mad, O Divine Mother!
> There is no more use for knowledge and discrimination.
> Make me intoxicated with the wine of Thy love.
> O Mother! Enchanter of the devotee's hearts!
> Immerse me in the ocean of love.
> In this, Thy lunatic asylum, some laugh, some cry, and
> others dance in excess of joy.
> O Mother, Jesus, Moses, and Caitanya were unconscious in
> the ecstasy of love
> Alas, O Mother, when shall I be blessed, mixing with them?

In heaven there is a fair of lunatics, there master and disciple are alike.
Who can fathom the mystery of the play of love?
Thou art mad with love, O Mother, crown of lunatics
Make poor Prasāda rich, O Mother, in the treasure of love.[150]

However, sometimes this madness is associated specifically with Śiva and Śakti:

It is all mad [*kṣepā*] Mā's play.
The three worlds are overwhelmed by her illusions.
The secret drama has been revealed:
That you are mad, your husband is mad, your two disciples are mad.
It cannot be described in any form or fashion or *bhāva*.
I have chanted her name, yet my fate is miserable,
And my throat burns with poison.[151]

As in the tantric literature, such divine madness is associated with the intoxication that comes from drinking alcohol:

Mind, do not be deceived.
Let people call me a drunkard.
I do not drink wine,
But I delight in nectar!
Today my mind is spinning, and I am maddened [*māta*]
Though wine drinkers call me drunk [*mātal*].
Always sit at the feet of Śiva's queen,
Or you will be lost
By drinking the deadly wine of the senses.[152]

For Rāmprasād, the Śākta rituals transformed the wine into another substance, purifying it into nectar. It is this substance that may induce divine intoxication:

O, I do not drink wine, but rather nectar, chanting "Jaya Kālī!"
My intoxicated heart makes me drunk
And drunkards call me plastered!
With *guṛ* [hardened molasses] given by the guru
I am mixing spices, Mā.
My distiller of knowledge is dripping into the still.
When I drink it, my mind becomes mad.

Filled with sound and image[153] I sanctify it by saying, "Tārā
Mā!"
Rāmprasād says of such wine,
"If you drink it, you shall gain the four goals of life."[154]

During a period of famine, he wrote a poem on devouring the goddess and called himself a *gaṇḍāyogi* (one born in a planetary arrangement that predicts the son will cause the mother's death):

This time, Kālī, I shall eat you.
You, who are so compassionate to the poor
I shall eat!
I was born in *gaṇḍāyoga,* Tārā.
If a son is born at this time
He will devour his mother!
This time, either you will eat me, or I will eat you
One or the other must happen.
I will cook Ḍākinī and Yoginī into a curry
And then I will eat them!
I shall seize your necklace of skulls
And make them into a sour sauce.
I am telling you, Mā, I shall eat you.
But I will not swallow you.
I shall sit you in my heart-lotus,
And mentally worship you.
Though you tell me that if I eat Kālī
I shall be touched by Death's hand
What have I to fear? I shall say Kālī's name, and show Death
the banana.[155]

Kālī is the mad Mother, who dwells inside the person:

She's playing in my heart.
Whatever I think, I think Her name.
I close my eyes and She's in there
Garlanded with human heads.

Common sense, know-how—gone.
So they say I'm crazy. Let them.
All I ask, my crazy Mother,
Is that You stay put.

Rāmprasād cries out: Mother, don't
Reject this lotus heart You live in,

Don't despise this human offering
At Your feet.[156]

Rāmprasād describes the visions of tantric meditation:

> Jagadamba's watchmen go out into dread, black night, Jagadamba's watchmen! "Victory! Victory to Kali!" they cry, and, clapping their hands and striking upon their cheeks, they shout *Bam, Bam*. That worshippers may tremble, the flowery chariot is in the sky and in it rides the ghosts, in it too are *bhairavas* and *vetālas*. Upon their heads is the half-moon crest, in their hands the dreadful trident; to their feet hangs down their matted hair. With them first come the serpents strong as death, then follow mighty tigers, monstrous bears. They roll their red eyes before the worshippers, who, half-dead with fear, cry out, no longer able to sit at their devotions. . . .
>
> Ramprasad, a poet and her slave, is swimming in a sea of happiness. Can misfortune come to one who worships? What cares he for these dread things? He sits *vīrāsana* at his devotions and takes the name of Kālī as his shield.[157]

For Rāmprasād, the goal of tantric yoga was not *samādhi,* but rather love of the goddess. It is a secret *bhāva,* a part of the older system of esoteric practice:

O mind, won't you search for her nature![158]
O madman, you are in a dark room.
In the room is a secret chamber
It is hidden from the light of day.

The object of this *bhāva* is beyond *bhāva*
But can she be grasped without *bhāva?*
From the beginning, my heart was enchanted by the moon,
Thinking of the depths of your power.
I got nothing from the six philosophies,
From the tantras or the Tantrasāra.
[But] in devotion, the lover is in constant bliss.

There is a *bhāva* which the greatest yogi desires,
He performs yoga for it age after age.
If this *bhāva* appears, the yogi grabs it
As iron is drawn by a magnet.
Rāmprasād says, I search for her secret in mother—
bhāva. . . .
O mind, understand by means of signs and gestures.[159]

He is believed by many Śāktas to have practiced a variety of spiritual techniques:

> Rāmprasād performed tantric practices [*divya-kulācāra sādhana*]. At the highest stage of this practice were experiences of *bhāva* and *tattva,* and the goals of this worship were union with the Mother and drinking the pure nectar. . . . Rāmprasād's songs were songs of life experience. He had visions of Mahāśakti and gained the essence of Śiva and Śakti.[160]

Such experiences were believed to be the source of his poetry, and he was called the *svabhāva kavi*—the poet of the true, inner self. His spontaneous trances and visions are seen by modern Śāktas as divine madness (*divyonmāda*) or the attainment of perfection (*siddhi lābh karā*), for the Mother is there when he calls and dwells within him in all situations:

> Blissful Divine Mother dwells in my heart, and always plays there.
> I never forget her name in whatever condition I live.
> When I close my eyes, I see Her with a garland of skulls in my heart.
> My worldly wisdom is gone, all call me mad;
> Let them call me whatever they please; let me get my mad Mother at the end.[161]

Rāmprasād was a devotee, although he practiced yoga and rituals involving sexuality and death (*vāmācāra*). His ecstatic states are first described after his initiation, when he would have visions and fall into trances during the day and during work. At that time, there was no developed system of Śākta devotion; meditation on the goddess was esoteric, by mantra and *kuṇḍalinī* visualizations. To express his religious experiences, Rāmprasād joined the poetic (*pada*) style of the Vaiṣṇavas, which emphasized spontaneous grace and devotional love, with the lyric style of the Buddhist *cārya* songs and their emphasis on divine mystery. He originated Śākta poetry (*śāktapadāvalī*) as a literary genre.[162] He wrote songs of divine play (*līlā*), using mythic themes about the goddess, and of meditation (*sādhana*) which expressed his experiences during tantric practice. His poetry proved that he was not mad, but rather inspired.

Out of the Cradle, Endlessly Rocking: Madness and Ecstasy among Bengali Śāktas

All Śāktas are children of the Mother, who creates and destroys the universe. However, the relationship between Mother and child is interpreted differently in the different Śākta strands. The devotee is rocked in a fiery cradle, seeing the Mother's power and beauty in the flames of destruction. Her inner tenderness and nurturing are sensed beyond her frightening exterior; the devotee's love burns for her. For the yogi, her fires destroy the attachments that bind him to the world; her fires are in his ascetic practices (*tapas*) and in his burning of the seeds of future karmic actions. For the magician or exorcist, fire is the greater power, which chases away lesser spirits and empowers his magical rites.

The mad, fiery love of the Mother is a stage in the process of bringing her into the heart. The worshiper attracts her by his madness—being mad herself, she recognizes a kindred spirit. The more intense his passion and the more irrational his behavior, the more he is her child. Yet after this is the state of divine madness (*divyonmāda*), in which the fires are cooled and the devotee is eternally a child on the Mother's lap; he need not yearn for her, as he has been accepted. At this stage, his madness is action that is beyond human understanding, totally free and spontaneous, beyond good and evil. All acts are in relation to the Mother, rather than toward other persons. While the person's body is on earth, his mind is in Kailāsa, and he communicates with deities rather than people. His acts do not follow any earthly order.

Both Śākta and Vaiṣṇava informants quoted the rules of mad behavior from the *Bhāgavata Purāṇa,* on the four states of inertia, madness, impurity, and childlike behavior (*jaḍa/unmātta/piśāca/bālaka*). One Śākta informant described his experience of these states as a part of his own condition of mad desire for the goddess (*bhagavān pāgal*).[163] He described the state of madness as love in separation (*viraha*), when the deity has been seen, but is now gone. The person always thinks of the beauty of the goddess and wonders, "Will she come again?" In the state of divine madness (*kṣepā* or *divyonmāda*), love in union, the deity is achieved, and the worshiper is always with the goddess, or has access to her. He associated the mad symptoms with the state of desire: in the inert (*jaḍa*) state, he was like a corpse, finding it hard to break out of the meditative trance to deal with the world; in the crazed (*unmatta*) state, he would laugh and cry and speak incoherently, and there was no social concern or decorum—he forgot responsibility to home and family; in the impure or demonic (*piśāca*) state, he was fascinated by filth and would immerse himself in it; in the childlike (*bālaka*) state he developed childish appetites, alternately fasting and gorging himself.[164]

Several Śākta practitioners discussed their understandings of divine madness:

> A person who is divinely mad (*divyonmāda*) performs spiritual practices: he goes to the cremation ground, temples, places where religious discussions are held. He will do rituals in the burning ground with a corpse, and it will speak and tell him everything. But an ordinary man will not visit such places and do rituals. He is mad for a reason, such as loss of wife or service.[165]
>
> The one who is mad for the goddess [*divyonmāda*] has only the awareness of the goddess and no sense of body. He talks to deities and gestures to them; he gets along well with animals, and he will play with snakes and they will not bite him. He dedicates his food, and everything else, to Bhagavān. However, an ordinary madman [*pāgal*] is without sense, he is "crack-minded,"[166] his brain has failed. He will bite and hit people; he has no control over himself.[167]
>
> The person who is *divyonmāda* is in a state of religious insanity [*pāgla bhāva*]. In this state, there is no separate self, no manifestation. All action leads to direct religious experience. Sometimes he is naked, sometimes he acts insane, sometimes he speaks as the goddess, or as a child. He sees no distinctions between stool and meat, and has no envy or fear. But a madman [*kṣepā*] has "brain-*khārāp*" [his mind is bad]; he will do wrong actions. He does not see himself, for he does not do meditation, which is like a mirror—it allows a person to see himself.[168]

The madman will appear as divinely mad (*divyonmāda*) to other *tāntrikas,* but he will seem mad in an ordinary sense (*pāgal*) to others:

> Normal people cannot tell the difference, they do not have the ability to distinguish. . . . But really there are three different states. In religious madness [*divyonmāda*], the deity is attained [*siddhi labh kara*], and the person's sight of her is continuous—she is always there for him. In madness [*pāgal*], there is continual striving. In ordinary insanity [*unmāda*], there is a disturbance of the brain, rather than the soul. The person talks to himself, and his appearance and movements are strange. He does not seek after the goddess.[169]

Sometimes the state of divine madness is the peace after the storm. Mahendranātha Bhaṭṭācārya (Premika) writes of these states:

> You're not going to get mad [*kṣepā*] Mā,
> Unless you go mad yourself.

If you only pretend to be crazy
Nothing will result from that.
You haven't listened to matters of *bhāva*,
Your strivings are like the labor pains of a barren woman.
You don't open up your eyes
To the essence of Śiva's teachings.
You are like a mute, you do not respond to the summons.
Go inwards, and travel the path of the spirit
Dance, mad with love
And shout Kālī always.
There is enjoyment in this madness
You will come to know it when you become a true madman.
Saying, "Come, mad one"
You will be taken into the lap of the crazy Mother.
When the period of madness is over
The burning of the three pains will disappear.
You will then enter the abode of peace
Premika tells of this union.[170]

Sometimes divine madness is seen as closer to a trance state. A Kālī priest and healer stated:

> When a person is *divyonmāda*, then his external knowledge has fallen away, and knowledge of *brahman* has emerged. Even his external appearance changes. His body appears as if dead. He does not react if he is pinched or touched by fire. His face looks like that of a skeleton, and his eyes are fiery when they are open.[171]

And sometimes it is seen as pure ecstatic love, as Rāmprasād writes:

Will such a time come, O Tārā!
When tears will stream from my eyes on uttering thy name,
    Tārā, Tārā, Tārā!
When my heart-lotus will bloom, the mind's darkness will
    vanish
And I shall roll on the ground in the ecstasy of joy, crying
    Tārā!
When I shall cast aside all distinctions, and my heart's pangs
    will disappear!
Hundreds of scriptures declare, 'My Tārā is formless.'
Rāmprasād says, 'Mother exists in all forms.
O blind eyes, do see Mā; She dispels all darkness in the
    dark.'[172]

There are also a variety of Śākta meanings for the term *bhāva*. It may refer to thought, behavior, desire for the deity, ability to visualize the deity, detachment from the physical world. One practitioner, who sang both Śākta and Vaiṣṇava hymns, felt that *bhāva* was an inner substance, like a liquid, which leaves through the pores of the body; however, the deity did not cause the flowing, but rather prevented it:

> *Bhāva* is like filling a pail full of tap water—when it fills up, the sound will be changed. The body is a vessel that can understand things, and whenever you feel or understand, you have a sort of *bhāva*. But it is not called *bhāva* until it is overflowing. When the pail flows over, the eight *sāttvika bhāvas* emerge—these are the eight ways of overflowing. They are divine and supernatural.[173] *Bhāvas* are temporary because the body is full of pores. It is like a beautiful glass with holes in it—there is leakage. You put water in it, and it comes out. The body is made in such a way that whatever you fill it up with, it will come out.
>
> Feelings [*bhāvas*] and intense feelings [*mahābhāva*] come out through the pores of the body. But if the memory is powerful [*śakti*] an energy remains. . . . If we love the Mother, we can maintain the *bhāva,* concentrating on chanting her name. All the holes are plugged up. Yet one looks just like an ordinary man—all the *bhāva* is inside. Outside, he looks normal, but inside he is in deep trance [*samādhi*]. This is called *sahaja bhāva.*[174]

Another Śākta practitioner in Bākreśwar felt that the seven Śākta styles of behavior were *bhāvas,* so that acting like a Vaiṣṇavite or a Śaivite were appropriate actions for a Śākta, as were practices with corpses and women. In the highest state (*brahmabhāva*) the person loses distinctions and becomes mad—he is always seeking Kālī, and his separate self is destroyed.

The *Rudrayāmala Tantra* emphasizes the importance of *bhāva:*

> Everything is gained by *bhāva,* and the deities are seen through *bhāva,* so it is to be followed. *Bhāva* is the essence of all śāstras, situated in all senses and organs. When the devotee has the *bhāva* of Devī, he has all attainments, and his meditation is firm.[175]

It also mentions a typology:

> There are three categories of the divine [*divya*] state: low, middle, and highest. The first category refers to those who have reached the *divya* state by the study of the Vedas; the second to those who have attained the state by the study of tantra; and the third refers to those whose experience is born suddenly and based on their own discrimination.[176]

Bhāva may be striving or attainment. As one Śākta informant states:

> *Bhāva* is when the worshiper forms an image of his deity in his mind and seeks after the god. Then he does not like to talk to others. He tries to bring his object of worship before his eyes; that light [*jyoti*] which he has seen in slender form, he tries to see magnified. His deity may be Durgā, Kālī, Tārā, or another. If he can bring his god before his mental eye, then he is intoxicated in his *bhāva*. In the ray of light that sometimes flashes before his eyes, he tries to identify the image or the object of his worship. He has no time to look at his own clothing; he does not care if it is clean or soiled. He has no appetite for food. He forgets meals, and when he does eat, he does so carelessly. He is always searching for his goddess. This is *bhāva*.[177]

Bhāva is also associated with the roles one may play toward the goddess, and the *rasa* or mood of these roles. However, the term *rasa* is rarely used by Śāktas; it is not a goal in itself. The major roles are those of child and parent, and goddess and devotee may exchange these roles. Bhagavatī may be the loving guardian of the infant Śākta, or the devotee may be the parent of Kanyākumārī, the beloved daughter. Both of these roles are seen in the poetry of the Bengali Śāktas. Jahnavikumār Cakravarti writes of the two major Śākta *rasas* as *vātsalya* and *prativatsālya*—parental love and its corresponding opposite, the love of the child for its mother. He describes this latter *bhāva,* which is not found among the Vaiṣṇavas:

> The devotee's emotion is like that of a child—his pouting and demands are aimed toward the mother. Sometimes he feels pride, sometimes he makes earnest requests, sometimes he feels anger or desire for her grace, sometimes humility and fear, sometimes dependence. Above all, there is the agitated cry of the child, "Mā, Mā." It suppresses all other cries. [The

> devotee is] a mother-crazy child. At the end of his longest complaint, his final prayer is: "Brush away this dust, take me into your lap, Mā" or "Whatever is good, do that, Mā, I have unloaded my burden at your feet."[178]

In Rāmprasād's *āgamanī* and *vijaya* poetry (which is sung on Durgā Pūjā), the mother feels anxiety and love for her daughter, who lives far away, in a place that is difficult to visit. Both feel great sorrow at this separation; it is the longing of the devotee who is separated from his own divine mother, or from Umā as a young girl.

However, sometimes the rebellious nature of the child toward his mother is emphasized, in which he demands gifts and attention. One Śākta practitioner related this to two tantric lineages:

> In India, there are two schools of Tantra. In the south is Śrī-kula; they worship Lakṣmī, seeking wealth. In the north is Kālī-kula—in Bengal, Assam, Bihar, and Orissa. We worship the ten forms of the goddess [*mahāvidyās*], especially Kālī, Tārā, Cinnamastā, and Bagalā, and our greatest wealth is the wisdom of *brahman* [*brahmajñāna*]. We of the Kālī-kula are different from the Śrī-kula. We start from night and reach toward the day, while they start from light but then go toward night.
>
> The Kālī-kula says, "Let the darkness come first! I will fight against darkness—come with your sword, Mother! I am in the fight, Mā, come and help me. Let all the other *mahāvidyās* follow—but first, let us fight!" If Mā does not come, we say, "I hold a gun to you, goddess, give me knowledge! You are my mother, you are rich, so I am rich—it is my birthright! I have been deprived of my wealth, so now I am poor—but I come from my Mother, and I demand my wealth!"[179]

Struggle with the goddess is also seen in this poem by Rasikcandra Ray:

> Come, Mother, join battle with me as I worship.
> Let us see, Mother, who will be conquered, the mother or
> the son. . . .
> Today the battle shall decide the issue.
> What fear have I of death?
> With beating of drums, I will seize the wealth of salvation.
> In battle after battle you have overthrown the Daityas.
> This time, O Goddess, come and fight with me.

> Rasikcandra your votary says: It is in your strength, Mother
> That I shall conquer you in battle.[180]

At times, Śākta devotion may be toward a saint.[181] A monk of the Rāmakṛṣṇa order described his experience of Rāmakṛṣṇa and Śāradā Devī, both of whom he saw as aspects of the Mother. The monk had been frustrated by his inability to keep a vow of celibacy (sexuality was "a great mango tree, which eternally has new seeds"), and he had given blood and was fasting, hoping to die:

> On the ninth day of the fast, during Dūrgā Pūjā, I had a vision of the universe as flowing water, and then the image of Śāradā Devī. She brought Rāmakṛṣṇa, who said that my true desires would be fulfilled, and she put me in her lap and gave me sweets. After this, all of the men in the streets looked like Rāmakṛṣṇa, and the women all looked like Śāradā Devī. I saw a nude figure on a billboard and wept for how the Holy Mother was dishonored.
>
> This [experience] was repeated a year later, after another Dūrgā Pūjā. I had no sleep for three days and nights. I felt waves of joy and again saw all persons as Rāmakṛṣṇa and Śāradā Devī. For this period, I continuously heard a mantra, the name Rāmakṛṣṇa. For six months following this, I saw Rāmakṛṣṇa in dreams each night. I would look forward to this, as a bride to the coming of her bridegroom.[182]

However, Śākta visionary experience is described most often as occurring in the burning ground at night, when the Mother is seen amid the calls of jackals and dogs. Nigamānanda Sarasvatī, in his book *Māyer Kṛpa,* describes his own initiatory vision (although it is written in the third person). He took initiation from Vāmākṣepā, chanted mantras for twenty-one days, and was taken to the great burning ground at Tārāpīṭh. Vāmākṣepā left him there at midnight, near the ashes of three burned bodies, and told him to meditate on the deity in his heart:

> The young man chanted out in the dark burning ground, listening to the jackals in the distance. He had visions of various terrors. When he broke concentration, Vāmākṣepā would yell out, "Tārā, Tārā" from the temple, and he would again focus his attention. He felt his identity slide away and had a feeling of the supernatural.[183] He felt as if a liquid light were emerging from every pore of his body, rising like a vapor and be-

> coming as bright as lightning. It was like the light of a thousand moons, without beginning or end.
>
> He closed his eyes at the light, and when he opened them, he saw a beautiful woman standing in the midst of the light. He bowed down before her and praised her.[184] He could barely speak, for his voice was choked. He was filled with love, and tears flowed from his eyes. He asked, "Mother, who are you?" (She told him many secrets of knowledge and illusion, body and soul, one and many gods. . . .)
>
> He asked for a vision of her cosmic form, and he saw her image again reduced to the liquid light, and the light spread out across the universe. Her form became vast, with thousands of tongues of fire, grinding teeth, and eyes emitting fire, folding innumerable weapons of tremendous power. Her thousands of heads and bodies were brighter than millions of suns. He was filled with awe, chanted the *Devī stotra,* and fainted.[185]

The vision of the Mother, who appeared in her peaceful form, also told him about divine grace and the nature of devotion (*bhakti*):

> The signs of devotion are seen when a person chants the names of the Mother, and listens to My hymns and songs of praise, when the mind is full of good wishes, and it flows toward Me without a break, like a liquid. He worships without hope of reward, even liberation, for he desires to remain as My servant. . . . Because of his excessive love, his eyes are always full of tears, and his voice is choked. . . . When he attains the state of transcendent devotion [*parābhakti*], he cannot think of anything but Me and becomes absorbed in my aspect of pure consciousness. This kind of devotee gives up all sastric observances and ordinary responsibilities, and he always calls for me, saying "O Mā, O Mā." I come to him as the cow comes to the calf when it calls.[186]

One source for the madness in both Śākta bhakti and Śākta yoga is the *Pāśupata Sūtra.* It is the earliest known work of the Pāśupata sect. Its author is unknown (it is attributed to Lakulīśa), and there is a commentary by Kauṇḍinya. It describes stages of life for the yogi and appropriate behaviors for each of them. The stages involve progressive detachment from the world, and the major means for this separation is apparently mad behavior. The *vratas,* or vows of actions that are to be done in secret, include laughter, song (hymns to Śiva), dance, making sounds (like a bull, the *dunduṅkāra* or *huddukāra* sound), prostration before the deity, and concentration on mantra. A later stage, the *dvāras* (doors) or *upahāras* (gifts), includes feigning sleep, trembling, limping, flirting, and insane acts and speech (especially those associated with impurity).[187] In both, the practitioner is told that he should behave like a lunatic (*unmattavat*), to wander like a ghost or a *preta* (*pretavaccaret*), to act in a way that is hidden or unmanifest (*gūḍha*), and to appear as ignorant or dull (*mūḍha*). He may show the five types of madness—caused by bile, wind, cough, all three of these, or by a strong blow.[188]

The *Pāśupata Sutra* states that such behavior evokes rejection, and thus detachment and the destruction of bad karma (Daniel Ingalls refers to it as the "seeking of dishonor.")[189] However, there may be another dynamic at work here. The practitioner initially is told to keep his *vratas* concealed, but his *dvāras* public. However, he is later told to keep the *dvāras* concealed also (*sarvāṇi dvārāṇi pidhāya*).[190] If they are practiced in secret, they do not bring bad reactions from spectators. Kauṇḍinya states, "The doors get hidden when they are practised well by the false show."[191] It may be that the false practice of these states allows a hidden aspect to emerge—they may either induce the ecstatic states they imitate, or they may hide real states by claiming to be false ones. A spectator would not know if the Pāśupata pretends to tremble or is actually trembling. The Pāśupata *vratas* and *dvāras* may be compared with the Vaiṣṇava *sāttvikas* and *anubhāvas*,[192] as in table 1.

The Pāśupata states of simulated insanity have many parallels with Vaiṣṇava states of ecstasy. Such states may serve more than one function—to express false states and be rejected, but also to hide the true states from the eyes of the world. The goal of the Pāśupata is to attain union with Rudra, to dwell in the cremation ground in yogic stillness, or to wander the world absorbed in the deity (*devanitya*).

In Śāktism, the yogi becomes the *vīra*, the hero, whose one-pointed concentration conquers illusion and temptation, and attains the Mother. There is an opposition in Śāktism between the lover, the *premika*, and the hero, the *vīra;* between the lover's voluntary submission and lack of control, and the hero's desire to determine the relationship. The lover experiences ecstasy by submission to the Mother's will, receiving her love, while the hero experiences ecstasy from his dangerous voyage, the vigil at night, or the ascent of Kuṇḍalinī—the ecstasy of exploring the spiritual terrain.

There is often confusion about the hero's role. This role (*vīrācāra*) is a

TABLE 1 Pāśupata and Vaiṣṇava Ecstatic States

Pāśupatas	Vaiṣṇavas
laughing	laughing
singing	singing
dancing	dancing
making "sounds"	crying, shouting, sighing
prostration	
japa	
feigning sleep	yawning
trembling	trembling
no control of limbs	twisting of body
erotic gestures	
insane acts	disregard for society
speaking nonsense	giddiness
	foaming at the mouth
	hiccoughs
	stupor
	pallor
	perspiration
	horripilation

stage through which the Śākta passes on the way to divine consciousness, which is beyond good and evil, and requires no ritual. Madness and ecstasy are reactions to intense experience, to the identification with deities and visions of heaven-worlds. The hero's rejection of tradition is not the goal of tantric ritual practice, although often it is seen in that way. Benjamin Walker erroneously states of the *tāntrika:* "He must first learn to become indifferent to the traditional taboos. He must then positively reject them. And finally, he must become actively hostile to them."[193]

As the person progresses through the three tantric stages or *bhāvas,* his attitudes toward tradition differ. In the *paśu-bhāva* he accepts traditional morality, for he has not explored other options. In the *vīra-bhāva* he rebels against them, struggling against his own cultural beliefs and presupposition. In the state of *divya-bhāva* he has experienced all possibilities and extremes, and gone beyond traditional moralities to one in which all objects and actions are equally valuable.

Although there is wide acceptance of the idea of three stages of growth, there is little consensus of practices among Śāktas, and there is no single ideal Śākta or yogi whom all practitioners see as a model. Śiva is often seen as the ideal yogi, but in Bengal he is an irresponsible husband who smokes hashish at night with his unattractive friends and barely supports his family. He is Bom Bhola or Pāgla Bhola, who is seen as shiftless, mad, or merely eccentric. He is loved and pitied, but not imitated.[194] Kālī, too, is mad—dancing on the dead and drinking blood. Śāktas desire to be the child of the Mother, but they never imitate Ganeṣa or Skanda. They wish to be related to the goddess, but this relationship is not based on myth. It is new each time, and there are no set stages of proximity to the Mother. There are ritual models, but no mythic role models to be imitated.

There are human saints to be respected, but they are not emulated. Kṛṣṇānanda Āgambāgīśa is often considered the first Śākta, and by many the greatest, but his life is virtually unknown. Śāktas venerate Rāmakṛṣṇa and Vāmākṣepā, but they do not practice Islam or urinate on temple statues. Saints are great individuals, but not models to be followed. There is no Śākta *avatāra* after whom they can pattern their behavior. The lack of a model encourages madness and spontaneity; the images of the saint are as shifting as the understanding of his *bhāva*. It may be that in madness is the greatest commonality between the Śākta, his deity, and his saints.

In Vaiṣṇava ecstasy, there is the flowing of an ecstatic substance, as *rasa* or *prema,* a love that enters the heart and flows out in waves. For Śāktas there is an emphasis on the transformation of impurity into divinity and the continued proximity to this divinity. Wine becomes Tārā Mā and is swallowed; flesh becomes the goddess and is eaten; the consort becomes the goddess, and she is drawn close by sexuality. The transformation is a reversal: death becomes life, the corpse becomes the body of the Mother, the forbidden becomes the sacred.

Many forms of Śākta ritual practice include a heightening of dramatic tension between the devotee and his goddess. He seeks her in danger, when he is about to be overcome by demons, in the midst of magical rites, or when he is starving and rejected by others. The corpse ritual deliberately puts the devotee in danger, so that he may call on the Mother with true desperation. As Lois Lane would consciously put herself in danger in order to be saved by Superman, so the Śākta devotee seeks to draw down the goddess's grace, to save him from the demons and potential insanity of the burning ground. The goddess can reverse the situation of danger and turn it into bliss.

The great saints are called mad, but for Śāktas it is a term of affection. While the saints were initially considered mad in a negative sense, over time people came to respect their devotion and to see madness as an intense expression of yogic detachment or Śākta devotion. Rāmakṛṣṇa's spiritual status was proved by a conference of scholars, who interpreted his symptoms as Vaiṣṇava *mahābhāva*—intense love for the deity. Vāmākṣepā had no single event that changed the opinion of others toward him, but both the intensity of his devotion and his miraculous abilities to cure attracted a crowd of followers. Because his *bhāva* was so intense, people believed that it could change the fabric of reality, bring life to the dead, and change the will of the goddess. His madness was seen as a result of his love. Nityagopāl often fell into trances, but he followed traditional yogic rules (pilgrimages, asceticism, celibacy, renunciant initiation) and was accepted as a yogi and an avatar. Rāmprasād was seen as mad with love for the goddess, but his poetry gained him respect—he was not a madman, but a mad poet and a Śākta saint.

Each strand of Śāktism has an ascetic and an ecstatic aspect. The yogi who is silent and disciplined, following the instructions of his guru in Pātañjala or Kuṇḍalinī yoga, may be seated next to a mad yogi who becomes ecstatic from his experiences, leaping about like a fish or frog and speaking to the goddess in visions. The exorcist (the *ojhā* or *guṇin*) may do traditional healing in the village, curing ghost possession and other ailments, or he may become possessed himself, or involved in magical ritual, or enter into continuous contact with those deities who were once his business associates. The devotee may worship his Kālī statue each day with offerings of leaves and fruit, or he may go mad with love, dancing with the goddess whose anklets ring in the burning ground.

The yogi who is disciplined and does traditional ritual practice is respected for his efforts by the Śākta community. But the mad saint, intense and unpredictable, who spends his life in ecstasy (*bhāva*), is revered.

FOUR

Sexual Sādhana and the Love of the Bodily God: Auls, Bāuls, and Sahajiyās

Āsal pāgal bhagavān.
The true madman is God.
—Bāul expression

The Madness of the Unknown Man

The Bāuls are the madmen of Bengal, the mad lovers of Bhagavān, who lives within them. They are village singers who wander from town to town, begging and playing music. Their songs are emotional and often symbolic, describing in village language and images from their surroundings their religious experiences. The word *bāul* has several possible derivations: from the Sanskrit *vātula,* meaning crazy (affected by the wind disease); from the Sanskrit *vyākula,* meaning confused; or more distantly, from the Arabic *āwliya,* meaning friend or devotee. The Bāuls are seen as mad by outsiders, who consider their behavior and spiritual practices to be a reversal of normal religious actions; but the Bāuls also see themselves as mad—the term *kṣepā,* or mad one, is a term of great respect among Bāuls. Madness is sought by a variety of techniques—Vaiṣṇava, Śākta, Śaiva, Sahajiyā—for it is not the doctrine and tradition that matter, but the ability of the technique to induce a state of madness for the Man of the Heart. As a Baul song states:

O crazy mind
For this reason I have not become mad
I haven't found a madman up to my wishes
I haven't found any such madman.

Only false madmen everywhere,
True madmen nowhere.

Finding a madman like Śiva is difficult,
Whose food was the poison in the nectar. . . .

O crazy mind
Prahlād was the foremost of madmen.
While saying "Hare Kṛṣṇa," he fell unconscious
Though his house was wealthy
And he lacked for nothing.

Aside from him, there is one madman,
Who has made everyone mad.
Becoming maddened by the love of Rādhā,
He has purchased Goloka.
Saying "Kṛṣṇa" and again "Kṛṣṇa"
Jumping into the black waters
Why did he not die?

What more can I say?
The country was once full of madmen,
Where is there a madman like Rāmakṛṣṇa any more?[1]

A Bāul song describes the Bāul who lives in a way that others find strange and difficult to comprehend:

He who becomes the realizer of *bhāva,* the lover among lovers
His ways are reverse, unconventional
Who can understand them?
How does he live, the man of *bhāva?*
He has neither joy nor sorrow
Because he has attained the eternal bliss of love.
His eyes stream with tears, the waters of bliss.
Sometimes he laughs to himself, and sometimes he cries.
He has equal enjoyment if he smells sandal wood.
And if someone flings mud upon him.
He does not want fame, fortune, or followers.
All persons are the same to him, relatives and strangers.
He builds his castles in the sky.[2]

It is partially this detachment from the world and partially his intense emotional states which make the Bāul appear mad. However, madness has different meanings for the Bāul and the non-Bāul, the outsider. To the non-Bāul, the madman (*kṣepā*) is irrational, weak, escaping from the world, ill, or possessed. For the Bāul, madness is the glory of Bhagavān and shows commitment to a spontaneous love that defies traditional social rules. The madman does not hallucinate, but has visions of the Real.

The Bāul Śrī Anirvan tells of Khepa (*kṣepā*) Bābā, "whose hair was matted but the knots of his heart were untied," and whose madness acted as teaching:

> Once upon a time Khepa Baba was in Benares in the middle of a crowd of people who kept looking at him without daring to approach, for if anyone bothered him, he would brandish his stick and hurl insults. One daring woman came towards him moaning, "Oh Maharaj, have pity on me." "Daughter of a whore!" Khepa Baba shouted at her. "Come here and I will rape you in the street in front of everyone!" She fled!
>
> Khepa Baba had a jug full of wine in front of him. He calmly drank it down to the last drop without saying a word. The people were stupefied at this impious act, not understanding what was going on, but his disciples noticed that he had become white like Shiva; his body radiated light, Khepa Baba was in ecstasy.
>
> With his immense power and his heart of pure gold, Khepa Baba spread almost insurmountable obstacles around him and created dangerous reefs, thus provoking deep disturbances in all those living near him. . . . Khepa Baba did all this in his uncouth way, for he himself was beyond good and evil. He provoked people into constantly facing themselves.[3]

The outside world sees the mad saint (*kṣepā*) quite differently than do his disciples who understand his actions. There is a discrepancy between the public image, which is hostile and irrational, and the private self-image, which is that of ideal devotee. The traditional image of the holy man is a controlled yogi, peaceful and strong, while the mad saint or Bāul is wildly enthusiastic, passionate toward God, and erratic toward his fellow men.

Bāuls follow their own religion (*bāul dharma*), with its own belief system and practices. This religion is expressed primarily in song. Bāul songs express both belief and religious experience, and are often written in the first person. Bala writes:

> My mind is captivated by the blue lotus in the sky above my
> head.
> Its manifold petals illumine the blue heavens.
> The sky is full of blue lotuses
> And overflows with the nectar of their glow.
> The drunken bee soars
> And my mind becomes listless in this impenetrable void.[4]

Bāuls seek after the man of the heart (*maner mānuṣ*). The mysteries of sexuality reveal the powers of this divinity, and he is found in the perfection of the body and the realization of the inner self. Bāuls take this idea of perfection quite seriously—one Bāul informant stated that no person who had ever had an operation where something had been removed (such as tonsils or appendix) could ever be a Bāul, for his body could never be perfect. He reserved his greatest scorn for vasectomy (apparently confusing it with castration), saying that such birth control techniques took away the dwelling place of the man of the heart and that such a person could never find Bhagavān.[5]

The man of the heart has many names and forms for the Bāul. Sometimes he is associated with Kṛṣṇa and Caitanya, or with the prophet Muhammad. He may be called the unknown bird, or the man who is hidden and ungraspable. He may be called the unknown man, the man of aesthetic enjoyment (*rasa*), the man of *bhāva,* the golden man, and the man of jewels.

While the Bāul religion is largely a rebellion against traditional Indian religion, one source for the Bāul concept of man of the heart is the Upaniṣadic concept of the inner controller (*antaryāmin*). The *Bṛihadāraṇyaka Upaniṣad* describes his locale in the body:

> 21. He who, dwelling in the skin, yet is other than the skin, whom the skin does not know, whose body the skin is, who controls the skin from within—He is your Soul, the Inner Controller, the Immortal.
> 22. He who, dwelling in the semen, yet is other than the semen, whom the semen does not know, whose body the semen is, who controls the semen from within—He is your Soul, the Inner Controller, the Immortal.[6]

This deity who dwells in the body dwells in a more general sense in all mankind:

> 13. This mankind [*mānuṣa*] is honey for all things, and all things are honey for this mankind. This shining, immortal Person who is in this mankind, and with reference to oneself, this shining, immortal Person who exists as a human being—he is just this Soul, this immortal, this Brahma, this all.[7]

Upendranāth Bhaṭṭācārya, a respected writer on Bāuls and himself a practitioner of *bāul dharma,* finds five major elements that contribute to the Bāul outlook.[8] He first stresses its non-Vedic character and its affinities with tantra and other nontraditional (*aśāstrīya*) religions. He sees its reflections in the opposition of the Buddhist *tāntrikas* and Sahajiyās to the Vedas, the Sufi criticisms of the orthodox Shariat in favor of the experiential *marifat,* and the Gauḍīya Vaiṣṇava stress on spontaneous devotion over doctrine and formalism. Bāuls follow the Vaiṣṇava emphasis on love, and this leads to the state of *sahaja mānuṣ,* a realization of and union with the inner self, which is also called joyful divine madness (*mahā-ullāsa-mahābhāva*). It may be reached spontaneously, by worship of mankind (*mānuṣ-bhajana*) or by worship of passion (*rāger bhajana*).

The second major element of the Bāul outlook is worship of the teacher (*guruvāda*), in which the teacher is seen as the ideal human being and as the true form of God. Firm devotion toward the teacher leads to the grace of God and to the teacher's true essence, the perfected state.

The third element of *bhāṇḍa/brahmāṇḍa* states their belief that God dwells physically in the human body. God does not indwell in a metaphorical sense; rather, he literally lives in certain liquids of the body, in the waters of bliss (*mahārasa* or *ānanda-āmṛta*). Not only is God within the body, but the body also contains the fourteen realms, sky, sea, rivers, and mountains. All of these may be found through the ritual practices of the body (*deha-sādhana*).

The fourth element is that of the man of the heart (*maner mānuṣ*), the ideal form of the individual. The Bāul wishes to capture this man and to merge with him. Often he is equated with God (Bhagavān), or with Caitanya or Muhammad. The fifth element of *rūpa/svarūpa* states that appearance differs from reality—that the true nature of man and woman is the union of Kṛṣṇa and Rādhā or Śiva and Śakti (*jugala milana*). These deities in union dwell in a natural state of intense emotion.[9]

Such early writers on Bāuls as Kṣitimohan Sen and Rabindranāth Tāgore emphasized the Bāuls' freedom and spontaneity.[10] For them the Bāul was marked by avoidance of ritual, spontaneous enthusiasm and love of God, independence of tradition and social mores, and creativity. He was a rebel and artistic genius seeking inward truth, not bound to time and place as were traditionally religious people. His *bhāvas* came spontaneously (*sahaja*), without effort. Ritual was seen as unimportant, a degenerate habit that interfered with spontaneity and humanism. Later writers, notably Upendranāth Bhaṭṭācārya, emphasize the importance of sexual initiation, ritual practice, and yogic effort among Bāuls. Both early and later writers used Bāul songs as texts.[11]

These writers concentrate on the *bhāvagān,* the meditative and thoughtful songs, rather than on the *śabdagān* or word songs, which are not based on Bāul belief and ritual, and are primarily for entertainment. A major difference seems to be that early and later writers are talking about different sets of Bāuls. Sen and Tāgore were interested in the perfected Bāul, who has attained the state of mad love for Bhagavān.[12]

Such people are visionaries, writing of their experiences. Fikircanda writes:

My soul cries out
Caught in the snare of beauty
Of the formless one.
As I cry by myself,
Night and day.
Beauty amassed before my eyes
Surpasses numerous moons and suns.
If I look at the clouds in the sky,
I see his beauty afloat.
And I see him walk on the stars
Blazing my heart.[13]

Persons in such states do not need ritual practice. Many Bāuls feel that states of intense passion toward Bhagavān are either innate in the person (*sahaja*)—something that comes naturally—or a state that may arise from singing. Ritual practice performs a backup function, if *bhāva* is neither natural nor inspired. As one Bāul informant stated, "*Bhāva* is sudden, it occurs from absorption [*āveśa*] in singing and dancing. But if it does not come, then some Bāuls use drugs [*bhang* or *ganja*], or they perform other practices [*sādhana*] in order to bring on the *bhāva*."[14]

Those who perform the "other practices" are ordinary Bāuls, for whom true *bhāva* is not a common event. In such a situation, it requires effort to gain the Man of the Heart. He is the bird to be caged, the fish to be caught, the milk to be taken from the water. He is the divine beloved, to be held close; for Hindu Bāuls he is Caitanya or Hari, while for Muslim Bāuls he may be called Khoda, Allāh, or Muhammad.

To understand Bāul *bhāva,* we look at two Bāul groups, the Muslim and Sahajiyā Bāuls. Each has its own variants of ecstasy and madness.

Muslim Bāuls: Catching God Fever in the Marketplace

Muslim Bāuls are often called *āuls,* a word associated with the Arabic term *āwliya,* meaning "proximity" (a person who is close to God). It also has a Sufi meaning—the complete or perfect man, who has gained the essence of God. Upendranāth Bhaṭṭācārya gives a possible derivation from the Sanskrit *ākul*—to be moved by emotion, full of *bhāva,* behaving strangely, mad.[15] The Āul is associated with the Sufi *deoyana,* a fakir or wanderer who is forgetful of self or self-absorbed (*ātmabholā*) and who roams about as if mad.

Sufi Bāuls may also call themselves *bāul,* deriving the word from *baal* (one who frees himself from obligation, a desert wanderer who is madly in love) or from the sect of Buhluliyas, named after their founder Abu Walid Ibn Amre Seirafia Khufi, who was called *buhlul* for "blockhead" or "crazy."[16]

There is no clear line between Hindu and Muslim Bāul; indeed, Bāuls often deny that such distinctions are valid. Many Bāul songs speak of the equal uselessness of temple and mosque, sacred threads and prayer five times a day. However, the songs of Bāuls with Muslim or Sufi influence often use Muslim symbolism: God is called Allāh rather than Bhagavān, mantra is *dhikr,* and the stages of spiritual development are unique to Sufism.

There are four stages (*maqāmāt*) to the path of the Bāul who is also a Sufi. Sufis distinguish between the stage or station, the *maqām,* a long-term state, and the *hal* which descends suddenly from Allāh as a special and temporary grace. Allāh is light and beauty, seen briefly in ecstatic trance. To gain full union with Allāh, it is necessary to die to the physical world. This idea is based on the Muslim *hadith,* "You all will die before you [actually] die." It is later seen in the Bāul concept of death while the body is living (*jiyante mara*). The affirmation of God becomes the negation of the self, and the state of self-annihilation (*fanā*) precedes the state of abiding in God (*baqa*), a state beyond pleasure and pain.[17]

In contemplation, the disciple awaits the descent of light (*nur*) on his centers of energy (*latifahs*). These are specialized centers in the body, places where Allāh's light may descend. They include the heart, the place of Adam; the soul, the place of Noah or Abraham; the secret heart, where Moses dwells; the secret soul, where Muhammad is surrounded by green light; and the *nafs* or evil self, at the forehead or navel.[18]

The Sufi approach emphasizes love, as does the Vaiṣṇava outlook. Allāh created light in the darkness and fell in love with it. Allāh's light creation was Muhammad. The purity of love is important, as sensual love (*ishq-i-mizaza*) must be transformed into divine love (*ishq-i-haqiqi*). Love is a liquid, symbolized by wine, and the Sufi Sā̇i is the cup bearer.

In the Bāul adaptation of Sufism, the emphasis on love is maintained.

The beloved may be the preceptor (*murshid*), Muhammad, Allāh, or at times even woman, whose body is the temple of Allāh and within whom is the unwritten Quran.[19] The lover seeks a mystical union with the beloved, and ritual practice is the path to union. In a poem of the *Hārāmaṇi* series, Allāh and Muhammad are seen as a couple in union, like Rādhā and Kṛṣṇa. Thus, Muhammad becomes the beloved of Allāh. This occurred during the prophet's ascent to heaven (*mirāj*), which has been a basis for much Sufi speculation:

> Allāh and the Prophet are united as a couple (*jugal milana*)
> in the land of love, during the ascent.
> Look, Sǎi, at the lonely throne, two persons are speaking in
> love.
> And in the ascent, Allāh revealed himself on his throne
> The Sǎi was a comrade, and that pure one [Allāh] showed
> the form of a friend.
> With joyful mind, the two have mingled (*miśra*) in love.[20]

Saints may become absorbed in love from seeing the man of the heart:

> Sǎi Rabana made love [*prema korilen*]
> There has never been anything like it.
> Muhammed Bakhoda is absorbed in love, he is the
> gatekeeper of love.
> Seeing the man of love, the great one, the mind and tongue
> become senseless.
> In such a union, one makes love like water in water.
> Allāh, Muhammad and Adam, all made demands of love.
> It is difficult to understand,
> Like finding the spirit of the wind.[21]

At times Sufi writers may use Vaiṣṇava imagery. Pāgal Ārqam writes of the importance of divine love which begins early and spontaneously: "Whom would you spend this night with, Oh Śyām, forsaking me? The candles burn the night through over my bed-head; be kind, and please come to the lap of Rādhā. . . . Mad Ārkum says that the sweetheart does not come in the night unless there is love since childhood."[22]

Terminology from the Quran and the orthodox Shariah may also be reinterpreted. The Quran begins with the word *bismillah,* meaning "in the name of Allāh." For the Muslim Bāul, this word is extended into *bis mi Allāh,* or "Allāh is in the *bis* [sperm]." Other terms have multiple meanings: *alif* is Adam, and also the *linga; lam* is Allāh, or *lāhut mokam,* the world of the heart, or the angel Jibrail. *Mim* is Eve or Hawā, or

Muhammad. *Nur* is divine light, and *nukta* the drops of ink used in writing the Quran, but both also refer to semen. The breath of Allāh is the soul of Adam, and this breath/soul is the man of the heart. It is sometimes associated with Eve and sometimes with Jibrail; both are believed to be mediators between Allāh and Muhammad.[23] Thus Allāh may be seen as present in the body directly, or in the form of his light or his emanation Muhammad, when he is indirectly present to the Sufi Bāul.

Bāul practice may emphasize either Sufi or Hindu elements. A major Sufi practice is chanting the name of Allāh (*dhikr*). It may be done loudly or silently, saying "*Lā ilāha ill' Allāh.*" The mind is controlled by a visualized image of the teacher, and breath control and music are used. At times there may be a vision of the soul's guide.

One Bāul source is the book *Jñānasāgar,* by Ali Rajāh. He writes that the love of Allāh and Muhammad has been transformed into the love of man and woman, and that ritual practice cannot be performed without woman.[24] This is the love (*jugal-prema*) of Allāh and Muhammad, echoed in the love of male and female worshiper, and developed in such intermediate figures as Bibi Ayesha and Fātima, who are loved by the Prophet and the *deoyana,* the mad fakir.

To the Muslim Bāul, Allāh is the merciful moon (*dayāl canda*). A Bāul song by Iśhān describes his vision, which is so powerful as to cause pain. It emphasizes firsthand experience of Allāh, who appears in front of the writer:

> With the first flush of light in the sky,
> The generous God has appeared at last.
> I wake and see in the morning
> That the Gracious One is manifest before me—
> He is manifest before me.
>
> Blossoms fall, birds take flight, and dew is on the leaves.
> The light of the night melts away in the heat of the sun—
> Oh Lord, the moon-beams too!
> Pondering these things, Iśhān weeps—
> The agony is intense.
> The agony is intense.[25]

Allāh is also seen as a treasure house, found through the experience of *bhāva:*

> Look O mind, submerged in *bhāva,*
> In Allāh's name is a great treasure

The mind has oceans and rivers of *bhāva,*
And if you dive into them
You can get the priceless jewel.
This is not a river, for it is so deep
Hidden by black clouds, it shines like lightning. . . .
O this man is a vine of eternity,
Where does my man of *bhāva* stay, my man of *bhāva?*[26]

When Allāh is attained, the Sufi Bāul merges with him. His statements may then appear as the ravings of a madman, as Hasan found when he spoke in ecstasy:

I have come to the conclusion that everyone is me. . . .
Allah and his messengers emanate from me
From me springs the clan . . .
From me comes the earth and sky
From me is the whole universe. . . .
But, misunderstanding me, my countrymen brand me a
stranger.
Prince Hasan, the crazy one, babbles only nonsense.
If my countrymen take me at all seriously
They are bound to die.
One who knows oneself knows the Lord.
Knowing himself, Prince Hasan sings this song.[27]

This realization of unity came about during his wanderings in Love's eternal bazaar: "Prince Hasan has caught God-fever in the market-place. . . . / He dances, plays, and sings this song of love."[28]

This occurs when the *Āul* has realized Allāh, the deity that lives within him. He is in intense emotion (*mahābhāva*), like the Vaiṣṇava Bāul, mad with a divine fever. The bodily God has been realized, and now life is a loving dance with *dayāl canda,* the merciful moon of the mad.

Sahajiyā Bāuls: Boiling the Milk of Bliss

The woman must be a *hijṛā* [hermaphrodite]
And the man must be a *khojā* [eunuch]
And perform the practice very carefully.

O sir, you drink poison and disregard the nectar.
Throw away the poison, and drink the nectar instead.
—Kartā-bhajā major proverbs [*mūla sūtras*]

Sahajiyās are associated with Bāuls, although the exact nature of the relationship is debatable. Sometimes they are seen as subsects of one another, and at other times they are linked only by their opposition to traditional (*śāstrīya*) religions. Modern Sahajiyās are most often associated with Vaiṣṇavism, although their predecessors were tantric Buddhist.

Sahajiyās are probably the least mad of the Bāul groups, although they are ecstatics. Madness would be too revealing; because of the socially unacceptable nature of their practices, and even of their theology, many Sahajiyās wish to appear ordinary and conservative, to maintain a low profile. Their poetry is hidden and cryptic, and several Sahajiyā practitioners were hesitant to answer questions, insisting that initiation was necessary before one could hear the answers.

This social concern must necessarily limit any madness and spontaneity. Many Sahajiyās consider themselves orthodox Vaiṣṇavas with an esoteric ritual practice, and this is how they wish to appear to others. Many are householders and not yet ready to reject all traditional values. Sahajiyā renunciants are more detached from social values, and thus more mad.

The term *sahaja* may refer to both a goal and a path. *Sahaja* as a goal is a state of being, the ultimate inner nature of the self. The *sahaja*-self pervades the universe; it is also called the body of ultimate nature or spontaneous being (*svabhāvika-kāya*). *Sahaja* as a path refers to a process of spiritual development that is easy and natural. The Sahajiyā is one who paradoxically follows this natural way to achieve the goal of living beyond the limitations of the physical world.

The Buddhist Sahajiyās were an esoteric group, and little information about them remains. They are known primarily by the Caryāpadas, symbolic poetry written from approximately the eighth to the twelfth centuries A.D. by the Buddhist *siddhācāryas* of Bengal. These poems emphasize the goal of intense bliss (*mahāsukha*), which arises in the state of *sahaja*. Tillopada describes this as a state, known only by intuition, in which all thought constructions are dead and the vital wind is destroyed.[29] He also writes that in the *sahaja* state, consciousness and emptiness enter into a union of bliss, and the objects of the senses vanish away.[30] Saraha writes that the individual mind enters into *sahaja* like water into water; this state is the destruction of body, speech, and mind, and the mind becomes "like the vacant sky."[31] However, the more active aspect of *sahaja* may also be emphasized, when the practitioner becomes drunk with the liquor of joy (*mahāsukha*). Kānha-pada writes that he becomes "like an intoxicated elephant"[32] who tramples the posts of the moon and sun, until he rests in the lake of lotuses. Such mad behavior was not limited to meditation—the tantric Buddhist saints were not limited by social conventions and were known for their "crazy wisdom" and eccentric behavior.

The goal of *sahaja* as intense joy (*mahāsukha*) was realized through a physiological process, although it brought the person beyond the body. This process was *kāya sādhana,* when the body was ripened by exercises of haṭha-yoga and the practitioner gained control of his body's actions. He had to raise the sperm (*bodhicitta*) up along the spine, into a center in the head (*uṣṇīṣa cakra*) where its movement was stilled.[33]

The fluid is then stabilized and transformed into *sahaja,* the ultimate state. Raising the sperm was associated with a sexual practice in which the physical union of male *upāya,* "means," and female *prajña,* "wisdom," reflected the inner union of male and female principles, universal compassion and perfect wisdom.[34] This state was called ultimate union (*yuganaddha*) and the unity of blissful emotion (*samarasa*). These concepts, like that of *mahāsukha,* reflect the shift from the Mahāyāna emphasis on *nirvāṇa* (a state of emptiness) to the tantric emphasis on bliss (a fullness of light and joy).[35]

In the thirteenth and following centuries, while India was under Muslim rule, tantric Buddhism changed form. The remaining Sahajiyās began to adopt the outlook and language of the Bengali Vaiṣṇavas. The emphasis on Buddha and Śakti shifted to an emphasis on Kṛṣṇa and Rādhā, and the goal of the great bliss of the void (*mahāsukha*) shifted toward the joy of ecstatic love (*mahābhāva*).

The central focus remained on a primordial couple, not in a symbolic metaphysical union as in Buddhism, but in the emotional, simultaneous union and separation of Kṛṣṇa and Rādhā in Vṛndāvana. Several other Buddhist characteristics remain: sexual yoga as a way of attaining the ultimate state; the images of the three major nerves (*īḍā, piṅgalā,* and *suṣumnā*), and the energy centers or *cakras* (which became inhabited by Hindu gods rather than Buddhist *ḍākinīs* and *herukas*); raising a liquid from the lowest *cakra* into the highest one, located in the skull; and the necessity of perfecting the body in order to transform it. Both Buddhist and Vaiṣṇava practitioners "drank nectar from the moon," and the conversion of poison (*biṣ*) into nectar (*āmṛta*) became the transformation of lust (*kāma*) into love (*prema*). Both Buddhist and Vaiṣṇava Sahajiyās recognized the difficulty of this form of yogic practice, using such metaphors as "diving deep without getting wet" and "making the frog dance before the serpent."

Caitanya became a focus for Vaiṣṇava Sahajiyās, as he was considered both male and female—either inwardly female and outwardly male (because of his Rādhā-*bhāva,* his identification with Rādhā), or inwardly both male and female, as both Rādhā and Kṛṣṇa. He was believed by Sahajiyās to have experienced the intense love of Rādhā's state of *mahābhāva* and to have performed Sahajiyā rituals, as did the Goswāmins, Jayadeva, Caṇḍīdāsa, Vidyāpati, and others. Mention of their *sahaja* practice with female companions is included in the *Vivarta-vilāsa* of Ākiñcana-dāsa.[36]

Caitanya was believed to be the perfect lover, for he knew from direct experience the feelings of both Rādhā and Kṛṣṇa. Sometimes he is the urban playboy (*nāgarika*), inspiring mad desire in the women who see him (although this role was rejected by the orthodox Vaiṣṇavas):

> I saw the gold-complexioned Gora going in a swaggering manner: [on seeing him] my body, my mind and my life were no longer mine. I was drowned in his gracefulness. My feet became immobile, my voice became choked, and my patience and prestige were gone. Bereft of consciousness, [I became] like one mad, as if in an ecstatic [*agamya*] situation. There was nothing to be afraid of, yet I felt terrified: [I could not know] why my limbs trembled.[37]

In such poems, sexual passion is often the precursor of religious intensity:

> Look, look at the glorious dalliance of Gauranga! He has now adopted sannyasa—he who was the master-lover of the hearts of a hundred thousand young women. He who once remained spell-bound in the hard embrace of the young women of the Vraja, now horripilates all over his person, and is in a state of divine intoxication, and tears of love flow from his eyes.[38]

For Bāuls and Sahajiyās, Caitanya is "the best of madmen [*kṣepās*]" or the "madman of madmen." He is described as a Bāul in *Caitanya Caritāmṛta,* in a letter from Advaitācārya:

> Tell that Bāul that people have become Āul.
> Tell that Bāul that because of this, nothing is being
> exchanged in the market.
> Tell that Bāul that these Āuls are not doing anything.
> Tell him that this message is from another Bāul.[39]

Caitanya is an important figure to Sahajiyās and Bāuls because he holds within him the secrets of Kṛṣṇa and Rādhā, both of whom could ignore their own gratification in order to please the other. Both were controlled and detached in the midst of sexuality, and neither was subject to orgasm, the failure of that control. In the *Bhāgavata Purāṇa,* Kṛṣṇa is described at the dance of the *rasalīlā.* Although making love to large numbers of gopīs, he was called *ātmani avaruddha-saurata,* "he whose semen was held within himself," or "one who controlled his erotic energy."[40]

Such control is associated with a mature sexuality, based on love (*prema*) rather than lust (*kāma*). It is only a ripened love which contains sweetness:

> Let ripeness appear
> In its own time
> For the full flavor of the fruit.
> A green jackfruit
> Can be softened by blows
> But not made sweet.[41]

As Erfan Shah says of this process:

> To find nectar
> Stir the cauldron
> On the fire—
> And unite the act of loving
> With the feeling for love.
>
> Distill the sweetness
> Of the heart
> And reach the treasures.[42]

The imagery of ripening may also be seen in a Sahajiyā text by Taraṇiramaṇa, in which molasses (*guṛ*) is being purified, dried, combined with milk, and heated. This process is stated to be a metaphor for the creation of sweet emotion (*śṛṅgāra rasa*) in the practitioner:

> Adding milk to this, he puts it on the fire, and it is purified, and its sediment (*gada*) goes away. . . . Thereafter, adding milk, it is heated and without difficulty it becomes *sitā miśri.* The unbroken sweet *rasa* is called white *miśri.* Golden hued, it rains down ceaselessly. That eternal *rasa,* the origin of all, sports in eternity. Secretly it rains down on the limbs of both. . . . In both bodies ceaseless is that shining transformation (*ujjvala vikāra*). The organs of both will overflow with

> that hundred times purified essence. . . . If the *rasa* becomes sweet there is no disease or death.[43]

This liquid creates *ujjvala vikāras,* shining or intense changes that occur in the body as a result of ecstatic states.[44] In this text, the *rasa* brings not only ecstatic states (causing the person to "overflow") but also immortality.

Rasa is described as a literal fluid: "In this body the *prākṛta rasa* is a milk-like fluid. By being stirred around over a fire, it gradually becomes purified. Stir this *rasa* over a fire. It will be uninterrupted and sweet when the mind is pure. The fire for this is the companionship of *prākṛti.*"[45]

This fluid is heated, stirred, and concentrated by a variety of exercises. It is finally raised to the "house of the moon" in the skull, by breath control and meditation. During ritual sex, the partners remain still, "each with the feelings of both," and this causes the *rasa* to became matured (*pakva*). *Rasa* is a fluid of pure emotion, which can be condensed and thickened by erotic yoga. It is believed that Rādhā and Kṛṣṇa are together within the body as the *rasa* liquid matures.

Generally, the states discussed by Sahajiyā texts are those experienced only by the male. However, this text mentions the woman—she is "always enraptured in love and knows love to the essence. In rapture, the tears of love flow from her eyes."[46] She is opposed to the lustful woman, who steals the liquid (*rasa*) of the male to make her body smooth and lustrous.[47] However, the desire of the latter woman may not be her fault; she may be driven to such actions by a sperm-drinking worm.[48]

The function of the woman is to ripen the male substance—the milk in the man must be purified by the fire in the woman. The *Vivarta-Vilāsa* states: "Now, hear about the nature of the *bāhya-parakīya* [outer woman]. Just as milk is usually boiled with the help of fire, so the Gosvāmis have utilised the fire that is in women (for the purpose of purifying the passion)."[49]

Sahajiyās place great value on ritual sexuality, and many texts mention the importance of practice with a woman. Yet despite the fact that Sahajiyās have greater emphasis on love than do the Śaiva and Śākta *tāntrikas,* their attitude toward the woman is virtually identical: she is to be used as a ritual object and then cast aside. As the *Premavilāsa* states: "Beehives are filled up with honey collected from many flowers. When the honey is collected, the flowers are of no use to the bees."[50]

Women condense the milk (or sperm) in the man, basically still "doing the cooking," but are of no use after this. While the inner relationship of male and female is one of pure, self-sacrificing love, the outer (*bāhya*) relationship is strictly utilitarian.

Yet Sahajiyās claim that the goal of such practices is also love. The poet Rādhāśyāma states:

> While desire burns in the limbs
> Still there is time
> Boil the juice on the fire of longing
> To condense the fluid.
>
> The sweetness of syrup will ferment and sour
> Unless it is stirred on controlled heat
> Feelings evolve from desire
> And love shoots forth from lust.[51]

Some Sahajiyā beliefs are much closer to orthodox Vaiṣṇavism. The Sahajiyā text "Atha Deśakāla Patra Kathānam" describes the four stages of worship (*bhajana*)—*sthūla taṭastha, sūkṣma pravarta, sadhaka,* and *siddhi*—as stages of proximity to the *Vṛndāvana līlā.*[52] The worshiper traverses a sacred geography that spreads from Jambudvīpa, to Śrī Navadvīpa, to Śrī Vṛndāvana, to Bṛihat Vṛndāvana; he progressively worships Brahma the creator, Śrī Kṛṣṇa-Caitanya Mahāprabhu, Śrī Nandanāndana Śrīkṛṣṇa, and the blessed Śrī Rādhikā.

In the *stūla* (coarse) state, the worshiper is concerned with discipline and purification, and follows a Vaiṣṇava guru. He must be certain not to imitate a gopī, for it is beyond his capacity.[53] At the *sūkṣma* (subtle) stage, he learns about Śrī Caitanya. He meditates on the secret nature (*gambhīra līlā*) of Caitanya, in which he felt Rādhā's mad love. At the *sādhaka* (practitioner) stage, he inwardly sees Kṛṣṇa, who thinks of nothing but Rādhā, and with the help of his guru he will aid Rādhā and Kṛṣṇa in the play of love (*śṛṅgārātmakā-līlā*).

In the *siddha* state, Rādhikā is queen of Vṛndāvana, and the worshiper's guru is a handmaiden (*mañjari*). He chants Rādhā's name and is devoted to her. Both guru and disciple dwell in purified bodies in Bṛihat Vṛndāvana. The mantra "kliṅ" will also be heard, which holds within it the five elements and the five devotees who have been transformed into them: Earth, Gadādhara; Water, Śrīvāsa; Fire, Caitanyadeva; Wind, Nityānanda; and Sky, Advaitācārya.[54]

There has been some debate over whether Sahajiyās still exist. Sahajiyās interviewed in Bākreśwar, Navadvīpa, Ghoshpāra, and Rādhānāgar claim to practice today and were willing to describe a few of their rituals. Newer disciples of the Sahajiyā guru Vṛndāvana Dās described their practice as a set of haṭha-yoga exercises of the urinary sphincters, to gain strength and control. Some further advanced disciples, a young couple, stressed the practical advantages of the Sahajiyā method. They said that it kept them in good health and that it was a good form of birth control (this was necessary, as childbearing was seen as damaging to women, making them old before their time and obstructing their devotional life). The man explained that women require at least two hours of intercourse to "have their heat cooled off" and that he suspected Western males were incapable of this. Sahajiyā practice, however, made the men capable of thus satisfying women. The couple lived a normal life in a joint family during the day and did their practice from 2:00 to 4:00 A.M. This included breathing exercises, meditation, and visualization of the guru.

Vṛndāvana Dās was a man of forty years, with a black beard and long hair in a topknot. He had performed Sahajiyā practice for twenty-two years, learning from gurus and visiting shrines. His first guru gave him the Kṛṣṇa mantra, and his second one gave him the *yugala* mantra, of Rādhā and Kṛṣṇa together. He emphasized that the goal of Sahajiyā practice was to gain Kṛṣṇa and to experience love like that of the gopīs (*gopī bhāva*), divine love (*mādhurya*). Such love comes as a result of the grace of the guru, rather than the practice of mantra. From this perspective, only Kṛṣṇa is male and all other beings are female. Kṛṣṇa is the inner self, as a single sun reflects in many pots of water. The goal of the practitioner is to gain union with Kṛṣṇa: "It is the fifth end of life [*puruṣārtha*], beyond worldly objects, even heaven and liberation. It is only to have Kṛṣṇa, to become merged in him, to realize him."[55] This union with Kṛṣṇa is echoed in the physical world, by the love of man and woman:

> Unless the needs of the man are fulfilled by woman, and that of the woman by the man, it is impossible to have perfection. They must have fulfillment through their union, one merging into the other. That is why union of man and woman is the precondition of all spiritual exercise, of meditation and contemplation.

The physical union not only reflects the divine, but evens out some biological imbalances between male and female:

> Women contain more of the blood [*rajas*] element, while men have more of the seminal [*vīrya*] element. Thus, women are blood-oriented and men are semen-oriented. In our body there are three nerves: *īḍā, piṅgalā,* and *suṣumnā*. These three nerves have specialized functions. The nerve *īḍā* is symbolic of semen and knowledge, while the *piṅgalā* is symbolic of blood and joy. Intercourse while the *īḍā* force is active produces male children, and when the *piṅgalā* is active, there are female children. Thus, the male contains the element of knowledge [*jñāna*] and the female that of joy or bliss [*ānanda*]. Both are complementary to each other.

The goal is to balance these extremes:

> Man must extract the power of bliss from the woman and develop it in himself. Likewise women must extract the power of knowledge from the man and develop it in herself. This is directly stated in the Sahajiyā way and told from guru to disciple among tantrikas.

This balance must include yogic practice and a teacher with a lineage:

> Perfection is possible through yoga. Otherwise, it is merely hypocrisy, or the lower method [*nimna praṇāli*]. But from Caitanya back to Kṛṣṇa, all were followers of the higher method [*ūrdhva praṇāli*]. Unless one follows the true method, there is no hope of gain, like a false document which has no credibility.[56]

A Sahajiyā interviewed in Ghoshpāra felt that both Caitanya and Nityānanda were important figures for Sahajiyās, for they had both become women inwardly, and all the men with whom they associated were women inwardly. It is important that both partners should be inwardly female during ritual sex, for then the drive of lust is destroyed. When the semen is held inside, then the man becomes a woman.[57]

Another Sahajiyā in Navadvīpa (who claimed not to have "lost his seed" in forty years) stated that Caitanya was their main teacher, for he said that "the couple [*jugala*] teaches us everything." Caitanya descended to earth to teach people how to make love, for he knew the love secrets of Rādhā and Kṛṣṇa. This Sahajiyā felt that the couple who worshiped together and attained a state of purity (*brahmacarya*) together by changing lust into love were the ideal Vaiṣṇavas. Indeed, there were two categories of Vaiṣṇavas—the *sūkṣya* (fine, or totally celibate) and the *jugala* (joint, in which male and female practiced together). The latter type was believed to bring the person closer to Rādhā and Kṛṣṇa.

In the small village of Rādhānāgar, a Bāul couple was described by others as Sahajiyā. They lived in a thatched mud hut with an altar containing Rādhā and Kṛṣṇa statues, clay horses, and a picture of Gaur Nitāi (the image of Gaurāṅga and Nityānanda as a couple is common is Bengal). Both claimed to be of the Sǎi lineage (*sampradāya*). They said that there were four lineages: the *Āul* (who was like a child, for he had not been initiated into a mantra); the *Bāul* (who has taken initiation, and who meditates and performs religious practice; the *Darvesa* (who has gained wisdom, *jñāna*); and the *Sǎi* (who has become perfected in his practice). Kṣepā Cānda, the male Bāul, stated:

> The goal of practice is the vision of God [*bhāgavata darśana*]. One goes through these stages until reaching the Sǎi state, which is like a bird flying high, and from which one can see the other stages. In the Sǎi state, the soul mixes with God like water in water, and God is formless and of white color. In practice, one says "Hari Bol," and the five minds become one. The forms of different deities dwell in the body—Balarāma, Gadādhara, Advaita, Rūpa—nine in all. They are not directly perceived, but they are seen as family members are remembered.[58]

They did not wish to give details of ritual practice, but reverently showed a worn and well-used book, which included instructions on the "five M's" (*pañcamākara*) and other tantric rites.

Bholanāth Bhaṭṭācārya has interviewed female Sahajiyās, called *bhairavīs* or *sādhikās*. They were of both Vaiṣṇava and Śākta orientation, and the majority said that they had inherited the role from their mothers. They emphasized in practice sexual ritual (*bindu sādhana*), breathing exercises, and contemplation of rivers and mountains (to avoid lustful thoughts). These female Sahajiyās were neither mystics nor madwomen, but were rather professionals, ritual assistants for the male practitioners, who would in turn support them.[59] The women interviewed did not appear to enjoy great respect or status, but their relationships with the men were justified on the basis of their being relationships of ritual rather than love. To use a woman as a ritual object was acceptable behavior, but to love her would have been unworthy of a holy man.

Certainly there is no single group, or theology, or particular practice which fits all Sahajiyā subgroups. These range from the Kartābhajās founded by Āul Canda (believed to be a reincarnation of Caitanya in the form of a fakir), who worship family leaders and ancestors, to the Kiśorī-bhajanas (who believe in liberation by imitation of Kṛṣṇa's acts) in which Rādhā is Kiśorī, the Śakti or first cause, to the Sakhī-bhāvakas, in which men dress as women to better understand and be close to Rādhā and her friends.

Groups that follow sexual ritual and visualization of Rādhā-Kṛṣṇa include the Nedas (believed to be organized by Vīrabhādra, the son of Nityānanda); the Spaṣṭadāyakas (who practice the *cāricāndra* ritual, in order to reabsorb valuable bodily elements which are lost); the Darveśis (believed to be started by Sanātana Gosvāmin, when he fled from the court of the ruler of Gaur in the dress of a Darveśa); and the Sādhvīnis (who oppose religious traditionalism on principle). Sahajiyā sects begun by Muslims (which follow the goal of *sahaja* and sexual ritual, but also incorporate some Muslim doctrines) include the Hazaratis, the Gobrās, and the Pāgal-nathis. All of these have been influenced by the Kartābhajās of Ghoshpāṛa.

There is thus a wide variety of Sahajiyā groups. Vaiṣṇava Sahajiyās worship Rādhā and Kṛṣṇa; among them the guru is comparable to Kṛṣṇa and the disciple to Rādhā. They follow the two prescribed modes of pleasure—the *svakīya* or enjoyment of one's own wife, and the *parakīya* or relationship with a woman who belongs to another man. They hold that the forbidden nature of the latter makes it superior to the ordinary love of husband and wife. Vaiṣṇava Sahajiyās may consider themselves the "true" (*sahaja,* natural or real) Vaiṣṇavas, more true to Rādhā and Kṛṣṇa than the orthodox Vaiṣṇavas.

Other Sahajiyā groups emphasize the divinity of the guru and ritual sexuality and may worship Khoda (Allāh) and Śakti as well as Rādhā and Kṛṣṇa. The practitioner may worship the woman, have ritual sex with the woman, or become a woman (a smaller number start out as women).[60] No clear lines, by theology, ritual or practice, define the Sahajiyā religion.

One of the largest Sahajiyā groups, and also one of the most conservative, is the Kartābhajā sect. It began in Ghoshpāṛa in Nadia district, where there is still a yearly religious fair that attracts thousands of people. The founder of the Kartābhajās was Āulcānd or Āulecānd, who lived in approximately A.D. 1686–1779. Various legends say that he was an orphan, a Sufi, a fakir beggar, a criminal, a healer. Kartābhajā sectarian accounts say that he was Caitanya in disguise as a Muslim fakir, who had returned to combat false Vaiṣṇava orders and the unpopular ascetic bias of mainline Vaiṣṇavism (thus their expression, "The rice husked by the Gauḍīya Vaiṣṇavas remained unsold in the market.").[61]

Āulcānd was discovered by Rāmśaraṇ Pāl, who became his disciple and invited him home. Rāmśaraṇ and his wife, Sarasvatī (affectionately called Satī Mā by the sect), lived with Āulcānd in a strained relationship, for Āulcānd behaved in an eccentric manner—he danced naked before the women of the house and would play violently with young men, to the point that he accidentally killed a young cowherd boy (however, when Rāmśaraṇ kicked the dead boy's head, the boy opened his eyes and sat up). After Āulcānd left the Pāl household, Rāmśaraṇ and Sarasvatī became known as Ādipuruṣa and Ādyāśakti.

After Rāmśaraṇ's death in 1783, his wife became the leader of the sect and also showed miraculous powers. Their son Dulālcānd developed a theology for the sect, emphasizing his mother's miraculous abilities. Dulālcānd was regarded by disciples as the incarnation of both Caitanya and Kṛṣṇa. His songs and poems were written down by four disciples and published in 1882 as *Bhāver Gītā* (the song of *bhāva*). Some of the songs in this collection were composed by his disciples; in the songs Dulālcānd is called Lāl Śaśī, the red moon. The following are a few lines from *Bhāver Gītā* on Bhagavān:

> God is not dependent on social rules and custom. He may be driven off, but He returns. Denunciation makes him glad. God is mad [*kṣepā*] because he is so unusual.[62]

> The whole universe was washed away in a deluge. A big lotus with 100 petals was floating on the cosmic ocean. On that lotus was seated the poor, mad one.[63]

> If the devotee does not become mad for God, He does not care to reveal Himself to him. Even God sheds tears for the genuine devotee.[64]

The sect emphasizes the difference between social behavior (*vyāvahāra*), and spiritual goals and behavior (*paramārtha*). Kartābhajās were advised to respect social norms and perform duties maintaining a traditional facade, while secretly worshiping the Kartā (leader) and performing other forms of ritual practice. There are four stages: *pravarta* (beginner), *sādhaka/satī* (the disciple together with his wife), *siddhi* (a person in the state of *sahaja,* whose inner nature is like an active volcano, boiling over with love of God), and *nivṛtti* (a state of nonduality in which the person is *jīyante marā,* alive and dead at the same time). While the beginner may speak about the faith, the *sādhaka* is forbidden to do so. Little is known of Kartābhajā spiritual practice, although some writers claim that there is ritual intercourse.[65] According to Akṣaya Kumār Dutta, the main practice of this group is *premanusthāna* (the ritual or celebration of love), which leads to perfection. The members meet together, chanting mantras and following other forms of Vaiṣṇava worship, and share the signs of *bhāva*—crying, laughter, hair standing on end, tremors, grinding their teeth. These signs increase with the presence of love (*prema*).[66]

The goals of the Kartābhajās are both religious spontaneity, *sahaja,* and liberation, *nivṛtti.* The *Bhāver Gīta* states of *sahaja*:

> The *sahaja* is unaffected by the *guṇas.* The *sahaja* joy is the joy of the perception of non-duality.[67]
>
> The behaviour-pattern of the *sahaja* man is as follows: If one rebukes him, one is sure to be embraced by him. He even redeems his enemies. He does not distinguish between friends and foes, good and evil.[68]
>
> The *sahaja* is something beyond knowledge. The *sahaja* spiritual culture [*sādhana*] is meant for couples.[69]

Nivṛtti is final release, the end of desire, beyond the senses, nondual. It is symbolized by night, and the boat (the Kartābhajā sect) travels to the other bank only at night. The boatman is the Kartā, the *sahaja* Man of Ecstasy.[70] The Kartā and his ancestors are worshiped (gurus follow a family lineage), and the worshiper's own family and ancestors are also worshiped. This sect has inspired much dispute, and Dāśarathi Rāya wrote of the Kartā:

> The Kartā of Kartābhajā is like:
>
> a Dog in the wretched hut wherein the paddy-grinder is kept;
> a Ghost in the crematorium;
> a *Mārid* in the Muhammedan grave-yard;
> a Spook in a field strewn with rotten carcasses of cows;
> a Female Goblin in a place full of rubbish and dung;
> a Cowherd in a field;

a Nurse in a room where a woman has given birth
to a baby;
a Calf in a pen full of rams and ewes.[71]

The Kartābhajā sect includes Muslim followers as well as Hindu. Many disciples believe that the soul of Āulcānd entered the soul of Rāmśaraṇ Pāl (who was then called Tatsvarūpa or Kartāsvarūpa) and continues down in subtle form into the present Kartā. Others have a trinitarian doctrine—that Āulcānd, Kṛṣṇa, and Caitanya are mystically united. It combines a variety of orientations, primarily Vaiṣṇavism and tantric Buddhism, with elements of Sufism and yoga. These may be seen in the other names of Āulcānd—Āule Mahāprabhu, Kangali Mahāprabhu, Fakir Thākur, Siddha Puruṣa, Sȧin Gosāin, and Pūrṇacandra.

Another Sahajiyā group is the Sāhebdhanī, which originated in Dogachia in Nadia district in the eighteenth century. Their beliefs are expressed in the songs of Kabir Gosāin and include both Hindu and Muslim elements. They call on the mercy of Kartā Bābā and Dindayāl, feeling that Hari and Allāh listen only to the upper classes. Their founder is unknown, but thought to be a woman, the incarnation of Rādhā rather than Kṛṣṇa or Caitanya. A Sāhebdhanī proverb states: "The merciful Sāhebdhanī has been blessed by the name of Rādhā of Vraja. That Rādhā has been reborn in Nadia."[72]

Little is known of their rituals, sexual or otherwise. Chanting mantras is a very important practice, and Sāhebdhanīs accept the Sufi emphasis on the respiratory organs. The poet Kabir Gosāin emphasizes the unity of Hindu and Muslim thought, saying that Allāh-Muhammad and Rādhā-Kṛṣṇa are united souls, and that Allāh dwells in the throat, while Kṛṣṇa exists in the palate (thus the importance of mantra, with which the deities physically resonate). Allāh's power of delight, his bliss, is shown in Rādhā. Sāhebdhanīs have both male and female gurus, who give mantras and instructions to their disciples. Their major deity is Dīndayāl Dīnabandhu, the friend of the poor who is merciful to the poor. His mantra is "*Kliṅ Sāhebdhanī Allāhdhanī Dindayāl.*"

Sahajiyā groups place an emphasis on living direct ecstatic experience. Many are involved with the forbidden, as sexuality or as substance, and have found traditional (*śāstrīya*) religion too limiting. Their forms of practice are often close to those of the Bāuls. A Bāul woman devotee stated: "When I loved him, I did not know that he was a man and I a woman. Our hearts were simply ground into one paste in which two elements mingled."[73]

Bāul Practice: Fishing in the Waters of Ritual

When a person becomes a Bāul, he must realize that God lives within him. This is the stage of *padata*. When he knows God, he is *siddha*. He may sing and dance, but ritual practice is very important. Without knowing Bāul practice, one cannot understand a Bāul.

—Interview with a Bāul, in Calcutta, 1984

Bāul practice, like many forms of tantric ritual, is kept secret—it is not widely known or discussed outside the group. It is mainly described in symbolic songs and poems, and in small discussion groups within the Bāul community (*ākhaṛā*). A variety of texts are considered relevant: the *Caitanya Caritāmṛta* (interpreted in a Bāul fashion), the *Vivarta Vilāsa*, and verses of *kadacas* (notebooks) from various saints and sages. Among the Muslim Bāuls, the most relevant texts are the Quran, believed to be the words of Allāh or Īśvara, and the *hadith*, the words of Muhammad, often interpreted by later *darveśas* and fakirs.[74]

Bāul spiritual practice focuses on the body. Without reference to the body, practice is considered irrelevant or imaginary. A Bāul proverb states, "What is not in the body [*bhāṇḍa*] is not in the universe." As Upendranāth Bhaṭṭācārya states: "They call the conceptions of Vaikuṇṭha, etc. outside of the body inference [*anumān*]. Their own body [*bhāṇḍa*] they call existence [*bartamān*]. They do not accept inference, and without [physical] existence, they have no ritual practice."[75]

The greatest truth of the body is that it is the dwelling place of the highest being (*parama-tattva*), as Śrī Kṛṣṇa, the Sẵi, Alekh Nur, or the man of the heart. As a story by one Bāul informant went, this Supreme Self was at first one, and unable to taste aesthetic pleasure (*rasa*). Because he wished to do this, he divided himself in half, into a female form. She was created for pleasure and sexuality. Because of her existence, the Self could taste the best and sweetest of the emotions (*śṛngāra rasa*). Such emotion is both the joy of love and the foundation of creation.[76]

Bāul ritual practice is based on this primordial duality of male and female, and also on a quaternity, the four moons or elements. These four moons (*cāricāndra*) have four colors: black, yellow, red, and white. These are associated with the four basic elements of the body, in some cases conceived as earth, water, fire, and air. However, in the context of ritual practice, they become *biṣṭha* (excrement, or in Bāul language, *māṭi*); *mūtra* (urine, or *rasa*); *rajas* (blood, called *rūpa* or *strī-vīrya*); and *śukra* (semen, also called *rasa*). It is believed that, by absorbing these substances, the body becomes fully matured and ripened, and physically charged with fixed, calm energy. The body then becomes fit for emotional practice (*bhāva sādhana*).[77]

These substances are used for the ritual piercing of the four moons (*cāricāndra-bheda*). This ritual is believed to split the body into these four elements, so that the person may recognize and accept the components of the body.[78] It requires a detached state of mind[79] and includes chanting the name of Hari and *mantras* (with emphasis on the *kāma-bīja* and *kāma-gāyatrī*). Upendranāth Bhaṭṭācārya states that he has witnessed this ritual and that the participants do indeed remain calm.[80] Although the techniques of absorption are not clearly stated, it is implied that these substances are mixed together and drunk.

These moons are often mentioned in Bāul songs:

> The *bhāva* of the human soul is hard to understand.
> For a little while there is earth in the body,
> And for a while there is fire.
> And just for a moment, there is flowing water.
>
> Inside my body are four eternal moons
> In one moon is the origin of the exorcist [*ojhā*],
> In one moon is a palace.
> In one moon is day and night.
> In one moon is darkness.
> Four persons wait at the four doors of the body.
> At these doors, flowers blossom.
> Of these four fakirs, one is primordial
> And another is instrumental.
> The man in the mind waits on the other shore of creation.[81]

Blood (*raja*) is the main moon of the four. It is gathered on the third day of menstruation and used both for the *cāricāndra-bheda* ritual and that of *tīn-diner-krīyā,* the ritual actions of the third day. In this latter ritual, the Bāul seeks, by meditation during ritual intercourse, to find the man of the heart who dwells in the fluids of sexuality.

According to one interpretation, Īśvara, or the man of the heart, dwells in the sperm of the male (which is stored in a receptacle in the head). His female aspect, Kulakuṇḍalinī, dwells sleeping at the bottom of the spine, in the lowest or *mūlādhāra cakra* and is released during menstruation. When the blood flow (*rajo-rūpa*) of the woman is at its height (menstruation is believed to occur due to a buildup of blood), then

Īśvara descends from the crown of the head in the form of sperm (*vīrya*) to meet with it.[82]

Īśvara is man in his true or natural state (*sahaja mānuṣ*). He is made of love (*prema*), and when he is encountered, the Bāul feels a continuous bliss which arises from love. During ritual intercourse, Īśvara meets Kulakuṇḍalinī, who is also believed to be Prākṛti and another aspect of the man of the heart. Īśvara merges with her, and both return to his home in the crown of the head, with the help of various yogic practices, especially breath control. The Bāul phrase for this is *jāhākar bastu, tāhākare deoya* (to return something to where it really belongs). The feeling between Īśvara and Kulakuṇḍalinī is called the bliss of union (*milanānanda*) and is assumed to be identical to the union of Rādhā and Kṛṣṇa in the paradise of the body (*deha-Vṛndāvana*). To feel this way continually is the state of *sahaja*.[83]

According to another Bāul interpretation, the man of the heart shows himself in the woman. In this case, the imagery used for Īśvara or the man of the heart is that of a fish (*mīn-rūpa*). This fish swims in the "high tide" of the menstrual flow and is caught by the enjoyer (*rasika*), the Bāul who is full of love. This is the "tide time in the river," the overflowing of *rasa*. He catches the fish and causes it to move in an upward direction. The fish must be caught at the right time, or the waters dry and he is gone:

> The Sǎi plays in the form of a fish.
> Look for him in the waters of the river of love.
> If you do not dive into this river
> Having untied the bonds of the world
> [Then] the fish will burn with sorrow
> And be consumed, never to return.
>
> Release the ties to the shore of the river.
> The prisoner can untie the knot
> If he is submerged in love
> And the fish will come into his hand,
> Moving in its own way.
> The true form of woman is an ocean of love
> And the fish avatar is the friend of the poor.[84]

The fish avatar is a friend to both the poor in spirit, who cannot give up fascination with love and sexuality for traditional renunciation, and the poor in wealth, who cannot afford traditional worship. But one must be able to penetrate his disguise:

Who can recognize him?
My Lord plays in the water like an ordinary fish.
This fish pervades the universe.
In the midst of the waters of mercy
A person who understands the time
Can grasp the fish.

The man plays amazing games in the Ganga.
The water flows upon fire.
When the water will dry
Everything will be ruined
And the fish will escape into the void.[85]

The right time is once a month, at Mahāyoga. It includes new moon, the period regarded by the Bāuls as the time before the fish emerges; this is the time of lust (*kāma*). When the fish is present, it is the time of the menstrual flow designated as full moon. The third day is the time to catch the fish; he is not present before that, and there is the danger of the black crocodile of desire:

Pāgal Kanāi sits in the council of Dharmarāja [Yama].
On new moon and full moon, a high tide flows in the river
of lust
The black crocodile wanders about there!
If one goes to bathe in the new waters
The black crocodile will grab and eat him.[86]

On the third day, however, is the full moon, and the fish comes down to the Triveṇī. This term refers to the female genitals (*bhaga*), so-called because three courses of menstrual flow are believed to pass through here, each with different qualities and colors. The three currents are called the *kāruṇya bāri* (the waters of mercy), the *tāruṇya bari* (the young or tender waters), and the *lāvaṇya bari* (the charming or graceful waters).[87]

The value of the blood is seen in a poem quoted by Charles Capwell:

The flower blooms after twelve years,
month after month that flower falls.
To whom shall I speak about that flower?
Except for the enlightened, it is forbidden to say.
Others' is the desire for the fruit;
the enlightened immerses himself in the flower.
In Mādhuvan, Vraja's Balāi Dādā
is inebriated with drinking honey.[88]

Sexuality at this time is called the union of water and milk (*nīr* and *ksīr*). When they meet, the *ksīr* is extracted from the *nīr,* as the swan was believed able to separate milk and water. The pure milk is the treasure of the great ones (*mahājaner dhan*) and the inherited treasure (*poitrika dhan*).[89]

The mystical fish plays in these waters, and must be captured by meditation, control of breath and orgasm, postures, and alchemical techniques. All of these are part of the bodily practices leading to direct communion with God (*dehavāda* or *bindu sādhana*). The fluids may be mixed and drunk, leading to radiant health and physical or spiritual immortality.[90] In some cases, the fluids are seen as the physical representations of the divine male and female, as Rādhā and Kṛṣṇa, or the Săi and his Śakti Mā, and as the material manifestation of spiritual sweetness (*mādhurya* or *śṛngāra rasa*). The interaction of deities and fluids is *līlā,* the cause of the creation of the universe. In other cases, the mingling of fluids gives movement to the fish-avatar:

> Great sages cannot grasp this in their meditation.
> My unknown moon moves through the water in the form of
> a fish.
> This fish pervades the universe.
> It plays in Manasarovara, the lake of the heart.
> You desire to see him.
> Look, the *rasika* who seeks [him], seizes [him].
>
> He lives alone in the deep waters
> And searches for water [*nīr*].
> When the ebb meets the flow
> He begins to move independently.[91]

The most common metaphor is that of diving into the waters, to gain a treasure:

> The man plays in the milk and water.
> O my mind, understand your own house
> Why do you wander, seeking in the darkness of your
> heart? . . .
> It is difficult to dive deep into the river of *nīr.*
> When one is submerged, how many strange new things are
> seen!
> O, this full water jar is the universe [*brahmāṇḍa*].
> Just to say this, I begin to cry.

Indra's drum is not [heard] in this kingdom.
The flow of *sahaja* returns to *sahaja*.
O Lālan, dive down once.
And see with the true self.[92]

Diving reveals the true self (*svarūpa*), which allows true perception and understanding. Vaiṣṇava Sahajiyās interpret the true self to be Kṛṣṇa and Rādhā, opposing the ordinary forms of male or female. However, there is also a strand among Bāuls for whom the true self is Śiva and Śakti, and these Bāuls use Śākta imagery:

In another [kind of] love, a person is drowned in oblivion,
　　playing in love.
He plays in one burning ground after the other.
Around his neck is a bone necklace for Śakti.
He is mad [*pāgal*].[93]

Attitudes toward ritual practice vary among Bāuls. Some find it necessary to reach the state of perfection, while for others practice is only a preliminary stage for those who are not naturally close to the man of the heart and cannot become possessed by *bhāva* in song and dance. However, the desired end is to become a saint, caring yet detached, mad with ecstatic love, and dead while still alive.

The Country Was Once Full of *Pāgals:* Madness and Ecstasy among the Bāuls

What more can I say?
The country was once full of madmen
Where is there a madman like Rāmakṛṣṇa any more?

—Boidyanāth Sarma,
Calcutta, 1984

Madness is the highest goal of the Bāul—the madness of the *kṣepā* or *pāgal siddha.* He seeks after madness with a thirst, a desire, to be thrown from his normal outlook. The goal is to become mad by learning from a mad saint, rather than from those who pretend to be mad or are mad in a secular fashion. Of course, even divine madness has its disadvantages. Bāuls recognize that the person may be confused and his words incoherent or rambling. However, if this is due to experience of the divine, it is to be overlooked—the madman lives in a difficult place, the land of opposites:

After one becomes mad [*pāgal*], confusion [*gol*] remains.
The madman is one who comes and goes within the world.
Those who are mad in this world,
All know the confusion of the madman,
For he is dead while yet alive.

His heart is simple and fearless,
And within it is [both] darkness and golden light.
The temptations and the [senses] are great evils,
And they [always] irritate one together.
The madman in the world is he who can restrain them.

Those who are naturally mad,
Their words are not intelligible.
They have seen the divine couple [*jugala*] in human form.
And their vision is drowned in love [*jugala prema*].[94]

Such madness is generally too complex for ordinary people to understand:

How can you understand the language of madness?
At one moment forgetful, at another moment insane,
Then at another moment, someone's form is seen.
As I think of it, my mind goes mad,
My *bhāva* and mind are the play of madness.
This state stays day and night,
For how can the madman grasp time?

Saha Madar was mad,
He saw the vision of Allāh [*didār*] in Damsumara.
His state was neither stable nor unstable,
Yet he was called in *saṃsāra* a madman.
Panchanan was mad, he lived in the forest and burning
ground.
He knew the pleasure [*moeja*] of the madman.
He has attained the name of Mṛtanjaya [defeater of death]
in this life.[95]

Sometimes this state is described as apparent madness (*pāgalpārā*), as in the case of a Vaiṣṇava Bāul:

He thinks only of Rasarāja [Kṛṣṇa], and the path of the
aesthete
The fever [*jvāla*] of orthodoxy is gone.
He has renounced duty [karma and dharma].

He is not mad [*pāgal*], but appearing as if mad [*pāgalpārā*].
His eyes stream tears
Like rivers of melody,
All rules have flowed out with them.
Poor Gopāl says, he who is love-mad
Floats in a stream of *rasa*.[96]

One may deduce the madness of the Bāul by looking at his *bhāva,* his state of feeling or mood. *Bhāva* is an important term for Bāuls. When the singing is inspired, the Bāul is in a state of *bhāva* or *bhāvāveśa;* when he encounters the man of the heart, he is also in a state of *bhāva.* The man of the heart is the man of *bhāva* (*bhāver mānuṣ*), who lives in the city of *bhāva,* which is along the river of *bhāva.* One Bāul informant stated:

> Bāul *bhāva* is the last stage of practice. The person is without [secular] desire and passion; he only wants to see the man of the heart. You can see when he is successful, in his laughter, tears, and singing. . . . The *bhāva* comes and goes like breathing. But this *bhāva* is really Bhagavān. . . . Bāul *bhāva* is spiritual consciousness [*ādhyātmik bhāva, ādhyātmik cetana*]. In this state, the border is the universe, and the center is ultimate consciousness [*pūrṇa brahman*]. . . . Spiritual thought [*ādhyātmik cinta*] is the mirror that enables a person to see his own image.[97]

Bhāva includes both the highest states of spiritual bliss and the conditioning that keeps the person bound to the illusion of the body. A poem by Lālan Fakir states:

On this room there is a lock of *bhāva.*
In this room the Sǎi dwells.
Open the lock of *bhāva* by means of *bhāva,*
And you will see the play of that Man.
The torment of death will disappear
If your vision is fixed upon his beauty.

Wonderful is the image in the room of *bhāva*
Bhāva is the lantern, and *bhāva* is the lamp.
Lust is the enemy of *bhāva,*
It causes its beauty to disappear.

Of what use is devotion without *bhāva*?
Won't you see this, O king of men?
He who has *bhāva* is able to see,
Says Lālan with humility.[98]

Bhāva is sometimes considered to be a technique, a game, a way of grasping the inner God. The multiple meanings of the word are often used in Bāul songs:

In this city of *bhāva,* in what *bhāva* can I grasp him?
You tell me, mind, figure it out.
I cannot grasp him by thinking about him,
And if I try to use force
I shall never get the treasure.

This world is a fair of *bhāva,* a play of *bhāva,*
Everybody plays the game of *bhāva.*
Tell me, mind, in what *bhāva* can I grasp the treasure?
What is the nature of this *bhāva,* and what fruit does
it bear?[99]

Bhāva allows the person to reach the "red pearl," the drop of blood full of visionary images:

Why not see?
In the city of *bhāva,* in the house of *bhāva,* is the glory of
bhāva.
In the water burns a lamp.
The man of *bhāva* plays the game of *bhāva.*
Look in solitude for *bhāva* and *rasa.*
In the water and milk
A raft floats, shining.

The light of desire rises.
Can ordinary people understand it?
O, how many forms can be seen in
The red pearl.

When silence consumes sound
Then the game of *bhāva* will fall apart.
Lālan says, You will yet see
The means of escape.[100]

Such *bhāva* has the danger of driving the uninstructed person into a state of secular madness, in which he does not seek the man of the heart. Lālan writes of the mad Sufi Bāul (*pāgal deoyana*), who fears the mad *bhāva* of the Śākta:

If a person goes to the burning ground,
But he does not know about the *bhāva* of madness,

Does he then become [really] crazy, smearing his body with
ashes?
Thinking of such a madman I became crazy. . . .

Poor Lālan says: You forget what you possess.
Such is the state of the madman, when love comes.[101]

Thus Lālan recognizes several shades of madness—the unselfish love of the madman in devotion, and the madness that occurs when the unprepared worshiper goes to the cremation ground and is frightened out of his mind.

Lālan also writes of the states of possession by *bhāva* (*bhāvāveśa*), the only way to understand Bāul practice properly. It is the insight of this state which allows perfection (*siddhi*) to arise, easily and without effort:

Can this topic be discussed?
It can only be known in possession by *bhāva*.
When new moon and full moon are united,
[There are] amazing possibilities of enjoyment.
If one knows the fragmented and diseased [nature of the]
mortal world,
He can reach the world of wholeness,
He stays detached from sun and moon,
And at the end of the month he sees one day.
He enters into this union of unions.
If he practices, perfection comes naturally.[102]

Often the highest state is called *mahābhāva,* especially by Bāuls who emphasize Rādhā and Kṛṣṇa. However, the Bāul *mahābhāva* may include detachment, along with Vaiṣṇava emotionalism:

If you meet the man who is *mahābhāva,*
You will recognize him immediately.
His eyes are full of tears, and he smiles.
Sometimes he laughs, and sometimes he cries,
Sometimes he dances, and sometimes he begs.
His *bhāva* is always the same.
He does not pay attention to purity and impurity,
And he leaves at the doorway
Those things called good and evil.
His heart is unperturbed as a stone.[103]

Bāuls are mad because of God's proximity. He indwells not metaphorically, but literally—physically dwelling in the heart and bodily fluids. Religious experience is not seen in the sacred geography of the Vaiṣṇavas and Śāktas, where divine presence is in a physical locale or a heaven world. There is rather a sacred physiology—Bhagavān is present in the body, found not by travel but rather by erotic yoga and intense emotion.

Divine presence is seen primarily in terms of beauty—in visions, feelings of love, and mad desire. The Bāul and Sahajiyā are "trapped in the snare of beauty" of their deities. It is not possession—the god does not come down from another world to take them over. Instead, the Bāul or Sahajiyā grasps an elusive deity seen in instinct and instinctual imagery—the bird, the fish, the dance of the frog and the snake. The major ritual actions are also the acts resulting from instinctual drives—eating and sexuality. God is found through intensification of instinct—turning milk into cream, boiling away the water that dilutes the intensity, thickening the love of God by sexual control. In the saint, God's presence has been moved from the bodily fluids into the heart and vision, and religious and human drives have been fused. Religious behavior becomes instinctual and spontaneous.

The transfer of God's locale results in madness. Real Bāul madness does not result from separation from God (*viraha*), but rather from direct visual presence (*darśana*). Seeing the man of the heart makes a person mad in the world of illusion.

A poem in the *Bānglār Bāul O Bāul Gān* may best show the many concepts of madness and the place of the Bāul madman (*kṣepā*):

Mad, mad, everyone is mad,
So why are people criticized for it?
When you dive into the ocean of the heart, you see
That only the madman is truly good.

Some are mad for riches, others for people
Some grow mad from the pull of need.
Some are mad for form, and some for *rasa,*
And some are mad for love.
These madmen laugh and cry.
There is grandeur to this madness.

Everyone says, "Mad, mad,"
On what tree does madness grow?
When you do not care for truth or falsehood
Everything is equal, the bitter and the sweet.[104]

FIVE Saints, Seekers, and Bhor Ladies: Bengali Holy Women

The Door of Faith

> I think of generations of Bengali women hidden behind the barred windows of half-dark rooms, spending centuries in washing clothes, kneading dough and murmuring aloud verses from the Bhagavad Gita and the Ramayana, in the dim light of sooty lamps. Lives spent in waiting for nothing, waiting on men, self-centered and indifferent and hungry and demanding and critical, waiting for death and dying misunderstood, always behind bars, those terrifying black bars that shut us in, in the old houses, in the old city.[1]

It is only religion which holds the key:

> If I had religious faith, I could easily enough renounce all this. But I have no faith, no alternative to my confused despair, there is nothing I can give myself to and so I must stay.[2]

Religion has been both the way in and the way out for Bengali women. It has been the way into a ritual tradition that supports subservience, lowered status, and a limited sphere of activity. But it has also been the way out, for religious knowledge and practice have given women freedom and a wide range of action.

In this chapter, I look at the lives of five modern holy women. Two of these women—Ānandamayī Mā and Śāradā Devī—were famous saints, with literally millions of disciples. The latter three are holy women (*sādhikās*), with their own smaller groups of disciples. In all of these cases, religious experience (or in one case, the attribution of such experience) served to create and justify their religious status. In almost all cases, this religious experience was initially associated with madness or illness, and it was proven to be religious, not insane, only after testing, devotion, miracle, and the passage of time.

The theology of some of these holy women was idiosyncratic, while others followed a Śākta/universalist perspective. It was virtually impossible for me to find a Vaiṣṇava holy woman.[3]

The data on the saints come primarily through biographies and the writings of disciples, while the stories of the three holy women come from interviews and from the statements of disciples. In all of these cases, religious experience in these women was spontaneous, occurring from childhood and at unexpected times; practice was a later addition—to act as an object lesson for disciples, to gain control of the experience, and to develop an ordered life. There is no single practice that was followed by all, although many traditional kinds of experience—possession, visions, emotional extremes of religious passion and detachment—are present.

The initial association of ecstasy and madness is not uncommon in viewing budding holy men. As with male practitioners, madness is often the precursor of religious experience in a mode reminiscent of shamanism. This may be seen in the case of the "madwoman of Calcutta," described by the Bāul Śrī Anirvāṇ:

> About twenty years ago in a residential section of the city, people used to see a very young and beautiful woman stopping passers-by on the sidewalk in front of her house and asking them, "Where is Shyama Babu? Have you seen him? If you tell me where he is, I will go and fetch him." Her beloved was dead and she was still waiting for him, living from her love of him. And love had betrayed her. The passers-by played cruel tricks on her.
>
> Then another phase began for her. She clung to young men as they were going by and said to them, "You are my Shyama Babu, you have come back." Since she was not a prostitute, these men drove her away and ill-treated her, even threw stones at her.
>
> After several years, one of her neighbors who had known her in the past noticed her sitting all day long at the foot of the sacred tree of that district. She had aged but her face was radiant with joy. She recognized her neighbor. He asked her, "Have you found your Shyama?" "Yes," she replied with a lovely smile. "Look, there he is," and she pointed to her breast.[4]

In this case, the madwoman had become a holy woman. She drew her deepest desire within her, so that it became both eternal and attainable.

Bhagavān may be an inner love, or an inner emptiness, as in the case of Mā Ānandamayī.

Ānandamayī Mā: *Bhāvātīta*

"Am I Bhagavatī herself, or am I possessed by Bhagavatī? I really don't know."
—Gopināth Kavirāj, *Śrī Śrī Mā Ānandamayī: Upadeśa O Praśnottara*

Ānandamayī Mā was born in 1896 in Kheora, East Bengal. Although the area was primarily Muslim, her parents were devout Vaiṣṇavas. She was named Nirmalā Sundarī (immaculate beauty), and showed herself so cheerful during childhood that her neighbors called her Khuśir Mā (happy mother). She was obedient to an extreme toward her parents and had less than two years of schooling because of poverty. She also had no formal religious training.[5]

Her father, Bipin Beharī Bhaṭṭācārya, was the son of a guru, and people noticed early in him the qualities of divine love (*bhāgavata-bhāva-prema*). He sang Vaiṣṇava songs at all times and places, appearing as if intoxicated. He was the only son of a widow and grew up barely able to discharge his worldly responsibilities.[6] He would get up at 3:00 A.M. and sing hymns; often he would wander off for long periods—once for over a year. His wife would find him and bring him back. He would sleep in his outhouse, so as not to disturb anyone, and would roam about in the darkness without a light. When the roof of his house was blown off by a storm, he sat singing in the rain.[7]

Mā's mother, Mokṣadā Sundarī Devī (nicknamed Vidhumukhī Devī), was also known for her states of *bhāva*. Vidhumukhī's mother died when she was very young, and her father died soon after. At the age of seven she was brought to the house of her mother's daughter-in-law and lived there until she married at the age of twelve. She was visited periodically by avatars, gods, and deities, who glittered with light in the midst of her household work. While pregnant with Nirmalā, she would see visions of sages, and statues of deities which would suddenly disappear. She later took renunciant (*sannyāsa*) vows, taking the name Swāmī Muktānanda Giri Mahārāja.

Nirmalā also had a sister named Surubala, younger by nine years. Surubala was a moody child, subject to fits of anger in which her body would turn rigid and her face darken from anger and lack of oxygen. She died at the age of eighteen years, soon after her marriage.

The first daughter of the family died young, and for luck, Vidhumukhī would place Nirmalā at the foot of a luck-bringing *tulsī* plant and roll her to and fro on the ground. This was done every day until she was eighteen months old, after which she would go and roll there herself.[8]

Nirmalā was a happy child, but had peculiar reactions to everyday events. She was generally assumed by neighbors to be either absent-minded or slightly retarded. She was subject to trances and visions, and was seen talking to trees and inanimate objects. She stared at the sky so much that she was called "camel-faced," and she would play, jumping and laughing, with birds and ants. When the roof was blown off the house in Kheora, she laughed and clapped her hands and said that now she need not go outside to see the stars (her mother described this as "just like the joy of a lunatic on the killing of a cow").[9]

As a child she perceived gods, goddesses, and ghosts during group singing (*kīrtana*), but would not tell anyone about them:

> From her childhood, when listening to kirtan, Mother would exhibit in her person manifestations of Bhavas, extraordinary raptures and divine ecstasies. She said, "When Kirtan would be heard even from afar, many unusual manifestations of Bhavas (ecstasies) would appear in this body. Owing to the darkness of the room, it would pass unnoticed by its parents. Moreover there was this sort of feeling also in this body that nobody should notice these manifestations."[10]

Her parents arranged a marriage for her when she was thirteen years old, to Ramaṇi Mohan Cakravarti, later called Bholānāth, who was many years older. She lived with her husband's family for five years, while he moved around East Bengal looking for a job. She worked hard there, and her relatives assumed that her trances were due to fatigue. She got along well with them, and in 1914, at the age of eighteen years, she moved to Aṣṭagrāma to be with her husband.

It was a celibate marriage, as Bholānāth learned. Ānandamayī Mā later said that, whenever a worldly thought arose in Bholānāth, her body would assume the symptoms of death, and he would have to repeat a mantra to bring her back to consciousness. She has also said that her body would shrink or expand, or simply grow rigid. At one point, Ānandamayī Mā said that she gave him electrical shocks at such times. He initially thought the situation would be temporary, but it proved permanent. He accepted it, although his relatives suggested that he remarry.

At Aṣṭagrāma, Mā's *bhāvas* came to public notice during *kīrtanas,* and a neighbor predicted that the whole world would call her mother. These states occurred without any instruction or ritual practice and against the strong opposition of her relatives:

> As the sound of kirtan would reach Her, She would generally drop whatever work She might be doing and gradually Her body stiffened and fell on the ground. She would remain in this condition for varying periods. Afterwards or at times, She would stand erect resting only on the big toe or only on the forepart of Her feet, with both hands raised above Her head, Her eyes fixed steadily ahead without even a flicker of the eyelids. Sometimes Her head would bend backwards until it touched Her back. She would either stand there absolutely still and motionless, or sway rhythmically with the heaving of her breath. Often she would run dancing to the spot where kirtan was being sung, sometimes very gracefully undulating like a wave, and sometimes with incredible swiftness. Her movements then would be quick like a flash of lightning. . . . Frequently She would roll in ecstasy to and fro on the ground in a whirl over a distance of 15 or 20 yards like a dry leaf driven before a storm. It was impossible to stop Her at such moments. She who was usually so modest and never unveiled Her face before strangers would now run and dance bare-headed, entirely oblivious to the external world.[11]

Even stranger events would happen:

> There were occasions when Her body would stretch and become much taller than usual; or again it would shrink into an inconceivably small size. At times it would become rolled up like a round mass of flesh, as if there were no bones. Sometimes the entire body would so throb and thrill with strong emotions surging through it, that it would get swollen and red, with every single hair standing on end. She would sometimes shed profuse tears or laugh and become stiff as in a stupor. There was, in short, no end to the varieties of Bhavas and their expressions induced in Her by the chanting of God's holy name at Kirtan.[12]

In 1916 she became ill and moved to Vidyākuta to be with her parents. In 1918, she and Bholanāth moved to Bājitpur, where she began both Vaiṣṇavite and Śaivite spiritual practices. These continued until 1924. She would hear voices which told her which exercises to do, which mantras to chant, and which images to visualize. The voices would issue commands, and she would obey. She would fall into trances publicly and heal people by touch. Her body would move involuntarily into complex yogic postures, and often long strands of hair would be pulled out. Her *bhāvas* increased, and Bholānāth summoned exorcists to cure her. These attempts failed, and finally a physician told him that it was god intoxication rather than mental illness.

Her devotee Bhaiji met her in Bājitpur and suggested to Bholānāth that she be called Ānandamayī. Her ritual practices included extremes of eating (from virtual fasting to eating large amounts of food); later she gave up feeding herself and had to be fed by devotees.[13]

During her period of practice and meditation, she initiated herself and later initiated Bholānāth. She described her initiation as occurring on a full moon night, with invisible *pūjā* (worship) articles:

> But do you know what happened to this body that night? All the articles of worship were arranged, visibly, though nothing had been procured from outside as is usually done. Then the *yajñasthali* (platform) was made and various yantras were also drawn thereon. The particular *bīja* was inscribed . . . (there were also fire oblations and chanting). The various objects and articles of *pūjā* were as visible to this body as yours are to you. . . . After this *japa* started. At first the fingers stretched themselves and became still. This body was watching and admiring. Then slowly the fingers curved and attached themselves to the proper positions for *japa*. Now also as a suggestion arose in the mind that it should be done in a particular way there was confusion. But when again the conscious attempt was given up and the body waited quietly, it all went on slowly and correctly.[14]

She would see deities issue out of her body, complete with associates; she would worship them, and they would again merge into her body, after which another deity would emerge. Her yogic actions (*krīyās*) were involuntary, and she said of them: "Do you know how it all functioned? Just as has been observed in Tata's factories—the various machines were all working automatically, there being no one to guide them."[15]

After her self-initiation, she took a vow of silence and did not speak for three years. If speech were absolutely necessary, she would first draw a circle around her seat with her fingers. Her only free speech was during trance, when she spoke in a language resembling Sanskrit, which observers generally could not understand. Her disciple Bhaiji managed to write down a few lines and more or less translate them:

> By Me alone are all created in My own image; by Me are all sent into this world and in Me all find final refuge. I am the final cause indicated by the Praṇava in the Vedas. I am Mahāmāyā and Mahābhāva all in one. Devotion to Me is the cause of *mokṣa*. All are mine.[16]

During this time, Bholānāth lost his job in Bājitpur and found a new one in Dacca, as the manager of the Shāh-bagh Gardens, in 1924. Her period of silence continued, but she would laugh and cry for hours. Even after this period, she would sometimes go into trance for days and weeks, and then begin to mumble a few broken words. She would forget how to talk, walk, and even distinguish between different articles of food and drink. She would not remember what rice was, but would cry if she could not have some immediately. She would have tantrums like a child, and would alternately refuse to eat and eat large quantities of food—enough for eight or nine people. She stated: "At the time of eating I did not know that I was swallowing so much food. It was from you that I first came to learn about it. At that time, whatever things you would offer, good or bad, even grass and leaves, would have been eaten up."[17]

In 1925 she conducted a worship of Kālī (*pūjā*) in which she placed flowers and sandal paste on her own head, rather than on the statue. In 1926 people began singing hymns (*kīrtana*) at Shah-bagh, and she would fall into trances, dancing and rolling on the ground. As one devotee described her religious states:

> A variety of *bhāvas* manifested themselves on her body, all marvelous to behold. Now it seemed that she was engaged in a great battle—the expression on her face was fierce and even her complexion had darkened—then it appeared that she was performing *ārati* with her entire body. The fierce expression of a moment ago changed into a beautiful gesture of supplication. The *bhāvas* were too numerous and were changing too rapidly to permit more than a glimpse of them . . . her body was blown like a scattered dry leaf in the tempest.[18]

This tendency to change roles was also described by one of her foreign disciples, Arnand Desjardins, in "Mother as Seen by a Westerner": "At an interval of a few seconds I have seen her appear 30 and 70 years old, be the image of gentleness and the embodiment of severity; I have seen in her the laughing little girl and the terrifying man, the radiant saint and the inspirer."[19]

An *āśrama* was built for her in Ramna, Dacca, but she was unwilling to stay there. The night it was completed, she left with Bholānāth and her disciple Bhaiji for Dehradun, where she stayed in an abandoned room in a Śiva temple for almost a year. She was without blankets or money, and the weather often went below freezing. Her hair became matted, and she lived on little food and water.

She went on various pilgrimages and located hidden temple ruins by intuitions felt in trance. In 1928 she told Bholānāth to meditate at the Tārāpīṭh burning grounds. She later told him to move to the Rama *āśrama,* while she traveled through India. She refused to cook for him any longer, and told him that he had to sleep on the floor (she had his bed taken apart).

She continued to travel through India, stopping for short periods at *āśramas* built for her by devotees and participating in religious festivals. Bholānāth died of smallpox in 1938, and Ānandamayī's mother (who took renunciant vows) died in 1970, at the age of ninety-three years. Ānandamayī Mā died recently, in 1981.

Devotees felt that Ānandamayī Mā had miraculous powers (*siddhis*), such as the ability to make her body shrink and expand, and to read thoughts and know events at a distance. She stated that the thoughts and emotions of devotees were like the alphabet—she always knew how to read them if she thought it necessary. She could see inwardly the faces of distant devotees: "Just as at a flash of torchlight your faces gleam forth in their bold outlines, all your facial expressions appear in my mind when you meditate on me or talk about me or sit down to pray to me."[20]

She would speak with invisible deities, ṛṣis, (sages) saints, and ghosts. She would perform symbolic cures: to heal a child's ear abscess, she took a needle and scratched herself (at which time the abscess burst and the child was cured). Sometimes her actions were more shamanic, as when she grasped the spirit of one of her female disciples (who had been in a car accident):

> On enquiry from [the disciple], we learnt that just at the time the accident had happened, she had felt that she was dying and someone was carrying away her life substance. But Mother intervened and snatched away her life substance from the hold of that being and placed it in her body, which appeared to her to be a new one, because Mother had thrown away the old body in the form of a piece of steel on the road. The broken piece of mudguard was in the place of her corpse. That is

> why Mother did not allow any of us to know what had happened, lest we should bring with us the said broken piece representing her corpse. . . . Ma stated that the spirit had been leaving the body and soaring high, but it had been brought again into contact with the body.[21]

Ānandamayī Mā avoided questions about her identity. Devotees would guess her to be a goddess (Kālī, Durgā, Saraswatī, Rādhā), a human seeker, a reincarnated Vedic holy woman (*brahmavādinī*), an avatar, a saint, a person possessed by gods. Her answers were most often evasive: "I am who you think I am" or "This body is like a musical instrument—what you hear depends upon how you play it."[22] Indeed, she considered individual identity to be a disease. She called it *bhāva roga,* the disease of every person who looks on himself as a separate individual.[23]

When a devotee complained about the crowds of people who followed her, she stated:

> As you do not feel the weight of your head, of hands and feet . . . so do I feel that these persons are all organic members of THIS BODY; so I don't feel their pressure nor find their worries weighing upon me. Their joys and sorrows, problems and their solutions, I feel to be vitally mine. . . . I have no egosense nor conception of separateness.[24]

Her identity, or lack thereof, was a continuous one, sometimes interpreted as dependent on a personal god: "I have no sense of pleasure or pain, and I stay as I have always been. Sometimes He draws me outside, and sometimes He takes me inside and I am completely withdrawn. I am nobody, all of my actions are done by Him and not by me."[25] Sometimes, however, she claimed that her mind was empty and that only the sense of "I am" remained. Her mind was then lost in the great void (*mahāśūnya*): "My inner world is a vacuum, with nothing within. If you hit an empty drum, sound comes out of it. In this way, whatever I speak comes out spontaneously from the inner void."[26]

According to Ānandamayī Mā's philosophy, all is spontaneous action which is chaotic and incoherent (*elomelo*). This universal state of chaos arises due to spontaneous upsurges of divine will (*kheyāla*). Her *bhāvas* were not the acting of roles, as in drama, but rather the play of Bhagavān acting through her body. Her actions were spontaneous (*svakrīyā*), without individual will.

Bhāva is a broad concept for her, much more than a trance state. It is hidden and mysterious, both religious experience and the origin of life:

> The source of the Ganges lies in the depths of inaccessible jungles, hidden away from the eyes of men, yet its life-giving waters irrigate fields and pastures and bring prosperity to the smiling countryside along its shores. It is *bhāva* that is at the root of creation, preservation, and destruction of the universe.[27]

Bhāva arises from within and must be expressed—it creates an inner pressure which must be released:

> When something is boiled in a closed vessel, there comes a stage when the vapor will push up the lid and, unless force is used, the vessel cannot be kept covered anymore. In a similar manner, when, while being engaged in *japa* or some other spiritual exercise, a wave of ecstatic emotion surges up from within, it becomes difficult to check it. This ecstatic emotion is called *bhāva*. It emerges from deep within and expresses itself outwardly.[28]

Sometimes it shows itself as worship:

> In the whole of my body, worship is going on, and formerly sound used to rise up from my navel. When this sound would emerge, I used to feel as if my navel were being torn up. I felt that the sounds touched every part of my body, and then worship would take place in every pore of my body. This sound would rise into my head, and it would transform itself there into the mantra *Om*.[29]

But if there is any conscious thought or attempt to control it, the sound disappears:

> Mantras would express themselves spontaneously in me. Nothing would happen when I tried to exert my own will. When I spontaneously tried to will [the mantras], I was unable to utter anything, and I felt as if my mouth had been shut.[30]

In Ānandamayī Mā, *bhāva* was seen in two major forms: trance (*bhāva samādhi*) and possession (*āveśa*). In the former state she was cold and lifeless, appearing to be dead—in Aṣṭagrām the ants would gather around her eyes as she lay on the floor. In possession states, she would dance, sing, utter stanzas in unknown languages, roll back and forth rapidly on the ground, and take on different roles and identities. Sometimes she would interpret these *bhāvas* as part of a process, the progressive internalization of Bhagavān:

> Look, at first one believed the Lord to be present in one's prayer-room, but by and by one is able to perceive Him here and there. At a further stage, not anymore in particular places, but wherever one turns one's eyes: He is seen sitting in trees, standing in water; He is perceived within animals and birds. However, even here one's vision of Him is not uninterrupted.
>
> Then comes a time when the Beloved does not leave one anymore: wherever one may go, He is ever by one's side and His presence is constantly felt.
>
> What, now, is the next stage like? The form, variety, appearance of the tree—all is the Lord. At an earlier stage one perceived Him within all objects; but now He is not seen within the objects anymore, for there is nothing but He alone.[31]

Gopināth Kavirāj, a scholar and disciple of Ānandamayī Mā, organized her religious experiences into four hierarchical stages of the soul's evolution after many discussions with her. In the first stage (*citta samādhana*), the mind is dried due to the evaporation of the waters of desire and passion. The purified mind easily catches the fire of spiritual knowledge. This stage is also called *bhāvaśuddhi,* the purity of *bhāva,* and is seen when the person is overwhelmed by emotion.

In the second stage (*bhāva samādhana*), the body is paralyzed and the mind drawn inward, while *bhāva* flows into the heart like a stream. The body is insensitive and immobile. In the third stage (*vyakta samādhana*), the individual soul is absorbed in an individual deity, and the duality of form and formlessness remains. The fourth stage (*pūrṇa samādhana*) is the melting away of all duality. It is the state of *bhāvātīta,* "beyond *bhāva,*" beyond form and formlessness, in which the mind is free from the ripples of thought. There is continuous awareness, even in dream states.[32]

However, such a concept of stages contradicts her own statements that she has never undergone any changes of mental state or body, that she has always been the same and has never had an identity. Disciples have been compelled to invent identities for her, as a lack of identity seems too close to madness.

On the subject of madness, Ānandamayī Mā was of two minds. When a disciple asked her if visions were due to mental imbalance, she answered:

> An unbalanced mind is the cause of vision? How lovely. God is manifest everywhere and you have to attain to the vision of Him. How can this vision be due to an unsound mind? To go beyond the pairs of opposites in the characteristic of enlightenment. How can this be achieved by a deranged mind? The vision of God cures even insanity.[33]

However, madness also means attainment:

> Go forth to realize God—try at least. This is the genuine madman (otherworldly, visionary seer—like Śiva). Madman (*pāgal*) means *paoa gol* (to reach the goal). . . . When one becomes obsessed by his madness, the madness after the world of duality takes flight.[34]

Ānandamayī Mā is a holy woman without a formal tradition, whose spiritual status is based almost entirely on her ecstatic states. She had no guru, initiated herself, and learned ritual from invisible voices. When she was a child, she learned about repeating the name of Hari from her father; later she would repeat the name spontaneously, with *āsanas* and mantras. Bholānāth told her to repeat *Jai Śiva Śaṅkara Bom Bom Hara Hara,* and she did so. While she had a period of ritual practice, she did not see this as spiritual striving but as play. She claimed that her consciousness had never changed over her life, and that her practice was a game, to show others how they should act. She emphasized detachment and devotion, and while she has performed a few miraculous cures, these are hardly mentioned by her devotees—it might change her role from that of high-caste devotional saint to low-caste village healer.

She would sometimes refer to herself as a madwoman (*pāgli*), as indeed her relatives and neighbors initially believed her to be. However, her spontaneous worship, positions, trances, yogic powers, mantras and hymns, and strange Sanskritic speech convinced observers of her religious orientation. The ecstatic child of ecstatic parents, she has become a famous saint but stands where many holy women do—on the edge of several traditions, in the midst of none.

Śāradā Devī: Attribution of *Bhāva*

Śāradā Devī was the wife of Rāmakṛṣṇa and was worshiped as Mother of the Universe after his death. She initiated thousands of disciples and helped guide the Rāmakṛṣṇa order until her death in 1920. She did not claim to be an ecstatic, but was nevertheless seen as one due to her association with Rāmakṛṣṇa.[35]

She was born in Jayrāmbati, a small village in Bankura, West Bengal, in 1853. As Śāradā Mukherji, she was a serious child who preferred to play alone with dolls rather than play games with other children. She helped her parents with housework and care of her younger brothers while she was very young, and helped in the village worship of Jagaddhātrī, Śītalā, and Siṁhavāsinī. In 1859, at the age of six, she was chosen as wife by Rāmakṛṣṇa Paramahaṁsa, who came from the nearby village of Kāmārpukur. He was seventeen years older and in the midst of his early spiritual crises. After the wedding, he returned to Dakṣhiṇeśwar and she remained in the village. She heard little from him and grew up under the stigma of being married to a madman (in 1858 there had been an unsuccessful exorcism of Rāmakṛṣṇa in his home village, and rumors kept drifting into the villages of his erratic behavior as priest of the Kālī temple). When she was nineteen years old, she went to visit Rāmakṛṣṇa, as he had never sent for her, and she wished to know the status of her marriage. She traveled by foot to Dakṣhiṇeśwar, lived with Rāmakṛṣṇa for several months, and began a series of visits in which she alternately lived in her home village and in Dakṣhiṇeśwar.

In 1872 or 1873, Rāmakṛṣṇa declared that she was an incarnation of the goddess and worshiped her in the ritual Ṣoṛaśī Pūjā. This radically changed her religious status, as well as her state of mind:

> The master took some sanctified water from the pitcher and sprinkled it on her body. Then, after uttering the mantras appropriate to the occasion, he prayed to her: "O Thou eternal Virgin, thou Mother Tripura Sundarī, the Source of all Power, do thou open the gates of perfection. Sanctifying her mind and body, do Thou manifest thyself through her (the Holy Mother) and ordain all good." Then he mentally identified the different limbs of the Holy Mother with the corresponding parts of the Deity, with appropriate mantras, and considering her as none other than the Deity Herself, worshiped her duly with the usual 16 kinds of offerings.[36]

Rāmakṛṣṇa told others to worship her as the Divine Mother, for she had taken on his merit:

> In a state of divine afflatus the Mother accepted the worship as also the result of all the spiritual disciplines of the Master. In fact, she inherited the richest spiritual wealth without any corresponding conscious endeavor on her part; and in addition, she learnt how to look upon all beings as manifestations of the Universal Mother.[37]

Śāradā Devī was shy and self-effacing, subservient to Rāmakṛṣṇa and obedient to his wishes. For a time, she was allowed to help him in his spiritual practices, to use mantras to bring him out of certain moods, and to help him in those *bhāvas* in which he played roles:

> Whenever the Master came down to the conscious plane during this period, he was swayed by a feeling of womanliness within himself, so much so that he considered himself, as also the Holy Mother and others, as the maids or handmaids of the Universal Mother. The Mother then clothed and adorned him like a woman, and felt elated at the thought that just like the Master, she too was a maid of Kālī.[38]

However, when she mentioned being kept awake at night by Rāmakṛṣṇa's trances, he suggested that she live in the Nahabat, in a tiny room that was also a pantry and kitchen. She spent the rest of her time at Dakṣhiṇeśwar in this room, surrounded by pots and pans and vegetable baskets, bent low beneath the slings hanging from the ceiling. She would spend the day in this room, emerging only at night, and she stayed not only veiled but largely invisible to the disciples and visitors at Dakṣhiṇeśwar. She cared for Rāmakṛṣṇa's mother, who also lived in the building, and did the cooking for all disciples and visitors.

Rāmakṛṣṇa died in 1886, and Śāradā had planned to adopt the widow's dress and habits—shaved head, lack of ornaments, sari without borders. However, a vision of Rāmakṛṣṇa told her not to dress as a widow:

> At evening the Mother sat to remove her ornaments one by one, and when at last she was about to take off her gold bracelets, the Master suddenly appeared in his body just as it was before he had the disease, and taking hold of her hands said, "Have I died that you are removing the signs of a married woman from your wrists?" She then desisted from doing so.[39]

She would occasionally have other visions of Rāmakṛṣṇa and would worship his picture, or her own picture together with his. She performed austerities after his death, such as the *pañcatapas* rite (or five fires, in which the person sits in meditation in the midst of four fires, with the hot sun above as the fifth). She would be urged toward these practices by visions of a little girl and a monk with a shaven head.

After an initial period of chaos and poverty, she settled into a relationship with Rāmakṛṣṇa's disciples, who called her Mother. She began to initiate people in Rāmakṛṣṇa's name while continuing to cook and care for the stream of visitors who came to his disciples. During Durgā Pūjā at

Belur Math, the monks of the growing Rāmakṛṣṇa order offered flowers at her feet, as they did to the deity, and wrote poems to her divinity. Disciples began to follow her, saying that Mother was kinder than Father (Rāmakṛṣṇa) and that they desired healing:

> Hundreds of sufferers came to her with their burdens of sins and woes. Their touch often produced pain in her feet, but she bore this knowingly and willingly. . . . She said, "Don't allow anyone anymore to salute me by laying his head on my feet; thereby all sins enter there, and my feet burn, so that I have to wash them. That's why I fall ill. Ask them to salute me from a distance."[40]

Yet the majority of her time was spent cooking for the monks and serving the crowds of visitors and relatives who followed in Rāmakṛṣṇa's wake. In later life, she lived with Surubala, the insane widow of her late favorite brother, and Surubala's daughter Rādhu, who was both insane and hostile. Her other relatives attempted to gain money from her position, and there were many squabbles over funds and properties. She counseled many women devotees and went on several pilgrimages. She was frequently ill, and finally died in 1920.

One theme in Sāradā Devī's life is the attribution of *bhāva* and its effects on her. She was a modest, normal Hindu wife, until the Ṣoṛaśī Pūjā, and especially until Rāmakṛṣṇa's death. After these two events, people began to look to her for visions and revelations, believing that she was hiding her states of *bhāva* if she said that she did not experience them. Initially, she would wistfully say that she wished to experience such states; later, she had visions that made her into a saint, a guru, even a goddess, in which she would merge her identity with that of Rāmakṛṣṇa, and alternated grandiose claims with statements of her low status and ability.

Her lack of statement proved the state:

> The Mother often had her moods of rapt absorption, but we do not know whether along with that self-forgetfulness there was any external expression known to herself or to others. . . . Perhaps such exuberance of spiritual ecstasy was kept in check because of the Master's condemnation of it.[41]

Laughter was an indication of *bhāva*:

> One night somebody was playing a flute. The Mother was in the grip of a spiritual mood produced by that music, and she sat up and began laughing by fits and starts. (The disciple of

> Rāmakṛṣṇa) Yogin-Ma, too, sat up and withdrew herself to one corner of the bed thinking, "I am a householder, I should not touch her now."[42]

Rāmakṛṣṇa began this attribution of *bhāva,* in which falling asleep showed her spiritual status:

> When the Master spoke to village women of "higher things," the Mother often fell asleep. Rāmakṛṣṇa said, "No, my dear, no, don't awaken her. Don't think she is asleep without reason. If she hears these things, she will fly headlong away."[43]

Walking alone could demonstrate *bhāva*:

> Forgetful of herself she sometimes walked across the vast sandy shore to the waters of the Yamunā unknown to anybody, and she had to be searched out and persuaded to return. One does not know, she might have then thought of herself as Rādhā, the sweetheart of Kṛṣṇa, and of Śrī Rāmakṛṣṇa as Kṛṣṇa, and was thus lost in the bliss of union in the Vrindaban of her heart. It is said that she once told a devotee, "I, indeed, am Rādhā."[44]

Going to temples also demonstrated her states of *bhāva*:

> She went round the temples daily, seeing the different images and sitting for meditation at suitable places. She must have been blessed with many visions at that time, though she never gave them out.[45]

Resting while walking was also a sign of spiritual states:

> During this walk (in Vrindaban) the Mother seemed to be looking at the roads, fields and forests of the place with intense interest; at times she stopped altogether, lost in her reverie. To Yogin-Ma and others, it was clear that she was in a spiritual mood and was having some visions, too. So now and then they put questions to her out of curiosity. But the Mother put them off with a simple answer, "No, that's nothing, move on."[46]

She was described by Rāmakṛṣṇa's disciples as a "cat under the ashes," her true state hidden from sight, although everyone wished to see it. Her glory was seen in unlikely ways, such as the ability to eat food from low-caste people. Svāmī Premānanda stated:

> Who has understood the Holy Mother? There's not a trace of grandeur. The Master had at least his power of *vidyā* [knowledge] manifested, but the Mother? Her perfection of knowledge is hidden. What a mighty power is this! Glory to the Mother. . . . She grants shelter to everyone, eats food from the hands of almost anyone and all is digested! Mother, Mother, victory unto the Mother![47]

Such attributions of spiritual states contributed to a vacillation in her sense of identity. She would state:

> "The wisdom of God is in the palm of my hand. I can have it whenever I want"; "In the midst of worldly activities, whenever I desire, I understand with a flash that all this is nothing but a play of Mahamaya"; "Don't regard me as your relative, I can leave this body at once if I desire"; "No one will be able to know my real nature so long as I am alive."[48]

She also stated: "Don't you consider me an ordinary mortal. . . . Do you think you can have any escape if I am really offended? I can rend all ties asunder this very moment."[49]

Sometimes she would claim to be merely the daughter of Rām Mukherji, but her denials of divinity were not believed. She questioned: "People call me a goddess, and I too am led to think so. Or how could you explain all the strange things that have happened in my life?"[50]

The beliefs of others about her divinity allowed for a latitude in her behavior—she could violate caste rules, such as eating or sleeping with Westerners or people of lower caste, and this was called "an achievement of her maternal consciousness"[51] and a sign of maternal love, rather than impurity. When she was chased by an insane man, she threw him to the ground and slapped him; she stated that "then my true self came out." Rather than seeing unfeminine behavior, her disciples interpreted this incident to mean that her identity as Bagalā, one of the ten forms of the goddess (*mahāvidyās*), emerged.[52]

She inspired a fascination with the paradox of the highest becoming the lowest; as Svāmī Premānanda stated:

> You have seen with your own eyes how this Mother, who is in reality the Great Goddess ruling over those who wield the destinies of kings and emperors, has yet elected to become a poor woman plastering the house with cowdung, scouring

> utensils, winnowing rice and clearing the leavings of the devotees after their meals.[53]

Sometimes after his death she would feel close to Rāmakṛṣṇa, saying that they shared the same soul; at other times they would be separate, as in a vision of him she had one night:

> The Mother came out to the head of the steps leading to the water to enjoy that beauty, without any other thought in her mind. Suddenly Shri Ramakrishna emerged from behind and rushed down by her into the river, and his body of pure spirit got dissolved in the holy waters of the river, which has been washing away the sins of millions of people for ages. The sight made the Mother's hair stand on end. Dumbfounded, she kept her eyes fixed there, when all of a sudden, Swami Vivekananda burst upon the view from nowhere and shouting with elation, "Glory unto Ramakrishna" went on sprinkling handfuls of that water over the millions of people standing around, who, before her eyes, became freed from this world at the very touch of that water.[54]

The conflict between human and divine identities became an internal one:

> That day, as she sat for meditation on the roof of Balaram Babu's house, she entered into *samādhi*. When she emerged from it, she said to Yogin-Ma, "I saw, I was in a far-off place. All were treating me there with the utmost love. I became very beautiful. The Master was there, and with great tenderness they made me sit by his side. I can't describe the bliss that I enjoyed. When I regained my consciousness a little, I saw the body lying here. Then the thought came to me, 'How can I enter into this ugly body?' I had not the least desire to resume it. At long last I managed to get into it; and then consciousness returned to it."[55]

For Rāmakṛṣṇa's disciples, her identity as goddess became the dominant one. Svāmī Abhedānanda wrote a meditation on her:

> Let us meditate in the lotus of the heart
> On Mother Śāradā.
> Of golden hue;
> Seated cross-legged;
> Half of her dishevelled hair flowing down the chest;

Wrapped in white cloth. . . .
Bestower of devotion and salvation;
Redeemer of all Jīvas;
Giver of Divine Knowledge.[56]

Arcanāpurī Mā: *Ekātmika Bhāva*

Arcanāpurī Mā was a serious, sweet-faced woman and the head of an *āśrama* in Calcutta. She was part of a lineage—her guru was Satyānanda, whose guru was Abhedānanda, a pupil of Rāmakṛṣṇa. Her father, Nirvedānanda, was a holy man, and Arcanāpurī Mā became dedicated to a religious life at the age of twelve years.[57]

The *āśrama* was a clean, airy building with marble floors and a large altar at the front. On the altar was a large picture of Svāmī Satyānanda done in oils and smaller photos of Rāmakṛṣṇa and Śāradā Devī and other saints, Rādhā and Kṛṣṇa dolls, and a large Śiva *liṅga* of black stone in the middle. Arcanāpurī Mā had a shiny black braid and black-rimmed glasses, and an orange and purple sari. She sings with a harmonium and sits on a brocade cushion to give discourses to her disciples, who sit on blankets on the floor. They are a universalist group, with no objections to a woman guru—after all, Rāmakṛṣṇa worshiped Śāradā Devī. They are also a literary circle; they state that Satyānanda wrote sixty thousand songs, while Arcanāpurī Mā has written forty-eight plays (mostly about saints) and three thousand songs, as well as philosophy books and biographies.

Arcanāpurī Mā states that Satyānanda, the guiding force of the *āśrama*, was born in 1902, after his mother performed rituals as directed by Siddha Bilayat Āli of Birbhum. The child was named Satyavrata. He was a solitary child, who grew up fond of silence and meditation. He began an ascetic life shortly after entering college, and, after completing his M.A., he began to undergo severe austerities. He took his first initiation from Svāmī Abhedānanda, but for the renunciant (*brahmacari* and *sannyāsa*) initiations he took instruction from Mā Bhāvatāriṇī, who gave him the name Satyānanda. He stayed in Calcutta and Baranāgar, in different *āśramas* and temples. He died in 1969.

Arcanāpurī Mā said of her own life:

> I began to visit Śrī Ṭhākur Satyānanda in Siuri when I was twelve years old. I spent much time at this *āśrama* and began living there, rarely returning to my own home. I took initiation from him at that age—while he was playing with me,

> he grabbed my hand and whispered a mantra in my ear. He taught us about religion through games.

At first she was frightened by his spiritual power:

> In 1940, Śrī Ṭhākur was initiating a disciple, and I was watching. I was only twelve or thirteen years old at the time. I noticed the curtain blowing at the window. Ṭhākur was looking at the devotee in a strange way. I don't know what type of feeling or experience the disciple was having. I saw with open eyes a flow of light emerging from Ṭhākur's eyes, like a powerful flashlight. The rays of light seemed to enter right into the soul of the disciple. I felt that those rays had entered me, and I was terror-stricken. I began to tremble and ran home. My body felt as if it were burning, and I lay down on the cold cement floor. My parents and guardians at home did not pay much attention—they thought of the *āśrama* and spiritual things, rather than about children. So nobody asked all day how I was feeling. But a messenger came that evening from Ṭhākur, to ask me to attend worship. I ran to the *āśrama,* although it was night, for the midnight Kālī Pūjā. The vision of those dreadful eyes was still in my memory. I moved quietly to the well, to wash my feet. Ṭhākur beckoned me, and I prostrated myself before him. He patted my back, and asked, "Have you become afraid of me?" At that moment the burning in my body disappeared, and I felt blissfully cool. He asked me to sit close to him and explained that sometimes he would transfer his spiritual power into a disciple. He would stare at the disciple with a piercing look, but only he understood this transmission of energy.

Satyānanda was also an ecstatic, who would spend long periods of time in states of trance. Arcanāpurī Mā began to follow him in this:

> Ṭhākur would spend all day in *bhāva,* and when I had been going there for one or two years, I became completely lost in Ṭhākur. I, too, began to fall into *bhāva.* One day, I fainted and fell down a flight of stairs. This state of *bhāva* occurred continuously for several years—I was lost in Ṭhākur, I could think only of him.

Her disciples describe Satyānanda's validation of her *bhāvas*:

> When these trances occurred, Ṭhākur had to leave his own meditation in order to care for her. The devotees began to

> grumble that she was disturbing Ṭhākur and complained about her. Ṭhākur became angry with these devotees one day, and said, "I have taken her as my adopted daughter, so do not raise questions about her. I forbid the devotees to criticize her." Some of them suggested that she might be ill, but Ṭhākur said angrily, "This is not a disease, it is a *bhāva*. For your sake, I will do an experiment."
>
> Arcanāpurī Mā was lying senseless upstairs, and Ṭhākur brought a group of doctors and devotees into the house. He had one group sit in the room with her and the other sit nearby on the veranda. While Arcanāpurī Mā was unconscious, with her eyes closed and her hands in fists, Ṭhākur started striking his own body in different places. Wherever he struck his body, Arcanāpurī Mā put her hands on her own body and expressed pain. Her eyes were still closed, and Ṭhākur was not within range of her sight. Yet the devotees could walk from the bedroom to the verandah and see the similarity of the gestures, For another experiment, he had groups of people synchronize their watches and take notes on her behavior while in trance. Ṭhākur would make deliberate gestures, and she would echo them. She was upstairs in bed, while Ṭhākur was downstairs. They noted the gestures and times, and again they corresponded.

This experiment was made to show the validity of her states of *bhāva,* which she called *ekātmika bhāva,* in which the souls of guru and disciple are believed to be fused into one. Mā's state was believed to be that of trance rather than ordinary unconsciousness—she claimed she was not unconscious, but rather fully conscious, with the soul aware and the body like a wooden statue. In this state, thoughts, emotions and dreams are believed to be shared, and one person can sense directly the desires and thoughts of the other at a distance. The disciple may reflect the actions and wishes of the guru, or the guru may realize the desires and impulses of the disciple. Identification is changed—there are no longer two separate entities, but one center and one periphery. The roles of relationship are fluid—the guru may be Mother, seen in dreams in red Banarasi silk, while the disciple is the devotee, or the guru may be Gopāla, while the disciple is Rādhā.

In this relationship, the disciple may see the guru in visions. He develops the eye of love (*prema-cakṣu*), through which he may see the inner nature of the guru. The inner love acts as a screen upon which the divine images are projected, and the whole body becomes a body of love. These visions are comparable to dream images, except that the person is conscious at the time, and the images stay bright and clear in the memory—they do not fade over time.

This relation of *ekātmika* may continue even after death. Since Satyānanda's death fifteen years ago, Arcanāpurī Mā has been in a state of separation (*viraha*), as Rādhā was when Kṛṣṇa was in Mathurā. She states:

> I still fight with Ṭhākur for leaving me alone here on earth. I can still talk with him, although his physical body is not here. When I first saw him, I was only a child and did not understand Bhagavān or the spiritual world. But I loved him at first sight. When I entered the *āśrama,* he played with me, but soon he became my friend, philosopher, and guide. He had great spiritual power, but natural love and affection flowed from him like a fountain. Certainly this love was greater than that of a worldly mother and father, sister and brother, friend and relation. His love was a thousand times greater than the combined love of all of those. I did not feel any lack of worldly love.
>
> It was also true that he was fond of penance, as he was an ascetic. He directed his disciples to perform severe austerities involving torture of the body, like sitting in the scorching sun on summer days and being drenched in ice water on winter nights for hours together, and undertaking long fasts. These were just a part of life. But all of these gave us enormous pleasure instead of pain.

It was a happy time for the disciples, until Satyānanda's death:

> We lived with him for about thirty years. Though sad events happened from time to time, these could not move us or even touch us, because we floated in a current of joy. A chain of festivals with songs, music, dramas, and dances kept the *āśrama* and disciples joyful throughout the years.
>
> But then suddenly the dream broke, and it felt as if we had fallen down on stony earth from some sweet remote dreamland. Ṭhākur had left us. I felt myself as a newborn child having lost her mother. I wished and craved to go with him. The carefree feeling of endless happiness has now turned into a burdened feeling of worries and anxieties thrust onto these weak shoulders. Certainly, I feel his subtle presence,

> and his invisible grace is showered upon us at every moment, in every act. Yet I cannot stand alone.
>
> I depended on him so much, I was one with him to such an extent that I did not have a mind with a separate existence from his. Now I suffer because of this separation. I still cannot bear his physical absence. Sometimes I feel so helpless. I was so full in his presence, now I am empty in his absence.

Arcanāpurī Mā has spent most of her life in states of *bhāva*—in the continuous union of *ekātmika bhāva* and in the inspired *bhāvas* in which she wrote her songs, plays, and books. Possession by *bhāva* (*bhāvāveśa*) is absorption in the divine, a surrender to Bhagavān, an offering of love, and often a feeling of loss and bereavement. She distinguishes this state from deity possession (*bhor*), which she finds quite different:

> In *bhor,* a spirit temporarily descends on a person. There is no precondition, no ritual practice, no striving for Bhagavān. It is not realization of God, for such persons do not understand themselves. Usually deity possession happens to professionals, and it is usually possession by Kālī. Its goal is not to attain God.

She describes the state of divine madness (*divyonmāda*) and mentions that Satyānanda once met a person in this state:

> A person who is divinely mad has great knowledge. One glance will show such a holy man. Anybody can tell true spirituality from madness and drunkenness—people visit saints, but they do not go to visit drunks. Religion is not lunacy or whim or imagination. There are four signs of divine madness [*jaḍa, unmāda, piśāca, bālaka*]. Holy men become inert, like Trailaṅga Svāmī, but a *jaḍa* is just lazy.
>
> Ṭhākur once met a mad holy man who never allowed anyone to go close to him. He would throw stones and curse at people, and he was always covered with mud and dust. But there was something about his eyes. Svāmījī began to massage his legs one afternoon, and the man did not chase him away. They stared at each other for perhaps fifteen minutes, and the holy man's eyes were amazing—it was almost as if they glowed.
>
> Ṭhākur once met a person mad with knowledge [*jñānonmāda*], a sage who looked like a madman, but sometimes his words were full of wisdom. While eating, he gave his milk to the old woman next to him, saying "I will eat through her

> mouth. If this mother drinks, then I shall be fed. Her mouth and my mouth are the same."

She felt that religious experience is different in men and women:

> Women have a greater measure of devotion than men. They have a softness, a motherliness, which men do not have. Men are more suited for worldly action [*karma yoga*], in mind and in body. If the responsibility of worship is placed on a girl, she will do it in a way that is not possible for a man.
>
> It is difficult for women, because most religious texts were written by men. But in the Vedic age, Āmbhrer Ṛṣi had a daughter called Vāk, and the *Caṇḍī* was written with her *bhāva*. She calls herself Īśvarī, Mother of the Universe. Brahma himself is within her. In the Vedic age, many holy women acquired divine wisdom [*brahmajñāna*]. But since the Muslim era, women have been discouraged from remaining unmarried and leading a religious life.

Arcanāpurī Mā took renunciant (*brahmacarya*) vows at the age of fourteen and studied Sanskrit, Bengali literature, and philosophy at the *āśrama* school. The *āśrama* itself grew to include forty to fifty men and thirty women, all renunciants.

She grew up as a lonely child in a household of religious practitioners whose only value was spirituality. She accepted this value system and excelled. Her guru was also her first love, whom she met in early adolescence. Austerities became pleasurable, as they gained his attention and approval. Her trances gained the *āśrama*'s attention, and led to her status as the guru's "adopted daughter," or *mānasakanyā*, the "daughter of the mind." The *āśrama* was a shelter from the world, and now that she is in charge of it, only her "shared soul" maintains her through her extended period of mourning. Hers is a life of bittersweet emotion, expressed in poetry and prose. She writes:

> In the roots of the wild fig tree
> my essence in the depths keeps watch.
> The gusts of many a gale have left their touch
> Still I am not dead.
> My breathing has not stopped.
> In life's abyss, in suspense it's held.
> Do you think in the torrent of dead events
> floating and floating, I am drowned
> Turned to a fossil in some closed dark pit? . . .

Know that the eternal motion of the new star
at my ancient sky's bidding
Forever motionless abides.[58]

Lakṣmī Mā: *Pāgal Bhāva*

Lakṣmī was a strong-looking woman with a wide face, high cheekbones, and deep-set dark eyes. Her hair hung in long strands of matted knots (*jaṭā*) which reached down to the floor. She dressed in red and carried a Śiva trident and water pot. She wore heavy ankle bracelets and necklaces of *rudrākṣa* berries, and a red spot which took up most of her forehead. She was a married holy woman (*gṛhī sādhikā*), with a husband and five children, and was a worshiper of the goddess Tārā Mā.[59]

Lakṣmī was sixty-five years old when interviewed; she came from Nārāyaṇ Ganj near Dacca. Her father was Bipin Candra Dāsa, a Kṛṣṇa devotee and Vaiṣṇava singer who worked in the Dacca area. She had five sisters and seven brothers. From her childhood she was a Kālī worshiper to a degree that made her parents and relatives consider her mad. After her marriage, her husband and in-laws brought her to an exorcist because they thought she was possessed. He began an exorcism that lasted for seven days but that ultimately was unsuccessful—she continued her passion for Kālī, and her relatives deduced from the exorcist's lack of success that perhaps she was a true holy woman.

She took initiation from a Vaiṣṇava guru and then a Śākta guru. She has a small symbol (*pratimā*) of the goddess, which she claims has been growing larger over the years. She described her life:

> When I was seven or eight years old, I used to play with Mā [the goddess]. She would go away and then return again. Even at that age, I was very concerned with religion. I used to read books about Bābā Tārakanāth and Mā Kālī. I also read them out loud to my own mother. I never went to any school—Bhagavān has helped me to learn. Sometimes I went to our next-door neighbor's house to study, and there was a girl there of my age with whom I would study. I can read Bengali, but I cannot understand English, though I would like to learn.
>
> I got married at the age of fifteen years. My husband was also religious. His name was Nityānanda Aich. He died recently. He had matted hair like me and was a holy man. He used to follow Bacchagiri Nāga [Nāga Bābā] and was his disciple. He had not planned to marry. He used to visit burning ghats with Nāga Bābā, and he followed Nāga Bābā's wishes.

After nine years, Nāga Bābā told him that he would not be able to accomplish anything alone, that he needed a wife. Nāga Bābā told him to marry and gave him a description of the girl. He told my brother (whom he knew through work) about this description, and he said, "That is my sister." He came to our house and decided to marry me. I was very pretty at that time and had long hair like Mā Kālī. Nāga Bābā had *brahma śakti,* he knew everything. He had never seen me before.

Three months after my marriage, Mā came to me again. She asked me to make arrangements for an altar at my in-law's house, as they did not have one. After some time, I had a miscarriage. Three years later I had a daughter. After a child is born, we cannot touch the altar or perform ritual worship for one month. During that time, Mā used to come to me, she would complain that she was not getting food and water. Śiva and Durgā, and Śiva and Kālī appeared before me. I used to show them to my husband, but he could not see anything.

Such visions caused her a great deal of trouble with family and neighbors, who decided to call an exorcist:

Everybody thought that I was possessed by evil spirits, so they called an exorcist who bound me with ropes and started burning me.[60] For seven days this continued, but I didn't die, because I had the blessings of Mā. I still have the marks of the burning on my body. Then they bound me in my room, and bound me with thick iron chains. But I was so powerful that I would break the locks and chains, and go to the temples of Śiva and Mā Kālī.

My husband was very good. He used to find where I had gone and bring me back home. He would give me food to eat. Gradually, I started having matted hair [*jaṭā*]. First I had six large knots, but my in-laws forcibly cut them off. Then I became mad; I had no sense. I used to open all my garments, to tear them off and tie them on my head. I rarely ate. I remained in this state for many years. They had cut my matted hair off several times, and I grew insane each time, but now they have grown again, and now I am sensible. When I became mad, my husband took good care of me and served me.

The initial call to become a holy woman was associated with madness:

One day while I was sitting and cooking food, suddenly I saw Lord Śiva with his trident in his hand, standing in front of me. I was terrified and closed my eyes. He said that he had come to see me. He asked me not to put oil in my hair, and not to use a brush. At that time my mother was alive, and she used to comb out my matted hair. But after I saw Śiva, I asked my mother not to do this. But later that hair was cut, and I became mad again. Then I ran away for seven days. My husband found out where I was, and brought me back home. There they used to pour water on me [as a treatment]. As I was fond of bathing, I asked them to pour a hundred mugs of water on me. I became normal for a while, but then I returned to the state of madness.

I used to listen to songs about Śiva and visit Śiva temples. My husband scolded me, but he could not do anything. I used to cry and pray to my Śiva. Then my husband started having matted hair, but he did not like this—he thought of cutting his hair. I prayed to Lord Śiva to make him a devotee—make him equal to me. But he decided to go to Gayā to perform a funeral [*śrāddha*][61] ceremony in which he was supposed to cut his hair. I told him not to do this, but he came back from Gayā bald, a week later. I yelled at him for this and again prayed to Lord Śiva. And again my husband started growing matted hair. He had one great knot at the back and two at either side. After growing the matted hair again, he became a devotee.

The exorcist about whom I told you put two legs of a chicken inside my nose, and much blood came out. But still I didn't die. I was possessed [*bhor*] by a good spirit. I used to drink a bucket full of milk and remained nude [all of the time]. I heard about these events from my husband later on. The exorcist could not cure me because Bhagavān was present within me, not an evil spirit. My husband came to know this in his dreams. Mā Kālī told him in a dream to make an altar for me. Then my husband calmed down. He made an idol of Mā Kālī and worshipped her.

In response to a question about her spiritual life, she stated:

My Vaiṣṇava guru was Pavitra Gosvāmi. He is no longer in this world. He worshiped Rādhā and Kṛṣṇa. My Śākta guru is Himaṅgalu Gosvāmi, and he stays in Nainital. I have transferred from Rādhā-Kṛṣṇa to Mā because she was fond of me and would visit me.

I have seen the goddess Tārā like I am seeing you. I can see a light here which you cannot see. She is present with me always, but she takes different forms. Her complexion is black. I have seen her without doing any ritual practice, because I have done good deeds in my previous births. I saw her first in Dacca.

On Kālī Pūjā day I experience possession trance [*bhor*]. I don't remember what I say during this time. Sometimes my disciples will tell me afterward what I have said.

She then told the myth of Kṛṣṇa and Pūtana, and the story of Pūtana's poisoned milk was followed by the story of Śiva's drinking poison and then Satī's milk:

We believe in thirty-three crores of gods. All of them wished to drink nectar from the great ocean, which causes immortality. The gods didn't invite Śiva when they were going to drink the nectar. Śiva was angry when he realized that he was not invited, and he came to drink it himself. But no nectar was left, and all he drank was poison. After drinking it, he had a burning sensation, and went to Brahma for relief. But Brahma said that if he would suck the nipple of Satī's breast, he would feel better. He did this, and the burning left. But the poison left a dark mark around her nipple. Satī was frightened that because of this the gods might consider her unfaithful rather than *satī* [faithful to her husband]. Then Śiva blessed her that all women will have a dark ring on their breasts.

Kālī is the most powerful goddess, she was created from the ashes of Śiva's body. Satī worshiped Śiva and obtained him. Satī once said to Śiva, "You never keep me company, you always stay in burning ghats and your body is always covered with ashes." Śiva also realized this and started dusting the ashes from his body. From those ashes Kālī appeared. She is powerful and kills demons. At first she was maddened and killed anyone who came near her. The gods were frightened and asked Brahma and Nārāyaṇa to stop her, but they could not. So the gods went to Śiva for help. Śiva lay down near Kālī, and Mā Kālī stepped on him without realizing. When she saw that it was Śiva, she stopped and put out her tongue in shame. This is the image which you see.

When asked about Śakta ritual practices, she said:

When the corpse ritual [*śava sādhana*] is successful, Mā appears. I have seen it. This ritual is performed on dead bodies;

> it is a very difficult practice. One performs it on floating dead bodies or on dead bodies in the burning ghats. If the time comes, I will perform that practice. The dead body wakes up, and the person must chant the *bandhana mantra* to cause the body to lie down again. The corpse ritual worships one form of Mā; she has 108 forms.
>
> I have gone to Tārāpīṭh several times. Sometimes I go and stay there. I have also seen ghosts, but I was not frightened of them. I am only frightened of human beings. I can hold a snake with my hand. I am scared of people because they do not let one be honest. People used to stare at me when I walked.

Lakṣmī lived in the back of a market, and in the one room of her hut was a large statue of a black Kālī standing on a blond Śiva. The hut was full of pictures, statues, and objects for ritual worship. On one occasion, a man dressed in white was huddled in the corner, staring wide-eyed at the statue. He clutched his arms around himself, and would shiver violently and periodically fall to the ground, with his eyeballs rolled back into his head. The shaking resembled malaria, but Lakṣmī pointed him out as divinely mad (*divyonmāda*), a diagnosis echoed by others in the area, who referred to him as *bhagavān pāgal* or *ṭhākur pāgal*. Lakṣmi perceived his situation as similar to her own condition, and she was proud that he took her as guru; because of her experience, she felt uniquely qualified to deal with him. But when she started to talk about Tārā, he was horror-stricken and started screaming, "No, not Tārā! Don't talk about Tārā! Don't say her name!"

Lakṣmī said of her own states of madness:

> There is a difference between ordinary madness and divine madness. One who has seen Bhagavān and has become a madman loses all sense and is not conscious of his belongings. One who becomes insane for other reasons always remains conscious of his belongings. And one who has become mad by seeing Bhagavān can be easily distinguished. He will not concentrate on any worldly objects. He will forget even his close relatives and think only about God.

Though Lakṣmī came from a religious family, she was considered by family and neighbors as mad from her childhood. While this state had certain disadvantages (notably the attempted cures), it allowed her to gain power over both her husband and his family, for her husband would serve her when she was in fits of madness, and he eventually followed her as a holy man. It also allowed her to gain an identity as healer and Kālī devotee, and to lead a life of visions and adventures. And it allowed her to become the celebrity of her Calcutta street when she was interviewed by a Westerner.

Yogeśvarī Devī: Snakes, Liṅgas, and Miracles

Yogeśvarī lived in a small *āśrama* with a large Kālī statue off a winding dirt road in Rājpur, surrounded by jungle and banana plants. She had an orange sari and long matted hair worn in a sort of beehive hairdo. She was a holy woman who had been married but was now separated from her husband. She blamed this on his family and appeared to be still fond of him.[62]

Yogeśvarī was famous locally for her miracles (*vibhūtis*). She would go into possession trances in which cures for various ailments and bowls of food would be materialized for her devotees. At one point, according to a disciple, when a visitor doubted her sincerity and thought she had a pot beneath her sari, she started taking off her sari until she was stopped by the disciples present. However, she had proved to those present that there was nothing hidden in her clothing. Her guru warned her against such states, saying they would cause her to lose spiritual power, and she avoided them while he was alive. After his death, however, she would again become possessed, alternately by Bābā (Śiva, when she would speak in a deep male voice) and Mā (Kālī, when she spoke in a female voice).

Her description of her life includes both history and mythical images:

> I was born in the village of Marakathi in the Barisala district. My father was Ānanda Kumār Canda, and my mother was Hiraṇ Bala. My father was a Kavirāja [Āyurvedic doctor], but he was ill with tuberculosis. When he became ill, our family was very poor, and he decided not to hold Durgā Pūjā. But shortly before the holiday, after my father took a bath, he heard the voice of the goddess asking to stay in his house. He was in a state of *bhāva,* and he saw a great image of the goddess standing before him, with a great light around her. As he returned to a normal state, the image disappeared.
>
> Durgā also appeared to Sūrya the sculptor, asking him to make an image for my father. Sūrya came to our house the next day. He fell at my father's feet and said, "I cannot take money from you any longer. I saw Mā Durgā in my dreams

yesterday." The image was made, but my father was worried because he had no money. My mother heard the sound of jingling anklets while drawing water and saw a fair girl with dark hair, who said, "Worship me with cucumber and coconut from that tree" and disappeared. Then the village zamindar left us a sack of rice, and another man brought a black goat for sacrifice. My father cried through the worship ritual. I heard this from my mother.

I was born that year, ten months after a *sādhu* [holy man] gave my mother a triple wood-apple leaf and asked her to eat it. After I was born, a large snake coiled around me, and it left after my father prayed to the goddess. When I was young, I would often play with a snake. I would also play at the nearby temple, where Śiva, Kālī, and Manasā were worshiped.

A famine broke out in the middle 1940s, and my father died. My mother would feed us [four children] with a little food from the neighbors. I would go to the temple and lick the image of Lord Śiva for food and drink from the teat of a white cow. The priest and some men of the village wanted to beat me for this, while I was in the temple, but the snake came and barred their way.

When I was six years old, I met Rām Ṭhākur, at Kaivalya Dhām in Jādavpur. He took me on his lap and chanted a mantra in my ear. I used to stare at the sky, and sometimes I would see Rām Ṭhākur there, and sometimes Śiva or Kālī.

Two years later, my elder brother brought us to Calcutta. I studied and did music for two years, until when I was ten, a vender gave me two pictures of Kālī and Śiva, which a *sādhu* had given him. After this, I would worship them and was always in a state of *bhāva*. I always saw Kālī and Śiva before my eyes. I could not concentrate on anything.

It became difficult for her to maintain this state of *bhāva* in the midst of family life:

When I was twelve years old, my older brother married. His wife would always speak against me, complaining that I did not work hard enough at my studies. My brother and I used to be close, but my sister-in-law complained about me every day. One day she lied about me, saying that I spent time with boys, and my brother believed her and beat me until blood came from my mouth. I was angry and asked Śiva for justice. I tore Śiva's picture. I brought poison from the room of my brother's friend, who sold medicine, and I drank it. My mother prayed to the three snakes to save me, who then came and moved over my body. After that, I regained consciousness.

From that day I stopped talking to anyone in that house, and I did not eat there. At night someone would come and give me milk. Three days after the beating, my brother's small daughter died. He understood that this was because he had acted wrongly. Afterward, he asked me to take food and forgive him.

A bad marriage caused her to wish to leave the family situation:

Then I got married, and I had four daughters and one son. My husband was very poor. My in-laws gave us money for a while, but then they stopped, and we suffered greatly. Most of the time, we had nothing to eat. This was before I obtained Śiva. But later, when my relatives wanted the gifts from my disciples, I left home.

My married life was very unhappy. I used to pray to Bhagavān, I used to cry before him. I got a Śiva *liṅga* on the bank of the river Ganges. For a few days I dreamt that a snake coiled around a Śiva *liṅga,* and someone was indicating to me that I should take that *liṅga.* I told my relatives about the dream, but they did not believe me. I was suffering very much at that time. I thought that I will fast on behalf of Śiva. On the ninth of Śrāvaṇ, I went to take a bath in the Ganges.

Cūṛāmaṇi Joga is celebrated on that day. Thousands of people go to take holy baths in the Ganges on that day. Suddenly I felt as if I were drowning. People at the bank of the river thought that I was being carried away by a shark. Then I lost consciousness. When I was again conscious, I was being taken back home. In my sari was a Śiva *liṅga,* and people saw that I had obtained it.

Finding the *liṅga* in the river began her time as a wandering *sādhikā*:

From then I gained disciples, and they made a temple for me. That place was called Śiva *bāṛi*. But I could not stay there, for there were many troubles in our house. Before obtaining the Śiva *liṅga,* we were very poor. But then my disciples started giving me many things, and my brothers-in-law wanted to take this property. I was hurt, and I wanted to leave the family. My husband helped me when I was living at the family house; he wanted me to remain spiritual. But my brothers-in-law wanted to earn money by exploiting me. So I began to travel.

I went to Kedarnāth, Badrināth, and South India. Then I came and stayed in Dakṣiṇeśwar for a week. One day while I was staying there, a little girl came and asked me to take a dip in the Ganges, and she said that I would get something there. It was full moon, and the month was Māgh. I dipped myself in the river twenty-one times and got an image of the goddess Kālī. Some of the people there came to know of this, and they said that I must stay in the temple. They also said that Rāmakṛṣṇa used to worship that image when he as a child. So they asked me to stay. But two of my disciples helped me to leave the temple. From there we went to Khārdaha.

Periods of madness occurred while she was wandering through India:

Sometimes when I traveled, I was in a state of madness, and then I had no awareness. I came out of my house with only a Śiva *liṅga*. I used to move about from one place to another, and often I had nothing to eat. Sometimes I would sleep on the footpaths. I traveled to different shrines, and at last I have settled here for three years. I stayed for some time at the Kāmadhenu Āśrama at Rāmgarh, and then I took initiation from Viśvapraṇava Svāmī.

I once became mad and jumped in the Ganges. I was rescued somewhere near Tārākeśwar. All I had with me at that time was a small Śiva *liṅga* and a picture of the guru. The men wanted to hand me over to my kinsmen, but I fled. My husband, his brother, and my son came to take me. But I escaped. I met a Nirmal Mukherjee who tried to persuade me to go home. But I fled. Eventually I reached Howrah Station, and a beggar woman gave me shelter. I used to beg with her. But then one of my disciples saw me there, so I fled again.

My husband is also very religious. But he cannot come to see me now because of his brothers. He came here twice. He is twenty-two years older than me. My daughters have gotten married, and my son is now a student. My children have often seen me while I am in possession trance, and sometimes they come here and stay with me.

Her spiritual experiences began spontaneously in her childhood:

I could see a light when I was very young. After seeing the light, I would feel quite strange. I could not understand what

> was happening inside me. I found that I had strange abilities. I could cure patients, and they made a temple for me. I could convert a wood-apple leaf into a Śiva *liṅga*. I could give idols of Lakṣmī and Nārāyan.
>
> First I sit for meditation [*dhyāna*], and then I see a blue light, which gradually becomes yellow and then disappears. Then I become unconscious. People say that I change during that state. I only feel sleepy.
>
> Now sometimes I experience god possession. Suppose I see a patient who is in a very bad condition. While looking at him, I will suddenly have a state of trance [*bhor*] descend on me. Then I will give the patient an amulet or something else. But I don't know where these things come from.

Her guru was conservative and did not approve of her powers and possession trances:

> But Gurudev was frightened. He realized that I had attained powers [*vibhūti*], and he stopped them. He did ritual worship to me, and then gradually I lost the power. But again, a few days ago, it happened again. I gave amulets to several people. But I did not realize what was happening; at such times I am unconscious.
>
> I do many kinds of meditation. When I start doing haṭha-yoga, I first sit and pray to Bhagavān to help me. I don't do anything else by myself. While I sit for haṭha-yoga, you can put a twenty kilogram weight on my hand, and I can remain in that position for four or five hours. But I don't know how I do that.
>
> I chant mantras as well as do visualizations. At first I worship Bhagavān, and this is ordinary worship. The second stage is chanting [*japa*], the third stage is visualization [*dhyāna*], the fourth stage is *bhāva*, and the fifth stage is *mahābhāva*. I was under the influence of *bhāva* while I was in Khārdaha, but one cannot remain in this state forever. . . .
>
> When I was in Khārdaha, my disciples saw me playing with snakes, and a little girl used to come out of me and play with me. My disciples have seen this, but I did not feel anything at the time. I was under the influence of *bhāva*.
>
> I sit for worship and meditation every day. Although now I am trying to limit my powers, sometimes they come spontaneously. There is no end of practice. I don't do anything for myself, I perform *homa* fires and other rituals for others.

Possession trance (*bhor*) occurs suddenly, often after experiences of *bhāva*:

> I do not experience possession whenever I sit, but I desire it very much. It comes according to Bhagavān's wishes. I have seen God in many forms. In Khārdaha when I had *bhāva*, I spoke in Sanskrit. But I don't know Sanskrit. People used to surround me. They also said that they smelled the scent of flowers and incense sticks in my presence.
>
> Before, I used to experience possession on Monday and Friday. I used to bang my head against the wall. Now I do not have these experiences. Possession trance is a type of *bhāva*. *Bhāva* comes first. Before experiencing trance, my heart fills with tremendous joy, and I can see a bright light. I don't feel then like talking to others. When I used to experience possession, a man once came and touched a hot iron to my body, but I did not feel anything. Many people came to examine me.
>
> Before marriage, my name was Nibhā. Then I was named Karuṇamayī by Gurudev of Kāmadhenu Āśrama. Now I am called Yogeśvarī. I was named Karuṇamayī because I had sympathy for the poor.
>
> A few days ago I had the experience of becoming Śiva. Mostly I see Śiva—he comes and corrects my errors. Every day I sit for meditation early in the morning, then in the evening, then at night after twelve.

Snakes have played an important part in her life:

> As soon as I was born, a great snake surrounded me and stretched its hood over my body. Since then, that particular snake has appeared at different times in my life. Other snakes have also appeared before me, and I would play with them. This happened until I was married. During my times of spiritual aspiration, I was always guarded by snakes and one dog. Wherever I went, they accompanied me. Often, I could not see them, but my disciples saw them.

She described a sort of inner split in which a part of her would separate out as a child and the rest of her would play with the child:

> Sometimes I have lost all consciousness. My disciples and persons known to me have seen that a small girl would often come out of my body, and I would play with her. This often happened at night, when I was in an open field. I could not

> feel this happen, but they saw it. Sometimes I was imprisoned in my room with the door locked, but they saw me outside, playing with my miniature self, in the form of a little girl, in the paddy fields on moonlit nights.

She understood *bhāva* as both external and internal:

> An ordinary *bhāva* is based on perception—objects are seen, they create an impression on the mind, and an idea about them is formed. An object can give you an impression or idea or feeling or *bhāva*. But in the case of spiritual *bhāva*, the sense organs have no function. The sense of the divine is not produced from perception of external objects. It has an inward side, which comes in certain forms of realization obtained through meditation. This is spiritual [*ādhyātmika*] *bhāva*.

Two of her disciples told of their experiences with her. A male disciple who has followed her for about ten years described her miracles (*vibhūtis*) and his faith in her as Mother:

> I did not want to go to her—I come from a Brahmo family, and we are related to Keshub Sen. My grandfather was a Brahmo priest, and we never believed in worship or images. We often insulted pictures of the goddess Kālī by stamping on them with shoes on, and we took a Nārāyaṇa stone from a neighbor's house. But I felt bound to go to Yogeśvarī Mā.
>
> When I was addicted to drugs and ill, I got a message from her to come. I took initiation from her, but later became again involved with drugs. Then she called me again, and I visited her, and she kept me with her. She didn't say anything, but in that one day my mind was totally changed.
>
> I have faith in her; like a child on his mother's lap, I feel safe with her. I have seen her as Kālī and Devī, and her predictions come true. I have seen the Hare Kṛṣṇa mantra appear on her body in different designs, even on her nails. When she would fall into *bhāva*, she would run about like a drunkard, and her feet would smell of sandalwood flowers. At such times she asks Mā for alcohol. She would sing beautiful songs about Kālī. Many of these were spontaneous—not known to her before.
>
> Sometimes her hands would flow with *sindūr* [red powder for the part in a woman's hair], and sometimes rice and lentils [*khicaṛi*] would appear, the sacred food [*prasāda*] of Lord Śiva.

I have drunk honey which appeared dripping from her matted hair.

I think that she is the "hole in the wall" described in the *Kathāmṛta* [the biography of Rāmakṛṣṇa]. Through this hole we come to know Bhagavān.

A female disciple is also a relative of hers and describes her two forms of possession trance:

Yogeśvarī was a simple housewife, with many family problems. When she found a Śiva *liṅga* in the Ganges, she began to spend more and more time in meditation. Then gradually she started having possession trances, and people began to come to her.

I used to see her often and sing hymns with her. We would sing at a specific time, and she would go into states of *bhāva* and possession trance [*āveśa*]. She would tremble continuously, as if she felt great pain. Then gradually she would stop.

During trance, she would keep her eyes closed. She had two types of possession—one of Lord Śiva and the other of Mā Kālī. When she was possessed by Śiva, she spoke in a deep, resonant male voice, and when she was possessed by Kālī, she spoke in a female voice, like her own voice. When she was in Kālī trance, sometimes she would have blood coming from her mouth. When we asked about the blood, she would say that she had eaten a goat.

She could give [materialize] sacred food [*prasāda*], and during trance she could bring the food offered to her by her disciples [in different towns] to her house in Naihati. She could fill empty bowls with hot rice and lentils, and when asked where it came from, she said it was offered to her by a nine-year-old boy, who lives in a distant town. On new moon night, she worships Mā Kālī and goes into possession trance. At such times, I have seen honey dripping from her hands.

Many patients who could not be cured by doctors would come to her, and during trance she would give them medicines, sweets, and food.

Often she would wander off for several months, and nobody knew where she was. When she would write me a letter, I would contact her. At first she would only be possessed by Śiva, but after leaving her home, she began to be possessed by Mā Kālī also. Her guru told her not to have possession trance, for it affects her health badly. It is harmful to be in trance very often.

Yogeśvarī had *bhāvas* of Bābā Śiva, Mā Kālī, and a little girl who would emerge from her body. Thus there are father, mother, and child—an ideal family of which she was all three members. She is most of all the child—there is no divine husband. With this "internal family" of deities and doppelgänger, she could separate herself from a stressful physical family situation. Her states of madness came during the initial separation from family and tradition. When the chaos settled, both her identity and pattern of living had changed. Ecstatic states allowed her to express the *bhāvas* of father, mother, and child in a relatively controlled and religious setting. She appeared happy in her role as priestess to the Kālī statue in her temple and would not accept money. Yogeśvarī moved in a slow and dignified way, and smiled to see visitors. She had settled down, surrounded by disciples.

Siddhimātā and the Ripened Identity

Siddhimātā was a Bengali holy woman living in Benares; she was first interviewed by Gopināth Kavirāj in 1931. She was known locally as a great woman seeker (*mātājī*), who lived in a series of houses and *āśramas* and stayed heavily veiled. Like Ānandamayī Mā, she had no initiation (although she did have a childhood initiation by a family guru). She had spent much time in seclusion, without either religious instruction or the company of holy people.

She was a devotee from childhood, and had early visions of gods and goddesses, and a spontaneous and simple love. With the flowering of this devotion, she moved (at an unspecified age) to Benares to bathe in the Ganges, visit temples, and spend time in secluded worship. She became known because mantras would appear on her body while she was meditating, as well as images of the lotus feet of deities. Her body was "penetrated"[63] by sound and the mantras of gods. The marks on her body were often associated with spiritual practice.

She would analyze her various types of religious experience and their influence on identity. The "partial I" (*khaṇḍa āmi*) lasts until the great union (*mahāmilana*) of the different aspects of the self, when the "I" becomes ripe (*pakva*). The "ripened" or "full I" (*akhaṇḍa āmi*) is the union of innumerable partial, fragmented "I's" and is the root of all sense of identity, as well as the manifest universe. When this "ripened I" is established, it may transcend further—into *brahmabhāva*, the union of the inner and outer sun, in which there are visions of dazzling light, or the blue light of Kṛṣṇa's radiance. The "I" travels higher, until it reaches the great void (*mahāśūnya*), which destroys karmic debts (*saṁskāras*), finally entering the realm of greatest wisdom (*paramajñāna*), in which even potential karma is consumed by fire.[64] In its highest state, as blazing wisdom (*ujjvala-mahājñāna*), it is difficult to perceive the physical world. Siddhimātā stated:

> The world is no longer there for me; I cannot see anything except the One. I find it wherever I look. Human beings and world do not exist in reality. Yet if one looks at the world a little crookedly, he can be caught in the world of appearances, and everything will appear to exist.[65]

Gopināth Kavirāj tried to figure out where Siddhimātā's experiences fit in relation to traditional Indian religious and philosophical systems. He finally decided that she was closer to Śaivism than to Vaiṣṇavism or Śāktism, but her religious outlook was basically original.

Siddhimātā initiated Kṛṣṇamātā, a holy woman who was also interviewed by Gopināth Kavirāj. Kṛṣṇamātā was also a visionary, who would see gods and goddesses, ancient *sādhus,* and miraculous objects. She would then become the objects of her visions, which were seen by her inner eye. She had direct vision of Śiva and Śakti, and the experience of being one with the sun. She saw her own soul as bright light and as merged with the soul of Siddhimātā. She then passed through the state of the great void, to the world of supreme truth (*satya-jagat*). Again, Gopināth Kavirāj did not know how to classify her.

Madness and Ecstasy among Holy Women: *Bhor* and *Bhāva*

The terms used most frequently by holy women to describe their own religious experience are possession (*bhor*) and *bhāva*, an emotional or ecstatic state. While *bhāva* is a term with a range of meanings used by many groups, *bhor* is more specialized, used for specific instances of domination by a deity.

For some holy women, *bhor* has a negative connotation. One woman, called a "*bhor* lady" by others, was scandalized when asked about her experiences. "I do not have *bhor,* I have *bhāva*!" she replied proudly. Possession trance (*bhor*) is associated with the poor and low caste, while *bhāva* belongs to several venerable religious traditions. *Bhāva* is more justifiable, a state of divine love or awareness, while possession trance often has practical ends (diagnosing and healing disease, asking the deities for favors) and demonstrates neither love nor awareness (many possessed women state that they are unaware of what occurred while they were in the trance state).

While possession states were seen mostly among women ecstatics, there were other differences of emphasis in the experiences of ecstatic men and women. While the men often emphasized the importance of sexuality as a way to relate to deities, the women described here tended to emphasize kinship instead, and the roles of mother and daughter. Although most of the holy women were married, the marriage relationship was of secondary importance. The primary relationships were through spiritual kinship—as "mental daughter" (*mānasa-kanyā*), as celibate disciple married to the guru, as child of Bābā Śiva and Mā Kālī. If relationship was emphasized, the holy woman tended to be spiritual daughter rather than wife. It was more difficult for the women to forge an independent spiritual role, and they sometimes needed the nearby presence of husband or guru to be able to follow a spiritual path.

Ecstatic experience was spontaneous among these women. Most were childhood visionaries, and these visions continued through their lives. Ritual practice did not induce ecstatic states, but rather validated the experiences by making them appear as if voluntary, as if a product of disciplined yogic effort. However, this emphasis on practice was only needed for the more conservative observers. Most devotees respected spontaneous experience, holding that it was a divine gift or a sign that the holy woman was never totally deluded by worldly events.

Some religious outlooks appeared neither spontaneous nor learned from a formal tradition, but were acquired from parents. All of the holy women had at least one religious parent—some parents were mad or ecstatic, some distant and detached. These parents provided leeway for their daughters' unusual behavior and accepted their extreme emotional states and visions, and the alternative forms of identity described in this volume.

The role of holy woman in Bengal allows the woman some freedom and self-determination. Both her *bhāvas* and her states of possession trance show that she is close to a deity, and she gains authority from this. While the initial break from a traditional pattern of life is difficult (almost all of the holy women described in this chapter were thought to be mad, and several underwent exorcism), the new role and the presence of disciples strengthen the developing religious identity. The holy woman may orient herself around the *āśrama* or pilgrimages to sacred places rather than the extended family.

Bhāva is the major criterion for female saints and holy women in Bengal, for religious experience is the basis for their religious status. This may be seen in the necessity of attributing *bhāvas* to Śāradā Devī—since she is a holy woman, therefore she must have *bhāvas* and visions. Even Rāmakṛṣṇa's claims about Śāradā's divinity needed to be corroborated. Holy women require *bhāvas,* yet recognition of them is often preceded by accusations of madness. And the women must prove themselves beyond ordinary madness in order to be taken seriously.

Women may gain disciples despite such mad behavior as running around naked, regression to childhood, fits of unconsciousness, aimless wandering, claims of projected bodies, and shamanic healing. If they have *bhāvas,* their claims are considered probable and erratic behavior is overlooked. *Bhāva* takes precedence over caste rules, gender distinctions, lineage, and family obligations. In most cases, the guru comes after the *bhāvas,* if he comes at all.

Bengali holy women need not depend on institution and mainstream tradition—no Vaiṣṇava holy women were found, and no Śākta holy women saw themselves exclusively as daughters of the Mother. The holy woman may be worshiper or priestess, scholar or inspired sage, controlling or controlled. *Bhāva* transcends even gender, for the holy woman may be worshiped as Bhagavān or Bhagavatī, god or goddess, by her disciples.

Bengali holy women do not appear to follow the traditions for women saints in other areas of India. In "On Women Saints," A. K. Ramanujan has studied the reversals in saints:

> According to Manu the female is subordinate to the male and the outcaste to the upper-caste, but in the lives of the *bhakti* saints "the last shall be first": men wish to renounce their masculinity and to become as women; upper-caste males wish to renounce pride, privilege and wealth, seek dishonor and self-abasement, and learn from the untouchable devotee.[66]

In his study of women saints, primarily Vīraśaivas, he found a consensus: early dedication to God (no conversion needed); denial of marriage (with the married minority widowed or leaving their husbands); defiance of social norms (especially caste hierarchies); initiation by a male authority figure; and marriage to the Lord as divine bridegroom.

Among Bengali holy women, the pattern is similar but not identical. The early dedication to God is not seen in acts of faith (for the Vīraśaivas, notably worship and sacrifice), but rather in visions and trances, which make family and friends think of madness or illness rather than dedication. There is usually acceptance of marriage, and the married holy woman lives a life in relation to her husband, periodically leaving him and returning, initiating the husband as a disciple or converting him into a holy man, or considering her saint-husband to be God. Most women encountered who would fall into possession trance were married, and this phenomenon was accepted by their husbands.

Certainly there is a similarity between Bengali and Vīraśaiva saints in the defiance of social norms. A certain independence of character is necessary for a woman to leave a joint family (even temporarily), to roam about unclothed or at random, to defend her visions or run an *āśrama*. Even Śāradā Devī, the most traditional of woman saints, ignored caste rules. Holy women may accept these rules as part of society and necessary for others. (Ānandamayī Mā's *āśramas* followed caste rules, but she was not bound by them herself.)

The importance of initiation varies among holy women. Ānandamayī Mā initiated herself; Śāradā Devī was initiated by her husband; Arcanāpuri Mā was initiated as a child; while other holy women had various gurus. Initiation helps to legitimate the role, but is not crucial. None of the Bengali holy women spoke of initiation as being a turning point in their spiritual lives. There is no final "divine marriage"; the initial visionary relationship remains the major mode of interaction until an undramatic death.

Part of the difference between these two patterns may be due to the differing inclusion of mythic elements between the South Indian and Bengali biographies of saints. As Bengali cinema emphasized realism (opposing the fantasy, song, and dance of the Hindi cinema epics), so Bengali saint tales tend to dwell on life experience rather than miracle. Certainly there are strange events described, and myth does appear as saints become theologized, developing into founders of sects and incarnate deities. However, the biographies of most Bengali saints do not conform to an orthodox model; there are few stories of miraculous births, conquest of mythical beasts, great adventures, and wafting off to heaven bodily. In many biographies, the stresses and contradictions of life are included.

In *Medusa's Hair,* a work on holy women in Sri Lanka, Gananāth Obeyesekere speaks of ecstatic experience (which he calls "hypnomantic consciousness") as a symbolization of past conflicts, especially of those involving guilt. The women whom he studied often found their first ecstatic experience to be a spirit attack, and these spirits were often ancestors. The woman would then go mad (*pissu*) due to the attack by the ancestor—she would shout, scream, run away from her home, wander without eating. She was thus expiating her guilt toward the dead. As Obeyesekere states:

> The sequence of these initial events is as follows: the patient is attacked by a vengeful spirit, leading to rituals for exorcism of the spirit, leading to the spirit's refusal to leave (patient's resistance), leading to the patient's wasting away and suffering a dark experience. This sequence is an objectification and dramatization of the patient's guilt.[67]

However, the attitude of the god or ancestor eventually changes, and he or she becomes a force for good. When the character of the experience changes, the woman is no longer mad, but *arude,* subject to divine possession. She becomes a priestess, and the gods show their love for her by gifts of matted hair and true prophecy.

Here, the pattern of experience of Obeyesekere's Sri Lankan holy women was similar, but not identical, to that of the Bengali holy women. Both were viewed as mad before they were accepted as holy, but for different reasons. Further, the Bengali holy women spoke directly to the deities and were possessed by them with little resistance. The deities were kind and nurturing, and gave advice and instruction. They were like good parents or friends, and the real clash was with human relatives who would not accept them.

The Sri Lankan holy women were persecuted by their gods, who would reproach and punish them. These trials were often an excuse to separate from their husbands. As the persecution of the deities wanes, the gods visit in more positive forms, and the holy woman may show the proofs of her devotion: matted hair (a gift from the gods), the ability to walk on hot coals, and ascetic acts (such as piercing the body with needles and arrows). The major conflict was internal, between the holy woman and her possessing spirits.

One difficulty encountered by Bengali women ecstatics is that possession trance is an ambiguous state—the person may be possessed by a positive or negative entity. Possession trance occurs most often among women (out of a dozen cases seen or heard of, all were women), and the goddess Kālī is most often the possessing entity. There may be possession by other deities, as one holy woman states:

> Mā Kālī and Śītalā Devī and Manasā Devī are sisters. Often when they are worshiped, there is possession trance, even in small children. When worship [*pūjā*] is offered, the priest prays that possession trance may descend upon one person. Often there is *dhūma* [aromatic powder burnt in braziers], for trance will be deeper if the room is full of smoke. The person in trance gives practical advice, and many people feel that if they pray to a person in this state, then their prayers will be answered. On Caraka Pūjā day in Tārākeśvar, people prove that they are possessed by holding a hot iron.[68]

Possession trance may also occur with ghosts, demons, and other less attractive entities. In such cases, trance is generally involuntary, more a pathological symptom than a religious event, and often recognized as such by the families involved.

The psychiatrist L. P. Varma mentions cases of possession that he has run across: in one, a young wife was having sexual relations with her father-in-law, justifying this by saying that she was possessed by his dead wife (as both women had leg cramps) and that at such times, she had changed identities. In another case, an unhappily married woman claimed that she was pursued by both Śiva and Pārvatī, who would enter her body and disturb her sleep, dancing in front of her.[69] Possession trance often expresses conflict in the life of the person possessed; one sees this in many cases of newly married girls who become possessed by a ghost or an ancestor upon entering the houses of their in-laws.

Varma mentions the clinical features of the possession syndrome: the woman senses that the goddess is coming, she fasts and sleeps on the floor, shakes her head and unties her hair. She is careless about dress and appearance, has bright eyes, and makes odd movements. She becomes restless and overactive, and she shouts, curses, and blesses people around her. When she speaks as the god or goddess, people prostrate themselves before her, and she treats elders as children.

Some of these qualities were seen by the author at a possession trance on full moon night, in Calcutta (from field notes):

> My first image of the holy woman was feet—red-lined feet which kicked and moved on the inlaid floor of the temple.

She was lying in such a way that her head and most of her body were hidden by a wall, with only her feet showing toward her disciples. The slow, steady chanting of a Bengali song was dying away, and a steady stream of moans, screeches, grunts, and incoherent words began to issue from behind the wall.

This was the induction of *bhor,* as the holy woman entered trance. She was surrounded by a close circle of attendants, older women dressed in the white saris of widowhood. At a distance, a crowd of people watched, householders with children who wanted answers to questions or the blessings of Mā Kālī. The temple was a plaster and cement building with two major rooms, one with a statue of Śītalā, the smallpox goddess, and the other with a blue statue of Kālī, covered with garlands. Both statues wore large numbers of bracelets, in Bengal a sign of the married state. Many of their bracelets were of red wood, which symbolized the newly wed.

Induction of trance was accompanied by the singing of a variant of the Hare Kṛṣṇa mantra in a minor key. Even the children sang, and the woman lay flat on the floor, writhing and rolling rapidly back and forth. Her mouth was open, gasping for air, and her head moved from side to side. Her arms were outspread, and her feet kicked in random movements.

The goddess's presence was perceived in her voice, which gasped and screamed answers to questions. Her body continued to roll and twitch throughout. One of the older women took the role of organizer, having people ask questions, and then repeating them to Mā, who would answer in trance. The observers milled around, jockeying for position, and keeping up a steady stream of commentary on the situation. The questions were about family situations, marriage, health, future accomplishments, work. Her answers tended to be optimistic, with admonishments for people to do meditation and follow spiritual rules in their lives.

During the trance, an aisle was kept empty from her feet outward, and people generally did not sit directly in front of her. After about a half hour of questions, her voice became more hoarse and gasping, and the attendants began the chanting of a Śiva song to bring the trance to a close. During this song she lay slumped on the floor in a heap, but would periodically roll back and forth in a frenzy, screaming, and then slump down again. She would become stiff, with her face on the floor.

She gasped to the goddess not to make things so difficult for her, to ease her burden. The apparent response of the goddess was a lessening of trance, as her words became quieter and her body more still.

The women attendants began to move her unconscious body, which lay drooped like that of a doll. They rubbed her limbs, rearranged her sari (white silk with a wide red border, lying in total disarray), hugged her, and rubbed her head with oil. They threw sanctified food out into the crowd, and there was a mad scramble for it, especially among the children. As the woman returned to normal consciousness, the crowd dispersed, and she ate some *sandeśa* and other sweets.

The curious and casual observers left, and a smaller group of devotees remained. These sat with the holy woman and talked to her, asking for advice, telling her about their lives, asking how she felt and would she like them to do anything for her. Possession is a gift from the gods, a blessing, and seeing such a person is very auspicious. She appeared quite cheerful after the experience and very much the queen in the circle of devotees.

Mā is a thin, quick woman in her fifties, whose gray-white hair comes down into long matted knots in the back. Her skin is brown, dry, and wrinkled, and her teeth stained red by *pān*. She is voluble and anxious to communicate, telling of Mā Kālī who lives in her heart.

This is possession in its positive voluntary side—in which it is deliberately induced; the ability is respected and seen as a divine blessing. The woman described above stated that her husband was awed at her states of trance and that neither he nor his family minded her religious devotion and its results.

Possession brought on by the invasion of the person by other entities was recognized by Caraka and Suśruta in their medical texts as causes of mental illness—different entities caused different symptoms. Such states were seen as a form of madness (*unmāda*), caused by influences from outside the person (called endogenous or *agantu*). God possession is shown when the person is dignified, radiant, and avoids food and sleep, while possession by a sage or elder manifests as obsession. The Pitṛs (ancestors) cause a person to be fatigued, indifferent, and apathetic toward food, while the Gandharvas bring passionate emotions and luxurious living. Possession by Yakṣas causes weepy emotional states, laughter, and the revealing of secrets, while Rākṣasa possession causes insomnia and preoccupation with weapons, blood, and flesh. Possession by Brahmarākṣasas causes self-mortification and contempt for gods, Brahmans, and physicians, while possession by Piśācas causes incoherence, morbid thoughts, running about naked, loss of memory, and a liking for piles of garbage.[70]

In the medical texts these states are not considered blessings, but rather burdens. They are forms of madness that attack the person while he or she is vulnerable. A variety of techniques are available to rid the person of his or her unwanted possessor: mantras, herbs, amulets, sacrifices, gifts to Brahmans, rules and vows, fasts and pilgrimages. These rid the person of the unwanted possession, as ceremony, sacrifice, ritual word and song may induce the desired possession state.

Possession has been a frequent theme in Indian literature and dance. At the Kālāmandir in Calcutta, an Odissi dancer did a stylized possession dance that she called "a dance of Kālī, a dance of ecstasy, a dance of *mokṣa*."[71] The dance began slowly, leading up to the rapid movements and bulging eyes of *Kālī bhāva*, as the dancer stared into space and acted out Kālī's mythic actions. Ecstasy was the possession of the dancer by the goddess. At the end was her return to the void—she stood like a statue as the light on stage faded away.

In Bengali *bhakti*, *bhāva* and *bhor* are judged by different types of evidence. *Bhāva* is nonutilitarian; it is not judged on the basis of secular results. It is unpredictable and often different each time. *Bhāva* is judged by the intensity of the devotional love toward the deity and the person's humility and willingness to sacrifice for that love. Possession trance (*bhor*) is judged biologically, psychologically, and religiously. The person may be given herbs to bring the body back into homeostatic balance or instructions in yoga and sacrifice to balance the mental tensions. If these do not work, the state may be assumed to originate from outside of the person. In that case, exorcism will chase the possessing spirit away or frighten the person who is faking symptoms.

When none of the traditional cures work, and the ecstatic states are accepted by the individual and include religious contents, the person may be viewed as a devotee and the symptoms as religious ecstasy. The possession state is reclassified as a divine gift, and the person as blessed.

Bhāva and *bhor* may also be seen in religious gatherings, most flamboyantly in groups that reject concepts of caste (such as Vaiṣṇavas and Bāuls) and in low-caste groups, such as the Mātua. This sect believes that

Haricanda Ṭhākur was a *śudra* (low-caste) incarnation of the saint-*avatāra* Caitanya, and that by this birth he has blessed all low-caste and outcaste peoples.

Examples of such group ecstasies may be seen at the yearly festival (*mela*) at Ṭhākurnāgar in West Bengal, with hundreds of thousands of participants, mostly low-caste Hindus:

> In the street parades, people ran along, raising their arms, and shouting "Hari bol" loud enough to be heard over a bass drum. Most looked poor, their faces dripping with sweat. In a tent near the temple (which had an image of Haricanda Ṭhākur) there was a mass frenzy of ecstasy. Waves of people were leaping, screaming, twitching, and fainting. People lay on the floor, rapidly rolling from one side of the room to the other, their hair and clothes getting covered with dust. One robust *sādhu* with long gray hair and beard was leaping and then falling to the floor, twisting and rubbing his body against the ground—he was covered with sweat and caked with mud. His eyes were rolled up into his head, and he would spread his arms wide and fall spread-eagled to the floor. Others would leap and dance with their eyes closed, raising their arms in the air.
>
> The tent was full of long, coiling snakes of people, all moving one direction or another. Some played small cymbals (*kartals*), drums, or *ektārās* (one-stringed instruments), and many carried small sticks. Blessed food (*prasāda*) was thrown into the air, and the people scrambled for it in the dust.
>
> Women tended to be less demonstrative than the men, although both fell down in ecstasy. Women tended to be less loud in their screams and moans, and tended to keep their arms close to their bodies, even while rolling around on the ground. Most people there had faces burnt dark by the sun and faded clothes which had once been brightly colored. The masses of the poor beat the bass drums and danced, declaring themselves blessed, and possessed, by Bhagavān.[72]

Another example of group ecstasy was the *cāraka gājan* festival at Kālīghat temple in Calcutta. It was a street parade of ecstatic dancers, costumed as Śiva, Kālī, and various sages. Some looked like transvestites (*hijṛās*); others ran in circles carrying fire.

The ritual was circumambulation of the temple by people who had fasted for ten days before the parade, during a holiday of Śiva worship (*nīla pūjā*), drinking only water before sunrise and after sunset. At the front of the marchers were holy men holding tridents and flowers, and women with long, matted hair. They danced to chants and drumbeats, leaping, throwing their heads back, waving their arms in the air, and moving spasmodically. Some would fall on the ground, rolling and twitching, and then leap up again. They yelled chants and waved painted fans. At one point, a child in the crowd began having fits, and a man costumed as Kālī did a healing dance, and the fits slowly subsided.

Behind the ecstatics and costumed dancers were more subdued people, walking quietly and meditatively. Following them at a distance was a band wearing military-style jackets and turbans, playing the song "Disco Dancer." Large crowds watched, elbowing each other for better positions. Many were in wet clothes, for they had just taken a dip in the Ganges from the ghat at the Kālī temple.

There is great leeway for unorthodox behavior in such groups; indeed, there often seems to be a competition as to whose movements are the most extreme and whose dancing the most enthusiastic. Ecstatic behavior is a sign of devotion to the deity and interpreted as love rather than madness by the observers. When possession occurred, onlookers described it as the deity's gift (*prasāda*) to the person. It was also called a blessing (*āśīrvāda*).

Possession may also be seen in the worship of Manasā, the snake goddess. On her day of worship (*bāroyārī pūjā*) there is a public ritual at a temporary bamboo shrine. Manasā is represented by a pot (*bāṛi*) or clay image. Men walk on burning charcoal, and women carry a pot with the charcoal in it. At the offering of fruit (*kāliyā konṛā*) to the goddess, there is possession and inspired speech. During marriage processions in Birbhum, songs to Manasā are sung, and the goddess will possess married women in order to correct any ritual errors and to predict the future.[73]

At the *jhāpān* or *jhānpān* ceremony, exorcists and healers gather to worship Manasā. The word is associated with *jhānpāna* (to jump, especially away from snakes) and *jupar,* a local word for possession. The trance states are induced both by *jhāpān gān,* ritual songs repeated over and over, and by an intoxicating drink served to the participants. *Jhāpān* is celebrated in Midnapur, Bankura, and Birbhum, and it was first mentioned in the fifteenth-century version of the Manasā legend by Bibrada.[74] However, most worship of Manasā is ritual *pūjā* rather than ecstatic dance and song.

To sum up, there may be possession among both Vaiṣṇava and Śākta groups, with most of it occurring in women but occasionally in men. However, it is a folk tradition—it is generally not included in the mainstream literature. It does not reveal saints, but rather healers—when people are possessed by the deity, it is most frequently shown in healing and prediction, and sometimes in materializations.

Among Śāktas, there is folk worship of Bhagavatī, Manasā, Śītalā, Mangal Caṇḍī, Vasulī, and Visalakṣī, as well as Śiva Mahādeva, and these may involve the use of empowered objects which help to induce possession states. The person who seeks a trance state may use vermilion from a statue of Mā Kālī, or relics of bone and ash from the burning ground. He or she may pray for the goddess's *śakti* to enter into his body, and this power may be spread through the breath, or by word or touch. Salt, water, mustard oil, and turmeric may become empowered substances to be used for magic or healing, from the breath of the person who becomes possessed. At times, fruits and vegetables may take on these powers. In the village of Budge-Budge in West Bengal, there was a woman famed for going into possession trance and causing bananas to bleed.

Exorcists (*ojhās* and *guṇīns* if male, *ḍāins* if female) may also perform healing due to the goddess's presence within them. They may see spirits in glass or mirrors, or use their thumbnails as mirrors in which to see events. Spirits (*bhūtas, pretas,* and ancestors) may be summoned, banished, or fixed with iron nails to prevent their interaction with the community. Blessed mud may be made to blaze with fire to repel spirits, and the exorcist's touch may cure snakebite, disease, and blindness. He or she may claim to bring the dead to life by sprinkling them with water or to be able to bring rain and fertility due to the goddess's presence.

This is also the territory of the *piśāca tāntrika,* who may be possessed by or may control spirits. A wide range of folk practice has been incorporated into the Śākta tradition. Some *tāntrikas* worship a stone or metal statue of the goddess immersed in alcohol or burn liquor to the deity, who is believed to breathe in the fumes. She may return them materializations, *śakti* (power) to perform miracles (*siddhis*), or the gift of *bhor.* While these are often viewed by village Śāktas as a part of their tradition, many urban devotees of the goddess reject possession and magical belief as superstition and weakness, inferior to loving devotion to the Mother. Most holy women interviewed followed a Śākta universalist approach, accepting both urban and rural folk beliefs as parts of a complex religious tradition in which a deity lived both within and beyond them.

SIX Conclusion

And all should cry, Beware! Beware!
His flashing eyes, his floating hair!
Weave a circle round him thrice,
And close your eyes with holy dread,
For he on honey-dew hath fed,
And drunk the milk of Paradise.
—Samuel Taylor Coleridge, *Kubla Khan*

The Ecstatic as Guru

The ecstatics discussed in this book play many roles: they may be teacher, saint, lover, and madman. In this chapter I examine these roles and note the patterns of life of the ecstatic and the developmental process of destruction and rebirth. For the teacher or guru role, I discuss the status of the ecstatic in society, based on how observers distinguish true from false gurus. For the saint or *siddha* role, I talk about the paradoxical nature of the ecstatic, in which unification of opposites is valued over ritual purity. For the role of lover, I show how love and madness are intertwined and emphasize the sharing relationship between the ecstatic and the deity. For the role of madman, I reexamine the relationship between secular and divine madness and also discuss the contributions of mad ecstatics to Bengali society.

The most important aspect of the ecstatic to others in society is his or her role as teacher or guru. The ecstatic guru is a religious specialist who actually deals with the ultimate goals of the tradition—passionate love and liberation from illusion and death.

Not all gurus are ecstatics. Most nonecstatic gurus do not deal with salvation, but rather with *dharma*. Such gurus are counselors and ministers, giving good wishes, suggestions for penance, and even arranging marriages. They listen to problems, comfort the depressed, suggest foods and meditations to keep people happy and on an even keel, and give amulets and mantras for healing and good luck. Some *bhakti* gurus act as brahmin priests, keeping the family deities happy in their shrines in the home. Like Saint Augustine, their disciples wish for liberation, "but not yet," and the gurus oblige them by not asking for more religious commitment than they care to demonstrate.

Ecstatic gurus have a different specialization. They are generally not considered capable of conducting ordinary life in a proper manner—they cannot organize their own lives, let alone organize someone's marriage. People come to them for *aśāstrīya* goals—not dharmic life, but the religious violation of societal goals. They attract devotees who wish to reject the world; thus the parents of the young men and women who go to see them often object—like Socrates, ecstatic gurus corrupt the youth. Jagadbandhu was beaten by angry parents, while Vāmākṣepā rejected as disciple a person who had a fleeting thought of his business in Calcutta. The parents reject religious passion; the ecstatics tend to reject *dharma*.[1]

The true ecstatic is rare in Bengal. There are many potential devotees who seek gurus, descending en masse on the latest person whose claims of *bhāva* have gained him disciples and reputation. Many of these devotees travel from *bhakti* ecstatic to yogi to *tantrika*, seeking blessings and initiation. All seek someone they can believe in, but nobody (except perhaps a *pāgal* Westerner) would accept a guru without question, any more than one would buy a used car from a lot without question.

The Western mythos of meeting the guru is much like love at first sight—there is a spark when their eyes meet, there is a sense of the lost parent or beloved, there is an atmosphere of mystery and romance, full of bells and incense and exotic yogic disciplines. In contrast, the model devotee for most Śāktas was Vivekānanda, who was much more hesitant when he came to visit Rāmakṛṣṇa, and did not recognize him as guru for a long while. For Vaiṣṇavas, the guru is a representative of a lineage and tradition—he is not expected to have the Śākta charisma and is respected for his entrance into the *līlā* of Kṛṣṇa and Rādhā. The Bengali guru-disciple relationship is not based on romantic love, but more on the model of an Indian marriage—not passion, but growing compatibility.

For those seeking salvation, the ecstatic guru is the decisive figure. If the guru is a false ecstatic, a person claiming experience that he does not possess, he cannot save—he is unable to send the devotee to the deity's paradise or to some other *bhakti* form of liberation. However, if the guru is an ecstatic blessed by the gods (or at least known to them), then the devotee has a chance to attain his highest dreams. The guru can act as patron, introducing him to the gods and finding the disciple a place near him in Vṛndāvana or Kailāsa. While the disciple could conceivably attain this on his own, directly through the grace of the deity, this is believed to happen only in extraordinary cases.

It is thus important for the disciple, and for observers who may become disciples, to be able to find the true ecstatic guru. The major criterion is not a judgment of sanity or insanity, but one of true or false experience. Observers try to gauge if the person is a true guru with *darśana* (vision) of the deity or a false claimant, which includes conscious simulation of religious experience, possession by a demon or ancestor, physical disease, and secular madness. Dramatic imitation for the sake of gain is generally the first suspicion people voice in hearing about an ecstatic.

How can one verify a true guru? If his experiences appear genuine, then he may be judged a *siddha,* one who has attained, based on them. However, if the person is already believed to be a true guru, then his experiences will look genuine. We thus have the hermeneutical circle—interpretation and presupposition support each other. There is no single answer to this problem, but a number of factors must be weighed. The two most significant sets of distinctions deal with the content of the guru's experience and its expression, and the context in which it takes place.

The experiences themselves are analyzed for content—are they consistent with the tradition and internally consistent? The guru's *bhāva* is studied to see how he expresses his feelings about the deity and the *līlā,* to note the passion, sensitivity, sincerity, and seriousness. The religious imagery must be convincing and powerful, and recognizable to observers. In the various forms of *bhakti,* the eight *sāttvika bhāvas* (the ecstatic symptoms—changing skin color, hair standing on end, etc.) are proofs of ecstasy, for they are considered to be involuntary. As several informants stated, one or two of these symptoms may conceivably be simulated by a good actor, but not all eight at once.

The ecstatic is expected to act irrationally, overcome by love of the deity. While some parts of India include hatred of the deity as an acceptable state of passion (*dveṣa-bhāva*), this is not mentioned in the Bengali texts or in the oral saint tradition. Rādhā's love-madness included elements of jealousy and anger toward Kṛṣṇa (and some devotees feel anger toward Rādhā's rival Candrāvalī), but in general any expression of hostility is suspect, unless it can be linked to renunciate behavior.

In some forms of trance, the ecstatic may act out the mood (*bhāva*) of the deity, thus showing their close relationship. He may act as a person of the opposite sex, as an animal (especially if overcome by the mood of one of Viṣṇu's animal incarnations), or as a mythical figure in a specific situation, such as a warrior on a battlefield. Disciples may see the guru's visions imprinted on his skin or share his vision of a mantric symbol or deity. Although the trance is powerful enough to render the ecstatic immune to pain and unconscious of the physical environment, it should (according to Vaiṣṇava and Śākta practitioners) be able to be broken if necessary for the sake of compassionate action.

Moodiness is almost expected in *bhakti* ecstatics, who alternate between despair when the deity is far away and joy when the deity is present to vision, hearing, or touch. Stories of threatened suicide are frequent in saint biographies (such as those of Rāmakṛṣṇa Paramahaṃsa and Gaur Kiśora) as ways of forcing the deity to manifest and show love.

Some types of confusion are expected to accompany intense experiences. The ecstatic guru should ignore his physical body and the world around him, in favor of his spiritual body which dwells in the deity's paradise. He may claim that the rivers or mountains he sees are really rivers in the paradise or mountains that existed in a sacred past situation. Such disorientation is accepted as an accompaniment of ecstasy, when the person is believed to live in two worlds at once.

The ecstatic is also expected to be able to spread his *bhāva*—certainly to his disciples in initiation, but more broadly to all observers, who may be overcome at unexpected moments by the guru's spiritual love (*prema*) or power (*śakti*). The ecstatic's moods are expected to inspire both disciples and observers, instilling religious sentiments even in nonbelievers and skeptics.

Although miracles are not strictly a part of the *bhakti* tradition, if they occur, they may be understood as proofs of the deity's grace toward the ecstatic, and they show the power of intense love. Many disciples interviewed stated that they were called to recognize the guru in dreams—that the guru appeared, showed his love and/or power, and asked the disciple to follow. The ecstatic may demonstrate immunity to pain (Yogeśwarī Mā) and poison (Jagadbandhu). He gives miraculous healings, especially by touch or materialized amulet (popular among Śākta *tāntrikas*), or materializes food for the hungry (especially seen in stories about women ecstatics). Sometimes miracles reveal the "hidden" guru, who appears lazy but is really dynamic and alert, who appears dull but has divine knowledge. He is ignored until his meditation causes the temple to shake, or until the goddess visits other people in dreams to tell them of his true nature (as in the case of Vāmākṣepā).

Ecstatic gurus are also believed to have great insight into the thoughts and emotions of other people. Saint biographies abound with stories of people who simulate *bhāvas* in meditation and *kīrtana* singing, and how the saint (the true ecstatic guru) would expel the actor from the group, exposing his hypocrisy to all. It is a significant quality of the ecstatic that he can distinguish between true ecstasy and dramatic simulation with authority and credibility (Vijayakṛṣṇa would repeatedly expel false ecstatics from his *kīrtana* groups). The metaphors used are that the true guru can distinguish between gold and imitation metal, between jewels and colored glass.

Such simulation has become widespread in the *bhakti* tradition, as emotional states are not difficult to imitate. In yoga, the only real proofs are asceticism and miraculous powers (*siddhis*). It is difficult to imitate an ascetic life—people can see how the yogi lives and whether he looks well fed. Imitation of *siddhis* requires an ability at sleight of hand, if not some mechanical contrivance, and audiences are known to get angry if they feel deceived. But emotions are much more difficult to disprove, and some forms of *bhakti* include practices in which the person consciously tries to induce emotion in himself. When there are practices to evoke emotion in private, public attempts to feel strongly can follow close behind. Although the theological literature does not distinguish between acceptable and unacceptable simulations of religious emotion, informants tend to accept private and condemn public imitations.

In addition to content, a second criterion for ascertaining the truth of the ecstatic's religious claims is context. While content examines the ecstatic's relationship to the deity, context looks at his relationship to other persons and to society. The person's sociocultural environment is taken into account—his family, caste, and social background are examined, as well as his householder or renunciant status. If the person has taken vows of renunciation (*sannyāsa*), he may be judged according to his guru, lineage, and tradition. The status of renunciant is an important aspect of gauging ecstasy—such people are expected to have some sort of religious experiences, and their claims do not arouse the anxiety seen when householders report visions to their relatives. Exorcisms are often performed on householders making ecstatic claims, but such statements among renunciants would be accepted. It is difficult for a householder to be accepted as a guru.

The ecstatic is also judged by creativity and by contribution to society. Śāktas emphasize artistic creation—writing poems and stories or making religious images—as a sign of true inspiration. Bāuls also emphasize the beauty of poems and songs. Vaiṣṇavas write plays and poetry, but they expect ecstatics to be primarily role models, seeing modern ecstatics as following in the footsteps of Kṛṣṇa Caitanya. The ecstatic should spread love for Kṛṣṇa and Rādhā, and thus bring glory to his lineage. He may also create Vaiṣṇava subcastes, or new social organizations. Society as a whole may also be affected by group miracles, especially the averting of epidemics and natural disasters (seen in Jagadbandhu's attempts to stop a plague with Harināma, and Vāmākṣepā's control over storms).

A major contextual issue is whether or not the ecstatic has gained disciples. Even one disciple radically changes the status of the ecstatic, as one child changes the status of a woman from wife to mother. An ecstatic without disciples is like an unmarried woman or an independent goddess—there is suspicion of too much unbound power, too much loose *śakti,* which might be used toward destructive ends. If power is not harnessed by *dharma* and responsibility, it may be used against society. Once there is a disciple, there is respectability. As one informant pointed out, madmen and drunkards do not have disciples—only gurus do.

Disciples fulfill a variety of functions. For those "*bhor* ladies" and gurus who feel it is a violation of their humble status to talk about their religious experiences or claim miracles, their disciples can act as their voices while the gurus remain aloof. Disciples can beg so that the ecstatic need not break meditative trance, and they may defend the claims of their guru against the claims of rival gurus.[2] Disciples take responsibility for earthly interactions so that the ecstatic may concentrate on heaven—a division of spiritual labor. And they give love and support to the guru, orienting and stabilizing him in relation to society.

To study context, the ecstatic's life history is examined—is there a record of honesty and sincerity, or are there incidents of duplicity or criminal behavior? Unless a radical conversion is emphasized, knowledge of such a background can disqualify the ecstatic guru.

An ecstatic may be shown to be a false guru by a negative context. The classical problems are shown in Rāmakṛṣṇa Paramahaṃsa's phrase "women and gold." A true guru should not even handle money, let alone accumulate it. However, some gurus are known for their ostentatious wealth, which is associated by traditional observers with desire, greed, and too much care for the body—good food, silk clothing, perfumes, and thick mattresses. The guru is expected to renounce physical comfort in favor of something greater. He also should not seduce the wives of his disciples or his female disciples, although there have been many such scandals. *Tāntrikas* especially are known for their "cures for barrenness" and their "personal meditation instruction," while Bāuls and Sahajīyas may volunteer to teach their "esoteric techniques" to married and unmarried women.

Some gurus are concerned with name and fame, boasting about their abilities and gossiping and insulting other spiritual teachers, leaders, and fellow disciples of their own gurus. Such behavior is traditionally considered a sign of pride and a violation of the humility that the true guru must have, as well as a lack of loyalty to his own lineage and tradition.

False claims can almost instantly disqualify a guru. If his predictions of the future do not come true, if his own practices do not attain their stated goal, he will be judged a hypocrite, a *nakal* guru, rather than as a true guru. A guru's hypocrisy is shown in claiming poverty while owning land or valuable objects, or in claiming celibacy while having a family on the side. Such a person violates his own rules and cannot claim the inspiration of a deity for motivation, as do gurus who violate *dharma* or purity rules (*sadācāra*) due to divine madness.

While normally there are clear areas that will disqualify *bhakti* ecstatics and gurus, at times these may be circumvented—if either guru or devotee is sufficiently motivated to find reasons. One such area is illness (difficult to categorize as content or context). A guru is expected to be a healthy person—most practitioners begin with haṭha-yoga to gain control over the body so that they may lead a properly ascetic life—and a failure of health is a failure of spiritual practice. Health is the sign of success, such radiant health that the guru's face glows with light and he is immune to poison and snakebite. Good health also means that the guru can interact with low-caste people and eat their food with no ill effects. However, some disciples will defend a sick guru on the grounds that his illness is a deliberate sacrifice by the guru, who has taken on the terrible karma of the Kālī Yuga to help save the world, or that he has taken on the bad karma of the devotee in order to help save the individual. Thus, lack of health is no longer a failure—it is rather a compassionate act, showing the guru's willingness to take on the suffering and sin of others (it may also demonstrate Christian influence).

Probably the most difficult area is the failure of the ecstatic guru to grant his blessings (usually in the form of intense experiences) to the devotee. As it is heresy to doubt the guru's ability to do so, the fault must be understood to lie within the devotee. Such a disciple must contemplate his own unworthiness again and again, and yet realize that doubt makes gaining the desired blessings more and more difficult. Such a position virtually guarantees that the guru cannot be confronted, or even questioned, for he can easily accuse the disciple of lacking the requisite faith. The issue thus becomes the lack of faith of the devotee, rather than the lack of power of the guru. Indeed, for the truly faithful disciple, even a statue or photograph may give blessings and serve as guru (this is seen in both yogic and *bhakti* traditions).

While it is easy to violate the canons of proper behavior, it is more difficult to violate myth. The scope of mythic and religious imagery in India is so broad that there is scarcely a behavior for which a mythical precedent could not be found. There are gods who devour and cause death, who tie and bind, who attempt world dominance and destruction. Attempted arson could be possession by Śiva, lord of the burning ground, or Agni, god of the sacrificial fire. Stealing or philandering could be following the behavior of the flirtatious Kṛṣṇa and his tricky friends; breakdown and fragmentation of self could echo Satī, whose corpse was chopped to pieces, or Prajāpati, who fell apart to create the universe. Grandiose claims could fit not only the gods, but the Vedic priests and sages who swallowed the hallucinogenic *soma* juice (thus eating the god Soma).

A whole host of societal taboos can be justified by folklore and myth. Myth includes hatred of the parents, hatred by the parents, withdrawal from human society, emotional extremes, multiple personality symptoms, hallucinations, and delusions. It is difficult to find an action that cannot be justified as a *bhāva* by relating it to the religious literature. The only limit on the ecstatic guru's behavior may be his or his disciples' knowledge of myth. In such situations, traditional contextual judgments come into direct conflict with claims of religious content, with the *bhāva* of the deity or sage taking precedence over societal expectations.

Some falsification of ecstatic gurus is determined by testing, but this is relatively rare and seen mostly among disciples with some Western education. As emotion is a difficult thing to measure, most testing emphasizes yogic abilities: control of heart rate and blood pressure, the ability to be buried alive or be immune to heat and pain. Some tests may include checking claims of knowledge made at a distance and testing of telepathy and clairvoyance. A guru who claims the ability to materialize objects may be tested by search (as in the case of Yogeśwarī Devī), or the depth of trance may be gauged by observation and stopwatch (as in the case of Arcanāpurī Mā). More frequent is the observing and recording of bodily changes indicative of ecstasy, the counting of how many *sāttvika bhāvas* the ecstatic underwent at various times.

Some forms of testing, however, show a subtle hostility on the part of the testers, who may be working out their own ambivalence toward the religious life. Such "testing" frequently occurs during exorcism, when the person is clearly tortured (tied up, beaten, suffocated, burnt, splashed with caustic liquids), and in other sorts of tests: rocks are dropped on the person in trance; he is punched and kicked to gauge the depth of the trance; he is teased and tormented to see if he gets angry. Pin pricks turn into beatings as the testing becomes a competition between the sacred and secular worlds, to determine which is superior or dominant. There are several stories of saints who were practically killed while in meditative trance, by villagers who were "testing" their spirituality.[3]

One form of ecstatic trance subject to particular suspicion is possession. Possession is associated with impurity because its practitioners are often paid for their trances, which puts spiritual abilities to materialistic and worldly ends. Yet possession trance is a culturally useful skill: people in trance are believed to be able to predict the future, heal, influence the outcomes of exams and marital disputes, bestow jobs, give general blessings—all in the name of the possessing deity. Such were the desires of people visiting "*bhor* ladies," who would ask for these boons during the woman's trance. These goals have a venerable history—the Vedic priests sought such material ends as wealth and fertility. Yet there is an urban suspicion of possession, viewing it as village superstitition and ignorance. Simulating possession trance is a gamble for false ecstatics—they may raise their status and gain some money, but if they are believed to be lying or inhabited by a lying ghost or demon, their dramatic renditions of trance may cause them to be outcast from the community or be exorcized—with a vengeance.

In the final analysis, powerful and convincing ecstatic claims can outweigh violations of context—housewives such as Ānandamayī Mā can become gurus. However, if the ecstatic is not sufficiently charismatic and his *bhāvas* are not believed, he may well be condemned for social excesses and violations. Context cannot prove the true ecstatic, but it can disprove the claims of false ecstatics. Such a disproved ecstatic may be labeled a false guru or a madman.

The ecstatic cannot be a guru if he is understood to be mad in the secular sense. Ordinary madness comes from an imbalance of humors, from bad configurations of planets (*grahas,* those that grasp), from predatory spirits. It occurs due to desire, greed, frustration, disappointment, and impurity of various types. Epilepsy is a special variety of madness, associated with terror. The madman will bite and hit people, and it is said that his brain has failed or his mind is bad (terms such as *brain khārāp,* bad brain). Its origin is physical, a weakened or impure body or situation.

In contrast, religious madness is believed to come from focus on the deity—from desire for God or from the vision of God. The worlds of matter and spirit are suddenly seen to be united and the illusory barrier between them falls. Religious madness is not insanity; it is closer to the romantic definition of madness: genius, poetry, art, impassioned oration. To call Caitanya, Nityānanda, and Rāmakṛṣṇa mad was not to insult them, but to compliment them and show respect; theirs was a "good" madness. To understand these we may ask two questions: Why does the ecstatic act mad? Why does the nonecstatic act mad?

The ecstatic may act mad because he really is in a state of divine love and acting appropriately to his feelings. Or he may be possessed by the *bhāva* of a mad saint or deity and cannot help acting as they would. Or he may be expressing a transcendent religious truth, beyond the ability of ordinary words and actions to express, and again he cannot help acting as a channel.

The ecstatic may even act as if he is mad in a secular sense. His motive is humility—the mad have a low status in the society, while gurus are high and pure. To act lowly makes the ecstatic equal to others and may show an egalitarian impulse. Or acting mad may induce jeering and insults from others, so that the ecstatic may practice nonattachment to society. For the Śaivite Pāśupatas, such simulation of madness was a ritual practice.

There are other advantages to feigning secular madness for the ecstatic. Such madness gives privacy for meditation—even mad people prefer not to associate with other madmen. It also gives freedom of action, for there is no need to justify behavior—it is explained by madness. The ecstatic may also be trying to teach his disciples a lesson by violating their narrow understandings of religion with unexpected and hostile actions. He becomes a trickster, appearing both good and evil. Or he may be testing his observers as to who can see through illusions to the truth behind it. The ecstatic critiques the traditional religion by showing its limits and the absurdity of social norms, but he also supports it by both being a part of it and illustrating the dangers involved in leaving traditional behavior.

The nonecstatic may act mad in the religious sense for a variety of reasons. He may be mad in the ordinary sense, and this coincidentally resembles divine madness. He may be trying to look like an ecstatic and thereby gain money and secular status (risking the chance of rejection and exorcism) or religious status (raising his standing in a devotional group). Or he may be trying to accelerate spiritual growth by wishful thinking, feeling that public dramatic imitation brings the real thing. This view is almost universally rejected by ecstatic *siddhas* and potential devotees—it is considered an attempt to coerce the grace of the god, and thus a sign of magical leanings or vanity.

No normal nonecstatic would act mad in a secular sense. He would have to be mad to wish to appear mad: he could only attain low status, he would find no benefits, and he would risk painful exorcism. There is no Indian Hamlet, no strategic use of apparent madness to gain one's ends (except perhaps avoiding marriage), and there is no romanticizing of madness of physical origin. The person whose madness is due to too much heat, wind, desire, or impurity cannot be a guru.

The true ecstatic guru is distinguished from the secular madman and the false guru by the analysis of content and context, and it is not a simple task. For the devotee, the stakes are high—rebirth and wandering in the dark, or salvation. He must find the saint (*siddha*) who has united the opposites of the world within him.

The Ecstatic as *Siddha*

The role of saint or *siddha* defines the ecstatic as one who has attained the highest goal. *Siddha* (saint) is an inclusive term. It unites a variety of polarities, incorporating impurity, chaos, passion, and insanity. The *siddha* does not follow the traditional pan-Indian association of sacred and pure; the holiness of the *siddha* includes worship in the outhouse and seeking God in impure bodily substances.[4] The religion of the *siddha* is not a defense against chaos but a creative incorporation of disorder. The highest goal of devotion is to become *siddha,* transcending the illusory order of the world.

The brahminical and yogic images of the *siddha* describe a person who is high and pure, unattached to the body, balanced, beyond life and death. He is without preference, passionless, tranquil, storing large amounts of spiritual energy amassed from austerities. He is without impurity, without ignorance, without emotion.

In contrast, the Bengali *bhakti siddha* is not a purified person but a completed process. The term *siddha* has several meanings, according to the Bengali dictionary: realized, accomplished, attained, evolved. Though it is a qualifier, in Bengali it is used as a noun when referring to persons (as a short form of *siddha puruṣa,* the spirit which has attained). In some contexts, the word *siddha* is used to mean a proven truth, that is, that which is self-evident.[5] The *siddha* is eternal (*nitya*) and liberated (*mukta*), but also *miśrita,* meaning mixed or blended.[6] His attainment occurs during the process of becoming *siddha,* which is associated with boiling and sweating. The *siddha* is cooked by internal fires arising in ecstatic trance. He is not purified, but cooked, and his opposites are blended into a whole.

The *siddha* incorporates several types of polarities. Some of the principal ones are (1) embodied/disembodied, (2) emotion/detachment, (3) purity/impurity, (4) male/female, (5) auspicious/inauspicious, (6) reality/myth, (7) sanity/madness, and (8) life/death.

These are present in both theology and biography. The issue of embodiment is seen in the ecstatic states, in which the limitations of the physical body are both emphasized and violated. For the *siddhas* in this book, the body is shrunken (Ānandamayī Mā), stretched and bleached (Kṛṣṇa Caitanya), burnt (Rāmakṛṣṇa Paramahaṃsa and Vijayakṛṣṇa Gosvāmin), and psychically imprinted with mantras and scenes from meditation (Vijayakṛṣṇa and Siddhimātā). The ecstatic may appear to be different people (Ānandamayī Mā, Kṛṣṇa Caitanya). He is both beyond the body (in an inner vacuum or a spiritual body) and within it—the physical body is radically changed by the inner nature of the *siddha,* which influences and dominates it.

The role of emotion is seen in both Vaiṣṇava and Śākta *mahābhāva,* the highest devotional states, in which all possible emotions are felt toward the deity. The *siddha* feels both passion and detachment, love and hatred, joy and sorrow. Rather than the yogic avoidance of emotion and concentration on bliss, the *siddha* devotee seeks to incorporate all emotions as ways to approach God. He is not inwardly dissociated from passion; instead he accepts it as valuable if properly directed.

Indifference to purity and impurity is shown in the behavior of the *siddha.* In Bāul poems, the *pāgal siddha* equates filth and sandalwood paste, food and dung. He is sensitive to the *bhāvas* of others and can share their states of love, but he cannot be made impure—he is immune, like gold. He can eat the leavings of jackals and undergo no change; he can turn an outhouse into a temple, resonating with Kṛṣṇa's name. He may follow ritually pure behavior or totally violate it—his status does not depend on it.

The *siddha* is often an androgynous figure, uniting male and female identities. Vaiṣṇava males see themselves inwardly as young girls, flirting and playing, while Śākta males are inwardly children of the Mother, or the gentle handmaiden of the goddess, helping her dress and oil her hair. Śākta holy women may be possessed by Kālī or Śiva or both, or they may be inwardly empty and capable of both male and female identities. At times this can extend to the physical world, as, for example, hermaphrodites (when the *sādhu* Nityagopāl was born, the midwife thought him female), or as Sahajiyā Vaiṣṇavas or Śāktas who are male, yet dress in women's clothing.

Auspiciousness is shown in health, wealth, fertility, and good fortune. The *siddha* shows the extremes of both the auspicious and the inauspicious. He lives in poverty, yet can bring wealth; he often has no children, yet can cause fertility in others; he eats impure food and wears the cloth of corpses, yet he gives blessings. Although often in poor health himself, he may yet heal others. Śāradā Devī was a childless widow, yet she was visited by women who wished to have sons.[7]

In the lives of *siddhas*, myth is often interspersed with physical realities. Childhood memories include both relatives and gods, while visions and mysterious powers are included in casual conversation (Lakṣmī Mā mentioned how Śiva had come to see her while she was cooking dinner). Personal history is often understood in mythic terms: meetings with sages and gods may be remembered as the major events of adolescence. Mythic events can be taken literally by members of the group, such as the story of Lalitā Sakhī of Navadvīpa, a Gauḍiyā Vaiṣṇava *siddha*. A Vaiṣṇava informant stated that Lalitā Sakhī, born male, dressed himself as female and considered himself to be a girlfriend of Rādhā in the heavenly Vṛndāvana. When crass townspeople wished to disabuse him of this notion, they captured him and proceeded to strip off his sari. However, the sari grew infinitely long (like Draupadī's sari in the *Mahābhārata*), and the townspeople could not reach the end of it. Unable to prove that he was male, they left in a confused and disgruntled mob. Lalitā Sakhī's virtue was saved.[8]

The relation of sanity and madness has been discussed through this book. The *siddha* is mad in his divine love, but this madness is chosen and affirmed as a sign of his dedication to the deity. He may act sane or mad, as he chooses; his trance may be voluntary, in order to accomplish some social good. The *siddha* acts irrationally and the patient is healed; he screams and weeps and the statue becomes alive; he dances and sings and the people around him fall into ecstatic states. The world may be chaos, *elomelo,* but the *siddha* finds order through the chaos of a mad inner god. Both extremes are united, and the *siddha* walks with one foot in each world.

The *siddha* is believed to have conquered the distinction between life and death, to exist in a state that is beyond both. The Vaiṣṇava *siddha* lives in a spiritual body, which will continue to live in the celestial Vṛndāvana after his physical death. The Śākta *siddha* seeks the Mother in the burning ground and is rewarded with the gift of eternal life in her presence, without the fear of rebirth. The Bāul is dead while alive (*jiyānte marā*), literally brought back from the dead, beyond the limitations of either state.

Each devotional group has its own sets of opposites. Vaiṣṇavas emphasize emotions, especially those found in separation and union. In the state of passionate delirium (*mādana mahābhāva*), these emotions are felt together; bliss and joy mingle with fear and jealousy, love with sorrow, playfulness with loneliness and depression. The *Caitanya Caritāmṛta* compared Kṛṣṇa Caitanya's emotions to warring elephants, destroying his body. Śāktas unify opposite states of power—from total reliance on the Mother to total control of her; Vāmākṣepā was both beloved child and conqueror of storms and disease. The range is from dependence to autonomy, and the Śākta in *mahābhāva* is both child and adult, fearful infant and world-controlling magician. Bāuls unify opposite substances—gold and mud, pure and impure. Seeing God in sperm and menstrual blood violates the traditional dichotomy of pure and impure substances, yet Bāuls affirm the body as valuable, and in all aspects the temple of Bhagavān. Their *mahābhāva* links those opposites considered most extreme in the culture—pure spirit and impure substance.

These opposites are balanced in a fluctuation of worlds: the realms of myth and religion, and the arenas of history and social interaction. Myth and physical reality shift back and forth, and the *siddha* lives in many worlds at once. As we study these worlds, duality becomes multiplicity. Rāmakṛṣṇa Paramahaṃsa was told by Kālī to live in the state of *bhāva-*

mukha, an awareness of all worlds at once. Another understanding of such multiplicity is the state of *bahumānasa,* in which the person becomes capable of acting simultaneously in the many worlds he can feel and perceive. At the devotional extreme, the person is overwhelmed by many words; at the yogic extreme, he is a master of them. The *siddha* incorporates both of these perspectives. The Śākta text *Tripurarahasyam* describes the saints who are *bahumānasa*:

> 82. *Vairāgya* [indifference], etc. is of no use to them. Neither are reflection and meditation [useful]. They enter [the states of] reflection and meditation as soon as they hear [about them].
> 83. And at that moment they become aware of the root of the ultimate. They are liberated while living, like those of whom Jānaka was the foremost. . . .
> 86. There is not the slightest sullying of their intellects [by the traces of desire], and these people are referred to by the wise as fully liberated, as many-minded [*bahumānasa*].[9]

The text describes the yogic aspect of the saint, in which intellect and ability are emphasized:

> 97. Just as a very intelligent person can perform fifteen acts simultaneously, without faltering at all;
> 98. And as a person may be observed acting skillfully, simultaneously moving, speaking, and acting;
> 99. And as a teacher, for example, notices the errors in recitation of a number of students simultaneously. How can there be a single mind and complex action?
> 100. Your own enemy, Arjuna king of the Haihayas, was killed by you, O Rāma.
> 101. [He] had 1,000 arms and fought with many different weapons simultaneously, and made no mistakes at all. Here you have seen a person of this type of intellect.
> 102. The mind of such a person becomes manifold, [capable of] following a variety of paths, as one may perform a complex act. They are the many-minded [*bahumānasa*], the best of the brightest [*jñānins*], whose inner nature manifests freely.[10]

The *siddha* is thus understood as a person of complexity, in both scripture and folk tradition. A popular collection of saint biographies has a *parama siddha* or great sage, "shining like a great luminary," describe himself:

> I was born in all castes, I drank the milk of all mothers, I experienced the joys and sorrows of innumerable wives, children, friends and relatives. I did undergo great sorrows of separation, deaths, floods, destruction and devastation . . . the joys and gains of friends, the sorrows of friends becoming enemies, and enemies causing great losses, the troubles of thieves and of drunkards I experienced. I fell in many hells. The troubles, tortures, turmoils of life, birth and growth, agonies of diseases and deaths [would] comprise volumes of books if recorded.[11]

Some types of ecstatic states are more highly valued than others in the *bhakti* traditions. The less-valued types are also more public: divination, prophecy, healing, the types most valued by the Greeks and Hebrews. The more highly valued types are more private revelations—the visions and insights that affect the person inwardly, but make little impact on the world. The public ecstasies are considered utilitarian and associated with magic, while the private revelations have ecstatic love of the deity as a valuable end in itself.

Such public states and claims of occult power are often seen as the antithesis of *bhāva*. For the orthodox bhakta, *bhāva* is opposed to *sthūlatā*—the state of the materialistic person who does not understand religious faith and experience. The *sthūla* person is a householder, concerned with status and the social world. For the yogi, the opposition is between *bhāva* and *nakal*, imitation. The *nakal sādhu* is a person who is a phony, who imitates *bhāvas* so that others may think him religious or give him money. It is a technique of manipulation. For the urban Indian, *bhāva* is opposed to *pāglāmi*—the madness whose religious imagery covers up deprivations and desires, in the person attempting to find something of value in his misery. Śāktas may have false claims of power and Vaiṣṇavas false claims of love. Among Bāuls, there is skepticism as to whether a person is genuinely inspired and performs ritual and meditation, or whether he is only a singer, performing songs he does not really understand before large groups of people.

Some of the most highly valued states are expressed in metaphorical images of flowing or liquids.[12] Vaiṣṇavas speak of *rasa* and *āmṛta*, the nectar of love which is like ghee and honey. One drinks in the sweetness of the *Bhāgavata Purāṇa* through the ears and divine love (*prema*) through the heart. Śāktas drink the milk of the Mother and find her dwelling in the ritual wine, which is her substance. Bāuls and Sahajiyās find the Man of the Heart in sperm and menstrual blood, in the water and milk (*nir* and *kṣir*), and in the older Buddhist *mahāsukha* and *bodhicitta* liquids. Devotees may drink nectar from the moon or *rasa* from a text or play. In the yogic tradition, semen, believed to be stored in the head, aided in the attainment of concentration, trance, and immortality. In the devotional tradition, liquids are dynamic (although often not directed), and their movement and thickening create the waves of religious love.

The person who is dry, without the liquid of ecstasy, may have the power of *tapas* (stored heat or fire). It is a force that may be used destructively (to slay demons) or creatively, to give life—for fruits need heat to ripen, rain needs heat to fall, sexuality needs heat for reproduction. It is both the energy of the sacrifice and the human effort to concentrate that energy, as visibly shown by sweat (again, one of the associations of *siddha*).

In this area, most bhakti literature is closer to Āyurveda than to Veda—the person who is dry is hard-hearted, dusty, heated, blocked, selfish, and far from the deity. The ecstatic is soft, wet, open to the spirit, while the yogi is hard, dry, closed to the impure. The secular madman confuses these traits: he may be wet and soft, and open to the impure; or hard and dry, and closed to the pure. Devotional *siddhas* have a selective permeability—they are affected by love, but not pollution.

The danger for such ecstatics is not impurity, but rather hierarchy. The ecstasy of the *siddha* must remain in some sense chaotic. If he organizes it, he loses it—and the power is trapped in the hierarchies of purity, kinship, and caste. As the intensity lowers, the situation becomes *śāstric* and ecstasy becomes a part of the universe rather than beyond it. The problem of dilution of intensity is present in the major *bhakti* traditions: Śāktas become poets and pandits, Vaiṣṇavas become professional *kīrtana* singers and caste gurus, Bāuls become entertainers. It is also seen in theology, where the guru becomes the patron willing to introduce the novice to the heavenly hierarchies of the celestial realms of Navadvīpa and Vṛndāvana. The institutionalization of charisma may occur even in paradise.

This opposition is also present between the theological texts and the biographies in this book. The reader may notice that there is little correlation between them. Hierarchies and daily ritual practice seem to have very little to do with the ecstastic experiences of major figures in the traditions. The term *siddha* is often understood to refer to a person who has attained the religious goal by means of *sādhana* (ritual practice). Yet among the Vaiṣṇavas, Kṛṣṇa Caitanya's states were spontaneous, Haranāth had an unexpected death and rebirth, Vijayakṛṣṇa Gosvāmin was performing *kuṇḍalinī yoga* and other non-Vaiṣṇava practices, Jagadbandhu had apocalyptic visions by the age of thirteen, and we have no information on the origin of Gaur Kiśora's states (although he practiced traditional Vaiṣṇava ritual). Among the Śāktas, Rāmprasād had spontaneous trances, Rāmakṛṣṇa Paramahaṃsa practiced the techniques of many traditions while meditating in the temple of a low-caste widow (and was declared an *avatāra* by Vaiṣṇavas), and Vāmākṣepā and Nityagopāl were spontaneous ecstatics and had childhood trances.

If ecstatic states come without ritual, then why do ecstatics practice *sādhana*? There appear to be several reasons. Some seek control over the spontaneous ecstasies, to better understand them. *Sādhana* is said to refine these states, to polish them like jewels. It also brings people into the tradition, giving a context and a frame to their experiences. Ecstatic states are more acceptable to observers if the person is part of a tradition. The lineage and guru represent cultural acceptance, and the ritual practice shows that a person is willing to sacrifice worldly goals and spend time and effort seeking religious ones. Joining the lineage also means that the person is linked with a guru, somebody who will vouch for the person and take some responsibility for him. If the ecstatic begins to act in too extreme a manner (especially if he is aggressive and damages persons and property), there is an authority figure in charge. The ecstatic cannot be totally autonomous or he makes people nervous.

Sādhana also gives periods of time during which ecstasy may occur without disrupting other activities. It may be difficult to train insights and revelations to come on command, but at least there are times during which they may occur without ruining meals or putting saints in awkward situations.

In a way, *sādhana* is a magical practice—an attempt to coerce the love of the god or goddess. In *bhakti,* the best means of control is love: the person must consciously induce love to gain the deity's favor. Love must be forced, to force the deity's grace. Many ecstatics find such behavior inappropriate and instead emphasize waiting for grace, the *ajapa japa*—the mantra that chants itself. Others speak of the pride involved in visualizing the form in which the god will appear—it should be up to the deity to determine such things. This debate is particularly noticeable in

Vaiṣṇavism, between those who chant the Name as their only practice and those who perform visualization.

Some saints discuss how they themselves performed *sādhana,* but as a didactic method—a way of teaching other devotees discipline. Ānandamayī Mā went through a period of ritual practice which she said was solely for the sake of her disciples, who needed a role model; her own claim was that she was *siddha* from birth.

Generally the most useful forms of ritual practice seem to be relatively unstructured (such as *kīrtana* singing) or idiosyncratic. Gaur Kiśora performed worship in unorthodox ways for the Vaiṣṇava community, and Vāmākṣepā's rituals were mostly *aśāstrīya,* violating the rules, yet both found their practices successful. Ritual practice does not bring them to the goal, but it does define their social status while they are experiencing it.

Ecstatic and Ritual Profiles

Several themes are present in the lives of ecstatic devotees and *siddhas.*

Table 2 looks at five areas of characterization in the lives of fourteen ecstatics and helps us draw some general conclusions.

Most ecstatics were childhood visionaries, seeing nurturing deities, ghosts of dead friends and relatives, and magical animals. They did not feel persecuted by these entities, but rather welcomed them. From childhood on, many of the ecstatics occasionally fell into deathlike trances. Most ecstatics came from religious families, and several had mad or ecstatic parents. In fact, this is the case with some of the most widely known saints—Rāmakṛṣṇa Paramahaṃsa, Ānandamayī Mā, Vijayakṛṣṇa Goswāmin, Vāmākṣepā.

These early visions and trances caused relatives and neighbors to wonder about the sanity of these budding saints. All of them, except for Śāradā Devī (whose status was supported by Rāmakṛṣṇa), were considered possessed or mentally ill at some time in their lives, usually for months or years at a time. This diagnosis was generally made during childhood or early adolescence. Many of them were treated for madness, either by exorcism or with Āyurvedic remedies.

These remedies generally did not work; they rebounded onto the exorcist (in Ānandamayī Mā's case, he was struck by a severe stomachache), made the patient worse (Caitanya became frenzied after the application

TABLE 2 Ecstatic Themes

	CA	VK	PH	GK	PJ	RK	VA	RP	NG	AN	SD	AR	LM	YM
Early life														
Childhood ecstasy	x	x	x	ND	x	x	x		x	x		x	x	x
Ecstatic parents		x		ND		x	x			x				x
Religious parents	x	x	x	ND		x	x		x	x		x	x	x
Crisis														
Accusations of madness	x	x	x	x	x	x	x	x	x	x		x	x	x
Exorcism/Āyur-vedic cure	x	x	x	ND		x				x			x	
Social life														
Wandering or seclusion	x	x	x	x	x	x	x	x	x	x	x		x	x
Marriage	x	x	x	x		x		x		x	x		x	x
Adult ecstasy														
Adult visions	x	x	x	x	x	x	x	x	x	x	x	x	x	x
Trances	x	x	x	x	x	x	x	x	x	x	x	x	x	x
Bodily distortions	x	x	x	x	x	x	x		x	x				x
New identity/possession	x		x	x	x	x			x	x		x	x	x
Child *bhāva*	x		x		x	x	x	x	x	x				x
Miracles	x		x		x		x		x	x				x
Social role														
Called avatar	x	x	x		x	x			x	x				
Performed ritual	x	x	x	x	x	x	x	x	x	x	x	x	x	x

NOTES

CA = Caitanya
VK = Vijayakṛṣṇa Goswāmin
PH = Pāgal Haranāth
GK = Gaur Kiśora
PJ = Prabhu Jagadbandhu
RK = Rāmakṛṣṇa Paramahaṃsa
VA = Vāmākṣepā
RP = Rāmprasād
NG = Nityagopāl
AN = Ānandamayī Mā
SD = Śāradā Devī
AR = Arcanāpurī Mā
LA = Lakṣmī Mā
YM = Yogeśwarī Mā

ND = No data

of Nārāyaṇa oil), or simply did not change the situation in any appreciable way.

Almost all of the ecstatics had periods of wandering or seclusion, the only exception being Arcanāpurī Mā, who lived in an *āśrama* with her guru and took over responsibility for it after his death. The others all had periods of lonely reflection or traveled to meditate in distant places, went on pilgrimages, or simply avoided the distraction of others.

Most ecstatics were married, although it appeared to be of great importance only in the case of Śāradā Devī, whose husband was also her guru. Gaur Kiśora was a widower whose *bhāvas* began after his Vaiṣṇava initiation (or so it appears from his biography, which does not include information about his childhood), while Caitanya left his wife to become a *sannyāsin.* Ānandamayī Mā initiated her husband as a disciple, while Lakṣmī coerced her husband into becoming a holy man, and Yogeśwarī was informally separated from her husband. Some ecstatics never married, taking early vows of renunciation. The others remained married, and about half had children, but their lives were much more concerned with religion than with being householders. The yogic emphasis on celibacy was not seen as important among most ecstatics. The emphasis in their marriages is on emotional rather than physical separation.

All had visions and trances in their adult lives. In visions they saw specific deities, places, or situations, while in trance they would be overcome by a feeling or mood and be unaware of the outside world. In a majority of these cases, visions and trances were accompanied by bodily symptoms. These included expansion and contraction of the body, projection of a subtle body, feelings of dismemberment and separation of the limbs and head from the body,[13] extreme change in skin color, images of mantras and mythic scenes imprinted on the body, blood gushing from mouth or oozing from the pores, feeling of intense heat, and the *sāttvika bhāvas* (bristling hair, choked voice, fainting, trembling). Such distortions would act to validate the *bhāvas,* as would immunity to pain and extended trance states.

Most ecstatics describe a new personality that emerges out of such experiences. Sometimes it is understood as rebirth and sometimes as possession. The ecstatic may become Rādhā overcome with *bhāva,* or her confidante, or, like Haranāth, may be dismembered by Gauranga and possessed by Kṛṣṇa. He may be empty of everything except the sound of a mantra, or he may be the new world savior or emerge as a newborn child. The ecstatic is sometimes a child of the Mother, or possessed by her, or living in a "ripened" ego which includes awareness of many states. The exception is Ānandamayī Mā, who claimed to have the same lack of self-awareness throughout her life. However, she was frequently possessed by deities and had several periods in her life when she acted like a child or took on other roles.

Often this new identity shows itself in the child *bhāva,* in which the ecstatic will take on the role of an infant. It appears to be the most common *bhāva* which is not considered to be possession by a god. The person in child *bhāva* will crawl around like a child, lisp, attempt to nurse from others present (including men), babble, cry for his mother, and demand things from her. The Śākta becomes the child of the Mother, while the Vaiṣṇava becomes baby Gopāla (the child Kṛṣṇa). This is interpreted by disciples as a state of innocence and humility, showing blissful emotion and a lack of attachment to worldly things.

Miracles are rare among ecstatics—such accomplishments are too close to yogic powers (*siddhis*), which emphasize individual attainment and responsibility. As such, they are not a proof of true devotion to a deity. Caitanya's biographies describe a few miraculous events, which showed his status as avatar, while Vāmākṣepā's miraculous abilities showed his aspect as a magician, and Haranāth's demonstrated his love for his disciples. Yogeśwarī disclaimed responsibility for her miracles—they were the god's doing, not hers. Ānandamayī Mā's miracles were hardly mentioned by her disciples. Michael Williams notes that the miracle is a secondary rather than a primary sign of charisma; it serves to validate and support a religious role, but cannot initiate it.[14]

Miracles were one proof of avatar status, but they were not required. Half of the ecstatics on this list were considered by their disciples to be incarnations of deities. *Bhāva* gives the proof of devotion, while supernatural abilities are the proof of yogic advancement or the favor of the deity. After the *bhāvas* are present, it is up to the disciples to confirm and spread the guru's status. Ecstatics are generally concerned with their visionary states, while the disciples write books and build cults. The saints are the heart of the religion, their followers the mind and limbs.

The themes shown in table 2 are sufficient to propose an ecstatic *siddha* life profile. This may first be contrasted with the profile of the traditional ritual practitioner, which is found in the theological texts, worship manuals, and less detailed saint biographies. The process of spiritual growth in devotional yoga shows a dominance of ritual practice, and the yogi is admired for his self-control (as the proverb goes, he who controls his senses can make the world his slave). In these types of religious biography, ecstatic experience is secondary or irrelevant. The ritual pattern of *bhakti yoga* includes the following:

1. There is initiation by a guru into a lineage, after a conscious decision by the disciple. His social role is stabilized, and the guru "plants the seed" of future spiritual growth.

2. The disciple's attitude is one of faith and dedication, and he begins practice under the guru's watchful eye, learning from texts or from verbal instruction.

3. The practice of *sādhana* becomes more disciplined and intense. It may involve periods of austerity and isolation, or the disciple may live as part of a spiritual community.

4. The ritual begins to work—the mantras become "alive," the visualizations become real, there are feelings of love and glimpses of paradise. Devotion to the deity grows due to practice.

5. Continued practice brings reward—visions of the deity, disciples, the reverence of other devotees and townsfolk. The power of the tradition is proven. The spiritual role in relation to the deity is stabilized, and the person's outward demeanor comes to resemble that of the respected leaders of the tradition.

The ecstatic life pattern follows a different series of events—the erratic *divyonmada* state is emphasized, and the devotee is admired for his lack of control. According to this pattern:

1. Normal life is disrupted by a series of visions, trances, and uncontrollable emotions. However, there is usually not the physical illness that characterizes shamanism. The ecstasy often begins in childhood, worrying the family and relatives. The child welcomes the visions, which are friendly and nurturing.

2. Relatives and neighbors attempt to bring the child back to normal by medical and religious means, or the adolescent goes through a period of chaos. The ecstatic attempts to maintain normal life while trying to limit, control, or understand what is happening to him or her. Sometimes a marriage is arranged, if the symptoms are thought by the family to be due to celibacy.

3. The ecstatic withdraws into seclusion or wanders, plunging into spiritual practice with or without initiation. There may be no guidance, or there may be inner voices, the presence of a deity, or one or more gurus. Practice generally involves separation from society. The visions and trances become more pronounced.

4. There is a turning point in the person's experience—a sense of new birth or identity, an acceptance by the deity, a significant vision, or a gradual lessening of impulses toward isolation. There are often experiences of death and rebirth, and the deity's love becomes central. The person's spiritual role in relation to the deity is stabilized, although his behavior is often unpredictable to society.

5. The ecstatic is accepted as guru by others, gaining disciples and respect. Apparently mad behavior is assumed to show deep religious insight. Inner and outer worlds become harmonized, and his social role is stabilized. Knowledge from the ecstatic order (dreams, visions, trances) is balanced by knowledge of the traditional order (worship techniques, names and roles of major deities, local teachers and lineages). His extreme experiences, initially interpreted as madness, become the yardstick by which to gauge future ecstatics and saints.

The Ecstatic as Hero

The two patterns of devotion, the ritual and ecstatic paradigms, influence the ways in which saint stories are told. The ritual pattern is associated with the ascetic hero, the yogi who is initiated and renounces, struggles and achieves his goal after being tested. He studies to gain knowledge, practices renunciation to gain detachment from the world, and performs visualization to gain the love of the deity. Often the renunciant is a member of a spiritual community, and love for other disciples becomes as important as detachment from the world. Devotional love is an addition to the older yogic pattern of renunciation leading to *mukti* or liberation.

Biographies that follow the pattern of the ascetic hero emphasize certain qualities. The hero may shed golden radiance (gained from austerities), win acclaim, know the sacred texts, be capable of resisting the temptations of both natural and supernatural women, and be continuously immersed in contemplation of the deity. Such classically yogic themes as the gaining of miraculous powers and worship by the kings of heaven and earth may be added, but these will be unimportant compared to love of the chosen god. At times the ritual pattern may be superimposed on the life stories of spontaneous ecstatics and create an unexpected blend. An example of such an occurrence is the biography of the Śākta *tāntrika* Vāmākṣepā in the collection of biographies by Sobharani Basu, in which Vāmākṣepā (famed for drinking alcohol, eating flesh, throwing urine on a statue of the goddess, and other violations of ritual behavior) is called "Christlike" and a great yogin.[15]

In the feminine form of the ascetic hero, the woman may worship her husband as a god and gain miraculous powers through her obedience, or be unmarried and accepted by the deity. In the first type of story, there is often a child marriage and the wife becomes the ideal householder, humble and rising early to bathe and worship, and offer devotion and service to holy men. In the second type, the woman either may never marry (although she is respected, feared, and courted by handsome and wealthy men), or may leave her husband for the sake of the deity. In both cases, her austerity and penance impress the deity, who may then cause a miracle which will reveal her devotion.

The ecstatic pattern in biographies is associated with the paradoxical hero, whose strength is his weakness before the deity and who conquers by surrender. There is little emphasis on study—among ecstatics, spiritual knowledge is not what you know, but rather who you know—the deity who gives the true *darśana,* not philosophy but direct spiritual sight. Devotion occurs through a process of ripening rather than effort; texts often mention the uselessness of beating a fruit to make it sweet or of ripping the skin off a snake when the creature will shed the skin in its own time. There is a tension with the traditional authority, which the biographies sometimes attempt to ameliorate by comparing the ecstatic with a deity or paradigmatic figure of the tradition. The ecstatic is rarely in the mainstream of the tradition; more often he is an outsider who must prove himself to the religious hierarchy. While the male ecstatic must prove his vulnerability, the female ecstatic must also prove her strength.

In the feminine form, the women do not worship their husbands; they dominate them or leave them, or occasionally do both. Ānandamayī Mā initiated her husband; Lakṣmī coerced her husband into becoming a devotee. While male ecstatics emphasize a romantic relationship to the deity, holy women tend to see their role as part of a divine family, usually with themselves as the children. The worldly marriage is simply irrelevant.

Sacred biographies of the ritual/ascetic pattern include renunciants, writers, proselytizers, and defenders of the faith who have had little or no ecstatic experience. They usually have no childhood—life begins at initiation, the second birth which takes precedence over the first. The parental influence is usually male—in the older, epic stories of yogis and sages, they are often born without mothers (*ayonija*) or have divine *apsaras* mothers, who are known for their disinterest in their offspring.[16] Occasionally the town of birth and a few anecdotes about the ecstatic's purity and play at ritual during childhood may be included. But it is the lineage and tradition which determine the link with the divine; practice may make him perfect, but it is the initiation which allows this practice. Spiritual transitions are orderly, and empowerment is gained by renunciation.

The ecstatic pattern opposes this by idealizing desire. In ecstatic biographies, the childhood and difficulties of adaptation are emphasized—it is during the childhood of the ecstatic that he is chosen. Often the parents themselves are visionary or religious, and their influence may support and inspire the young ecstatic. The drama is not initiation, but instead the tension between fidelity to experience and adaptation to tradition and society.

These two biographical types, the ritual and the ecstatic, correspond closely to Max Lüthi's distinction between saint legends and wonder tales. In *The European Folktale: Form and Nature,* he contrasts these genres.[17] Saint legends (*legenden*) have different goals and styles than wonder tales. The legend portrays the saint in an idealized fashion, with the intention of affirming the religious tradition. It confirms the faith, showing miracles as revelations of divine power, and proclaims the demands of the god. It is dogmatic, systematizing otherworld phenomena and influences, and it demands faith in the truth of the story and the correctness of its interpretation.[18] The spiritual realm is distinct from historical daily life, and the legend is revelatory, giving a definitive and binding account of the nature and meaning of the supernatural.

Wonder tales (*märchen*) differ in style—the hero is not a product of a tradition. He is instead a person who gains the treasure by accident, unaware and unintentionally. He does not have abilities, but rather acquires gifts, and he lets himself be guided by unknown characters and objects, without questioning their history or background. The story itself does not interpret or explain; instead, it observes and portrays. It is bound to neither dogma nor physical laws.

Wonder tales mix the miraculous with the natural, without a sense of the extraordinary. Spiritual otherness is symbolically expressed in the strange forms and powers of characters, or through geographical separation (the hero visits other worlds as one might visit other countries, on his quest for a treasure or other object). Encounters lack historical detail—wonder tale heroes are isolated in time and space. They trick otherworld characters into yielding gifts, or receive gifts as a blessing. Lüthi calls such tales "a gift from visionary poets to the people."[19]

There are clear parallels between these genres and the ritual and ecstatic biographical patterns. Saint legends are associated with ritual—the traditional means of contacting and attaining the deity. Both saint legends and biographies of ritual heroes are primarily theological: they serve the purpose of an object lesson. The practitioner succeeds by dint of effort, will, and dedication, inspiring listeners to follow the correct path and follow in the footsteps of the holy person.

Wonder tales are associated with the ecstatic pattern. The ecstatic gains the religious goal by accident, and the stories emphasize gifts (spontaneous events, often the grace of the deity) rather than abilities. The ecstatic is guided, and the accounts are descriptive rather than explanatory. There is little or no historical detail, and there is no absolute distinction between sacred and profane worlds. The realm of the supernatural overlaps and interpenetrates the physical world.

The analogy between ecstatic and wonder tale hero is not exact. The major distinction between the ecstatic biography and wonder tale is in the characterization of the hero/saint. The folk hero is not really an individual but a type, flat and one dimensional, without an inner life or personal history. In a sense, he has no biography—Lüthi's term for this is "depthlessness." He reacts without questioning and acts without contemplation. The ecstatic saint, on the other hand, has a rich inner life. He is very human, complete with conflicts, confusion, family problems, and uncertainty about how to act. In the ecstatic pattern, we have the entrance of a fully human person into a supernatural world—a historical person entering the world of the folktale, a biography of a character who has no biography. Without the distinctions maintained by ritual and legend, the worlds are superimposed and the ecstatic moves between them. The ability to travel in this fashion is often gained by an experience of death and rebirth.

The Ecstatic Process

Ecstasy has been defined here as an experience of integration, a uniting of parts into a greater whole. The ritual texts emphasize the attainment of this goal by worship and visualization. The ecstatic texts, on the other hand, detail the process of destruction and fragmentation of self and gender which precedes or alternates with this new integration. This process is found in folktale, ritual, theology, and biography.

In the Indian folk tradition, ecstasy is symbolized by a journey, which often involves destruction and resurrection. Folk tales have the hero travel in the physical rather than the spiritual body, through other worlds and supernatural adventures. He does not travel by meditation on the light between his own eyebrows, but instead takes the *mānik,* the jewel that grows on the snake's forehead, and travels underwater by its light.[20] Instead of having an inner body in a paradise, Dālim Kumār has his life in a necklace in the stomach of a fish. The concept of eternal life appears in stories in which yogic mantras can give life to skeletons and in the story of the princess who is killed when touched with a silver stick, and brought back to life with a golden one. In another story, a decapitated maiden drips blood onto Śiva's matted hair. The drops become giant rubies, and a golden rod reunites her head with her body.

More broadly, Indian folk themes include such phenomena as rebirth by boiling, burning, or bathing (sometimes this is described as beautification); resuscitation by arrangement of separated limbs; magical restoration of the body by holy men or helpful animals (the body may be transformed or sewn together); re-creation of missing members (often from ashes, dust, or excrement); a separable soul which is lost or replaced by a ghost or an ancestor; and the piecemeal destruction of the separable soul. The folk hero sometimes has removable organs, or a life token (his life is mirrored in a plant, animal, or object, such as in breast milk that turns bloody or in a sword which rusts).[21] Other images of disintegration are present in the Indian rope trick (in which a person ascends a rope, is chopped to pieces, and later is brought back to life) and in the "half body dance" (in which half of the body dances and the other half remains still) mentioned in the Jātaka tales.[22]

Informants in Śāntiniketan stated that ritual human sacrifice to Dharma Thākur still occurred in several Bengali villages, where it was believed that if a body had its limbs ritually chopped off, the trunk and limbs would grow and cause flowers and vegetables to emerge.[23] Less extreme imagery of destruction is found in the practices of the exorcist (*ojhā*) who tortures himself to impress the spirits he must exorcise. The exorcist lashes himself with iron chains, sprinkles boiling oil in his hair, and puts burning wicks in his mouth as a means of showing his power to the offending ghost or ancestor. In some cases, he (usually exorcists are male) allows a more powerful spirit into his body, to chase away the being possessing his patient.[24]

Destructive actions are also present in those rituals to the god Śiva that involve austerity and self-torture. While devotion to Śiva as Mahādeva is more prominent in southern India, Śiva is the great god of asceticism in several Bengali villages and sacred centers. An example of devotion to him is the *caṛak-gājan,* which involves both rituals of welcoming Śiva and fertility, and such ascetic practices as the *hindol* (in which a person is tied upside down over a fire) and the *jihvā-puṛ* (in which the devotee's tongue is pierced with nails). The devotee (called the *puṛ-bhakta*) undergoes various painful experiences, such as having iron hooks put into his back while he is tied to a tree and hooks with string through them pierce his arms; the string runs through the wounds and is tied to other objects while he dances the *ranjā-lāch* or is spun around on a high platform (the *gājan tola*). When the devotee is asked how he can stand the pain, he will frequently say that at these times Śiva descends upon him, and Śiva's power dominates him, so that he does not feel the pain. Śiva fills his mind, both because it is the time of the Śiva *gājan* and because the actions fulfill a vow to the god. The vow may be his own or another's. The mother of the ascetic devotee at one *carak-gājan* had prayed to Śiva that if she were cured of her headaches, her son would be his devotee, as he now is each year. Such dedication to Śiva allows him to experience a form of *bhor* or possession, seen in his endurance of pain.[25]

The *gājan* shows the destructive aspect of devotion—pain evokes the presence of the deity. The devotee who suffers, emotionally and physically, calls forth the god or goddess. Thus destruction or disintegration leads to greater power or integration, for the entrance of the deity into the heart can strengthen the devotee and lead to rebirth. The alternation in *bhakti* of pain and joy, separation and union, death and love appears in both theology and hagiography.

From the theological perspective, Vaiṣṇava devotees seek to echo Rādhā's emotions in separation from and union with Kṛṣṇa. Her state of separation is understood as powerful, upsetting the universe and causing trees to burst into flame. Yet it is an intense and loving state, capable of drawing Kṛṣṇa to her, despite its intense sorrow, hallucination, and delusion. In Rādhā's most extreme experience of *mahābhāva,* she can no longer distinguish between separation and union. Among Śāktas, the disintegrative states are seen in the rituals of sexuality and death (which separate person and body in different ways) that precede the vision of the goddess. There is also the dissolution of *bhūtaśuddhi,* separating the body into its component elements, and the purification of the body parts, which leads to the goddess's entrance into the heart and mind of the worshiper. Tantric practice includes both *yoga* and *bhoga*—detachment from traditional life and ascetic control over the body, as well as enjoyment and fullness. In separation from the goddess, the ecstatic is a child or a lover, burning with devotion and longing.

The Bāul is united in vision and presence with the man of the heart, and his joy and wonder are expressed in song. However, when the deity is gone or invisible, the ritual involves a split between mind and body—a conscious control over instinct which allows an entrance into the bodily substances themselves, to find the god within them. This is a disintegration, an inner separation that allows a rearrangement of the bodily deity, bringing him to where he belongs. Holy women often show an initial stage of chaos and disintegration, when their states of possession and emotion are unpredictable and associated with madness. The ecstasy of union occurs when the deity is internalized and possession accepted and welcomed.

From the hagiographical perspective, disintegration and reintegration are prominent in the lives of ecstatic saints. Among Vaiṣṇava ecstatics, we see experiences of trance, death and dismemberment, and rebirth in purified form. The ecstatic communicates with god, ghosts, and ancestors, and he can give salvation to disembodied spirits. There are vivid dream experiences and journeys in shadow form, as well as division into multiple subtle bodies. In possession experiences, the ecstatic may be taken over by Vaiṣṇava or non-Vaiṣṇava entities, and travel with an invisible guru or invisible companions.

During the ritual practice, the Vaiṣṇava ecstatic may experience *nāmāgni*—intense burning which results from the chanting of mantras (especially the Kṛṣṇa mantra). *Nāmāgni* is great heat in which the limbs and organs of the body are pulled apart and later reorganized, or withdrawn and reshaped, as part of a process of purification. The burning is so painful that the person will cover himself with mud or water in an attempt to alleviate it. When the body is remade, it resonates with the Divine Name. The purified person can then take on disease or sin from disciples and remain detached, gaining insight into both persons and the world of nature.

Among Śākta ecstatics, disintegration is present in involuntary trance, separation from the goddess, and the projection of inner bodies. In trance, the goddess speaks through the person's mouth, and he is considered unconscious (as an individual). The person often cannot feel pain (this can be tested with a hot iron), and in Kālī possession there may be bleeding from the mouth. Traditional relationships fall apart—the husband calls his possessed wife "Mother," and a low-caste woman possessed by a goddess may strike a brahmin man or step on him with impunity. After the trance passes, the person generally lacks memory of what happened at that time.

When the ecstatic is separated from the deity, he may experience bodily pain and burning, may threaten suicide, and may destroy possessions. The ecstatic is inert, immersed in impurity, and acting in a deluded fashion or childishly gorging himself. He rubs his face against the walls and floor; he may be frozen with horror or dancing with statues, feeling sensations of death followed by great joy. At times the person's face resembles that of a skeleton, with fiery and piercing eyes. This is the state of Śākta *divyonmāda,* in which there is endless and extreme yearning for the Mother's presence.

The Śākta ecstatic often identifies himself as a child, or he may perceive a child projected from his own body, with whom he may play. This child can then enter the body and change aspects of it, or he may simply become reincorporated into the body. At times there are many figures whom the ecstatic perceives as dwelling in his body, and with whom he identifies. In some cases, the soul is projected from the body in order to accomplish a task. Ānandamayī Mā explained that she had gone to rescue the soul of one of her devotees and brought the soul back. This devotee had been in a car accident, and her soul had left her body. Because the body was then considered to be a corpse, the soul could not directly be returned to it. Ānandamayī Mā thus switched the body's essence to the mudguard of the car (which had fallen off), and it took on the impurity, while the soul could safely return to its old body.

Sometimes there can be alienation from the body in the state of *bhāva samādhi,* a union with the goddess in which the body becomes cold and lifeless, unable to eat or move. It might appear to be dead, with ants crawling across it. Loving union with the goddess is described most frequently as occurring in the burning ground, amid a background of death, when devotion becomes more powerful than fear.

In both Vaiṣṇavism and Śāktism, ecstasy includes shamanic aspects. There is no complex that can be isolated as classical shamanism, no initiatory illness, apprenticeship, public performances and contests, magical flight and journey to the realms of the dead in order to heal patients. However, there is supernatural designation, dreams and visions, death and rebirth, acceptance by a spirit or deity, some formal or informal instruction, and group acceptance. The Śākta *siddha* Vāmākṣepā had visions of ghosts and demons, an initiatory encounter with the goddess, and was said to control weather, illness, and natural disasters by his supernatural powers. He could read minds and gain knowledge at a distance, and many people came to him to be healed. He studied under a guru known as a *piśāca siddha,* a powerful man with control over spirits, who would sacrifice black goats to ghosts and send them out to do his will. Rāmakṛṣṇa Paramahaṃsa practiced tantra and would see dark figures emerging from his body and returning again, while Nityagopāl would become possessed and have blood pour from his mouth. Vaiṣṇava *siddhas* describe experiences of death and rebirth, bodily destruction and purification, miraculous healing and travel in a subtle body. However, these aspects are avoided by mainstream tradition—Vaiṣṇavism emphasizes the love within the individuals involved. Śāktism accepts the folk tradition more readily, and many devotees of the goddess accept the tantric association with magic. While this approach was rejected by Rāmakṛṣṇa in favor of a Śākta universalism (while all religions lead to the ultimate, love of the Mother is the most beautiful), it was accepted by Vāmākṣepā and is still seen in the *piśāca tāntrikas* of Calcutta.

Many ecstatic symptoms show a link between *bhakti* devotion and older religious ideas. Great heat was experienced by Rāmakṛṣṇa, Ānandamayī Mā, and Vijayakṛṣṇa Goswāmin as a part of their ritual practice—a link with the older idea of *tapas,* the spiritual heat of meditation. The idea of sacrifice was seen in the experiences of dismemberment and separation of limbs in Vijayakṛṣṇa and Haranāth, as purification and restructuring of the body. Withdrawal of limbs, symbolically showing the yogic withdrawal of interaction with the physical world, occurs in the experiences of Vijayakṛṣṇa, Caitanya, Rāmakṛṣṇa, and Ānandamayī Mā. The body as the universe, free of normal boundaries, is seen in its expansion and contraction, in Caitanya, Vijayakṛṣṇa, and Ānandamayī Mā.[26]

Ideally, the disintegration phase should be balanced by a new organization. However, some breakdowns do not appear to lead to renewal (as in the case of Jagadbandhu, who reverted to childlike and erratic behavior), while other crises lead to a higher level of functioning (as with Pāgal Haranāth). For most devotees, disintegration is a phase of the practice not covered in the texts.

When disintegration is included in the devotional path, it is often understood as a part of the process of *vairāgya,* detachment from worldly concerns. In ritual practice, *vairāgya* involves the breaking of attachments to the illusory world—human relationships, comfort and pleasure, power and reputation. The devotee leaves one world and realigns himself with another. This process is regulated by yoga. In spontaneous ecstatics, this separation is chaotic, occurring by the process of divine madness (*divyonmāda, thākur pāgal*). The imagery accompanying this process can come from folk or religious sources, or might involve idiosyncratic imagery, but in all cases serves to tear the person away from a mainstream, dharmic life.

The integration phase is seen in *bhakti* ritual practice in the processes of visualization (*bhāvana*) and superimposition (*āropa*). The spiritual world and the devotee's place in it are contemplated and visualized. A new world is created, with detachment and austerities blurring the edges between one world and another. The devotee is strengthened by faith in the tradition and love of the deity, and the worlds in meditation come to appear more real than the physical world.

Another alternation between disintegration and integration is seen in the ecstatic's own perception of gender. Male ecstatics expend a good deal of effort in dealing with the feminine, often destroying their sense of being a male adult in favor of integrating the feminine in some new way. Most women ecstatics interviewed tended to maintain gender, but emphasized new kinship relations instead, often experiencing themselves as young children. There is an awe of the power of the feminine in Bengal, especially its potential for creativity and love.

For Vaiṣṇavas, the locus of power is female—Rādhā, who conquers Kṛṣṇa with her beauty and love. The inner body of the disciple becomes a feminine one, one of Rādhā's handmaidens, who may share Rādhā's emotions and experiences. This body is like a bud on the same stem on which Rādhā is the flower, and the fluid love (*rasa*) that runs through Rādhā also runs through her budlike handmaidens (the term *mañjarī*, used for handmaiden, literally means "bud"). As the *Govinda-līlāmṛtām* states: "The *sakhīs* [in this case the *mañjarīs*] of Rādhā . . . are like the flowers and petals and buds of the vine of love, which is Rādhā, and they are equal to her. When she experiences the joy of being sprinkled by the *rasa* of the nectar of Kṛṣṇa-līlā, they experience a joy one hundred times greater than hers."[27]

The *Murali Vilāsa* states that the gooseflesh that appears on Rādhā's body also appears on the bodies of the *mañjarīs*.[28]

For Śāktas, the Mother may be a beautiful maiden or a powerful woman. The devotee worships her power (in her various forms) with submission, yet loves her for her beauty and protectiveness toward her children. The devotee can gain her love by taking on the role of a child, or he can act as the *vīra*, the hero, who struggles against the Mother and conquers her, taking on her power by ritual means. The statue most frequently seen in Calcutta is that of Kālī stepping on the chest of the god

Śiva, her consort. This image is often interpreted as the power of transcendence to conquer death, and many of Rāmprasād's poems speak of Kālī treading on Śiva and saving her devotee from the power of death. The wife may also save the husband, as did Savitrī in the *Mahābhārata* and Behulā in the *Manasā Maṅgala,* who returned their dead husbands to life. This is one of the powers of the *pativratā,* the woman who gains spiritual power by devotion to her husband. Bāuls and Sahajiyās use the feminine power to energize their spiritual seeking and to find the god within the body.

In these traditions, there is also a disintegration of intimacy, an element of sexual alienation and distancing. The *tāntrika* and Bāul have sex without sensuality, while the Vaiṣṇavas have sensuality without sex. In both cases, the interaction is incomplete, a symbolic act. There is no relationship of intimacy with an individual—the woman (or in rare cases the man) involved is an object, a representation of power itself or of other persons or deities. For the *tāntrika,* sensuality is reserved for the dark goddess of mystery and danger and for nonphysical women (such as *yoginīs* and *ḍākinīs*), while physical women are merely spiritual batteries, or at best one-half of a synergetic system. For the Vaiṣṇava, sensuality is reserved for the appreciation of Kṛṣṇa's love play with Rādhā and the gopīs; the devotee is ascetic, either unmarried or married but detached from his mate, with sexuality only allowable for reproduction. Sensuality is perhaps seen primarily in food, in literary descriptions and celebratory feasts.

Ascetic distancing allows the devotee to focus his love on the deity and to control the deity in this way. The devotee may thus become more powerful than the deity, as the son controls the mother by his love. The ecstatics in this study had to balance these forces, as most were or had been married. Some, such as Ānandamayī Mā, had celibate marriages (her disciples wrote that she gave her husband bodily electric shocks if he touched her with lust and that she fell into deathlike trances from which he could only awaken her by chanting mantras). Rāmakṛṣṇa Paramahaṃsa too had a celibate marriage, which he maintained partly by having both he and his wife identify themselves as female servants of the Divine Mother.

Pāgal Haranāth symbolically separated himself from his genitals, claiming that they were made of earth, added at the last minute when his body was cut apart and rearranged, while the rest of him was made of a spiritualized substance. Nityagopāl was initially thought to be female by the midwife; he avoided marriage entirely by claiming madness, but would later be possessed by the goddess. At times this conflict may be solved by homosexuality—Alain Danielou claims that large numbers of renunciants follow this approach.[29] However, this alternative is not accepted by any of the *bhakti* traditions. The most frequent means of resolving gender conflicts are worshiping a goddess living in the heart, taking on an inner female identity, and becoming possessed by a goddess.

As one holy woman interviewed stated, men are more capable of karmic action, but women have more natural ability at devotion.[30] While men are hard and resistant, giving to the children they engender bones and muscles, women are soft and yielding, giving children blood and internal organs. Men are capable of yogic self-sufficiency and containment, holding in their creative fluids, while women are dependent and sensitive, unable to hold back their creative fluids in menstruation and sharing their nurturing fluids in nursing children. Feminine love cannot be hidden and held back—it is protective, sheltering, spontaneous, uncalculated, drawing by its submissiveness. It is paradoxical, as the *siddha* must be. One of the major aspects of feminine power sought is its vulnerability. Such feminine associations are also present in those *siddhas* who spontaneously become children of the Mother. They usually experience themselves as younger than five years old, below the age of the sacred thread ceremony (*upanayana*), when the child's primary orientation is toward the mother. Vaiṣṇavas are both female and childlike—their spiritual bodies are those of girls on the edge of puberty.

The other major association with femininity is creativity—giving birth not only to worlds and persons, but to the arts. The most desired goal of the majority of Śākta practitioners interviewed was some form of creativity—literary, philosophical, poetic, or oratorical. The goddess was the guide who could bring forth the devotee's hidden sensitivity to beauty. While classically the goddess Sarasvatī was the patron of learning, Śākta *tāntrikas* interviewed usually worshiped Tārā Mā as the essence of knowledge and inspiration. Vaiṣṇavas as *mañjarīs* seek to serve Rādhā and Kṛṣṇa in ever new and more beautiful ways, not so much imitating women as seeking to embody the feminine qualities of grace and beauty. The male is yogic discipline, austere and inexpressive, while the female is shyness and romantic love.

For the male devotee to take on such qualities, the adult male body and mind must in some way be negated. Negation of self and natural gender can bring ecstatic vision and fullness of love, or inner emptiness and insanity. It is the quality of relatedness which makes the difference.

The Ecstatic as Lover

The role of lover allows intense interaction with the deity. Love madness shows the highest possible devotional state and is the sign of ecstatic transformation. The erratic uprisings of passion and signs of fragmentation show that the realm of the voluntary has been passed and that the changes within the person are now involuntary, due to a deity's grace, past incarnations, specifically, the fruits of present or past devotion. All of the devotee's attention is focused on the relationship with the beloved deity.

Love madness in Bengal is not a recent phenomena. At least seven centuries before Caitanya and his Kṛṣṇa *bhakti,* the *siddhācāryas* were called mad (*pāgal*) and poetically described themselves as intoxicated with the wine of bliss, like a bull elephant maddened from drinking the lotus-honey of the *yoginī.* They wrote of passion for the Dom girl or *caṇḍālī,* the figure of the lowest who represents the highest, dancing in the water and lightning of the interior cosmos. Such love united the extremes, violating dharmic love, which united persons of the same caste and qualities. The state of *sahaja* of which they wrote implied both love ecstasy and divine madness.[31]

Islam entered Bengal at the beginning of the thirteenth century, bringing with it an active tradition of Sufism. The Sufis sought to be intoxicated with love of God, entering states of passion and annihilation of individual identity (*fanā*). They drank the wine of love, becoming so maddened (*mast*) that they could think only of the divine Beloved. The Sufi *majdhūb,* the "enraptured one," was an ecstatic maddened by the "unveiling of God." Annemarie Schimmel calls him part of the "darker side of the Sufi world."[32] The most famous "enraptured one," known in both Sufi and mainstream Islam, was Majnūn.

In the twelfth century the poet Nīzami collected folk versions of the story of Layla and Majnūn and wrote a long poem that is one of the best known in the Islamic world. The child Qays fell in love with the child Layla and, "drowned in the ocean of love," he began to exhibit mad behavior, becoming known as Majnūn, or madman.[33] Her parents forbade their marriage, and he wandered the desert singing *ghazals,* bemoaning the loss of his beloved. He became a ragged nomad, with a wasted frame and matted hair, with wild beasts as his companions. A pilgrimage to Mecca caused his mad passion to be intensified rather than cured. His intense love was described in many metaphors: "his innermost being was revealed like the heart of a split fruit"; "everyone saw in his face the reflection of the fire scorching his heart"; he was like a moth rushing to a flame, who has "broken up the teeming bazaar of the senses in the body."[34] His body and personality were only veils, hiding the Layla within him. Many Sufi groups took this story as an allegory of the relationship between the person and God.

In the Sanskrit literary tradition, madness is a sign of genuine love. In the Araṇyakāṇḍa of the Vālmīki *Rāmāyaṇa,* Rāma is overwhelmed by the loss of Sītā, and he is said to be "wandering like a madman," questioning the trees, mountains, rivers, and animals about Sītā. He threatens to obliterate the boundaries between the worlds, to annihilate the cosmos and kill all living things.[35] Such love madness is also seen in the god Śiva, when he is driven to destruction of the world when his wife Satī dies by suicide. He flies into a rage, bursts into tears, and wanders like a madman.[36] In the *Vikramorvaśīya* of Kālīdāsa, mad king Purūravas is frantic with the loss of the *apsaras* Urvaśī and sees aspects of her all through nature. This is a fragmented vision of the beloved, reflecting his own fragmented psyche. When the god goes mad, the world is destroyed. When the person goes mad, it is the individual mind which is destroyed. Madness expresses the streak of disintegration and destruction that is a part of the devotee's passionate love.

Such fragmentation of the beloved is also seen in the ecstatics in this book. Ānandamayī Mā saw Bhagavān as permeating nature, Gaur Kiśora saw Kṛṣṇa and Caitanya in neighborhood children, and Svamī Naciketasānanda (in interview) saw Rāmakṛṣṇa Paramahaṃsa and Śāradā Devī in all of the men and women he passed in the street. Śāktas speak of seeing the Mother in all women and call even little girls Mā, while Vaiṣṇavas may see all infant boys as Gopāla. In union, the beloved is seen everywhere; in separation, the beloved is sought everywhere.

These conditions are understood as ripened states of love. Love in *bhakti* both maintains and overcomes distance—both affirming and denying the distinction between self and other. While in classical notions of ecstasy the person is "beside himself," in *bhakti* the ecstasy of the person is in relation to the deity, each within the other.

Kṛṣṇa states to Arjuna in the *Bhagavad Gītā* that "I am in them, and they are in me." The verb used is *bhaj,* to share—both deity and devotee share in each other. This is a traditional Indian marriage formula. One form in the *Mantra Brāhmaṇa* (1.3.9) states: "May your heart be mine, may my heart be yours." Archer Taylor notes numerous parallels to this formula in such varied sources as Goethe, Shakespeare, Ovid, the Song of Songs, the Babylonian Talmud, and James Joyce.[37] However, it is also a Vedic statement of relationship to a deity. As the sacrificer in the Ṛg Veda (8.92.32) says to Indra, "You are ours, and we are yours" (*"Tvam asmākaṃ tava smasi"*). In the *Taittirīya Saṃhitā* (2.11.1–2), the ritual relationship between the sacrificer and Agni is also formulated in this way: "That which is my body is in you, that which is your body is in me" (*"Yā mama tanūr eṣā sā tvayi, yā tava tanūr iyaṃ sā mayi"*).

The terms used to express close human and divine relationship are identical. A part of the self is understood to belong to the other—as an exchange of tokens, in which the token is the self. The process is reciprocal, so that both gain by expansion of the self and incorporation of the other. In the *Nāṭyaśāstra* (25.67), which also states "I am yours, and you are mine," the relational process is interpreted as *ātmopakṣepana* or the "projection of the self."

It is in this understanding of relationship of selves that the close relationship between yoga and *bhakti* may be observed. In the yogic tradition, bodies are consciously created and/or projected in order to attain a goal, usually power or knowledge. An example is Devaśarman, who asks his disciple Vipula to protect his wife from the god Indra. Vipula "made his way into her body, as wind makes its way through the air," making her unable to move or speak.[38] Such "ecstatic flight" was considered a power (*siddhi*), often used for entering the bodies of others or reanimating corpses. Such flight symbolizes the "autonomy of the spirit," according to Eliade, and is associated with shamanism and the magical tradition.[39] The true yogi can enter any situation as a result of an effort of will and remain untouched. Such projection is not reciprocal and does not involve love. Projection and introjection in yoga are conscious, temporary efforts, to prove ability or force obedience. Yogic entrance into another person means taking him over.

The processes of introjection and projection are prominent in devotional ecstasy. These terms have several meanings in psychology. Most frequently, introjection is the assimilation of qualities or aspects of another person, making these a part of the self such that they are not perceived as existing separately from the person, while projection is understood as the attribution of thought content (affective and cognitive) to persons outside oneself. The aspects and qualities involved in introjection are alternately inside and outside the self—"mine" rather than "me." It includes the idealization that is a part of devotional love, the incorporation of parts of the object, making them parts of the self, and the internalization of the whole love object within the person. Projection may be not simply getting rid of unwanted thoughts and emotions by attributing them to others, but rather recognizing that a part of the self is a part of the other, that the self has extension beyond the bounds of the physical body. For *bhakti* ecstatics, the self is projected when it dwells in another person, place, or thing. Introjection occurs in many cases, such as when the deity or guru is perceived to exist within the body of the ecstatic.

More specifically, these dynamics may be seen in certain descriptions of ecstatic states. These include perceiving the deity as dwelling in the heart, sensing the self to be in a celestial paradise, perceiving the deity in bodily fluids or in the limbs, having the heart and mind possessed by the god, being jointly possessed (when a group is possessed by the same god or goddess), sharing emotion by being a bodily extension of the deity (especially in the handmaiden or servant role), traveling in a subtle body, and sending out other bodies (often younger or of different gender) and then withdrawing them again. In these cases, the cycles of projection and introjection serve to consolidate the sense of self, determining its limits and boundaries in relation to both the deities and other persons. The spontaneous ecstatic is born and reborn, and his challenge is the same as that of the child—to differentiate out a separate self from fluid experiences of introjection and projection. The ritual practitioner has the opposite problem: he must reach toward a state of communion with the deity, from a consciously created self that is initially separate and private. Ecstasy and ritual practice are understood to increase devotion from both directions—both the devotee's love for the deity, and the deity's love for the devotee.

In devotional ecstasy, emotion is reciprocal and shared, continually increasing in intensity. While in psychoanalysis, the states of internalization and merger are understood as primitive, in the Bengali devotional case these are understood as advanced states of personality development, bringing the person closer to the ideal state of participation in the life and emotions of the god or goddess.[40] The ecstatic is joyfully permeable and vulnerable, with the deity both immanent and transcendent, both within and beyond the ecstatic. Ritualized devotion attempts to coerce the deity's grace by the Vaiṣṇava development of affection or the Śākta development of need and fear, drawing the deity into the heart. The spontaneous ecstatic surrenders both mind and body to a love relationship often conceived in romantic terms, and the deity enters the heart of the devotee by grace or sudden passion. While the earthly marriage is dutiful and arranged, the relationship with the deity is a love relationship—sweeter for being *parakīya* and forbidden (in the secular world). And too much emotional intensity, toward person or deity, brings accusations of madness.

The Ecstatic as Madman

We return to the beginning, to the issue of divine madness. This is the madness of the saints, the ecstatic experience which is so difficult to discern that the saints are treated with exorcism and Āyurvedic medicine. Yet it is also the guarantor of the highest spiritual status—the sign of *mahābhāva* and *divyonmāda* in Vaiṣṇavas, Śāktas, and Bāuls, and of *āveśa* in holy women.

This book has emphasized four points about Bengali ecstatics. One is the discrepancy between theology and lived experience, seen by comparing ritual text and biography; while the theological texts emphasize development by stages and yogic control, ecstatics in life have chaotic visions and experiences, and alternating experiences of inner destruction and reintegration. The second point is that this discrepancy is due to different understandings of ritual and spontaneous ecstasy. There are biographical patterns in both. The ritual pattern tends to be an organizational creation, a life that supports the claims of the tradition, while the ecstatic pattern is closer to folk belief and less involved with organizational and theological validation. The third point is the *bhakti* emphasis on inclusiveness and breadth of experience rather than brahminical purity, as seen in the understanding of what it means to be a *siddha*. This stress upon wide and firsthand knowledge includes impurity and sacrifice, as well as worship and sweetness. The fourth point is the difficulty in differentiating between the highest and lowest states that a person may experience, the ways in which ecstasy resembles pathology.

In the recent psychoanalytic literature, there have been two major approaches to apparent pathology in Indian saints. Writers such as Jeffrey Masson and Nathaniel Ross emphasize the psychopathology of ecstatic and mystical states, assuming Western paradigms to be normative.[41] Ultimate liberation is a failure of reality testing, Rāmakṛṣṇa Paramahaṃsa is psychotic, and the Buddha is simply a man struggling with depression. Opposing this approach are ethnopsychologists such as Sudhir Kakar who emphasize the importance of cultural concerns. In his review article in the *Journal of Indian Philosophy,* Kakar speaks of the dangers of "pathography"—biographies of religious figures based on their traumas rather than their cultures. This is "biographical explanation in terms of pathographic understanding," a view not sufficiently empathic to non-Western perspectives.[42] For Kakar, mysticism is a romantic quest, culturally sanctioned and rewarded.

In the biographies in this book, there appears to be pathology—fragmentation recognizable in both India and the West. However, it is part of the process of death and rebirth—the disintegration of the secular personality and the birth of the religious/ecstatic one. Psychopathology is a means rather than an end—the less idealized part of the romantic journey, which serves a function in India as it does with mystics and ecstatics cross-culturally. However, these states are considered neither normal nor acceptable: devotional ecstasy is chaotic, not the ordered and hierarchical path to *mokṣa*. Ecstatics cannot be called socially acceptable, even in India. Cultural context can to some extent justify their behavior, but this behavior will not be valued unless the ecstatics are understood to be saints. They will be worshiped or despised, but not accepted on the everyday level.

To determine where the ecstatic stands, he must be tested. The Bengali means of differentiation is Āyurveda, in which the emphasis is on permeability, especially blockage which must be opened to flow. Āyurveda describes channels (*srotas*) that are obstructed, in which humors build up, as well as invasions of impurity and defilement (from sorcery, poison, planetary influences, and sexual or family stresses). The person may be blocked so that there is too much heat or wind (prime sources of madness); he may have flowing into inappropriate channels; or he may be too permeable due to weakness of nerves or draining of spiritual energy and be driven mad. Such problems are cured by opening blockages with oil, cooling the person's heat, and strengthening him with prayers, amulets, and iron bracelets.

Ecstasy opposes madness in Āyurveda, as it is the overflowing of love. Ecstatics are not weak, but instead have great energy (*śakti*) and ability, enough to bear the vision of God. The mad extreme of blockage and invasion is opposed by the ecstatic extreme of emotional overflowing.

In the psychoanalytic model, the person must deal with conflicts, especially those of instinct and relationality, finding resolution via catharsis and sublimation. This is done with a therapist, who takes into account the person's needs and drives (orientations to dependency, pleasure, aggression) and the quality of his relations with others (merging, fearful, manipulative). Insanity (madness has disappeared from the psychiatric classification of disorders), when not of physiological origin, is a set of conflicts that has not been resolved, that cripples the person in interactions with others and fragments his sense of self. The older psychiatric model of drive theory used the image of dammed-up libido for neurosis, a blockage that must be overcome. In both cases, insanity is contrasted with the positive extreme of integration, which includes creativity and autonomy. Like *bhakti* ecstasy, it emphasizes the importance of expression and outflowing. However, instead of the intense *bhakti* flow of emotion, one sees the creative flow of ideas, and individuation is emphasized rather than merging. Both *bhakti* and psychoanalysis value a state of love and self-knowledge, but these are understood differently in the two traditions.

Autonomy is a problem for *bhakti siddhas.* Devotional love requires dependence, an interdependence of deity and devotee which sanctifies life in the physical world. *Siddhas* rebel against normal human relationships and are ambivalent toward or avoid human secular society. The extremes of avoidance and dependence are shown in Gaur Kiśora, who hid from people who wanted initiation from him and hit them with his umbrella, and Arcanāpurī Mā, whose ecstasy was based on her close relationship with her guru, who was her idealized love. The guru can give admiration and protection, a love unavailable in the human sphere, a merging with an idealized figure. In devotional communities, autonomy is always relative to hierarchy. Distance from parents and family may be balanced by dependence on the guru, or the guru may be left behind in favor of dependence on the deities themselves.

The devotional self exists in an idealized relationship with a deity, with whom it can merge and gain peace and satisfaction. There may be symbiosis, or a pact of peaceful coexistence, or at times the deity may dominate the ecstatic in trance. The sacred is understood and encountered through symbolic roles—as the mother, the first intense love, and as a divine couple or simply as the lover, the most intense adult passion. Ideally, the new self is both harmonious and strong, capable of maintaining cohesion in the face of stress, but open to being a channel for the deity's presence and love. It must also be capable of being a target for idealization and empathizing with the problems of disciples. When this is a longer-term state, rather than a fleeting experience that briefly appears in ritual, the world of the sacred becomes the norm, and the physical world and conditioned personality are relativized. The old self is sacrificed, understood as a false self which covers the true one, or as a tool through which to communicate with the world.

Bhakti ecstasy involves the creation of a new self that is intimately related to the deity. The ecstatic both exists in the god's paradise and has the deity dwell within his own heart. The ecstatic is appreciated for his service and loved as a beloved child, both a part of the deity and a separate person.

While devotional ecstatics are often emotionally volatile and have an elastic sense of self, most reach some state of relative stability over time, calmed by the continuous presence of deity and disciples. However, *bhakti* values instability; we could view crises of self-definition as almost institutionalized by the tradition. Too stable a state would be uncaring for the deity, smug and self-sufficient, without passion or true commitment. Yet some stability is necessary for them to affect society.

Part of the study of mad saints must include their effects on society. Secular madmen have little cultural influence, unless they are also gifted in other fields. In the West, intense vision and emotion are justifiable only if there is capacity to love and work, if there is creativity and integration.[43]

In Bengali *bhakti*, the *siddha* is flowing, spreading love of the deity and living an intense and dedicated life. He is a model of passion or attainment, and is not expected to work in the world. The saint is primarily an inspiration for others, who organize his experiences into songs and literature, and into a defense of his tradition against the influences that encroach upon it.

Kṛṣṇa Caitanya acted as the focus of the medieval Bengali Vaiṣṇava movement, inspiring literature and theology based on his experiences. This served to revive Hinduism against the growing dominance of Islam, and his *bhāva* as the man-lion Narasiṃha while fighting the Muslim Kāzi inspired others to support an egalitarian Vaiṣṇavism with Caitanya as an *avatara* (or real presence) of Kṛṣṇa. Vijayakṛṣṇa Gosvāmin initially joined the Brahmo Samāj, preaching in favor of its Christian goals. However, his ecstatic experiences caused him to turn away from them in favor of older and more traditional doctrines, and he became a strong voice for neoconservative Hinduism, moving away from adaptation and accommodation to the West. He drew millions of people toward a revived Vaiṣṇavism in the nineteenth century.

Gaur Kiśora Dās Bābājī Mahārāj attempted to lead an isolated life, but was nevertheless pursued by Vaiṣṇavas; he became a major inspiration for the widespread translation and publication of Vaiṣṇava texts, through Bhaktisiddhānta Sarasvatī and the Gauḍīya Math.[44] Prabhu Jagadbandhu actively opposed the conversion of Hindus to Christianity, spreading Vaiṣṇava practice and creating a Vaiṣṇava subgroup specifically intended to prevent the group from converting to Christianity. He predicted a future in which Hindu practice would spread throughout the world, and thousands of people joined his *kīrtana* groups.

Rāmprasād influenced the practices of Śāktism, changing worship of the goddess from tantric esotericism into mainstream public devotional worship.[45] He sang Śākta songs in the court of the Muslim king and wrote that all religions had divine madmen who sought God. His songs are an important part of Kālī worship, the dominant tradition of Calcutta and much of Bengal. Rāmakṛṣṇa Paramahaṃsa incorporated other religions into Hindu *bhakti* by practicing Islam, Christianity, and Advaita Vedanta and revealing that they all reach toward the same goal. He was believed to have united them and surpassed them by maintaining his worship of the Mother throughout his life. He was the inspiration for Vivekānanda and the Rāmakṛṣṇa Mission, with its publishing, schools and clinics, monastic organization, and charitable activities. The biographies written by his disciples made *bhakti* ecstasy known in both India and the West. After his death, his widow, Śāradā Devī, had a major role in the organization—feeding visitors, making peace among the disciples, and acting as a guru.

Vāmākṣepā popularized folk Śāktism, with its focus on death and miracles. He brought the socially unacceptable aspects of Śāktism into the mainstream, incorporating magical belief and tantric practice into Śākta devotionalism. Ānandamayī Mā began a series of charitable organizations, emphasizing medicine, education, and publishing. Other ecstatics led *āśramas,* educated disciples, led congregations in religious practice, organized medical care, wrote books and gave lectures, or worked intimately with disciples in small-scale prayer and ritual practice, acting as a model for the religious life. All had close devotees and followers.

These ecstatics clearly affected both individuals and society as a whole. In *bhakti,* there is love of the god or goddess and also of their manifestations, which may be understood as the religious community, humanity as a whole, even the universe itself. People are loved not as individuals or for what they can accomplish, but for what is understood as their deepest nature. Relationships based on attraction and repulsion are rejected in favor of selfless affection. Certainly this is not attained in all instances, but it is the goal of spiritual love. Such love is directed toward both the deity and the community.

However, this is offset by the dangers of extreme religious states. Certainly ecstasy enhances regression and may also bring out archaic parts of the person which have not been integrated. There is the possibility of grandiosity, of the person claiming to know or feel more than the true situation, of claiming broad abilities or identification with Bhagavān (God). In *bhakti,* such grandiosity is restrained through the ethical imperative of humility, the necessity for devotees to be servants or children of the deity. The person may temporarily be the beloved (in *vīrabhāva* or some forms of Vaiṣṇava Sahajiyā practice) or identified with the deity, but these are not long-term states. Although the guru may be God or the gatekeeper for God, the one who gives access, there is an awareness of narcissistic and corrupted gurus.

Introversion and avoidance of society have always been problematic. The ancient sages (*ṛṣis*) spent years in meditation and were known for knowledge and control of the body, yet were very much subject to grandiosity, to easily wounded pride and outbursts of anger and lust. The unacceptable aspects of the personality were dissociated rather than integrated, and thus never disappeared: asceticism led to displacement of drives. The sages were respected for their dedication, but feared for their tempers.

The process of introversion has different connotations in Western psychoanalytic thought and in Bengali *bhakti.* In the West, the negative aspects are emphasized, to the virtual exclusion of the positive ones.[46] It is regression, a lack of adaptation, a loss of intelligence and maturity, the dissociation of affect or the emergence of instincts in primitive form. Sometimes internal objects, beings only the individual can see and hear, are substituted for human relationships. The regressed ego is depleted, weak, empty, helpless, and hopeless; it is confused and frightened of life in relationship. Such a self is largely dysfunctional, an infantile ego terrified by maternal deprivation, dreading abandonment, feeling strong anxiety or lifeless apathy. There may be fantasies from the various stages of psychosexual development and masochistic attachments to hostile individuals. The only way to gain something positive from such a state is to reestablish relationships with stable others and strengthen the ego to the point where it may interact almost normally with the world, renouncing its imaginary compensations and its defenses.[47]

In some ways, this is the image of the *bhakti* saint. The ego is deliberately weakened, and the person consciously withdraws from life to seek a deity others cannot see or hear. The ecstatic avoids normal human relationships, is neutral or hostile toward them, and looks toward the deity with longing and dread of being abandoned. There may be erratic behavior, eccentric views of sexuality and aggression, delusions of grandeur, extreme concern with food or purity. The ecstatic does not fit into the secular community and does not seek such adaptation. It can be argued that his capacity for genuine closeness has been impaired, that he undergoes the sort of hysterical conversion described by Freud in which bodily tensions and symptoms are substituted for emotional states, where emotional deprivation and longing are transformed into physical ailments.

There are, however, also major differences. In Bengali *bhakti,* knowledge is not understood to be lost but rather gained, and this knowledge brings insight into both the deity and the problems of devotees and society. The lack of adaptation to the physical world is secondary to the gain in adaptation to the spiritual one. Rather than a loss of emotion there is intense love and enthusiasm, and instead of primitive sexual and aggressive impulses there is *prema,* spiritual love, toward the deities and the devotees. The ecstatic does not avoid emotion when the ecstatic symptoms emerge; instead he welcomes intense emotion. The symptoms do not substitute for emotions, but accompany them. The ecstatic is full, overwhelmed, instead of empty; capable of inspiring *āśramas* and disciples, rather than helpless; full of faith in the grace of the deity, rather than hopeless.

For the observer, the distinction between ecstasy and madness is based on the attribution of motivation. But for the ecstatic, the distinction rests on the issue of faith. This is not the sort of faith that is a belief in a doctrine or tradition, but the faith that is an orientation, a sense of direction, that pulls him out of normal society and its values. Both ecstatic and secular madman are plunged into a sea of chaos, surrounded by confusion, impulses, and winds of passion. How can they cross the stormy ocean? The secular madman does not recognize another shore, and his only choice is to return limp and battered, back to where he began. Madness here is inadequate depth and commitment. The ecstatic, however, sees a distant light, and struggles through the world of regression—the memories, the attractions and repulsions, the intense emotions—to the far shore. Faith in a divinity beyond the waters guides the ecstatic so that his struggles have meaning, his traveling has a goal, and he may take on a new role as saint. On the far side of madness is the shining god, dancing.

APPENDIX A Yoga and Ecstasy

This appendix looks briefly at yoga as a background to the devotional ecstasy explored in this book. Yoga includes both ritual and spontaneous paths, called by Eliade "differentiated enstasis" (*saṃprajñāta samādhi*) and "unprovoked enstasis" (*asaṃprajñāta samādhi*).[1] For Patañjali, yoga was a discipline whose goals were the suppression of changing mental states (*samādhi*) and the liberation of the spirit from the dominance of matter, a state of absolute isolation and peace (*kaivalya*). In the state of *samādhi,* the yogi perceives the true essence of the object, without the use of imagination. In *saṃprajñāta,* the *samādhi* "with support," this state is attained with the help of an object or idea, using techniques of concentration and meditation. It has four stages[2] which must be experienced serially, unless the grace of Isvara[3] allows the yogi to skip the preliminary stages. It gives absolute knowledge and the revelation of the self (*puruṣa*).

Asaṃprajñāta samādhi is not acquired by yogic techniques, although it often follows them; neither is it a gift of grace. It is "unprovoked"; as Eliade states: "But it comes without being summoned, without being provoked, without special preparation for it. That is why it can be called a raptus."[4]

However, Patañjali says that this state may be attained in two ways: by technique (*upāya*), the method of the yogis, and by *bhāva,* which is used by gods, disincarnate entities, and superhuman beings in the material realm.[5]

Another aspect of yogic ecstasy is the *siddhis,* the powers or visions that arise during meditation. These include knowing one's past lives; knowing the sounds of all living beings, other minds, death, and the heaven-worlds; control of the senses and elements; and the knowledge of the seer.[6] These arise in *saṃprajñāta samādhi,* often as temptations from deities. They are ecstatic experiences, but minor ones—the yogi must transcend them in order to reach liberation.

APPENDIX B Vaiṣṇava *Bhāvas*

There is a detailed description of Vaiṣṇava *bhāvas* in the *Bhaktirasāmṛtasindhu,* which discusses the *vibhāvas, anubhāvas, vyabhicāribhāvas,* and *sāttvika bhāvas. Vibhāvas* are excitants, which make an emotional state more extreme; *anubhāvas* express emotion, as do the *sāttvika bhāvas*; the *vyabhicāribhāvas* are transitory emotions, which accompany other, more long-lasting emotional outlooks.

> 1. The *annubhāvas* are the indicators of *bhāva* within the mind [*citta*]. They are mostly external manifestations, called *udbhāsvaras* [the shining ones].
> 2. [They include] dancing, rolling on the ground, singing, screaming, stretching the body, roaring or bellowing, yawning, breathing heavily, indifference toward the world, drooling, reeling, hiccoughing, and wild laughter.[1]

Examples of these ecstatic states are given: Rādhā's singing, which entrances her friends and causes stones to melt, and the sage who is drooling, bitten by the snake of *prema.* Some of the rarer symptoms are also briefly mentioned, such as spurting blood and swelling of the body. These *anubhāvas* are believed to follow and strengthen emotions.

The *sāttvika bhāvas* are spontaneous organic manifestations of emotions, which originate from pure spirit.[2] These include immobility (the person is conscious, but his mind is blank and he is unable to move), horripilation (the bristling of hair and gooseflesh), trembling (including quivering and throbbing), sweating, crying (several different types of tears), changing skin color, and total loss of consciousness.[3]

Rūpa divided the *sāttvikas* into categories:

> 1. When the mind is overpowered by *bhāvas* related to Kṛṣṇa, either directly or indirectly, it is called *sattva* by the wise.
> 2. Those *bhāvas* produced from this *sattva* are called *sāttvika bhāvas.*

These are of three kinds: *sneha* [soft or moistened], *digdha* [anointed or saturated], and *rukṣa* [dry or harsh].[4]

Sneha may be further subdivided into *mukhya* (primary, directly related to Kṛṣṇa) and *gauṇa* (secondary, related to him indirectly). *Digdha* is induced by fear for Kṛṣṇa (such as when hearing of his struggles with demons), while *rukṣa* occurs in people without deep feeling for Kṛṣṇa, who become temporarily excited about his exploits, such as his relationship with the gopīs.

The *sāttvikas* are also categorized by their degrees of intensity. *Dhūmayita* or "smoking" has one ecstatic symptom, capable of being suppressed; *jvalita* or "kindled" shows two or three symptoms and is difficult to suppress; *dīpta* or "burning" has four or five symptoms, which are impossible to hide; and *uddīpta* or "blazing" has six to eight ecstatic symptoms at the highest degree of intensity.[5]

The *sthāyī-bhāvas* are described as the dramatic roles and emotions in relation to Kṛṣṇa. The four major roles are *śānta-rasa* (quiet contemplation), *prīti-bhakti-rasa* (being a servant, younger brother, or son of Kṛṣṇa), *preyo-bhakti-rasa* (a relation of friendship), and *vātsalya-bhakti-rasa* (parental affection). The fifth and most important *sthāyī bhāva,* the *madhura-bhakti-rasa,* is discussed in the *Ujjvala-Nīlamaṇi.*

The *Ujjvala-Nīlamaṇi* describes the more advanced stages of ecstasy as well as the varieties of feminine emotion. It overlaps the *Bhaktirasāmṛta-sindhu* in its descriptions of the *sāttvika bhāvas* and the nature of *bhāva* and *prema,* but it adds stages of love that occur as *prema* grows more intense. These include *sneha, māna, praṇaya, rāga, anurāga,* and *bhāva* or *mahābhāva.*

Sneha occurs as *prema* becomes thicker, and causes greater melting of the mind.[6] It is of two types: love that is like ghee—basically tasteless, not sweet—and love that is intrinsically sweet, like honey. The love of Candrāvalī, Rādhā's rival, is compared to ghee, while Rādhā's love is like honey. *Māna* is sulking, hiding an excess of emotion. It, too may be like ghee (dignified sulking) or like honey (graceful sulking). *Praṇaya* is a feeling of confidence and deep sharing, so that there is no shame or hesitation in relation to the beloved one.

Rāga is a passionate attachment described in two colors: *nīlimā* or blue is a subtle, veiled love, while *raktimā* has both safflower yellow (a bright but inconstant dye) and madder red (a permanent dye). *Rāga* is self-existing[7] and independent of other emotions. In this state, pain is experienced as pleasure if it leads to Kṛṣṇa.[8]

Anurāga makes the beloved appear as eternally new and fresh. It includes such aspects as mutual submissiveness (shown outwardly by both male and female); sudden fear of the loss of the beloved, even while both are together; the desire to be born as inanimate matter in order to be near the beloved; and the vision of the beloved during separation (appearing as if he were actually present). It is contagious, appearing in one devotee and spreading to others as soon as they perceive it.[9]

Bhāva or *mahābhāva* is a state felt powerfully, overwhelming the individual with bliss so sweet that the personality is obliterated. At least five or six of the *sāttvika bhāvas* arise, and it may also affect other devotees by increasing their emotions. It is so intense as to be contagious. *Mahābhāva* is the highest goal of the devotee, the emotion of Rādhā that he may share.

Among Vaiṣṇavas, there is some debate over the dynamics of *sādhana siddhi,* the attainment of *bhāva* by ritual practice. Two terms relevant to this process are *anukaraṇa* and *anusaraṇa.* The *anukaraṇa* is commonly translated as imitation and glossed by the technical dramatic term *abhinaya. Anukaraṇa* involves acting like another person verbally, physically, ornamentally (in dress), and mentally (imitating their emotional states). The person imitated in a play is the *anukārya,* the acting is *anukaraṇa.* The actor's own identity is submerged and a new one taken on.

Anusāra or *anusaraṇa,* the term used to describe the relationship of the *bhakta* to Kṛṣṇa's eternal associates, is usually translated as "following." Rūpa Goswāmin does not use the term *anukaraṇa* in his works; he uses *anusāra* or *anugati,* which is never used in connection with drama. For *anusaraṇa,* one does not take on the identity of the model, but follows his teachings or example. He writes: "*Ragānuga bhakti* is that which follows [*anusaraṇa*] the spontaneous passion of the Vraja inhabitants."[10]

In a commentary on Rūpa Goswāmin's three verses on *ragānuga bhakti* (1.2.294–96) in the *Bhaktirasāmṛtasindhu,* Viśvanāth Cakravartin writes,

> *Anugāminī* in the verse means *anusāriṇī* [following] but not *anukāriṇī* [imitating], because of being so explained. This means following in a favorable manner the opinion [*mata*] of those [gopīs], but not having to act in entirety [as they do], just as an explanation based on the Vedānta being enlarged by oneself with arguments, and so forth, is called *vedāntanusāriṇī,* "following the Vedānta."

Thus, "following" requires more individuality than does imitation.[11] Indeed, Bhaktivinode Thakur writes a warning against dramatic imitation in *Jaiva Dharma:*

> Some people with naturally slippery minds practice shedding crocodile tears, and horripilation, for the sake of dramatic performance, or for the attainment of a material object. This hypocritical exhibition of tears or joy is called *nissattva* [simulated emotion]. Sometimes hard-hearted men, through constant practice, make crocodile tears natural. These men are called slippery-minded by nature.[12]

Perhaps another perspective is that of drama once removed—the devotee creates the *mañjarī,* who in turn is based on the *gopī.* The logical end of direct imitation is possession, as in a dance-drama in which the masked dancer is considered to be "possessed" by the character he portrays. The devotee is not "possessed" by the *mañjarī*—body; rather, he seeks to pattern its emotions after the feelings of the *gopīs.* In *anukaraṇa,* one portrays directly and in a dramatic fashion, while in *anusaraṇa* one follows indirectly—not becoming the pattern, but creating a character similar to the pattern, under the wing of the guru, who "hatches" the disciple into his (or her) new spiritual body.

APPENDIX C Yogic Perception

Amid the imagery and visions of yoga, it is often difficult to distinguish between hallucination and supernormal perception. Some varieties of yogic perception include *pratibhājñāna* (a flash of true intuition, showing accurate knowledge of the future); *ārṣajñāna* (the intuition of a *ṛṣi* due to merit from meditation and austerities, a valid immediate cognition of past, future, and remote events); and *siddha-darśana* (occult perception due to merit, herbs, or mantras).[1] Yogic perception has been characterized as true perception of subtle, hidden, and remote events. Two definitions include that of Praśastapāda (the essential nature of self, other selves, ether, space and time, perceived without the use of the senses), and that of Udayana (in which the *manas* or mental substance is withdrawn from the sense organs and supersensible events are perceived in a trance state).[2]

Nonecstatic (*viyukta*) yogic perception uses the sense organs, and perceives distant and hidden objects, while ecstatic (*yukta*) yogic perception involves only *manas,* perceiving the essence or event directly, without the use of the senses. Yogic perception perceives true events. To perceive an illusion is to corrupt this perception, and to live in a world of illusion is yogic madness.

There are various rituals described throughout the tantras, whose goal is the unification of the tantric yogi's identity with that of Śiva or Kālī. The body is ritually purified and its parts identified with deities. In *bhūtaśuddhi,* the five elements are each purified with mantra and yogic exercises. In *atmásuddhi,* the soul is purified. The yogi surrenders his identity before the deity and ritually places the deity in his heart. During the process of *nyāsa,* the deity or several associated deities are placed in different parts of the body. There are many types of *nyāsa*; in *mātṛkanyāsa,* mantric syllables are placed in the body, while in *śodhanyāsa* the *vidyās* or goddesses are located within the person. In *pīṭhanyāsa* the physical

Sakta *pīṭhas* (such as Kāmarūpa and Jalandhara) are felt in different parts of the body.[3]

In the *pañcaśuddhi,* there are five purifications: of self, place, mantra, articles of worship, and deity. These are often associated with the rites of *prāṇa-pratiṣṭhā,* which causes a god to dwell in an image. The worshiper first places the deity in his heart and then transfers it to the image or statue of the deity, so that the statue becomes "alive." All of these involve an identification with a form of Śiva or Kālī, and the human body transformed into a temple for the deity. Such identifications may be consciously shifted by yogic control. Like the supernormal perception of yoga, such states do not require the use of the outer senses.

These types of perception are direct and unmediated by the senses, which are believed to limit information by filtration or distortion. Such yogic perception may occur spontaneously or in ritual contexts.

Notes

Chapter One

1. Mircea Eliade, *Myths, Dreams and Mysteries* (New York: Harper Torchbooks, 1957), p. 96. See also idem, *Shamanism: Archaic Techniques of Ecstasy* (Princeton: Princeton University Press, 1974).

2. The soul is potentially separable from the body in this tradition. There are instances of devotees traveling to Goloka in their spiritual bodies in the Vaiṣṇava literature, although this is not frequent.

3. See Jan Gonda, *Vision of the Vedic Seers* (The Hague: Mouton, 1963) for a discussion of visionary experience in the Vedas.

4. See Diana Eck, *Darśan: Seeing the Divine Image in India* (Chambersburg, Pa.: Anima Publications, 1981) for a discussion of the meanings of the term.

5. Gilbert Rouget, *Music and Trance: A Theory of the Relations between Music and Possession,* trans. B. Biebuyck (Chicago: University of Chicago Press, 1985), p. 11.

6. William James, *The Varieties of Religious Experience* (New York: Collier Books, 1974), p. 156.

7. Ibid., p. 168.

8. Ibid., p. 187.

9. Karl Potter, *Presuppositions of Indian Philosophy* (Englewood Cliffs, N.J.: Prentice Hall, 1963), p. 99.

10. A few references specifically on divine madness: M. A. Screech, "Good Madness in Christendom," in W. F. Bynum, Roy Porter, and Michal Shepherd, eds., *People and Ideas,* vol. 1 of *The Anatomy of Madness* (London: Tavistock Publishers, 1985); Alexander Y. Syrkin, "On the Behavior of the Fool for Christ's Sake," *History of Religions Journal* 22, 2 (1982); and Glenn E. Yocum, "Madness and Devotion in Manikkavacakar's *Tiruvacakam,*" in Fred Clothey and J. Bruce Long, eds., *Experiencing Śiva: Encounters with a Hindu Deity* (New Delhi: Manohar, 1983).

11. *Phaedrus* 265a, b; quoted in Rouget, *Music and Trance,* p. 189.

12. *Phaedrus* 244a, ibid., p. 198.

13. See Ruth Padel, "Madness in Fifth-Century (B.C.) Athenian Tragedy," in Paul Heelas and Andrew Lock, eds., *Indigenous Psychologies: The Anthropology of the Self* (London: Academic Press, 1981). A good discussion of Greek concepts of madness may also be found in Rouget, *Music and Trance,* chap. 5.

14. David Kinsley, "Through the Looking Glass: Divine Madness in India," *History of Religions* 13, no. 4 (May 1974).

15. Such imitation has been a problem for the Sahajiyās, acting out the relationship of Rādhā and Kṛṣṇa, and the Vallabhācāryas, acting out Kṛṣṇa's *rasa* dance. The problems have been both theological and legal.

16. These symptoms include visions, trances, claims to have contact with gods or goddesses, possession, and claimed miracles, such as prophecy or healing.

17. Psychologists and psychiatrists were interviewed at Lumbini Park Mental Hospital, Calcutta Medical College, Samikshani Clinic, Calcutta University (Science College), N.R.S. Medical College, and R. G. Kar Medical College.

18. In Bengali, *Kālī siddhi lābh koreche.*

19. Interview, in Bākreśwar, 1984.

20. The most prominent advocate of schizoid breakdown as mystical insight is probably R. D. Laing. He suggested calling schizophrenia "metanoia," literally "beyond the mind," to suggest that the person moves "beyond the horizons of our communal sense." See R. D. Laing, *The Politics of Experience* (New York: Pantheon, 1967), and also John Weir Perry, *The Roots of Renewal in Myth and Madness* (San Francisco: Hossey-Bass Publishers, 1976). Kenneth Wapnick, "Mysticism and Schizophrenia," in Richard Woods, ed., *Understanding Mysticism* (Garden City, N.Y.: Image Books, 1980), pp. 321–37.

21. Wapnick based this comparison on Saint Theresa and Lara Jefferson. See "Mysticism and Schizophrenia."

22. See Venkoba Rao, "India," in John Howells, ed., *The World History of Psychiatry* (New York: Brunner/Mazel, 1975), p. 628.

23. Ibid., p. 629.

24. In Bengali, *dhātu sāmya.*

25. K. R. Srikantamurthy, *Clinical Methods in Āyurveda* (Delhi: Chowkhamba Orientalia, 1983).

26. *Caraka Saṃhitā*, trans. R. K. Sharma and Vaidya B. Dash (Varanasi: Chowkhamba Sanskrit Series Office, 1977), 2:94.

27. Frank Blackford, "Belief and Psychotherapy in Benares," Ph.D. diss., University of Pennsylvania, 1979.

28. J. C. Oman, *Cults, Customs and Superstitions of India* (London: T. Fisher Unwin, 1908), p. 312.

29. *Caraka Saṃhitā,* 2:89.

30. Ibid., 2:93.

31. Ibid., 2:98.

32. *Suśruta Saṃhitā,* ed. Kaviraj K. L. Bhishagratna (Calcutta: K. L. Bhishagratna, 1907), p. 284.

33. G. F. W. Ewens, *Insanity in India: Its Symptoms and Diagnosis, with Reference to the Relation of Crime and Insanity* (Calcutta: Thacker, Spink, 1908), p. 281.

34. Ibid., p. 276.

35. It is also called *māthā khārāp* (a bad head), *māthā garam* (hot head), or *māther doṣa* (a defect of the head).

36. Deborah Bhaṭṭācārya, "Madness as Entropy: A Bengali View," in Clinton

B. Seely, ed., *Women, Politics, and Literature in Bengal* (East Lansing: Asian Studies Center, Michigan State University, 1981), pp. 31–40. Further data on these themes may be found in idem, *Pāglāmi: Ethnopsychiatric Knowledge in Bengal* (Syracuse, N.Y.: FACS Publications, 1986).

37. Heinrich Dumoulin, *Zen Enlightenment: Origins and Meaning,* trans. John Maraldo (New York: Weatherhill, 1979), p. 44.

38. Ibid., pp. 49, 51.

39. A comparison of Catholic theologians' views on the distinctions between mystical and ascetical theology may be found in Antonio Royo and Jordan Aumann, *The Theology of Christian Perfection* (Dubuque, Iowa: Priory Press, 1962), p. 5. See also Auguste Saudreau, *The Mystical State: Its Nature and Phases* (London: Burns, Oates and Washbourne, 1924).

40. A. Poulain, S.J., *The Graces of Interior Prayer: A Treatise on Mystical Theology,* trans. Leonora L. Yorke Smith (St. Louis: B. Herder Book Co., 1907), p. 243. Alienation of the senses refers to a withdrawal of the senses from the outside world.

41. See Poulain's section, "Errors Regarding Ecstasy: How It Is Confused with Certain Conditions of Ill-health," pp. 257–65. On this point see also Albert Farges, *Mystical Phenomena Compared with Their Human and Diabolical Counterfeits,* trans. S. P. Jacques (London: Burns, Oates and Washbourne, 1926).

42. Poulain, *Graces,* p. 263.

43. Interview, in Navadvīpa, 1984.

44. Rouget, *Music and Trance,* p. 320.

45. In Bengali writing, the spelling would be *bhāb.* Here the Sanskritized spelling is used.

46. *Rasagullās* are sweet desserts based on grain and sugar.

47. Classical sources on mysticism include Evelyn Underhill's 1911 *Mysticism* (New York: Dutton, 1961); Rudolf Otto's 1932 *Mysticism East and West: A Comparative Analysis of the Nature of Mysticism,* trans. B. L. Bracey and R. C. Payne (New York: Macmillan, 1970); W. T. Stace, *Mysticism and Philosophy* (London: Macmillan, 1961); and Joseph Marechal, *Studies in the Psychology of the Mystics,* trans. Algar Thorold (New York: Benziger Brothers, 1927). A good source on the structure and content of mystical ecstasy may be found in Ernst Arbman, *Ecstasy or Religious Trance, in the Experience of the Ecstatics and from the Psychological Point of View*; vol. 1, *Vision and Ecstasy*; vol. 2, *Essence and Forms of Ecstasy*; vol. 3, *Ecstasy and Psychopathological States* (Stockholm: Uppsala, 1963–70). For a broad study of cases of mystical experience, see Marghanita Laski, *Ecstasy: A Study of Some Secular and Religious Experiences* (London: Cresset Press, 1961). A good discussion of verification, interpretation, and classification of mystical experiences may be found in Stephen Katz's collection of essays, *Mysticism and Philosophical Analysis* (New York: Oxford University Press, 1978).

48. Two more polemical sources include R. C. Zaehner's 1957 *Mysticism Sacred and Profane: An Inquiry into Some Varieties of Praeternatural Experience* (London: Oxford University Press, 1975), and Agehananda Bharati, *The Light at the Center: Context and Pretext of Modern Mysticism* (Santa Barbara, Calif.: Ross Erikson, 1976).

49. See George Devereux, "Normal and Abnormal," in *Basic Problems of Ethnopsychiatry* (Chicago: University of Chicago Press, 1980) for a discussion of schizophrenia and psychopathology among shamans.

50. On denial and depression, see J. Moussaief Masson, *The Oceanic Feeling: The Origins of Religious Sentiment in India* (Dordrecht: D. Reidel, 1980). See also idem, "The Psychology of the Ascetic," *Journal of Asian Studies* 35: 611–25, for an argument that religious striving and experience in Indian ascetics is due to childhood abuse.

51. B. D. Lewin, in *The Psychoanalysis of Elation* (New York: Psychoanalysis Quarterly, 1961), discusses depression and anxiety as underlying states of mystical elation and mania, and the fears of being isolated, killed, and eaten which are present.

52. Rudolf Bell, in *Holy Anorexia* (Chicago: University of Chicago Press, 1985), argues that religious asceticism in medieval Catholic women saints follows the same dynamics and goals as anorexia in modern adolescents and women.

53. The most famous proponent of mystical experience as regression was Sigmund Freud, in his writings on Romain Rolland's "oceanic feeling" in *Civilization and Its Discontents,* and throughout his *Interpretation of Dreams.* However, Freud himself was not doctrinaire about being a Freudian. He gives ascetics credit for sublimation in his discussion of Jung's ideas on introversion of libido leading to asceticism rather than dementia: "How little this inept comparison can help us to a conclusion may be learnt from the reflection that an anchorite who 'tries to erase every trace of sexual interest' (but only in the popular sense of the word 'sexual') does not even necessarily display any pathogenic disposition of the libido. He may have turned away his interest from human beings entirely, and yet may have sublimated it to a heightened interest in the divine, in nature, or in the animal kingdom, without his libido having undergone introversion to his phantasies or retrogression to his ego." See Freud, "On Narcissism: An Introduction," in *Collected Papers,* trans. Joan Rivière (London: Hogarth Press, 1956), 4:38.

54. For a collection of sources on possession and trance, see Irving Zaretsky, *Spirit Possession and Spirit Mediumship in Africa and Afro-America: An Annotated Bibliography* (New York: Garland Publishing, 1978). Other useful sources include Raymond Prince, *Trance and Possession States* (Montreal: R. M. Bucke Memorial Society, 1968); I. M. Lewis, *Ecstatic Religion: An Anthropological Study of Spirit Possession and Shamanism* (Harmondsworth, England: Penguin Books, 1971); William Sargant, *The Mind Possessed: A Physiology of Possession, Mysticism and Faith Healing* (New York: Penguin Books, 1973); and Erika Bourguignon, *Religion, Altered States of Consciousness and Social Change* (Columbus: Ohio State University Press, 1973).

55. Various understandings of ecstatic altered states may be found in Abraham H. Maslow, *Religion, Values and Peak Experiences* (Columbus: Ohio State University Press, 1964); Stanislav Grof, *Realms of the Human Unconscious: Observations from LSD Research* (New York: E. P. Dutton, 1976); Ken Wilbur, *The Spectrum of Consciousness* (Wheaton, Ill.: Theosophical Publishing House, 1985); R. E. L. Masters and Jean Houston, *The Varieties of Psychedelic Experience* (New York: Dell Publishing, 1966); and Roland Fischer, "A Cartography of the Ecstatic and Medi-

tative States," in Richard Woods, ed., *Understanding Mysticism* (Garden City, N.Y.: Doubleday, 1980).

56. Some relevant studies of Indian ethnopsychology include G. Morris Carstairs, *The Twice-Born: A Study of a Community of High-Caste Hindus* (Bloomington: Indiana University Press, 1967); Sudhir Kakar, *Shamans, Mystics and Doctors: A Psychological Inquiry into India and Its Healing Traditions* (New York: Alfred Knopf, 1982); Prakash Desai, *Health/Medicine in the Hindu Tradition* (Crossroads, forthcoming); Susan Snow Wadley, *Shakti: Power in the Conceptual Structure of Karimpur Religion* (Chicago: University of Chicago Press, 1975); and the largely unpublished work of McKim Marriott on the fluid nature of Indian personal identity.

57. For a discussion of the use of myth in the Caitanya biographies, see Tony K. Stewart, "Perceptions of the Divine: The Biographies of Caitanya," University of Chicago, 1985. For an examination of the problems involved in the analysis of sacred biography, see Frank Reynolds and Donald Capps, eds., *The Biographical Process: Studies in the History and Psychology of Religion* (The Hague: Mouton, 1976).

58. David N. Lorenzen, "The Life of Sankaracarya," in Reynolds and Capps, *Biographical Process,* pp. 89–90.

59. Mircea Eliade, *The Sacred and the Profane: The Nature of Religion,* trans. Willard R. Trask (New York: Harcourt, Brace and World, 1959), p. 232.

60. On empathy, Van der Leeuw states that it is "utterly impossible contemplatively to confront an event which, on the one hand, is an ultimate experience, and on the other manifests itself in profound emotional agitation, in the attitude of pure intellectual restraint." While he tended to polarize the "cold-blooded spectator" from the "loving gaze of the lover upon the beloved object," he focused on the importance of phenomena, appearance, and the intuition of types and structures. While the writer cannot reflectively enter the experiences of another person, or even fully understand his or her own, still the writer may look at its reflection in words and actions, seeing themes, essences, and categories. See G. Van der Leeuw, *Religion in Essence and Manifestation,* trans. J. E. Turner (New York: Harper and Row, 1963), 2:684.

61. James, *Varieties of Religious Experience,* p. 36.

Chapter Two

1. Friedhelm Hardy, *Viraha Bhakti: The Early History of Kṛṣṇa Devotion in South India* (Delhi: Oxford University Press, 1983), p. 27.

2. Ibid., p. 333.

3. Ibid., p. 346.

4. Ibid., p. 351.

5. A. K. Ramanujan, *Hymns for the Drowning* (Princeton: Princeton University Press, 1981), p. 54.

6. *Bhāgavata Purāṇa,* trans. G. V. Tagore (Delhi: Motilal Banarsidass, 1978), X.11, 12, 13. Hereinafter cited as *BP.*

7. *BP* X.30.4, 5, 14, 15.

8. *BP* VII.4.38–41.

9. *BP* X.38.26.

10. *BP* X.90.14.
11. *BP* VII.13.10.
12. *BP* XI.14.23, 24.
13. *BP* XI.18.29.
14. *BP* XI.7.28.
15. *BP* VII.7.35.
16. *BP* XI.13.36.
17. *BP* X.21.4.
18. The major secondary sources include A. K. Majumdar, *Caitanya: His Life and Doctrine, A Study in Vaisnavism* (Bombay: Bharatiya Vidya Bhavan, 1969), and S. K. De, *Early History of the Vaisnava Faith and Movement in Bengal* (Calcutta: Firma KLM, 1961).
19. In Bengali, *mantra dīkṣā*.
20. Kṛṣṇadāsa Kavirāja, *Caitanya Caritāmṛta*, ed. Sukumar Sen (New Delhi: Sahitya Akademi, 1977), II.1.87, 88. Hereinafter cited as *CC*.
21. In Bengali, *bhāvera taraṅga-bale*.
22. *CC* II.2.35.
23. *CC* II.2.36–42.
24. *CC* II.55, 56.
25. *CC* II.2.63.
26. The term used here for madness is *unmāda*.
27. *CC* II.2.57.
28. *CC* II.2.45.
29. Vṛndāvana Dāsa, *Caitanya Bhāgavata*, II.8.147–227. From Tony K. Stewart, "Perceptions of the Divine: The Biographies of Caitanya," Ph.D. diss., University of Chicago, 1985.
30. Kṛṣṇadāsa Kavirāja, *Caitanya Caritāmṛta*, trans. Edward C. Dimock, manuscript, 1985, III.10.67–73.
31. Ibid., III.10.9–22.
32. Ibid., III.18.44–69.
33. Ibid., III.17.59–60.
34. Rūpa Gosvāmin, *Śrī Śrī Bhaktirasāmṛtasindhu*, ed. with a Bengali translation by Haridāsa Dāsa, with the commentaries of Jīva Gosvāmin, Mukundadāsa Gosvāmin, and Viśvanāth Cakravartin, 3d ed. (Navadvīpa: Haribol Kuṭhir, 495 Gaurabda), I.3.6. Hereafter cited as *BRS*.
35. *BRS* I.1.35.
36. In Bengali, the term for such spontaneous experience is *sādhanabyatita*.
37. *BRS* I.3.15–16.
38. *BRS* I.3.17–20.
39. Such inborn love is termed *nisarga rati*.
40. *BRS* I.4.9.
41. *BRS* I.2.295.
42. *BRS* I.4.16.
43. Rupa Gosvāmin, *Śrī Śrī Ujjvala-Nīlamaṇi*, ed. in Bengali translation by Viṣṇ*udāsa Gosvāmin* (Navadvīpa: Haridāsa Dāsa, 497 Gaurabda, p. 124; 14.160.
44. Ibid., p. 125; 14.164.

45. This charm is called *uddīpta* (blazing) *sāttvika.*
46. Gosvāmin, *Ujjvala-Nīlamani,* p. 125; 14.174.
47. Ibid., p. 126; 14.180.
48. Ibid., p. 126; 14.186.
49. Ibid., p. 127; 14.193.
50. Ibid., p. 131; 14.220.
51. O. B. L. Kapoor, *The Philosophy and Religion of Śrī Caitanya* (Delhi: Munshiram Manoharlal, 1977), p. 210.
52. In Bengali, this is the *nāma cintamaṇi.*
53. *BRS* 1.2.231.
54. Raghava Caitanya Das, *The Divine Name* (Bombay: R. C. Das, 1954), p. 46.
55. Further sources on *nāma*: Manindranāth Guha's *Harināmāmṛta sindhubindu,* Kanupriya Gosvāmin's *Nāma cintāmaṇi,* Kedarnath Bhaktivinode's *Nāma cintamani,* Sundarānanda Vidyavinode's *Nāma cintāmaṇi khanika.* See also the "Nāma mahātmya" section of the *Prema Vivarta* by Jagadānanda Paṇḍita.
56. This process is called *mantra dīkṣā.*
57. Interview, in Navadvīpa, 1983.
58. This mantra is discussed in the *Gopāl Tapini Upaniṣad,* one of the recent Upaniṣads of the main 108.
59. One form of the Kāma *gāyatrī* is *kāmadevāya vidmahe puṣpabāṇāya dhīmahi tan no' naṅgaḥ pracodayāt.* It is a mantra to the god of love and is associated with the tantric tradition.
60. See the *paddhatis* of Gopāl Guru, Dhyānacandra, and Siddha Kṛṣṇadās.
61. Sanātana Goswāmin, *Śrī Bṛihad Bhagavatāmṛtam,* trans. Bhakti Vilās Tīrtha Goswāmi (Madras: Sree Gaudiya Math, 1975), p. 149.
62. Ibid., p. 151.
63. Sources include M. Guha's *Harināmāmṛta-sindhubindu,* and *Padakalpataru* (The desire tree of songs), compiled by Rādhācharandās.
64. Philip Lutgendorf, "Kṛṣṇa Caitanya and His Companions, as Presented in the *Bhaktamālā* of Nābhā Jī and the *Bhaktirasabodhini* of Priya Dāsa," typescript, 1980.
65. Śrīla Narahari Cakravarti Thākur, *Śrī Śrī Bhakti Ratnākara* (Calcutta: Gauḍīya Mission, 1967), p. 326.
66. *BRS* 1.2.295.
67. For a study of Vaiṣṇava *smaraṇa* based on the Vṛndāvana *līlā,* see David Haberman, "Acting as a Means of Salvation: Rāgānugā Bhakti Sādhana," Ph.D. diss., University of Chicago, 1984. It is a study of ritual emotion in Vaiṣṇavism, emphasizing the place of drama and conscious effort.
68. These are described in the *Govinda līlāmṛtam* of Kṛṣṇadās Kavirāj and the *Kṛṣṇanika kaumudi* of Kavikarṇapura.
69. Narendra Nath Law, *Śrī Kṛṣṇa and Śrī Caitanya* (London: Luzac, 1949), p. 78.
70. Interview, in Navadvīpa, 1983.
71. Thākur, *Bhakti Ratnākara,* p. 324.
72. Sukumar Sen, *A History of Brajabuli Literature* (Calcutta: University of Calcutta, 1935), p. 186.

73. Thākur Bhaktivinode, *Jaiva Dharma* (Madras: Gaudiya Math, 1975), p. 268.

74. *CC* II.8.236.

75. The first text of a *siddha rūpa* as revealed by a guru is the sixteenth-century *Gaura Govindarcanā smaraṇa paddhati,* by Gopālguru Gosvāmin. Other texts on *līlā smaraṇa* include the *Gaura ganoddesa dipika* of Kavikarṇapūra (which mentions the correspondence between *Vṛndāvana līlā* and *Navadvīpa līlā*), and songs, poems, *paddhatis* and *gutikās* of *siddha bābājīs,* Vaiṣṇavas who have entered the paradise and written maps, guidebooks, and general instructions. Siddha Kṛṣṇadāsa of Govārdhana was famed for his detailed maps of the villages of Rādhā and Kṛṣṇa.

76. Interview, in Navadvīpa, 1983.

77. Bhaktivinode Thākur and Bhaktisiddhanta Saraswatī, *Vaiṣṇavism and Nām-Bhajan,* ed. Bhakti Vilās Tīrtha Goswāmi Mahārāj (Madras: Śrī Gauḍīya Math, 1968), p. 89.

78. The major source for this biography was a chapter of volume 2 of the *Srī Śrī Gauḍīya Vaiṣṇava Jīvana* of Haridāsa Dāsa (Navadvīpa: Haribol Kuṭhir, 465 Gaurabda). It is a collection of biographies of Gauḍīya Vaiṣṇava *bhaktas.*

79. Ibid., p. 40.

80. Ibid.

81. Ibid., p. 42.

82. Ibid., p. 45.

83. Ibid., p. 44.

84. Tridandi Śrī Bhakti Prajñān Yati Mahārāj, ed., *The Renaissance of the Gaudiya Vaisnava Movement* (Madras: Sree Gaudiya Math, 1978), p. 49.

85. The main sources for this biography are a series of books written by Harañth's disciple A. S. Śāstri, based on the three *līlās* of Caitanya (Adi, Madhya, and Antya Līlās) in the *Caitanya Caritāmṛta* of Kṛṣṇadāsa Kavirāja. However, the *bhāvas* of Haranāth do not imitate those of Caitanya.

86. A. R. Śāstri, ed., *Madhya Līlā,* vol. 2 of *Lord Haranāth* (Calcutta: G. S. Ghar and A. R. Śāstri, 1971), p. 567.

87. A. R. Śāstri, ed., *Upadeshāmṛta or The Divine Voice of Śrī Śrī Thākur Haranāth* (Rajahmundry: A. R. Śāstri, 1965), p. 139.

88. A. R. Śāstri, ed., *Adi Līlā,* vol. 1 of *Lord Haranāth* (Bisnupur: Girija Shankar Ghar, 1970), p. 9.

89. These are called *aprakṛta mahābhāva dehas.*

90. Atal Behary Nandy, *Pāgal Haranāth* (Calcutta: Chintaharan Ghosh Gooha, 1915), p. 12.

91. Śāstri, *Upadeshāmṛta,* p. 29.

92. Ibid., p. 24.

93. A. R. Śāstri, ed., *Antya Līlā,* vol. 3 of *Lord Haranāth* (Calcutta: G. S. Ghar and A. R. Śāstri, 1971), p. 366.

94. Śāstri, *Upadeshāmṛta,* p. 127.

95. This biography is based on the works of Vijayakṛṣṇa's disciple Kuladānanda Brahmacārī, who later became a guru himself. Kuladānanda's major work, *Sadguru Saṅgha* (Calcutta: Sansad Prakāśani, 1388 B.S.), is a five-volume biography and description of Vijayakṛṣṇa's teachings. Kuladānanda's *Ācārya Prasanga*

(Calcutta: Sansad Prakāśani, 1383 B.S.), is a shorter and earlier work, with many anecdotal stories.

96. Kuladānanda, *Sadguru Saṅga,* 2:243.

97. Kuladānanda, *Ācārya Prasanga,* p. 46.

98. Ibid., p. 10.

99. Ibid., p. 9.

100. Ibid., p. 11.

101. Ibid., p. 62.

102. In Bengali, *bhāva-boicitryer biśṛnkhal saundarya.*

103. Kuladānanda, *Sadguru Sàngha,* 1:70.

104. The Bengali term is *mantra-mugdhavat.*

105. Kuladānanda, *Ācārya Prasanga,* pp. 138–40.

106. Ibid., p. 150.

107. In Bengali, *adbhuta ākāra.*

108. Kuladānanda, *Ācārya Prasanga,* pp. 95–96.

109. Kuladānanda, *Sadguru Saṅgha,* 4:196–97.

110. In Bengali, *kālpana* or *bhāvanā.*

111. Kuladānanda, *Sadguru Saṅgha,* 2:242.

112. Ibid., 3:188.

113. The major source for Jagadbandhu's biography was written by his disciple Navadvīp Chandra Ghosh, *The Life and Teachings of Śrī Śrī Prabhu Jagadbandhu* (Calcutta: Mahāuddharaṇa Granthalaya, 1973).

114. Ibid., p. 8.

115. Ibid., p. 18.

116. Ibid., p. 21.

117. Ibid., p. 60.

118. Sobharānī Basu, *Modern Indian Mysticism* (Vārānāsī: Bhārat Sādhana Publishers, 1974), 2:378.

119. Ghosh, *Life and Teachings of Prabhu Jagadbandhu,* p. 95.

120. Śrī Śrī Jagadbandu Advent Centenary Committee, ed., *A Glimpse of Indian Spiritual Culture* (Calcutta: Śrī Śrī Jagadbandu Advent Centenary Committee, 1971), p. xi. The year of publication was also given as Haripurushabda 100.

121. Jyotirmoya Nanda, "The Bhakti Śāstras and Contribution of Prabhu Jagadbandu," in *Glimpse of Indian Spiritual Culture,* p. 54.

122. Goswāmin, *Bṛihat Bhagavatāmṛtam,* p. 242.

123. Ibid., p. 217.

124. Ibid., p. 2.

125. K. R. Srikantamurthy, *Clinical Methods in Ayurveda* (Delhi: Chowkhambha Orientalia, 1983), pp. 627–28.

126. When Caitanya was first believed to be mad with the "wind disease," he was given blessed oil as a cure, but it made him even more ecstatic. The blessings of the deity cure madness, but intensify ecstasy.

127. Francis Zimmerman, "Oils and Spices," lecture at the University of Chicago, May 1985.

128. *Caraka Saṁhita,* trans. R. K. Sharma and Vaidya B. Dash (Delhi: Chowkhamba Orientalia, 1983), 2:89.

129. Haridāsa Dāsa, *Gauḍīya Vaiṣṇava Jīvani*, p. 356.
130. Lutgendorf, "Kṛṣṇa Caitanya and His Companions," p. 61.
131. Some Vaiṣṇavas are branded with a symbol, to show their devotion.
132. Haridāsa Dāsa, *Gauḍīya Vaiṣṇava Jīvana*, p. 21.
133. Interview, in Navadvīpa, 1983.
134. Kuladānanda, *Sadguru Saṅgha*, 2:244.
135. *CC* I.7.74.
136. Interview, in Navadvīpa, 1983.
137. Edwin Gerow, "Rasa as a Category of Literary Criticism," in Rachel Baumer and James R. Brandon, *Sanskrit Drama in Performance* (Honolulu: University Press of Hawaii, 1981), pp. 250–51.
138. Edward C. Dimock, Edwin Gerow, C. M. Naim, A. K. Ramanujan, Gordon Roadarmel, and J. A. B. van Buitenen, *The Literatures of India: An Introduction* (Chicago: University of Chicago Press, 1974), p. 217.
139. There are both aesthetic and psychological forms of depersonalization. The aesthetic type is temporary and voluntary; it is useful for enjoying a poem or a play. The psychological type is long term and involuntary; it is a way of relating to the world in which genuine emotion is excluded.
140. See Helene Deutsch, "Some Forms of Emotional Disturbances and Their Relation to Schizophrenia," in *Neuroses and Character Types: Clinical Psychoanalytic Studies* (New York: International Universities Press, 1965), As a form of borderline schizophrenia, the "as-if" personality is among the most difficult forms of psychosis to treat. Patients do not recognize the shallowness of their affect, believing that they feel as others do.
141. Jadunath Sinha, *Indian Psychology: Emotion and Will* (Calcutta: J. Sinha Foundation, 1961), 2:263.
142. Epilepsy has many symptoms. Bharatamuni lists trembling, labored breathing, violent shaking, running, falling down, perspiration, immobility, foaming at the mouth, licking the lips, and unconsciousness. Hemacandra adds throbbing, loud crying, and panting, while Saradatanaya adds terrible eyes and a frightening sound from the throat. Epilepsy is associated with possession by spirits, with impurity, imbalanced humors, and bad planetary influence. Vidyanātha attributes it to intense emotion, such as sorrow or infatuation, and calls it mental confusion (*vaikalya*). Sarveśvarācārya blames it on possession by evil spirits due to the practice of black magic. Rūpa Goswāmin also associates it with mental suffering and Jīva Goswāmin with separation from the beloved. Ibid., p. 260.
143. Ibid., p. 262.
144. *BRS* IV.8 and 9.

Chapter Three

1. Interview, in Calcutta, 1983.
2. Interview, in Risra, 1984.
3. R. S. Dineschandra Sen, *Folk Literature of Bengal* (Calcutta: University of Calcutta, 1920).
4. As the child grows, he continually gets into trouble, from which she saves him. After suffering rejection by his father, she finally becomes his chief queen and is recognized for her virtues by his subjects.

5. *Śākta pīṭhas* are places in which it is believed that pieces of Satī's corpse fell after being chopped to pieces by Viṣṇu's arrows or, in some cases, his discus. Because Śiva was so fond of Satī, he remained in the places where these pieces fell—thus both god and goddess dwell there. He told the Devas that whoever would worship in these places will gain everything he wishes. See the *Śrī Mad Devī Bhāgavatam,* trans. Swāmī Vijñānānanda (Allahabad: Bhuvaneśwarī Āśrama, n.d.), VII.30.42–48.

6. Interview, in Risra, 1984.

7. These are the three inevitable relations of man to woman—the woman bears him, makes love to him, and, as death, finally destroys him. See Sigmund Freud, "The Theme of the Three Caskets," in Vol. 12 of *The Standard Edition of the Complete Psychological Works of Sigmund Freud,* ed. James Strachey (London: Hogarth Press, 1962).

8. See the *Kulārṇava Tantra,* XV.64–65, on *mantra-caitanya.*

9. His songs of Durgā as a daughter returning to her parents have influenced the image of Durgā, who was otherwise seen as an agricultural and warrior goddess.

10. Swāmī Śāradānanda, *Śrī Śrī Rāmakṛṣṇa Līlā-Prasaṅga,* trans. Swāmī Jagadānanda as *Sri Ramakrishna: The Great Master* (Mylapore: Śri Rāmakṛṣṇa Math, 1952). The original English title was *The Play of the Divine Mother as Sri Ramakrishna.* Hereinafter cited as RLP.

11. Mahendranāth Gupta, *Rāmakṛṣṇa Kathāmṛta,* trans. Swāmī Nikhilānanda as *The Gospel of Sri Ramakrishna* (Mylapore: Sri Ramakrsna Math, 1980). Hereinafter cited as *RK.*

12. *RLP,* p. 47.

13. *RK* 2:544.

14. *RK* 2:564.

15. *RK* 1:14.

16. Romain Rolland, *The Life of Ramakrisna* (Calcutta: Advaita Asram, 1960), p. 41.

17. *RLP,* p. 167.

18. *RLP,* p. 169.

19. *RLP,* p. 172.

20. *RLP,* p. 200.

21. *RK* 1:18.

22. Rāmakṛṣṇa's status as a saint was thus determined by Vaiṣṇavas, on the basis of Vaiṣṇava scriptures. However, modern Vaiṣṇavas do not accept him because of his Śākta initiation and his worship of Kālī as Mother.

23. *RK* 1:24.

24. *RK* 1:25.

25. *RK* 2:747.

26. *RLP,* p. 377.

27. *RK* 2:32.

28. *RK* 1:116.

29. *RK* 1:244.

30. *RK* 2:595.

31. *RK* 2:603.

32. Rolland, *Life of Ramakrisna,* p. 37.
33. *RK* 1:265.
34. *RK* 1:491.
35. F. Max Mueller, *Ramakrishna: His Life and Sayings,* ed. Nanda Mookerjee (Calcutta: S. Gupta and Brothers, 1974), p. 90.
36. *RK* 1:245.
37. *RK* 1:405.
38. *RK* 2:813.
39. *RK* 2:830.
40. Rolland, *Life of Ramakrisna,* p. 185.
41. *RK* 2:760.
42. *RLP,* p. 400.
43. Dilip Biswas, "Rammohan Raya Dharmmata Tantrásāstra," *Viśvabhārati Patrikā,* no. 4 (1367 B.S.): 234–35.
44. *The Tantra of Great Liberation* (*the Mahānirvāṇa Tantra*), trans. and ed. Arthur Avalon (London: Luzac, 1913), V.51, 55–56. Hereinafter cited as *MT*.
45. *MT* III.140.
46. *MT* VII.39–41.
47. *MT* VI.38–39.
48. *MT* XI.105–6.
49. *MT* XI.114–15, 118.
50. *MT* VIII.180.
51. *MT* VIII.170–203.
52. *MT* VIII.205–20.
53. *Kulārṇava Tantra,* ed. Upendrakumār Dāsa (Calcutta: Nababhārata Publishers, 1383 B.S.), XVII.51. Sanskrit text, with Bengali translation and commentary. Hereinafter abbreviated as *KT*.
54. *KT* XIV.40–60.
55. *KT* XIV.61–62.
56. *KT* XIV.64–65.
57. *KT* XIV.89.
58. *KT* XV.64–65.
59. *KT* XV.66–68.
60. *KT* XI.84–85.
61. *KT* VIII.62.
62. *KT* VIII.59–61, 63–64.
63. *KT* VIII.67–77.
64. In Bengali, *parā-murchana.*
65. In Bengali, *parā-mantra.*
66. *KT* VIII.81–90.
67. *KT* VII.94–95.
68. *KT* VII.100–2.
69. *KT* VIII.107–9.
70. *KT* IX.86.
71. *KT* IX.67, 72, 74, 82.
72. *KT* IX.73.

73. In Bengali, *prakāśita hoe.*
74. *KT* II.28.
75. Early Śākta sources include the "Devī Sukta," a late hymn in the Vedic style, the Śākta Upaniṣads (including the *Bhāvanopaniṣad, Bahvṛcopaniṣad, Devī Upaniṣad,* and *Sītā Upaniṣad*), and medieval puranas, such as the *Devī Purāṇa* and the *Kālīkā Purāṇa,* and the Caṇḍī from the *Mārkaṇḍeya Purāṇa.*
76. *Śrī Mad Devī Bhāgavata Purāṇa,* trans. Swāmī Vijñānānanda (Allahabad: Bhuvaneśwarī Āśram, n.d.), vol. 26, VII.xxxvii, 13–20. Hereinafter cited as *DB.*
77. *DB* VII.xxxvii, 24–25.
78. *DB* VII.xxxvii, 25–30.
79. *DB* XL.vii, 23–24.
80. *DB* VII.xl, 30–31.
81. *DB* IV.iii, 4–7, 22–23.
82. *DB* III.V, 13–15. Śiva is generally considered to be Devī's husband.
83. *Śrī Kaalee Sahasranaama,* trans. Premlata Paliwal (New Delhi: Nilima Harjal, 1979).
84. *Śrī Lalitā Sahasranāma,* trans. C. I. Suryanarayanamurthy (Bombay: Bhāratiya Vidyā Bhāvan, 1975).
85. *DB* IX.xlvi.38–58.
86. *DB* IX.xlvi.40–42.
87. Sen, *History of Brajabuli Literature,* p. 449.
88. Chintaharan Chakravarty, *Tantras: Studies on Their Religion and Literature* (Calcutta: Punthi Pustak, 1963), p. 95.
89. Ibid., pp. 90–91.
90. Śākta practitioners interviewed emphasized worship as the major practice of Śāktism—yoga was practiced by a minority, as was healing and astrology. One Śakta practitioner estimated that 80 percent of the Śāktas known to him were *bhaktas,* or devotees.
91. Tantras warn of the great danger of improperly performed ritual, especially if the person involved is weak or unprepared. The result of such a ritual is not divine madness but rather permanent disintegration of the personality. See the last chapter of this volume for a discussion of the dangers.
92. Interview, in Calcutta, 1983.
93. Sanjukta Gupta, R. Hoens, and Teun Goudriaan, *Hindu Tantrism* (Leiden: E. J. Brill), p. 169.
94. The name Kuṇḍalinī comes from the term *kuṇḍala,* or coiled. Kuṇḍalini is a snake that lies coiled until she is awakened.
95. Swāmī Viṣṇu Tīrtha, *Devātma Shakti* (*Kuṇḍalinī*) (Rishikesh: Yoga Shri Peeth Trust, 1980), pp. 102–5.
96. Arthus Avalon, *The Serpent Power, Being the Sat-Cakra-Nirupana and Paduka-Pancaka* (Madras: Ganesh, 1964), p. 235.
97. Narendranath Bhattacarya, *History of the Tantric Religion* (New Delhi: Manohar, 1982), p. 338.
98. Gupta, Hoens, and Goudriaan, *Hindu Tantrism,* p. 180.
99. John White, ed., *Kundalini, Evolution, and Enlightenment* (Garden City, N.Y.: Anchor Books, 1979), p. 356. A detailed description of madness due to

Kuṇḍalinī meditation is given in this volume by Gopi Krishna, in "The Phenomenon of Kundalini," pp. 221–53.

100. Gupta, Hoen, and Goudriaan, *Hindu Tantrism,* p. 162.

101. *Kālī Tantra,* ed. Pandit Nityānanda Smṛtitīrtha (Calcutta: Nababhārata Publishing, 1388 B.S.), VI.8–11, 35–38, 40. Sanskrit text, with Bengali translation.

102. P. H. Pott, *Yoga and Yantra: Their Interrelation and Their Significance for Indian Archaeology* (The Hague: Martinus Nijhoff, 1966), p. 78.

103. Ibid., p. 77. The author uses this term for the graveyard rituals of Nepali tantric Buddhists.

104. F. Max Mueller, *Ramakrishna: His Life and Sayings,* ed. Nanda Mookerjee (Calcutta: S. Gupta and Brothers, 1974), p. 134.

105. The term *pītha* refers to a pilgrimage place and shows the *yoni-pītha to be a place of cosmic importance.*

106. Kāmākhyā Tantram, ed. Jyotirlāl Dāsa (Calcutta: Nababhārata Publishers, 1385 B.S.), IV.35–37. Sanskrit text, with Bengali translation and commentary.

107. The term used is *parakīya latācakra.*

108. *Samayācāra* includes the practices of the *samaya* family of Tibetan tantric Buddhism, whose *dhyāni buddha* is Amoghasiddhi, with his *Śakti* Tārā. This indicates Buddhist influence on the text.

109. *Māyā Tantram,* ed. Jyotirlāl Dāsa (Calcutta: Nababhārata Publishers, 1385 B.S.), XII.1–8. Sanskrit text with Bengali translation.

110. Kulāvalīnirnaya IV.15, VIII.223–25. Quoted in Bhattacarya, *History of the Tantric Religion,* p. 121.

111. The term *puṣpa* refers to both flowers and menstrual blood.

112. These stories generally dealt with the cowardly fright of friends or relatives, or the genuine danger that reawakened corpses presented.

113. In Bengali, *pavitra o mādhura bhāva rasa.*

114. In Bengali, *sthira sāttvika bhāva.*

115. Promode Kumar Chatterji, *Tantrābhilāsir Sādhu-saṅgha* (Calcutta: Mitra Ind Ghosh, 1980), 1:213–59.

116. *Śiva Sutra,* ed. I. K. Taimni (Adyar: Theosophical Publishing House, 1976), p. 20.

117. Ibid., II.5.

118. Bengal has many such Kālī *bāṛi* temples; a proverb says: *jekhāne bāngālī, sekhāne kālībāṛi* (wherever there are Bengalis, there is a Kālī *bāṛi*). From P. C. Roy Chaudhuri, *Temples and Legends of Bengal* (Bombay: Bharatiya Vidya Bhavan, 1967), p. 10.

119. Field notes, in Calcutta, 1984.

120. In Bengali, the seat of five skulls is called a *pañcamuṇḍi āsana.*

121. Interview, in Risra, 1984.

122. This biography is primarily from Subodh Kumār Bandopadhyāya, *Tārāpīṭh Bhairava* (Calcutta: Bāmdeva Sangha, 1376 B.S.), and also from the story of Vāmākṣepā in Gangescandra Cakravarti's collection of biographies, *Bānglār Sādhaka* (Calcutta: Viśvavāṇī Prakāśani, 1387 B.S.).

123. S. K. Banerjee, *Śrī Śrī Bāma Kṣepā* (Calcutta: Śrī Byomkesh Bysack, 1971), p. 36.

124. Bandopadhyaya, *Tārāpīṭh Bhairava,* pp. 69–73.
125. Banerjee, *Śrī Śrī Bāma Kṣepā,* p. 67. Here he attempts to suck out her life at the breast, as Kṛṣṇa did with Pūtana.
126. Interview, in Calcutta, 1984.
127. Interview, in Rishra, 1984.
128. Here he imitates the god Śiva.
129. Interview, in Calcutta, 1984.
130. Bannerjee, *Śrī Śrī Bāmākṣepā,* p. 97.
131. The lowest *cakra* or energy center in the body, at the base of the spine.
132. In Bengali, *anubhāva kare jae.*
133. Chatterji, *Tantrābhilāsir Sādhu-saṅgha,* 2:1–70.
134. In Bengali, *brahmatālu.*
135. This biography is primarily from a biography of Nityagopāl, *Śrī Śrī Nityagopāl* (Nabadwip: Mahanirban Math, 1948), written by Nityagopāl's disciple Swāmī Nityapadanda Abadhūta.
136. Ibid., p. 79.
137. Ibid., p. 83.
138. Ibid., pp. 87–88.
139. These styles were called *lāsya nṛtya* and *tāṇḍava nṛtya.*
140. Abadhūta, *Śrī Śrī Nityagopāl,* p. 282.
141. Ibid., p. 322.
142. Quoted in Jyotirindarnath Sengupta, *Nityagopal: A Superb Spiritual Teacher* (Calcutta: Sri Dhiresh Sen, 1372 B.S.), p. 40.
143. Srimat Swami Nityapadanda Avadhūta, *The Philosophy of Union by Devotion* (Navadvip: Mahanirban Math, 1953), p. 33.
144. The major source for this biography was the section "Mātrī Sādhaka Rāmprasād" in Gangescandra Cakravarti, *Bānglār Sādhaka* (Calcutta: Nabendu Cakravarti, 1379 B.S.), 1:173–94.
145. Cakravarti, *Bānglār Sādhaka,* 1:175.
146. This type of seat is called a *pañcamuṇḍi āsana.*
147. See Avalon, *Principles of Tantra,* p. 345.
148. A bird believed to drink nectar from the moon.
149. Satyanarayan Bhaṭṭācārya, *Rāmprasād: Jivanī O Racanasamagra* (Calcutta: Śrī Dharmadāsa Samanta, 1975), p. 138.
150. Sinha, *Ramaprosada's Devotional Songs,* p. 75.
151. Bhaṭṭācārya, *Rāmprasād,* p. 129.
152. Ibid., p. 184.
153. In Bengali, *mula-mantra* and *yantra.*
154. *Chants à Kālī de Rāmprasād,* trans. Michele Lupsa (Pondichery: Institut Français d'Indologie, 1967), p. 130. Poems in Bengali, with French translation.
155. Ibid., p. 104. To "show the banana" is an idiom with a hand signal, like the American "give someone the finger." It is a show of defiance.
156. Ramprasad Sen, *Grace and Mercy in Her Wild Hair: Selected Poems to the Mother Goddess,* trans. Leonard Nathan and Clinton Seely (Boulder, Colo.: Great Eastern, 1982), p. 55.
157. Edwin Thompson and Arthur Spenser, ed. and trans., *Bengali Religious Lyrics: Śakta* (Calcutta: Association Press, 1923), p. 47.

158. In the text, *tattva*.

159. Bhaṭṭācārya, *Rāmprasād,* p. 177.

160. Swāmī Prajñānanda, "Śrīrāmprasāder Gāne Jīvan-Anubhuti," in Debasis Mitra, ed., *Sādhaka Rāmprasād* (Calcutta: Adhyayana, n.d.), p. 13.

161. Sinha, *Ramaprosada's Devotional Songs,* p. 4.

162. Teun Goudriaan and Sanjukta Gupta, *Hindu Tantric and Śākta Literature* (Wiesbaden: Otto Harrassowitz, 1981).

163. Despite the fact that he was mad for Tārā, a goddess, both he and his disciples called the state *bhagavān pāgal* rather than *bhagavatī pāgal.*

164. Interview, in Calcutta, 1984.

165. Interview, in Bainchi, 1984.

166. The term was used in English.

167. Interview, in Calcutta, 1983.

168. Interview, in Bakreswar, 1984.

169. Interview, in Calcutta, 1984.

170. Amarendranātha Raya, ed., *Śākta Padāvalī* (*Cayana*), (Calcutta: Calcutta University, 1957), p. 174.

171. Interview, in Calcutta, 1983.

172. Sinha, *Ramaprosada's Devotional Songs,* p. 8.

173. These are *divya* and *alaukika.*

174. Interview, in Calcutta, 1984.

175. *Rudrayāmala Tantra,* ed. Bhagiratha Prasāda Tripathi Vāgīśāstri (Vārānāsī: Sampurnānda Saṃskrita Viśvavidyālaya, 1980), Yogitantra-Granthamala, vol. 7; Uttaratantra I.115–17.

176. Ibid., Uttaratantra XI.6–7.

177. Interview, in Bainchi, 1984.

178. Jahnavikumār Cakravarti, *Śaktapadābalī O Śaktisādhana* (Calcutta: D. M. Library, 1367 B.S.), pp. 228–29.

179. Interview, in Calcutta, 1984.

180. Thompson and Spenser, *Bengali Religious Lyrics,* poem no. 76.

181. Major Śākta saints (*siddhas*) include Kṛṣṇānanda Āgambāgīśa (the writer of the *Tantrasāra,* generally considered to be the first Bengali *tāntrika*); Sarvānanda of East Bengal (who achieved Kālī in a single night by the corpse ritual and saw all ten forms of the goddess at that time); Brahmānanda Giri of East Bengal; Rāmprasād Sen of Halisahar; Kamalākānta of Burdoman; and the two most significant: Rāmakṛṣṇa Paramahaṁsa of Dakṣiṇeśwar and Vāmākṣepā of Tārāpiṭh.

182. Interview, in Calcutta, 1984. After this, he no longer wished to die. He appeared quite healthy when interviewed, after performing a large *homa* fire ceremony.

183. In Bengali, *alaukika.*

184. Calling her Sarvakāma Pradāyinī, Nikhiljananī, Bhuvana-Mohinī, Brahmajñāna-vinodhinī.

185. Nigamānanda Saraswatī, *Māyer Kṛpa* (Halisahar: Swāmī Ātmānanda, Saraswatī Math, 1382 B.S.), pp. 3–13.

186. Ibid., pp. 11–12.

187. These last behaviors are called in Sanskrit: *krāthana, spandana, maṇḍana, śṛṅgāraṇa, avitat-karaṇa, avitad-bhāśaṇa.*

188. *Pāśupata Sūtram* (with the Panchartha-Bhasya of Kauṇḍinya), trans. Haripada Chakraborti (Calcutta: Academic Publishers, 1970), IV.6, p. 140. Hereinafter abbreviated as *PS.*

189. Daniel H. H. Ingalls, "Cynics and Pāśupatas: The Seeking of Dishonor," *Harvard Theological Review* 55, 3 (1962): 281–98.

190. *PS* IV.4, p. 139.

191. Ibid.

192. The Vaiṣṇava list is from Sushil Kumar De, *Early History of the Vaisnava Faith and Movement in Bengal, from Sanskrit and Bengali Sources* (Calcutta: Firma KLM, 1961), pp. 188–89.

193. Benjamin Walker, *Tantrism* (Wellingborough: Aquarian Press, 1982), p. 31.

194. Still, Śiva is more faithful than Kṛṣṇa, who flaunts his affairs with other women. As such, Śiva is considered to be a good husband, or at least preferable to Kṛṣṇa. See Manisha Roy, *Bengali Women* (Chicago: University of Chicago Press, 1975), p. 53.

Chapter Four

1. Sung by Boidyanāth Sarma, Calcutta, 1984.

2. Upendranāth Bhaṭṭācārya, *Bānglār Bāul O Bāul Gān* (Calcutta: Orient Book Company, 1388 B.S.), poem 515, p. 911. Hereinafter cited as *BBG.*

3. Srī Anirvan, *Letters from a Bāul: Life within Life* (Calcutta: Śrī Aurobindo Pathamandir, 1983), p. 118.

4. Alokeranjan Dasgupta and Mary Ann Dasgupta, *Roots in the Void: Baul Songs of Bengal* (Calcutta: K. P. Bagchi, 1977), p. 23.

5. Interview, at Jayadeb-Kenduli *mela,* 1984.

6. *The 13 Principal Upanisads,* trans. R. E. Hume (Madras: Oxford University Press, 1965), III.7.21, 22, p. 117.

7. Ibid., II.5.13, p. 103.

8. These are described in *BBG,* pp. 291–368.

9. The experience of this state is called *mahāsukha* by Bāuls who follow Buddhist tantra, *mahābhāva-anubhuti* by Vaiṣṇava Sahajiyās, and *śiva-śaktir samarasya* or *kevalānanda-upalabdhi* by Śakta *tantrikas.*

10. See Kṣitimohan Sen, *Bānglār Bāul* (Calcutta: Calcutta University, 1954).

11. Major collections of Bāul songs include Muhammed Mansur Ud-Din, *Hārāmaṇi: Loka saṃgīta saṃgraha* (Calcutta: University of Calcutta, 1942); Matilāl Dās and P. K. Mahāpatra, eds., *Lālan Gītikā* (Calcutta: University of Calcutta, 1958); P. M. Islam, *Kavi Pāgla Kanāi* (Dacca: Rajshahi University, 1959); and the latter half of *Bānglār Bāul O Bāul Gān.*

12. Bāul informants have variously named as *pāgal siddha* such Bāuls as Lālan Fakir, Padmalocana, Kṣepā Bāul, Rādhā Śyāma Dās, and Ananta Gosāin.

13. Deben Bhattacarya, trans., *Songs of the Bards of Bengal* (New York: Grove Press, 1969), p. 58.

14. Interview, in Calcutta, 1984.

15. *BBG,* p. 150.

16. Anwarul Karim, *The Bauls of Bangladesh* (Kushtia: Lalan Academy, 1980), p. 61.

17. Ibid., p. 80. *Fanā* is a temporary state. Mohammad referred to *fanā* as *faqr* and called it "the blackening of the face in both worlds" (when the face is blackened, it disappears).

18. Muhammed Enamul Haq, *A History of Sufism in Bengal* (Dacca: Asiatic Society of Bangladesh, 1975), p. 101.

19. The ordinary Koran is in thirty sections, but there are ten remaining sections, to be found in the experience of the fakirs. To know oneself is *faqiri.*

20. M. A. Hai and M. Mansur Ud-Din, *Hārāmaṇi* (Dacca: Dacca University Press, 1961), 5:13.

21. Ibid.

22. Asim Roy, *The Islamic Syncretistic Tradition in Bengal* (Princeton: Princeton University Press, 1983), p. 201.

23. Karim, *Bauls of Bangladesh,* pp. 122–23.

24. *BBG,* p. 513.

25. Dasgupta and Dasgupta, *Roots in the Void,* p. 43. The Bengali original of this song is in *BBG,* poem 668, p. 1043.

26. Hai and Ud-Din, *Hārāmaṇi,* p. 77.

27. Dasgupta and Dasgupta, *Roots in the Void,* p. 56.

28. Ibid., p. 42.

29. Shashibhushan Dasgupta, *Obscure Religious Cults* (Calcutta: Firma KLM Pvt. Ltd., 1976), p. 80.

30. Ibid., p. 82.

31. Ibid., p. 80.

32. The term used was *asava māta,* mad with wine.

33. The term *bodhicitta* originally referred to a mental state in which wisdom and compassion were united. In the change from Mahāyāna to tantric Buddhism it was redefined, first to mean semen, and then becoming identified with the union of male and female substances and having the nature of the five elements. It is this later, liquid *bodhicitta* which is raised along the spinal cord.

34. Dasgupta, *Obscure Religious Cults,* p. 91.

35. According to the *Guhyasamāja Tantra,* the *bodhicitta* may penetrate the body during intercourse, causing the "dark light" to arise in the "place of the androgynes." The sexual union of "diamond and lotus" destroys the Tathāgatas, or the five states of the womb, used here to mean attachments to form. See Alex Wayman, *Yoga of the Guhyasamājatantra* (Delhi: Motilal Banarsidass, 1977), p. 265.

36. See Edward C. Dimock, *The Place of the Hidden Moon,* (Chicago: University of Chicago Press, 1966), p. 44.

37. Sen, *History of Brajabuli Literature,* p. 341.

38. Ibid., p. 284.

39. *CC* III.19.

40. *BP* 10.33.26.

41. Bhattacarya, *Songs of the Bards of Bengal,* p. 55.

42. Ibid., p. 58.

43. A. N. Sarkar and N. Delmonico, "Two Texts from a Vaiṣṇava Sahajiyā Notebook," manuscript, 1983, p. 72.

44. In Vaiṣṇava literature, the *ujjvala* is the greatest intensity of the *sāttvika vikāras* or *sāttvika bhāvas*.

45. Sarkar and Delmonico, "Two Texts," p. 73.

46. Ibid., p. 79.

47. Ibid., p. 80.

48. Ibid.

49. Quoted in Manindra Mohan Bose, *The Post Caitanya Sahajiya Cult of Bengal* (Calcutta: University of Calcutta, 1930), p. 76.

50. Ibid.

51. Bhattacarya, *Songs of the Bards of Bengal*, p. 109.

52. In Haridāsa Cakravarti, *Saṭīkā Pañcatattva O Jñānāmṛta Kathānam* (Navadvīpa: Devīmādhava Cakravarti, 1983).

53. In Bengali, *gopīkar anukaraṇa korben nā*.

54. Cakravarti, *Satīkā Pancatattva*, p. 43.

55. Interview, in Bākreśwar, 1984.

56. Ibid.

57. Interview, in Ghoshpāra mela, 1984.

58. Interview, in Rādhānāgar, 1984.

59. Bholanath Bhattacarya, "Some Aspects of the Esoteric Cults of Consort Worship in Bengal: A Field Survey Report," *Folklore*, December 1977, pp. 385–97.

60. Most Sahajiyās encountered were male.

61. Ramalakanta Chakraborty, *Vaisnavism in Bengal, 1486–1900* (Calcutta: Sanskrit Pustaka Bhandar, 1985), p. 354.

62. Ibid., p. 369.

63. Ibid., p. 370.

64. Ibid.

65. Ibid., p. 364.

66. Akṣaya Kumār Datta, *Bhāratbarsiya Upasaka Sampradāya* (Calcutta: Pathabhaban Sanskaran, 1376 B.S.), p. 125.

67. Chakraborty, *Vaisnavism in Bengal*, p. 371.

68. Ibid., p. 372.

69. Ibid., p. 373.

70. Ibid., p. 380.

71. Ibid., p. 382.

72. Sudhir Cakravarti, *Sāhebdhanī Sampradāya: Tāder Gān* (Calcutta: Pustak Bepani, 1985), p. 23.

73. Anirvan, *Letters from a Baul*, p. 145.

74. *BBG*, p. 370.

75. *BBG*, p. 371. *Anumān* (*anumāna*) and *bartamān* (*vartamāna*) are only superficially similar.

76. According to Kṛṣṇadāsa Kavirāja in the *Caitanya Caritāmṛta*, this was also Kṛṣṇa's reason for incarnating in Caitanya.

77. Viewing such bodily substances as sacred is not unique to the Bāuls. Ac-

cording to Buddhist tantra (which was prominent in Bengal from approximately the eighth to the twelfth centuries A.D.), the five Dhyāni Buddhas were identified with the five kinds of nectar (*āmṛta*): Ratnasambhava with blood, Amitābha with semen, Amoghasiddhi with flesh, Akṣobhya with urine, and Vairocana with excrement. These substances were used in meditative ritual. See Alex Wayman, "Totemic Beliefs in the Buddhist Tantras," *History of Religions Journal* 1, 1 (1961): 91.

78. In this way, it is similar to the yogic *bhūtajaya,* in which all phenomena are broken down into their elements so that these elements may be understood and rearranged by the yogi's will.

79. In Bengali, *nirvikāra avasthā.*

80. *BBG,* p. 424.

81. Hai and Ud-Din, *Hārāmaṇi,* p. 18.

82. As the buildup of *tapas* could compel Indra, king of the gods, so the buildup of *rajas* can compel Īśvara.

83. *BBG,* pp. 369–437, for a discussion of these forms of *sādhana.*

84. Dās and Mahāpatra, *Lālan Gītikā,* poem 138, p. 94.

85. Ibid., poem 21, p. 15.

86. Hai and Ud-Din, *Hārāmaṇi,* poem 245, p. 148.

87. This flow is believed to have three tastes (bitter, salty, and sweet) and four colors (red, yellow, black, and white). It is called flower (*phul*) by the Bāuls. The blood of a young virgin is called *akhaṇḍa rasa* and is used for healing and long life. See Karim, *Bauls of Bangladesh,* pp. 124, 140.

88. Charles Capwell, "The Esoteric Belief of the Bāuls of Bengal," *Journal of Asian Studies* 33, 2 (1974): 262.

89. *Nīr* and *ksīr* are terms used in traditional Indian erotics. The *ksīra-nīraka* is one of the four embraces, like the mixing of milk and water. It is mentioned in the *Rati-rahasya* and the *Kāmasūtra.* See Rām Kumār Rai, *Encyclopedia of Indian Erotics* (Varanasi: Prachya Prakashan, 1983), p. 81.

90. This literalizes the Vaiṣṇava "drinking of *rasa,*" showing the Bāul to be a true lover or *premika.*

91. Dās and Mahāpatra, *Lālan Gītikā,* poem 37, p. 36.

92. Ibid., poem 34, p. 24.

93. Ibid., poem 172, p. 116.

94. *BBG,* poem 528.

95. Hai and Ud-Din, *Hārāmaṇi,* p. 67.

96. *BBG,* p. 774.

97. Interview, in Calcutta, 1984.

98. Dās and Mahāpatra, *Lālan Gītikā,* poem 380, p. 263.

99. *BBG,* poem 459, p. 867.

100. Dās and Mahāpatra, *Lālan Gītikā,* poem 150, p. 102.

101. *BBG,* poem 107, p. 611.

102. Dās and Mahāpatra, *Lālan Gītikā,* poem 15, pp. 10–11. This paradox is mentioned in several poems—one practices to be spontaneous. It is a topic of debate whether *sādhana* can actually lead to a state of *sahaja* or whether it must come on its own.

103. *BBG,* poem 516, p. 913.

104. *BBG,* poem 614, p. 1007.

Chapter Five

1. Anita Desai, *Voices in the City* (New Delhi: Orient Paperbacks, 1978), p. 120.
2. Ibid., p. 122.
3. The general response of Vaiṣṇava practitioners was a look of amazement, followed by, "A holy woman [*sādhikā*]? Why would you want to speak to one of *them?* Look at all the holy men here—they are much better to speak with." None could or would suggest specific women to interview.
4. Śrī Anirvāṇ, *Letters from a Bāul: Life within Life* (Calcutta: Śrī Aurobindo Pathamandir, 1983), p. 111.
5. Several sources were used for this biography. Ānandamayī Mā's mother, who later became a renunciate, narrated her own biography, along with that of her daughter, in *Svakrīya Svarasāmṛit,* ed. Brahmacarinī Kumārī Chandan Purāṇācārya (Kankhal: Śrī Vīrajānanda Mahārāj, 1981), 2 vols. Many devotees and disciples wrote of Ānandamayī's life and teachings, and perhaps the most vivid descriptions of ecstasy are in Bhaiji, *Mother as Revealed to Me* (Varanasi: Shree Shree Anandamayee Sangha, 1972), and Devotees, *Mā Ānandamayī* (Bhadaini: Ma Anandamayi Asram, 1946).
6. Purāṇācārya, *Svakrīya Svarasāmṛit,* 1: 49.
7. Ibid., 2: 98.
8. Devotees, *Mā Ānandamayī,* p. 166.
9. Purāṇācārya, *Svakrīya Svarasāmṛit,* 2: 23.
10. Devotees, *Mā Ānandamayī,* p. 166. From early on she would speak of her physical self as something different from herself, not as "I" but as "it." She later described her body as a doll, which plays as the viewer wishes it to play.
11. Ibid., p. 172.
12. Ibid., p. 174.
13. She never gave a reason for this refusal, merely saying that she had forgotten how to eat by herself. However, this is common in Indian *sādhu* lore as a sign of the *turīyātīta.* One eats with his mouth without using his hands and is thus called "cow-mouthed one." He has no belongings and regards his body as a corpse. See G. S. Ghurye, *Indian Sadhus* (Bombay: Popular Book Depot, 1953), p. 88.
14. Devotees, *Mā Ānandamayī,* pp. 177–79.
15. Ibid., p. 77.
16. Ibid., p. 188.
17. Bhaiji, *Mother as Revealed to Me,* p. 118.
18. Shyamananda Banerjee, *A Mystic Sage: Mā Ānandamayī* (Calcutta: S. Banerjee, 1973), p. 109.
19. Ibid., p. 135.
20. Gopināth Kavirāj, ed., *Mother as Seen by Her Devotees* (Varanasi: Shree Shree Anandamayee Sangha, 1967), p. 95.
21. Ibid., pp. 148–49.
22. Alexander Lipski, *Life and Teaching of Śrī Ānandamayī Mā* (Delhi: Motilal Banarsidass, 1977), p. 32.
23. Bhaiji, *Sad Vani* (Bhadaini: Shree Shree Ma Anandamayee Charitable Society, 1975), p. 32.
24. Kavirāj, *Mother as Seen by Her Devotees,* p. 94.

25. Gopināth Kavirāj, *Śrī Śrī Mā Ānandamayī: Upadeśa O Praśnottara (Calcutta: Pasyant Prakāśani, 1382* B.S.), p. 1.
26. Ibid., p. 2.
27. Bhaiji, *Sad Vani,* p. 61.
28. Ibid., p. 68.
29. Kavirāj, *Śrī Śrī Mā Ānandamayī,* p. 9.
30. Ibid., p. 10.
31. Atmananda, *The Words of Śrī Ānandamayī Mā* (Varanasi: Sree Sree Anandamayee Charitable Society, 1978), p. 147.
32. Devotees, *Mā Ānandamayī,* pp. 27–29.
33. Narayan Chaudhuri, *That Compassionate Touch of Ma Anandamayee* (Delhi: Motilal Banarsidass, 1980), p. 155.
34. *Matri Vani,* trans. Atmananda (Calcutta: Shree Shree Ananda Mayee Charitable Society, 1982), 1: 152.
35. Major sources for this biography include two detailed accounts of Śāradā's life: Swāmī Gambhirānanda, *Holy Mother Shri Śāradā Devī* (Mylore: Sri Ramakrishna Math, 1969), and Swāmī Tapasyānanda, *Śrī Śāradā Devī: The Holy Mother* (Madras: Sri Ramakrishna Math, 1977). Both authors are swamis of the Rāmakṛṣṇa order.
36. Gambhirānanda, *Holy Mother Shri Śāradā Devī,* p. 49.
37. Ibid., p. 51.
38. Ibid., p. 52.
39. Ibid., p. 137.
40. Ibid., p. 368.
41. Ibid., p. 111.
42. Ibid., p. 112.
43. Ibid., p. 116.
44. Ibid., p. 141.
45. Ibid., p. 143.
46. Ibid.
47. Ibid., p. 115.
48. Tapasyānanda, *Śrī Śāradā Devī,* p. 101.
49. Gambhirānanda, *Holy Mother Shri Śāradā Devī,* p. 329.
50. Tapasyānanda, *Śrī Śāradā Devī,* p. 101.
51. Ibid., p. 133.
52. Ibid., p. 144.
53. Ibid., p. 145.
54. Gambhirānanda, *Holy Mother Shri Sāradā Devī,* p. 174.
55. Ibid., p. 164.
56. Tapasyānanda, *Śrī Śāradā Devī,* p. 209.
57. The major sources for this biography were interviews with Arcanānpuri Mā and several of her disciples.
58. Arcanāpuri Mā, *A Sheaf of Waves,* trans. Jyotsna Nāth Mallik (Calcutta: Sree Satyānanda Devayatan, 1976), p. 20.
59. The sources for this biography were interviews with Lakṣmī Mā.
60. She acted out how they tied her to four stakes, spread-eagled on the

ground, with the fire between her legs. She showed the inside of her thighs, which was a mass of thick scar tissue.

61. A ceremony in memory of the dead, in which rice balls are offered so that the spirit can build a body in which to dwell.

62. Sources for this biography were interviews with Yogeśvarī and several of her disciples.

63. In Bengali, *kayabhedi.*

64. This fire is called *brahmāgni.*

65. Gopināth Kavirāj, *Sādhu Darśana O Sat Prasaṅga* (Calcutta: Himadri Sansad, 1373 B.S.), 2: 140.

66. A. K. Ramanujan, "On Women Saints," in John Stratton Hawley and Donna Marie Wulff, eds., *The Divine Consort: Rādhā and the Goddesses of India* (Berkeley: Religious Studies Series, 1982), p. 316.

67. Gananath Obeyesekere, *Medusa's Hair: An Essay on Personal Symbols and Religious Experience* (Chicago: University of Chicago Press, 1981), p. 78.

68. Interview, in Jadavpur, 1984.

69. L. P. Varma, D. K. Srivastava, and R. N. Sahay, "Possession Syndrome," *Indian Journal of Psychiatry* 12, nos. 1 and 2 (January–April 1970).

70. Ganesh U. Thite, *Medicine: Its Magico-Religious Aspects according to the Vedic and Later Literature* (Poona: Continental, 1982), p. 7. Also see Caraka, Cikitsa 9.20, and Susruta, Uttara 60.8.

71. The dance was described in English.

72. Field notes, Thākurnāgar, 1984.

73. Pradyot K. Maity, *Historical Studies in the Cult of the Goddess Manasa* (Calcutta: Punthi Pustak, 1966), p. 247.

74. Ibid., p. 305.

Chapter Six

1. However, there are ecstatic gurus whose approach may be characterized as "Do as I say, not as I do." Such gurus will themselves act in an extreme manner, but tell their disciples not to do so, that they are not ready, not worthy, or not capable of following such a difficult path.

2. Defense of the guru is widespread. On a Calcutta train I spoke to the people sitting near me about *bhāva* and gurus. Within three stops, virtually the entire train car was arguing about the techniques, sincerity, and general superiority of their own gurus in comparison to others.

3. Stories were told by informants of the heroic resistance of saints and of their own gurus in such situations. Some saints simply ignored the testing, others became immaterial and dissolved into vapor, yet others later took revenge on their tormentors.

4. See the biographies of Vāmākṣepā, Gaur Kiśora, Vijayakṛṣṇa Goswāmin, and the chapter on Bāuls.

5. In Bengali, *pramāṇīkrita* or *phalita.*

6. See Jñānendramohan Dāsa, ed., *Bāngālā Bhāṣār Abhidhān* (Calcutta: Sahitya Sansad, 1979).

7. Women who desire children normally avoid barren women.

8. Interview, in Navadvīpa, 1983.

9. *Tripurarahasyam* (*Jñānakhaṇḍam*), with the commentary of Śrīnivāsa, ed. Gopīnāth Kavirāja (Varanasi: Sarasvatī Bhāvana Granthamālā, 1965), XIX.82–83, 86.

10. Ibid., XIX.97–102. The Rāma mentioned here is Paraśurāma, famed for his ability as a warrior.

11. Bulusu Venkateswarulu, *Lives of Ancient Indian Saints* (Gandhinagar: B. Venkateswarulu, 1981), 4:44.

12. For a discussion of liquid metaphors in Vedic and post-Vedic India, see Wendy O'Flaherty, "Sexual Fluids," in *Women, Androgynes, and Other Mythical Beasts* (Chicago: University of Chicago Press, 1986).

13. These were described by the ecstatics, but not witnessed by any disciples.

14. Michael Williams, "Charisma and Sacred Biography," *Journal of the American Academy of Religion* 48, nos. 3–4 (1982): 4.

15. Sobharani Basu, *Modern Indian Mysticism: A Comparative and Critical Study* (Varanasi: Bharat Sadhana Publications, 1974), p. 337.

16. These themes may be found in B. Venkateswarulu's series of hagiographies from the epics and puranas, *Lives of Ancient Indian Saints*, virtually all of which follow the ritual pattern. This pattern is also widespread among shorter biographies of gurus, saints, "godmen," swamis, and the like.

17. See especially Max Lüther, "Function and Significance of the Folktale," in *The European Folktale: Form and Nature*, trans. John D. Niles (Philadelphia: Institute for the Study of Human Issues, 1982).

18. Lüthi here is more extreme than many folklorists, who find a wide range of belief expected for legend.

19. Lüthi, *European Folktale*, p. 99.

20. See the story of Phakir Chand in Lal Behari Dey, *Folk Tales of Bengal* (London: Macmillan, 1883). The other stories mentioned in this paragraph are also from Dey's book.

21. See Stith Thompson and Jonas Balys, *The Oral Tales of India* (Bloomington: Indiana University Press, 1958), for a motif index of Indian folktales.

22. E. B. Cowell et al., trans., *The Jātaka* (Cambridge: Cambridge University Press, 1895–1907), 1–6: 489.

23. Interview, in Śāntiniketan, 1984. This echoes the primordial sacrifice of Puruṣa, through which humanity was created.

24. However, it is rare that an exorcist allows himself to become possessed. There is a Bengali proverb for a person who is supposed to help one out of a difficult situation and turns out to be in the same situation: "the *ojhā* is [himself] possessed by a *bhūta*."

25. Field notes, Chilkigor, 1984.

26. Many actions of the ecstatics echo actions of the gods: turning blue like Śiva or gold like Rādhā or Caitanya; alternating passion and detachment, like Śiva; madly leaping and dancing; possessing clairvoyance and telepathic powers, inspired speech. These ecstasies relate *bhakti* saints to other religious figures: sages, yogis, ancient holy women (*brahmavādinīs*), exorcists, and liberated sages (*jivanmuktas*).

27. Kṛṣṇadāsa Kavirāja, *Govinda-līlāmṛtām* (Navadvīpa: Haribol Kuthir, 463 Gaurābda), 10.16.

28. In the sixth chapter of the *Murali Vilāsa,* Jahnava Thākuranī states, "Everyone [in Vṛndāvana] is equal to Rādhā, only their bodies are different. One breath, one self [*ātman*], all are expansions [*tantra*] of Rādhā. At the time of enjoyment [*sambhoga*] the couple experience the heightening of joy, and the gooseflesh on Rādhā's body appears on (the bodies of the) *sakhīs*. Her friends experience seven times as much pleasure as Rādhā does. [But] when Rādhā, on some excuse, causes one of her friends to meet [with Kṛṣṇa], she experiences ten million times more pleasure than does her friend." This is quoted in Kuñjabihārīdāsa Bābājī, *Mañjarī svarūpa nirupaṇa* (Rādhākuṇḍa: Śrī Kṛṣṇa Caitanya Śāstra Mandir, 489 Gaurābda), pp. 9–10. The inconsistencies in the amount of the *mañjarīs'* pleasure between the *Govinda-līlāmṛtām* and this text doubtless show the difficulties of comparative quantifying of nonphysical enjoyment.

29. See Alain Danielou, *Les fous de Dieu: Contes gangetiques* (Paris: Editions Buchet/Chastel, 1975).

30. See the section in this book on Arcanāpurī Mā.

31. See Atindra Majumder, *The Caryapadas* (Calcutta: Naya Prokash, 1967). Note especially poems 9 and 28.

32. Annemarie Schimmel, *The Mystical Dimension of Islam* (Chapel Hill: University of North Carolina Press, 1975), p. 19.

33. The word *majnūn* is related to *jinn*—a madman is like one who is possessed by a *jinn*. The term *divana* or *deoyana* is also derived from possession—in this case by a *div* or *daiva* (demon).

34. See Nizami, *Layla and Majnūn,* trans. R. Gelpke (Boulder, Colo.: Shambhala, 1978).

35. See Sheldon Pollock, "Rāma's Madness," in *Wiener Zeitschrift für die Kunde Südasiens und Archiv für indische Philosophie,* vol. 29 (Leiden: Brill, 1985). Seeking to find the lost beloved by questioning nature is also seen in the gopīs of the *Bhāgavata Purāṇa.*

36. The story of Śiva and Satī is in the *Kālīkā Purāṇa,* XVIII.1, and the *Devī Bhāgavata Purāṇa,* II.40.

37. Archer Taylor, *Comparative Studies in Folklore* (Taipei: Orient Cultural Service, 1972), pp. 267–74.

38. *Mahābhārata* XIII.40.56–57, quoted by Mircea Eliade, *Yoga: Immortality and Freedom* (Princeton: Princeton University Press, 1969), p. 79.

39. Ibid., p. 335.

40. I am indebted to Prakash Desai for a detailed discussion of the dynamics of introjection.

41. See Nathaniel Ross, "Affect as Cognition: With Observations on the Meaning of Mystical States," *International Review of Psychoanalysis* 2, 1 (1975).

42. Sudhir Kakar, "Reflections on Psychoanalysis, Indian Culture and Mysticism," *Journal of Indian Philosophy* 10 (1982): 289–97.

43. Philip Woollcott, Jr., and Prakash Desai, "Religious and Creative States of Illumination: A Psychological Perspective," typescript.

44. There is some disagreement as to whether or not Gaur Kiśora initiated

Bhaktisiddhānta as his disciple. Whatever the case, Bhaktisiddhānta considered himself to be Kiśora's disciple and to be honoring both Gaur Kiśora and Vaiṣṇavism by the Gauḍīya Math literature.

45. See Chintaharan Chakravarti, *Tantras: Studies on Their Religion and Literature* (Calcutta: Punthi Pustak, 1963), p. 92, on public worship of Kālī.

46. One such acceptable view of this process is Kris's "regression in the service of the ego."

47. See Jay R. Greenberg and Stephan A. Mitchell, *Object Relations in Psychoanalytic Theory* (Cambridge: Harvard University Press, 1983), pp. 210–17.

Appendix A

1. Mircea Eliade, *Yoga: Immortality and Freedom* (Princeton: Princeton University Press, 1969), p. 80.

2. These states are *vitarka, vicāra, ānanda,* and *asmitā.*

3. In yogic thought, Īśvara is a soul that has never been incarnated and that may on occasion help other souls striving for liberation.

4. Eliade, *Yoga,* p. 80.

5. Vijñānabhikṣu, a commentator on Patañjali's *Yoga Sūtras,* compares these two:

> For him, the *upāyapratyaya,* the "artificial" method (in the sense that it is not "natural," that it is a construction), consists in practising *saṃyama* on Īśvara, or, if one has no mystical vocation, on one's own Self; this is the method commonly employed by yogins. As to the second way, the "natural" method (*bhāvapratyaya*), some yogins can obtain undifferentiated enstasis (and hence final liberation) simply by desiring it; in other words, it is no longer a conquest achieved by technical means, it is a spontaneous operation; it is called *bhāva,* birth (*bhāva*) of the beings who obtain it ("birth" meaning birth at a propitious hour, as a result of having practiced Yoga in a previous existence). (Quoted in Eliade, *Yoga,* p. 92)

6. S. N. Dasgupta, *Yoga as Philosophy and Religion* (Delhi: Motilal Banarsidass, 1978), p. 157.

Appendix B

1. *BRS* II.2.1–2.

2. In Ayurvedic thought this pure spirit is called *sattva guṇa.*

3. Writers of *alaṅkāraśāstra,* Sanskrit rhetoricians, drama critics, and aestheticians have also written on the *sāttvika bhāvas.* Texts include the *Sāhityadarpaṇa* of Viśvanātha Kavirāja, the *Nāṭyaśāstra* of Bharatamuni, the *Bhāvaprakāśa* of Śāradatanaya, the *Rasārṇavasudhākara* of Śiṅga Bhūpāla, and the *Saṅgīta-Ratnākara* of Śārṅgadeva.

4. *BRS* II.3.1–2.

5. *BRS* II.3.64–80.

6. Rūpa Gosvāmin, *Śrī Śrī Ujjvala-Nīlamaṇi* (Navadvīpa: Haridāsa Dāsa, 497 Gaurābda), 115. Edited in Bengali translation by Viṣṇudāsa Gosvāmin.

7. In Bengali, *svataḥsiddha.*

8. Gosvāmin, *Ujjvala-Nīlamani,* p. 120.
9. Ibid., p. 122.
10. *BRS* I.2.272.
11. A large number of Vaiṣṇava *sādhus* warned against false (*nakal*) *sādhus* who would imitate the *bhāvas* of others. Sometimes there would be a positive side ("counterfeit gold proves the existence of real gold"), but generally such falsification was attributed to the influence of the Kālī Yuga.
12. Thakur Bhaktivinode, *Jaiva Dharma* (Madras: Gaudiya Math, 1975), p. 398.

Appendix C

1. Candrakānta calls it strengthened perception through the sense organs, purified by unguents.
2. Jadunath Sinha, *Indian Epistemology of Perception* (Calcutta: Jadunath Sinha Foundation, 1969), pp. 128–33.
3. Each *pīṭha* is believed to hold a limb of Satī, the Śakti of Śiva. The person thus places the limbs of Satī within himself.

Bibliography

Bengali and Sanskrit Sources

Bandyopādhyāyā, Subodh Kumār. *Tārāpīṭha Bhairava.* Calcutta: Vāṁadeva Sangha, 1396 B.S.

Bhagiratha, Śrī. *Śrī Śrī Vāmākṣepā.* Calcutta: N. Talukdar, n.d.

Bhaṭṭācārya, Satyanārāyaṇa. *Rāmprasāda: Jīvani O Racanasamagra.* Calcutta: Śrī Dharmadāsa Samanta, 1975.

Bhaṭṭācārya, Upendranāth. *Bānglār Bāul O Bāul Gān.* Calcutta: Orient Book Co, 1388 B.S.

Biswas, Dilip. "Rāmmohan Rāya Dharmmata Tantraśāstra." *Viśvabhāratī Patrikā,* no. 4 (1367 B.S.): 234–36.

Brahmacārī, Śrīmat Kuladānanda. *Ācārya Prasaṅga.* Calcutta: Sansad Prakāśani, 1383 B.S.

———. *Śrī Śrī Sad Guru Saṅgha.* Calcutta: Sansad Prakāśani, 1388 B.S.

Cakravartī, Gangeścandra. *Bānglār Sādhaka.* Vol. 1. Calcutta: Nabendu Cakravartī, 1379 B.S.

Cakravartī, Haridāsa, ed. *Saṭīkā Pañcatattva O Jñānāmṛta Kathā.* Navadvīpa: Devīmādhava Cakravartī, 1383 B.S.

Cakravartī, Jahnavikumār. *Śāktapadāvalī O Śaktisādhana.* Calcutta: D. M. Library, 1367 B.S.

Cakravartī, Narahari. *Śrī Śrī Bhakti-Ratnākara.* Calcutta: Gauḍīya Mission, 1967.

Cakravartī, Sudhir. *Sāhebdhanī Sampradāya: Tāder Gān.* Calcutta: Pustak Bipani, 1985.

Cattopadhyaya, Pramode Kumār. *Tantrābhilāṣīr Sādhusaṅgha.* Calcutta: Mitra and Ghosh, 1390 B.S.

Dāsa, Haridāsa. *Śrī Śrī Gauḍīya Vaiṣṇava Jīvanī.* Vol. 2. Navadvīpa: Haribol Kuṭhir, 465 Gaurābda.

Dāsa, Jñānendramohan. *Bāṅglā Bhāṣār Abhidhān.* Calcutta: Sāhitya Sansad, 1979.

Dāsa, Matilāl, and P. K. Mahāpatra, eds. *Lālan Gītikā.* Calcutta: University of Calcutta, 1958.

Dāsa, Vṛndāvana. *Caitanya Bhāgavata.* Ed. Sukumar Sen. New Delhi: Sāhitya Akademi, 1982.

Datta, Akṣaya Kumār. *Bhāratavarṣīya Upāsaka Sampradāya.* Calcutta: Pathabhāvana Saṅskārana, 1376 B.S.

Gosvāmin, Rūpa. *Śrī Śrī Bhaktirasāmṛta-sindhu.* Ed. with a Bengali translation by Haridāsa Dāsa, with commentaries *Durgasaṁgamanī-ṭīkā* of Jīva Gosvāmin, *Artharatnālpadīpikā* of Mukundadāsa Gosvāmin, and *Bhaktisārapradarśinī-ṭīkā* of Viśvanātha Cakravartin. Navadvīpa: Haribol Kuṭhir, 495 Gaurābda.

———. *Śrī Śrī Ujjvala-Nīlamaṇi.* Ed. with a Bengali translation. Navadvīpa: Haridāsa Dāsa, Gaurābda 497.

Gosvāmin, Sanātana. *Śrī Śrī Bṛhad Bhāgavatāmṛtam.* Bengali *pāyar* translation by Kanāi Dāsa. Navadvīpa: Haridāsa Dāsa, n.d.

Hai, M. A., and M. Mansur Ud-Din. *Hārāmaṇi.* Vol. 5. Dacca: Dacca University Press, 1961.

Kālī Tantra. Ed. Paṇḍit Nityānanda Smṛtitīrtha. Sanskrit text, with Bengali translation. Calcutta: Nababhārata Publishing, 1388 B.S.

Kāmākhyā Tantra. Ed. Jyotirlāl Dāsa. Sanskrit text, with Bengali translation and commentary. Calcutta: Nababhārata Publishers, 1385 B.S.

Kavirāja, Gopināth. *Sādhu Darśana O Sat Prasaṅga.* Vol. 2. Calcutta: Himadri Sansad, 1373 B.S.

———. *Śrī Śrī Mā Ānandamayī—Upadeśa O Praśnottara.* Calcutta: Pasyant Prakāśani, 1382 B.S.

Kavirāja, Kṛṣṇadāsa. *Śrī Śrī Caitanya Caritāmṛta.* Ed. Sukumar Sen. New Delhi: Sāhitya Akademi, 1977.

Kulārnava Tantra. Ed. Upendrakumār Dāsa. Sanskrit text, with Bengali translation and commentary. Calcutta: Nababhārata Publishers, 1383 B.S.

Māyā Tantra. Ed. Jyotirlāl Dāsa. Calcutta: Nababhārata Publishers, 1385 B.S.

Prajñānanda, Swāmī. "Śrīrāmprasāder Gāne Jīvan-Anubhūti." In Debasis Mitra, ed., *Sādhaka Rāmprasād.* Calcutta: Adhyayana, n.d.

Rāya, Āmarendranātha, ed. *Śākta Padāvalī (Cayana).* Calcutta: Calcutta University, 1957.

Rudrayāmala Tantra. Ed. Bhagiratha Prasāda Tripathi Vāgīśaśāstri. Yogitantra-Granthamālā, no. 7. Vārāṇāsī: Sampūrṇānanda Sanskrit Viśvavidyālaya, 1980.

Sarasvatī, Nigamānanda. *Māyer Kṛpā.* Halisahar: Swāmī Ātmānanda, Saraswatī Math, 1382 B.S.

Tārā Tantram. Ed. A. K. Maitra. Rajshahi: Varendra Research Society, 1913.

English Translations of Vaiṣṇava and Śākta Texts

Bhāgavata Purāṇa. Trans. V. Tagore. Ancient Indian Tradition and Mythology Series. Delhi: Motilal Banarsidass, 1987.

Bhaktivinode Thākur, Sacidānanda. *Shri Chaitanya Shikshāmṛtam.* Trans. Bijoykrisna Rarhi. Navadvipa: Sree Gaudiya Math, 1983.

———. *Jaiva Dharma.* Madras: Sree Gaudiya Math, 1975.

Devī Māhātmya or Śrī Durgā-Saptaśatī. Trans. Swāmī Jagadīśvarānanda. Madras: Ramakrishna Math, 1955.

Gosvāmin, Sanātana. *Śrī Bṛihad Bhagavatāmṛtam.* Trans. Bhakti Vilās Tīrtha Gosvāmin. Madras: Sree Gaudiya Math, 1975.

Kavirāj, Kṛṣṇadāsa. "Caitanya Caritāmṛta." Trans. Edward C. Dimock. Typescript, 1985.

Kulārnava Tantra. Ed. Arthur Avalon [John Woodroffe]. Madras: Ganesh, 1965.

Mahānirvāṇa Tantra. Trans. and ed. Arthur Avalon [John Woodroffe] as *The Tantra of Great Liberation.* London: Luzac, 1913.

Maharāj, Śrīyukta Śiva Candra Vidyārṇava Bhaṭṭācārya. *Tantra-Tattva.* Trans. John Woodroffe as *Principles of Tantra.* Madras: Ganesh, 1978.

Murthy, C. Suryanarayana. *Śrī Lalitā Sahasranāma.* Bombay: Bharatiya Vidya Bhavan, 1975.

Nārada. *Bhakti Sūtras.* Trans. Swāmī Tyagisānanda. Madras: Śrī Rāmakṛṣṇa Math, 1978.

Pāśupata Sūtram, with the *Padārtha-Bhāṣya* of Kaundinya. Trans. Haripada Chakraborti. Calcutta: Academic Publishers, 1970.

Śaṅkarācārya. *Saundaryalaharī* (The ocean of divine beauty). Trans. V. K. Subramanian. Delhi: Motilal Banarsidass, 1977.

Sen, Rāmprasād. *Grace and Mercy in Her Wild Hair: Selected Poems to the Mother Goddess.* Trans. Leonard Nathan and Clinton Seely. Boulder, Colo.: Great Eastern, 1982.

The Serpent Power, Being the Sat Cakra Nirupana and Paduka Pancaka. Trans. John Woodroffe. Madras: Ganesh, 1964.

Sinha, Jadunath, ed. *Ramprasada's Devotional Songs.* Calcutta: Sinha Publishing, 1966.

Sree Kaalee Sahasranama. Trans. Premlata Paliwal. Delhi: Nilima Harjal, 1979.

Vijñānānanda, Swāmī, trans. *Śrī Mad Devī Bhāgavatam.* Allahabad: Bhuvaneśwarī Āśrama, n.d.

Warrier, A. G. Krishna, trans. *The Śākta Upaniṣads.* Madras: Adyar Library and Research Centre, 1967.

Biographies in Translation

Atmananda. *The Words of Sri Anandamayi Ma.* Varanasi: Sree Sree Anandamayee Charitable Society, 1978.

Bannerji, Shyamananda. *A Mystic Sage: Ma Anandamayi.* Calcutta: S. Bannerji, 1973.

Bannerjee, S. K. *Śrī Śrī Bāmā Kṣepā.* Calcutta: Sri Byomkesh Bysack, 1971.

Bhaiji. *Mother as Revealed to Me.* Benares: Shree Shree Anandamayi Sangha, 1972.

———. *Sad Vani.* Bhadaini: Shree Shree Ma Anandamayee Charitable Society, 1978.

Chaudhuri, Narayan. *That Compassionate Touch of Ma Anandamayee.* Delhi: Motilal Banarsidass, 1980.

Chaudhuri, Pramathanath. *Ramprasad and Western Man.* Calcutta: Gautam Mallick, 1976.

Das, Bishnu Charan. *Life of Vijaykrishna.* Benares: Sree Sree Bijaykrishna Muth, 1940.

Devotees. *Ma Anandamayi.* Bhadaini: Ma Anandamayi Asram, 1946.

Gambhirananda, Swami. *Holy Mother Shri Sarada Devi.* Mylore: Sri Ramakrishna Math, 1969.

Ghosh, Navadwip Chandra. *The Life and Teachings of Śrī Śrī Prabhu Jagadbandhu.* Calcutta: Mahauddharana Granthalaya, 1973.

Gupta, Mahandranath. *Rāmakṛṣṇa Kathāmṛta.* Trans. Swami Nikhilananda as *The Gospel of Sri Ramakrishna,* 2 vols. Mylapore: Sri Ramakrishna Math, 1980.

Kaviraj, Gopinath, ed. *Mother as Seen by Her Devotees.* Varanasi: Shree Shree Anandamayi Sangha, 1967.

Lipski, Alexander. *The Life and Teaching of Sri Anandamayi Ma.* Delhi: Motilal Banarsidass, 1977.

Mookerjee, Nanda. *Sri Sarada Devi: Consort of Sri Ramakrsna.* Calcutta: Firma KLM, 1978.

Mueller, F. Max. *Ramakrishna: His Life and Sayings.* Ed. Nanda Mookerjee. Calcutta: S. Gupta and Brothers, 1974.

Nandy, Atal Behary. *Pagal Haranath.* Calcutta: Chintaharan Ghosh Gooha, 1915.

Nityapadanda Abadhuta, Srimat Swami. *Śrī Śrī Nityagopāl.* Nabadwip: Mahanirvan Math, 1948.

Puranacharya, Brahmacharini Kumari Chandan. *Svakrīyā Svarasāmrita.* Hardwar: Shree Virajanandji Maharaj, 1983.

Rolland, Romain. *The Life of Ramakrishna.* Calcutta: Advaita Asram, 1960.

Saradananda, Swami. *Śrī Śrī Rāmakṛṣṇa Līlā-Prasaṅga.* Trans. Swami Jagadananda as *Sri Ramakrishna: The Great Master.* Mylapore: Sri Ramakrishna Math, 1952.

Sastri, A. R. *Lord Haranath.* Vol. 1. *Adi-Lila.* Bishnupur: Girija Shankar Ghar, 1970.

———. *Lord Haranath.* Vol. 2. *Madhya-Lila.* Calcutta: G. S. Ghar and A. R. Sastri, 1971.

———. *Lord Haranath.* Vol. 3. *Antya-Lila.* Calcutta: G. S. Ghar and A. R. Sastri, 1971.

———, ed. *Upadeshamrita* (The divine voice of Śrī Śrī Thākur Haranāth). Rajahmundry: A. R. Sastri, 1965.

Sengupta, Jyotirindranath. *Nityagopal: A Superb Spiritual Teacher.* Calcutta: Sri Dhiresh Sen, 1372 B.S.

Tapasyananda, Swami. *Sri Sarada Devi: The Holy Mother.* Madras: Sri Ramakrishna Math, 1977.

Sources in English and French

Anirvan, Sri. *Letters from a Baul: Life within Life.* Calcutta: Aurobindo Pathamandir, 1983.

Arcanapuri Ma. *Katakgulo Ḍheu.* Trans. Jyotsna Nath Mallik as *A Sheaf of Waves.* Calcutta: Sree Satyananda Devayatan, 1976.

Bagchi, Subhendugopal. *Eminent Indian Sakta Centres in Eastern India.* Calcutta: Punthi Pustak, 1980.

Bannerji, S. C. *Tantra in Bengal.* Calcutta: Naya Prakash, 1978.

Basu, Sobharani. *Modern Indian Mysticism.* Vols. 1–3. Varanasi: Bharat Sadhana Publishers, 1974.

Bhaktivinode Thakur, Saccidananda, and Bhaktisiddhanta Saraswati. *Vaisnavism and Nam-Bhajan.* Ed. Bhakti Vilas Tirtha Goswami Maharaj. Madras: Sri Gaudiya Math, 1968.

Bhattacarya, Bholanath. "Some Aspects of Esoteric Cults of Consort Worship in Bengal: A Field Survey Report." *Folklore,* December 1977, 385–97.

Bhattacarya, Deben, trans. *Songs of the Bards of Bengal.* New York: Grove Press, 1969.

Bhaṭṭācārya, Deborah. "Madness as Entropy: A Bengali View." In Clinton B. Seely, ed., *Women, Politics and Literature in Bengal.* East Lansing: Asian Studies Center, Michigan State University, 1981.

Bhattacarya, Narendranath. *History of the Śākta Religion.* New Delhi: Munshiram Manoharlal, 1973.

———. *History of the Tantric Religion.* New Delhi: Manohar, 1982.

Blackford, Frank. "Belief and Psychotherapy in Benares." Ph.D. dissertation, University of Pennsylvania. Ann Arbor: University Microfilms, 1979.

Bose, Manindra Mohan. *The Post-Caitanya Sahajiā Cult.* Calcutta: University of Calcutta, 1930.

Capwell, Charles. "The Esoteric Belief of the Bauls of Bengal." *Journal of Asian Studies* 33, 2 (1974): 255–64.

Chakraborty, Ramalakanta. *Vaisnavism in Bengal, 1486–1900.* Calcutta: Sanskrit Pustaka Bhandar, 1985.

Chakravarty, Chintaharan. *Tantras: Studies on Their Religion and Literature.* Calcutta: Punthi Pustak, 1963.

Choudhury, P. C. Roy. *Temples and Legends of Bengal.* Bombay: Bharatiya Vidya Bhavan, 1967.

Collins, Alfred, and Prakash Desai. "Selfhood and Context: Some Indian Solutions." Typescript.

Daniélou, Alain. *Les fous de Dieu: Contes gangétiques.* Paris: Editions Buchet/Chastel, 1975.

Das, Raghava Caitanya. *The Divine Name.* Bombay: R. C. Das, 1954.

Dasgupta, Alokeranjan, and Mary Ann Dasgupta. *Roots in the Void: Baul Songs of Bengal.* Calcutta: K. P. Bagchi, 1977.

Dasgupta, Shashibhushan. *Obscure Religious Cults.* Calcutta: Firma KLM, 1976.

Dasgupta, Surendranath. *Yoga as Philosophy and Religion.* Delhi: Motilal Banarsidass, 1978.

Datta, Bhupendranath, trans. *The Mystic Tales of the Lama Taranatha.* Calcutta: Ramakrishna Math, 1944.

De, Sushil Kumar. *Early History of the Vaisnava Faith and Movement in Bengal, from Sanskrit and Bengali Sources.* Calcutta: Firma KLM, 1961.

Desai, Anita. *Voices in the City.* New Delhi: Orient Paperbacks, 1978.

Deussen, Paul. *The Philosophy of the Upanishads.* Trans. A. S. Geden. New York: Dover Publications, 1966.

Deutsch, Eliot, trans. *The Bhagavad Gītā.* New York: Holt, Rinehart and Winston, 1968.

Deutsch, Helene. "Some Forms of Emotional Disturbances and Their Relation to Schizophrenia." In *Neuroses and Character Types: Clinical Psychoanalytic Studies.* New York: International Universities Press, 1965.

Devereux, George. *Basic Problems of Ethnopsychiatry.* Trans. B. Gulati and G. Devereux. Chicago: University of Chicago Press, 1980.

Dimock, Edward C. "The Place of Gauracandrikā in Bengali Vaiṣṇava Lyrics." *Journal of the American Oriental Society* 78, 3 (1958): 153–69.

———. *The Place of the Hidden Moon.* Chicago: University of Chicago Press, 1966.

Dimock, Edward C., Edwin Gerow, C. M. Naim, A. K. Ramanujan, Gordon Roadarmel, and J. A. B. van Buitenen. *The Literatures of India: An Introduction.* Chicago: University of Chicago Press, 1974.

Eliade, Mircea. *Yoga: Immortality and Freedom.* Princeton: Princeton University Press, 1969.

Ewens, G. F. W. *Insanity in India: Its Symptoms and Diagnosis.* Calcutta: Thacker, Spink, 1908.

Foucault, Michel. *Mental Illness and Psychology.* Trans. M. Sheridan. New York: Harper Colophon Books, 1976.

Freud, Sigmund. "The Theme of the Three Caskets." In James Strachey, ed., *The Standard Edition of the Complete Psychological Works of Sigmund Freud.* Vol. 12. London: Hogarth Press, 1962.

Freud, Sigmund, and Josef Breuer. *Studies on Hysteria.* Ed. and trans. James Strachey. New York: Avon Books, 1966.

Gerow, Edwin. *Indian Poetics.* Vol. 4 of *A History of Indian Literature.* Ed. Jan Gonda. Wiesbaden: Otto Harrassowitz, 1977.

———. "Rasa as a Category of Literary Criticism." In Rachel Baumer and James Brandon, eds., *Sanskrit Drama in Performance,* pp. 226–57. Honolulu: University Press of Hawaii, 1981.

Ghosh, J. C. *Bengali Literature.* London: Oxford University Press, 1948.

Ghurye, G. S. *Indian Sadhus.* Bombay: Popular Book Depot, 1953.

Gonda, Jan. *Vision of the Vedic Poets.* The Hague: Mouton, 1963.

Goudriaan, Teun, and Sanjukta Gupta. *Hindu Tantric and Śākta Literature.* Ed. Jan Gonda. *History of Indian Literature.* Wiesbaden: Otto Harrassowitz, 1981.

Greenberg, Jay R., and Stephen A. Mitchell. *Objects Relations in Psychoanalytic Theory.* Cambridge: Harvard University Press, 1983.

Gupta, Sanjukta, R. Hoens, and Teun Goudriaan. *Hindu Tantrism.* Leiden: E. J. Brill, 1979.

Haq, Muhammed Enamul. *A History of Sufism in Bengal.* Dacca: Asiatic Society of Bangladesh, 1975.

Hardy, Friedhelm. *Viraha Bhakti: The Early History of Kṛṣṇa Devotion in South India.* Delhi: Oxford University Press, 1983.

Hiriyanna, M. *Outlines of Indian Philosophy.* London: George Allen and Unwin, 1932.

Hume, R. E., trans. *The Thirteen Principal Upanisads.* Madras: Oxford University Press, 1965.

Ingalls, Daniel H. "Cynics and Pāśupatas: The Seeking of Dishonor." *Harvard Theological Review* 55, 3 (1962): 281–98.

Jung, C. G. *The Structure and Dynamics of the Psyche.* Bollingen Series. New York: Pantheon Books, 1960.

Kakar, Sudhir. *Shamans, Mystics and Doctors: A Psychological Inquiry into India and Its Healing Traditions.* Boston: Beacon Press, 1982.

———, ed. Identity and Adulthood. Delhi: Oxford University Press, 1982.

Kapoor, O. B. L. *The Philosophy and Religion of Śrī Caitanya.* Delhi: Munshiram Manoharlal, 1977.

Karim, Anwarul. *The Bauls of Bangladesh*. Kushtia: Lalan Academy, 1980.

Kinsley, David. "Through the Looking Glass." *History of Religions Journal* 13, no. 4 (May 1974).

Lalye, P. G. *Studies in the Devī Bhāgavata*. Bombay: Popular Prakashan, 1973.

Laski, Marghanita. *Ecstasy: A Study of Some Secular and Religious Experiences*. Bloomington: Indiana University Press, 1961.

Law, Narendra Nath. *Śrī Kṛṣṇa and Śrī Caitanya*. London: Luzac, 1949.

Leff, Julian. *Psychiatry around the Globe: A Transcultural View*. New York: Marcel Dekker, 1981.

Lewis, I. M. *Ecstatic Religion: An Anthropological Study of Spirit Possession and Shamanism*. Harmondsworth: Penguin Books, 1975.

Lupsa, Michele, trans. *Chants à Kali de Ramprasad*. Pondichery: Institut Francais d'Indologie, 1967.

Lutgendorf, Philip. "Kṛṣṇa Caitanya and His Companions, as presented in the *Bhaktamālā* of Nābhā Jī and the *Bhaktirasabodhinī* of Priya Dāsa." Typescript.

Mahapatra, P. K. *The Folk-Cults of Bengal*. Calcutta: Indian Publications, 1972.

Maity, Pradyot K. *Historical Studies in the Cult of the Goddess Manasa*. Calcutta: Punthi Pustak, 1966.

Majumdar, A. K. *Caitanya: His Life and Doctrine*. Bombay: Bharatiya Vidya Bhavan, 1969.

Masson, J. Moussaieff. *The Oceanic Feeling: The Origins of the Religious Sentiment in Ancient India*. Dordrecht: De Reidel Publishers, 1980.

Nityapadanda Avadhuta, Sri Srimat. *The Philosophy of Union by Devotion*. Navadvip: Mahanirban Math, 1953.

Obeyesekere, Gananath. *Medusa's Hair: An Essay on Personal Symbols and Religious Experience*. Chicago: University of Chicago Press, 1981.

O'Flaherty, Wendy Doniger. *Women, Androgynes, and Other Mythical Beasts*. Chicago: University of Chicago Press, 1982.

Pott, P. H. *Yoga and Yantra: Their Interrelation and Their Significance for Indian Archaeology*. The Hague: Martinus Nijhoff, 1966.

Rai, Ram Kumar. *Encyclopedia of Indian Erotics*. Varanasi: Prachya Prakashan, 1983.

Ramanujan, A. K., trans. *Hymns for the Drowning*. Princeton: Princeton University Press, 1981.

———. "On Women Saints." In John Stratton Hawley and Donna Marie Wulff, eds., *The Divine Consort: Rādhā and the Goddesses of India*. Berkeley: Religious Studies Series, 1982.

———. *Speaking of Śiva*. Harmondsworth: Penguin Books, 1985.

Reynolds, Frank, and Donald Capps, eds. *The Biographical Process: Studies in the History and Psychology of Religion*. The Hague: Mouton, 1976.

Rouget, Gilbert. *Music and Trance: A Theory of the Relations between Music and Possession*. Chicago: University of Chicago Press, 1985.

Roy, Asim. *The Islamic Syncretistic Tradition in Bengal*. Princeton: Princeton University Press, 1983.

Roy, Manisha. *Bengali Women*. Chicago: University of Chicago Press, 1975.

Sargant, William. *The Mind Possessed: A Physiology of Possession, Mysticism and Faith Healing.* New York: Penguin Books, 1975.

Sarkar, A. N., and N. Delmonico. "Two Texts from a Vaiṣṇava Sahajiyā Notebook." Typescript.

Sen, R. S. Dineschandra. *Folk Literature of Bengal.* Calcutta: University of Calcutta, 1920.

Sen, Sukumar. *A History of Brajabuli Literature.* Calcutta: University of Calcutta, 1935.

Sharma, R. K., and Vaidya P. Dash, trans. *Caraka Saṃhitā.* Vol. 2. Varanasi: Chowkhamba Orientalia, 1983.

Sinha, Jadunath. "The Bhagavata Religion." In Haridas Bhattacarya, ed., *The Cultural Heritage of India,* vol. 4. Calcutta: Ramakrishna Mission, 1956.

———. *Cult of Divine Power: Śakti Sādhana.* Calcutta: J. Sinha Foundation, 1977.

———. *Indian Epistemology of Perception.* Calcutta: J. Sinha Foundation, 1969.

———. *Indian Psychology, Emotion and Will.* Vol. 2. Calcutta: J. Sinha Foundation, 1961.

Sivananda, Swami. *Kundalini Yoga.* Sivanandanagar: Divine Life Society, 1971.

Srikantamurthy, K. R. *Clinical Methods in Āyurveda.* Delhi: Chowkhambha Orientalia, 1983.

Stewart, Tony. "Perceptions of the Divine: The Biographies of Caitanya." Ph.D. dissertation, University of Chicago, 1985.

Thite, Ganesh U. *Medicine: Its Magico-religious Aspects according to the Vedic and Later Literature.* Poona: Continental, 1982.

Varma, L. P., D. K. Srivastava, and R. N. Sahay. "Possession Syndrome." *Indian Journal of Psychiatry* 12, 1 and 2 (1970): 65–70.

Wach, Joachim. *The Comparative Study of Religion.* Ed. Joseph Kitagawa. New York: Columbia Press, 1958.

Walker, Benjamin. *Tantrism.* Wellingborough: Aquarian Press, 1982.

Wayman, Alex. *Yoga of the Guhyasamājatantra.* Delhi: Motilal Banarsidass, 1977.

White, John, ed. *Kundalini: Evolution and Enlightenment.* Garden City, N.Y.: Anchor Books, 1979.

Woollcott, Philip, and Prakash Desai. "Religious and Creative States of Illumination: A Psychological Perspective." Typescript.

Yocum, Glenn. "Madness and Devotion in Māṇikkavācakar's Tiruvācakam." In Fred Clothey and J. Bruce Long, eds., *Experiencing Śiva: Encounters with a Hindu Deity.* New Delhi: Manohar, 1983.

Index